Computers in a Changing Society

first edition

John Preston

Sally Preston

Robert L. Ferrett

Prentice Hall

Library of Congress Cataloging-in-Publication Data

Preston, John M.
  Computers in a changing society / John Preston, Sally Preston, Robert L. Ferrett.
    p. cm.
  ISBN 0-13-145193-6
1. Computers and civilization. 2. Human-computer interaction. I. Preston, Sally.
II. Ferrett, Robert. III. Title.

QA76.9.C66P746 2004
303.48'33—dc22

2003027113

Executive Aquisitions Editor:
  Jodi McPherson
VP/Publisher: Natalie E. Anderson
Editorial Assistant: Alana Meyers
Developmental Editor: Mark Cierzniak
Project Manager, Supplements:
  Melissa Edwards
Senior Media Project Manager:
  Cathi Profitko
Senior Marketing Manager:
  Emily Williams Knight
Manager, Production: Gail Steier de
  Acevedo
Project Manager, Production:
  Vanessa Nuttry

Manufacturing Buyer: Vanessa Nuttry
Design Manager: Maria Lange
Interior Design: Pre-Press Company,
  Inc.
Cover Design: Janet Slowik
Cover Illustration: Carolyn Cole,
  Untitled Abstract #6, 2001
Manager, Print Production:
  Christy Mahon
**Composition/Full-Service Project
  Management:** Pre-Press Company, Inc.
Cover Printer: Phoenix Color
Printer/Binder: Von Hoffman Press

Credits and acknowledgments borrowed from other sources and reproduced, with permission, in this textbook appear on appropriate page within text (or on pages 267–268).

Microsoft® and Windows® are registered trademarks of the Microsoft Corporation in the U.S.A. and other countries. Screen shots and icons reprinted with permission from the Microsoft Corporation. This book is not sponsored or endorsed by or affiliated with the Microsoft Corporation.

Pearson Education LTD.
Pearson Education Singapore, Pte. Ltd
Pearson Education, Canada, Ltd
Pearson Education–Japan

Pearson Education Australia PTY, Limited
Pearson Education North Asia Ltd
Pearson Educación de Mexico, S.A. de C.V.
Pearson Education Malaysia, Pte. Ltd

10 9 8 7 6 5 4 3 2 1
ISBN 0-13-145193-6

ABOUT THE AUTHORS

John Preston is an associate professor in the College of Technology at Eastern Michigan University, where he teaches microcomputer applications courses at the undergraduate and graduate levels. He has been teaching, writing, and designing computer training courses since the advent of PCs, and he has authored and coauthored more than 60 books on Microsoft Word, Excel, Access, and PowerPoint. He is a series editor for the *Learn 97, Learn 2000,* and *Learn XP* books. Two books on Microsoft Access that he coauthored with Robert Ferrett have been translated into Greek and Chinese. He has received grants from the Detroit Edison Institute and the Department of Energy to develop Web sites for energy education and alternative fuels. He has also developed one of the first Internet-based microcomputer applications courses at an accredited university. He has a B.S. from the University of Michigan in physics, mathematics, and education, and an M.S. from Eastern Michigan University in physics education. His doctoral studies are in instructional technology at Wayne State University.

Sally Preston is president of Preston & Associates, which provides software consulting and training. Teaching computing in a variety of settings provides her with ample opportunity to observe how people learn, what works best, and what challenges people face when learning a new software program. This diverse experience provides a complementary set of skills and knowledge that is blended into her writing. Sally has been a coauthor on the *Learn* series since its inception and has authored books for the *Essentials* and *Microsoft Office User Specialist (MOUS) Essentials* series and the new *Go!* series. Sally has an M.B.A. from Eastern Michigan University. When she is away from her computer, she is often found planting flowers in her garden.

Robert L. Ferrett recently retired as the director of the Center for Instructional Computing at Eastern Michigan University, where he provided computer training and support to faculty. He has authored or coauthored more than 60 books on Access, PowerPoint, Excel, Publisher, WordPerfect, and Word, and was the editor of the *1994 ACM SIGUCCS Conference Proceedings*. He has been designing, developing, and delivering computer workshops for nearly two decades. Bob was a series editor for the *Learn 97, Learn 2000,* and *Learn XP* books and is an author for the new *Go!* series. He has a B.A. in psychology, an M.S. in geography, and an M.S. in interdisciplinary technology from Eastern Michigan University. His doctoral studies are in instructional technology at Wayne State University. As a sidelight, Bob teaches a four-week Computers and Genealogy class and has written genealogy and local history books.

DEDICATION

We dedicate this book to John Mitchell Preston, who is enjoying the 94th year of his life. He has seen the sweeping changes that computer technology has brought to our society since he was born in a log cabin in the mountains of eastern Kentucky. Through hard work and the help of a tuition-free community college, he got his start in life. His love of life and learning has been inspirational. For example, he learned to use a computer for the first time at the age of 84 because, in his words, "I've been retired for 20 years and I'm bored!" Within three years he sold his computer and bought another one; "I need more power!" he said. He needed a faster computer to run a voice recognition program so he could dictate all of his e-mail. He installed a broadband Internet connection and a Web camera so he can attach snapshots to his e-mail and browse the Internet for recipes for the healthful food that he enjoys preparing.

We are grateful for the opportunity Caney Community College (now Alice Lloyd College) in Pippa Passes, Kentucky, provided to him and the opportunity such schools provide to people like him in other parts of the country.

Brief Contents

Contents

Preface

TO THE STUDENT

Welcome to *Computers in a Changing Society*! This book will show you the basic tools you need to operate a computer and will teach you how computers are changing and affecting the world around us. So whether you are a novice to computers or an experienced user, this book will guide you through the fascinating world of computer concepts.

It became apparent that a computer concepts book was needed that focused on how computers affect us as a society. With input from students and professors, this idea became a reality. Now, not only can you learn the basics of computers and their uses, but you will be able to see how they are used in the world and how that affects you in everyday life.

USING THIS BOOK
This text is arranged in such a way as to help you understand computers and their societal impact.

First, Chapter 1 gives you a broad overview of where computers are found in our society and how they are used. The next chapter, Chapter 2, shows you how we all connect personally and in the business world through the Internet. Chapter 3, on hardware, gives you an inside view of your computer. Next, Chapter 4 is about software, how it works, and how it can work for you.

Ethical usage of the computer is covered in Chapter 5. Security, privacy, and some of things you need to do in order to protect yourself are the topics of Chapter 6. Last, you can see the effects of computers on the past, present, and future in Chapter 7.

Along the way, special features will teach you more about these concepts.

chapter boxes

- **Diversity Issues**
- **Voter Issues**
- **Mastering Technology**
- **Critical Thinking**

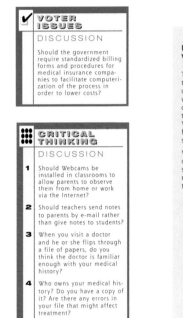

DIVERSITY ISSUES

DISCUSSION

1. How can distance education benefit people with disabilities?

2. What groups have less access to the Internet than others? Are they located in a particular geographic location?

3. If a child grows up in a home without a computer or Internet connection and does not have access to either at school, what effect will a very limited exposure to the Internet have on that child's future? Can you name five things that this child would not know how to do that most of his or her peers would know?

VOTER ISSUES

DISCUSSION

Should the government require standardized billing forms and procedures for medical insurance companies to facilitate computerization of the process in order to lower costs?

CRITICAL THINKING

DISCUSSION

1. Should Webcams be installed in classrooms to allow parents to observe them from home or work via the Internet?

2. Should teachers send notes to parents by e-mail rather than give notes to students?

3. When you visit a doctor and he or she flips through a file of papers, do you think the doctor is familiar enough with your medical history?

4. Who owns your medical history? Do you have a copy of it? Are there any errors in your file that might affect treatment?

mastering technology

USING FEATURES OF WINDOWS XP TO HELP THE VISUALLY IMPAIRED

The Windows and Macintosh operating systems have a group of accessibility features that allow users to modify the way the operating system interacts with them. There are options for those who have visual or hearing impairments and other options for those who have trouble using a mouse or keyboard. Elderly people are using computers to communicate with their children and grandchildren by e-mail, but many people in this age group have vision problems. Here are some tips for making changes to the Windows XP environment to assist someone who has some visual impairment or simply for customizing the visual environment to your own tastes. The Macintosh system has similar features.

Windows XP has a program that allows you to modify the font size, cursor width, color contrast, and mouse pointer to make them easier to see. It also can open a panel on the screen that acts like a magnifier to show details. If you are working in a computer laboratory, changes to the operating system may not be allowed. If they are, be sure to undo the changes before you leave to leave the computer the way you found it.

1. On the Windows task bar, click Start, All Programs, Accessories, Accessibility, and Accessibility Wizard. The Accessibility wizard starts.
2. Click Next. Click Use Microsoft Magnifier, and large titles and menus.
3. Click Next. A panel opens at the top of your screen, and the font size increases in all the Windows dialog boxes. Three dialog boxes open that may overlap.
4. Click the Microsoft Magnifier dialog box to select it. Click OK to close the dialog box.
5. Click the Accessibility Wizard dialog box. Confirm that *Change the font size* and *Use Microsoft Magnifier* are both selected. Click Next.
6. Click *I am blind or have difficulty seeing things on screen*. Click Next.
7. Click one of the larger scroll bar options. Click Next.
8. Choose *Large* or *Extra Large* icons. Click Next.
9. Choose one of the high-contrast display color schemes. Click Next.
10. Choose a different mouse and cursor combination. Click Next.
11. Click the middle of the *Cursor Width* bar to select a wider cursor. Click Next.
12. If you are sharing a computer in a lab, click Cancel. Click *No* to undo the changes. Everything changes back to normal except the Magnifier.
13. Click the title bar of the Magnifier Settings dialog box. Click Exit. The magnifier pane closes.

If you want to change the settings, you can run the wizard again or choose Start, Control Panel, Display to change the settings individually.

problem solving

- **Using help features**
- **Element analysis and troubleshooting methods**
- **Getting help from a professional**

---

critical thinking–research

How does the digital divide within the United States compare with the digital divide between the United States and developing countries?

1. **Teamwork**—Join one to five other students. Decide how to divide up the work. Possible divisions could be: within the United States, between the United States and other countries, diversity issues, editing the group paper, and preparing the class presentation.
2. **Research**—Use a Web browser and go to the companion Web site at **http://www.prenhall.com/preston**. Use the resources provided for use with this book. Follow the links by clicking on the Web addresses that are highlighted and underlined. Read about the digital divide in the United States and between the United States and other countries. Use a Web search engine such as Google.com or Yahoo.com to search for keywords and phrases such as "digital divide." Make a list of the sources you find to be relevant that you may want to reference later. Include the title of the page or article, the name of the organization responsible for the Web page, the date the page or article was written, and the Web address.

You may also go to the library and look up books, articles, and news reports that are relevant to this topic. Many libraries have the full text of articles and news reports in proprietary databases that are not available to the public online.

3. **Diversity issues**—Look for differences based on race, geography, religion, and economic status.
4. **Analysis**—Write an essay that compares the digital divide within the United States to that between the United States and the rest of the world. Form and express an opinion. Go beyond simple reporting of the facts. Support your opinion with references to the articles you read. Ask your instructor for guidance regarding the required length of the essay.
5. **Communication**—Prepare a presentation in which you present your opinion and the supporting facts to the class. Depending on your computer skill, you could give the presentation using a program like PowerPoint and save it as a Web page or you could prepare a paper handout with your Web references for use while you talk to the class.

problem solving

The objective of this exercise is to learn valuable processes for solving computer problems, not just the solution to this particular problem.

Occasionally a component of your computer stops working. If the mouse stops working in the middle of an important document, you need to know how to save the document and shut down your computer without a mouse. Operating a computer without a mouse is a situation that some people with mobility limitations face every day, and you can use the accessibility features provided for them to solve this problem.

search for help on the topic

Use the extensive library of Help topics that is included with your computer's operating system. In Windows, click Start, Help and Support. Look under the Accessibility section for help on using a computer if your mobility is limited. When you find a topic that appears to be appropriate for this problem, write down the sequence of choices that leads you back to it for future reference.

read the instructions and try it

Attempt to follow the instructions for replacing your computer's mouse with keyboard functions. Write a description of the process. If you are not successful, describe what you tried and what did or did not happen. Be specific. If you were successful but found that the instructions were not clear at some point, write a description of the problematic instructions, and suggest improvements.

troubleshoot

If your first attempt is unsuccessful, determine whether there are some alternative interpretations of the instructions that you can try. Record the results of these efforts.

BEYOND THE FACTS   29

- **Career challenges and opportunities**
- **Workplace interactions**
- **Social interactions**
- **Home life**
- **Lifelong learning**
- **Leadership**

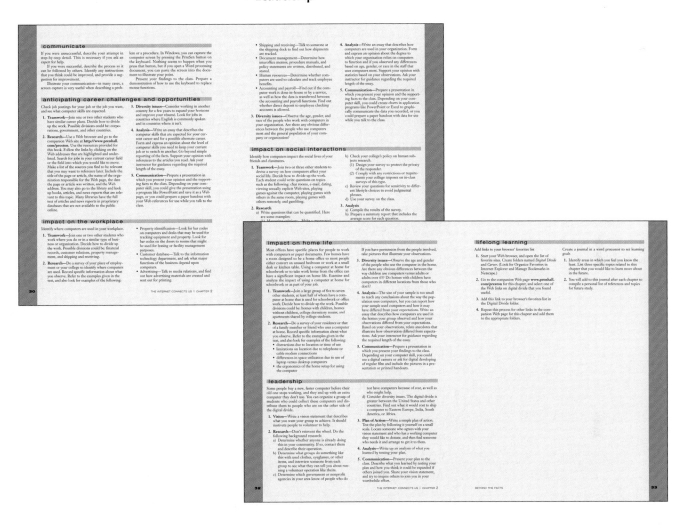

Student Web Site

Please visit the companion Web site for this book at **www.prenhall.com/ preston**. The site includes online exercises, Web projects, Internet links, an interactive study guide, careers center, TechTV videos, and much more—all designed to help you learn about computers and information technology. Other online learning tools, videos, software, and so on are described in the preface to the instructor.

FOR THE INSTRUCTOR

Welcome to *Computers in a Changing Society*! This text not only teaches the student about basic computer use, but also shows how society is greatly affected by information technology. This book has been designed with your needs in mind. Along with the wealth of supplements that are available to enhance the classroom experience, you can be assured that this text will provide you with the tools that will enhance your students' learning experience.

It became apparent that a computer concepts book was needed that focused on how computers affect us as a society. With input from students and professors, this idea became a reality. Now, not only can your students learn the basics of computers and their uses, but they will be able to see how they are used in the world and how that affects them in everyday life.

Below is a list of some of the concepts that your students will learn as they use this book.

> Ethical use of computers
> Computer skills
> Understanding culture and society in relation to computers
> Career challenges and opportunities
> Impact of computers on social relationships
> Impact of computers on home life

This text is arranged in such a way as to help your students understand computers and their societal impact.

First, Chapter 1 gives you a broad overview of where computers are found in our society and how they are used. The next chapter, Chapter 2, shows you how we all connect personally and in the business world through the Internet. Chapter 3, on hardware, gives you an inside view of your computer. Next, Chapter 4 is about software, how it works, and how it can work for you.

Ethical usage of the computer is covered in Chapter 5. Security, privacy, and some of things you need to do in order to protect yourself are the topics of Chapter 6. Last, you can see the effects of computers on the past, present, and future in Chapter 7.

The following chapter features will help students understand these concepts.

> Chapter Boxes
>   • Diversity Issues
>   How something is done in another country
>   How this affects other countries
>   How people from other countries view the current topic
>   How this affects the economy or politics of other countries
>   • Voter Issues
>   Examples of government regulation that relate to the current topic
>   Possible new laws that may be needed
>   Positions by major political parties
>   • Mastering Technology
>   Used to describe a procedure

- Critical Thinking

   Provocative questions intended for research and discussion with links to resources on the companion Web site

❱ Problem Solving—This section describes a situation and challenges the student to develop a strategy to deal with the problem.

- Using help features

- Analyzing elements and troubleshooting methods

- Getting help from a professional

   Describing the problem and what's been tried

   Capturing screens to illustrate the problem

   Allowing access to your computer by LAN or Web

❱ Projects—This section develops an integrated approach to analyzing technology's influence on four principle areas. There are projects in each of the four areas: research, cross-cultural issues, analysis, and communication.

- Career Challenges and Opportunities—projects addressing how technology affects the student's current career choice. Students evaluate threats to the status quo and opportunities created by new technology.

- Workplace Interactions—projects addressing how technology affects the work environment and the work itself

- Social Interactions—projects addressing how technology affects interactions between people

- Home Life—projects addressing how technology affects how we live at home

❱ Lifelong Learning—This section will help students to develop a set of skills for learning about technology and using technology for learning that persists beyond the end of the course.

INSTRUCTOR RESOURCES

The new and improved Prentice Hall Instructor's Resource CD-ROM includes the tools you expect from a Prentice Hall Computer Concepts text like:

❱ The Instructor's Manual in Word and PDF formats

❱ Solutions to all questions and exercises from the book and Web site

❱ Multiple, customizable PowerPoint slide presentations for each chapter

❱ Computer concepts animations

❱ TechTV videos

❱ Image library of all of the figures from the text

This CD-ROM is an interactive library of assets and links. This CD writes custom "index" pages that can be used as the foundation of a class presentation or online lecture. By navigating through this CD, you can collect the materials that are most relevant to your interests, edit them to create powerful class lectures, copy them to your own computer's hard drive, and/or upload them to an online course management system.

TestGen Software

TestGen is a test generator program that lets you view and easily edit testbank questions, transfer them to tests, and print the tests in a variety of formats suitable to your teaching situation. The program also offers many options for organizing and displaying testbanks and tests. A built-in random number and text generator makes it ideal for creating multiple versions of tests that involve calculations and provides more possible test items than testbank questions. Powerful search and sort functions let you easily locate questions and arrange them in the order you prefer.

QuizMaster, also included in this package, allows students to take tests created with TestGen on a local area network. The QuizMaster utility built into TestGen lets instructors view student records and print a variety of reports. Building tests is easy with TestGen, and exams can be easily uploaded into WebCT, Blackboard, and Course Compass.

Train & Assess IT www2.phgenit.com/support

Prentice Hall offers performance-based training and assessment in one product—Train & Assess IT. The training component offers computer-based training that a student can use to preview, learn, and review Microsoft Office application skills. Web or CD-ROM delivered, Train IT offers interactive, multimedia, computer-based training to augment classroom learning. Built-in prescriptive testing suggests a study path based not only on student test results but also on the specific textbook chosen for the course.

The assessment component offers computer-based testing that shares the same user interface as Train IT and is used to evaluate a student's knowledge about specific topics in Word, Excel, Access, PowerPoint, Outlook, the Internet, and computing concepts. It does this in a task-oriented environment so students can demonstrate proficiency as well as comprehension of the topics. More extensive than the testing in Train IT, Assess IT offers more administrative features for the instructor and additional questions for the student.

Assess IT also allows professors to test students out of a course, place students in appropriate courses, and evaluate skill sets.

TechTV is the San Francisco–based cable network that showcases the smart, edgy, and unexpected side of technology. By telling stories through the prism of technology, TechTV provides programming that celebrates its viewers' passion, creativity, and lifestyle.

TechTV's programming falls into three categories:

1. **Help and Information**, with shows like *The Screen Savers*, TechTV's daily live variety show featuring everything from guest interviews and celebrities to product advice and demos; *Tech Live*, featuring the latest news on the industry's most important people, companies, products, and issues; and *Call for Help*, a live help and how-to show providing computing tips and live viewer questions.

2. **Cool Docs**, with shows like *The Tech Of . . .* , a series that goes behind the scenes of modern life and shows you the technology that makes things tick; *Performance*, an investigation into how technology and science are molding the perfect athlete; and *Future Fighting Machines*, a fascinating look at the technology and tactics of warfare.

3. **Outrageous Fun**, with shows like *X-Play*, exploring the latest and greatest in video gaming; and *Unscrewed with Martin Sargent*, a new late-night series showcasing the darker and funnier world of technology.

For more information, log onto **www.techtv.com** or contact your local cable or satellite provider to get TechTV in your area.

TOOLS FOR ONLINE LEARNING

Companion Web Site www.prenhall.com/preston

This text is accompanied by a companion Web site at **www.prenhall.com/preston**. Features of this new site include an interactive study guide, downloadable supplements, online end-of-chapter materials, additional Internet exercises, TechTV videos, Web resource links such as Careers in IT, and crossword puzzles, plus technology updates and bonus chapters on the latest trends and hottest topics in information technology. All links to Web exercises will be constantly updated to ensure accuracy.

EXPLORE IT www.prenhall.com

Prentice Hall offers computer-based training just for computer literacy. Designed to cover some of the most difficult concepts, as well as some current topical areas, EXPLORE IT is a Web- and CD-ROM-based product designed to complement a course. Available for free with any Prentice Hall title, our new lab coverage includes: Troubleshooting, Programming Logic, Mouse and Keyboard Basics, Databases, Building a Web Page, Hardware, Software, Operating Systems, Building a Network, and more!

Online Courseware for Blackboard, WebCT, and CourseCompass

Now you have the freedom to personalize your own online course materials! Prentice Hall provides the content and support you need to create and manage your own online course in WebCT, Blackboard, or Prentice Hall's own CourseCompass. Content includes lecture material, interactive exercises, e-commerce case videos, additional testing questions, and projects and animations.

CourseCompass www.coursecompass.com

CourseCompass is a dynamic, interactive online course-management tool powered exclusively for Pearson Education by Blackboard. This exciting product allows you to teach market-leading Pearson Education content in an easy-to-use, customizable format.

Blackboard www.prenhall.com/blackboard

Prentice Hall's abundant online content, combined with Blackboard's popular tools and interface, results in robust Web-based courses that are easy to implement, manage, and use—taking your courses to new heights in student interaction and learning.

WebCT www.prenhall.com/webct

Course management tools within WebCT include page tracking, progress tracking, class and student management, a grade book, communication tools, a calendar, reporting tools, and more. Gold-level customer support, available exclusively to adopters of Prentice Hall courses, is provided free of charge upon adoption and provides you with priority assistance, training discounts, and dedicated technical support.

ACKNOWLEDGMENTS

We would like to acknowledge the efforts of a fine team of editing professionals, with whom we have had the pleasure of working. Jodi McPherson, Mark Cierzniak, and Alana Meyers did a great job managing and coordinating this effort. We would also like to acknowledge the contributions of other members of the Prentice Hall team as well as the editors and reviewers who gave invaluable criticism and suggestions.

Joe Delieria, *Arizona State University*

Donna Madsen, *Kirkwood Community College*

Israel Yost, *University of New Hampshire*

William Rust, *SpetralNoise*

Bhushan Kapoor, *California State University*

The faculty and staff of the College of Technology and the Interdisciplinary Technology Department in particular, have provided an environment of creativity and intellectual stimulation that made this book possible. Thanks to Dean John Dugger for suggesting that we include leadership as one of the goals of this book. Paul Kuwik, Department Head, has created a department whose faculty are encouraged to be creative and to excel. The faculty and staff of that department all contributed to an environment that supports scholarly activity. Those who deserve special mention are:

Wayne Hanewicz—an exceptional leader and thinker who first introduced us to challenging reading on the subject of technology

Alphonso Bellamy—stimulating discussions on the theory of technology

Denise Pilato—perspective on historical and cultural impact of computers

Carol Haddad—discussions on diversity and women's perspectives on technology

Ronald Westrum—international perspective on computers and technology

Anthony Adamski and Timothy Doyle—practical applications of computer technology in flight and airport management

David Gore and Paul Majeske—use of computers in communication

Gerald Lawver—insights on security, privacy, and law enforcement

Pam Becker and Cheryl Hanewicz—lecturers who enjoy teaching and discussing new ideas regarding computers and technology

Kathleen Powers—our department secretary whose competence reduced stress and distractions while we were writing this book

Computers Are Everywhere

outline & objectives

WHAT IS A COMPUTER?

- Identify the four main functions of a computer and give examples of each.
- Identify data flow among the four functions.
- Identify a typical sequence of functions.

AWARENESS OF COMPUTER INFLUENCE

- Identify at least one way that computers are used in each of the following: business, education, health professions, the military, transportation, and recreation.

PROTECTING YOUR PERSONAL HEALTH WHILE USING COMPUTERS

- Define ergonomics
- Identify examples of proper alignment between the user and computer components such as the monitor, keyboard, and mouse
- Identify key adjustments to chairs for proper posture
- Identify proper alignment of lighting sources

UNIVERSAL ACCESS

- Define "Digital Divide"
- Cite statistics on computer and Internet use for the United States as a whole and for select groups such as children, blacks, Hispanics, whites, Asians, and single mothers.
- Compare Internet usage in developed countries that charge a flat fee for access with usage in those that charge by the minute.
- Identify three major factors that limit poor nations' access to the Internet.
- Cite statistics on the percentage of people in the United States, by age group, who report they have at least one disability that could affect computer use.

Computers affect the way we live, work, and play. Computers are widespread in the United States and they impact virtually every facet of our world—from the food we eat to the cars we drive, computers are used to analyze, diagnose, record, and communicate.

The popularity of the Internet has changed the way we communicate, find information, shop, and go to school. The influence of computers and the Internet have shrunk the world in many respects because ideas and information can be shared with ease across the globe. Nearly all college students in the United States have access to computers, which gives some of them the impression that computers are everywhere and everyone has access to one. However, a Department of Commerce survey of 57,000 households in September 2001 indicates that only slightly over half of all Americans have computers in their homes; and there are many parts of the world where computers are rare.

In this textbook, you examine the impact of computers on our lives and the effect they have on our society and the world at large. Because computers are used in so many areas, you need to understand how they function and how to use them safely. Many of you may already be using computers at your jobs and in your homes. The uses of and applications for computers are likely to increase, and their effect on society will continue to grow as more and more people gain access to computers.

This chapter introduces you to the basics of computer technology—both the physical components and the functions involved in the computer process. You will explore where and how computers are used in several key areas of your life. Because many jobs involve extensive use of a keyboard, monitor, and mouse, you need to know how to use them for hours at a time without endangering your health. A few simple but effective guidelines will help prevent or reduce problems with your eyes, wrists, neck, and back. Finally, it is also important to understand that many people do not have convenient access to computers, and this disparity can become a significant social problem.

DEFINITION OF A COMPUTER

A computer is a device that can sit on a desk or be implanted in a pacemaker next to your heart. It can fill a room or fit through the eye of a needle. A computer has four major functions: input, processing, storage, and output. It can be any size or located almost anyplace.

INPUT

Input refers to the action of transferring instructions or data into the computer. *Data* is a collection of unprocessed facts and figures, such as names and addresses, or items purchased. A keyboard and mouse are examples of input devices, and so are the bar code reader and the magnetic card swipe used at a grocery store (see Figure 1.1).

PROCESSING

A computer manipulates data according to a set of instructions, resulting in the creation of *information*—data that is organized in a useful and meaningful manner. This data manipulation is known as *processing*. Instructions for early computers were provided by changing gears or wires, which limited their flexibility. Later-model computers were designed for a variety of tasks, and sets of instructions could be stored and used as required. A set of specific instructions for accomplishing a task that a computer can follow is called an *algorithm*. Writing algorithms for a computer is called *programming*, and computers that can change programs are *programmable*.

FIGURE 1.1

A variety of input devices can be used to enter data, commands, or responses into a computer.

People who write programs are called *programmers*. The physical device that does the processing is called the **central processing unit** or **CPU**. Common manufacturers and examples of their processors are Intel (Pentium 4), AMD (Athalon), and Motorola (PowerPC).

STORAGE

A computer must have the capability to store data and instructions while it is processing data. This type of storage is known as **primary storage** or **memory**. Computers must also be able to store the results of the processed data for later retrieval. This type of storage is referred to as **secondary storage**.

Primary Storage—Memory

There are two distinct types of memory in a computer:

) **Erasable programmable read-only memory**, **EPROM**—This type of memory contains the instructions used by the computer when it starts up and communicates with its internal components. It is programmed at the factory and does not need constant power to function.

) **Random access memory**, **RAM**—The processor retrieves data from memory, processes it, and returns it to memory. RAM is designed to keep up with the processor, and the time it takes to read or write data to it is measured in **nanoseconds**, which are billionths of a second. Its capacity is rated in **megabytes**. A **byte** of memory can store enough data to identify one character of text, and a megabyte of RAM can store a million characters of text. RAM consists of computer chips that are mounted on small plastic boards (see Figure 1.2) inside the computer case. Present technology uses devices that must have constant power to function; otherwise the data is lost.

Secondary Storage

Secondary storage includes any device on which information can be stored for later retrieval and which does not require constant power. There are three main types of secondary storage devices, which are classified according to the technology that is used to store the data.

) **Magnetic media**—Coatings of magnetic material on a disk can record and store data by magnetizing small spots on the disk in one

FIGURE 1.2

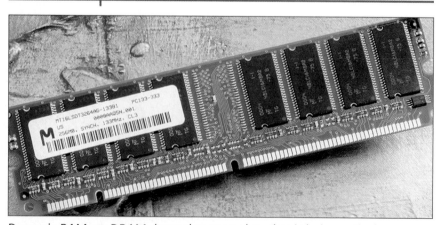

Dynamic RAM, or DRAM, is used to store data that is being actively processed by the computer.

FIGURE 1.3

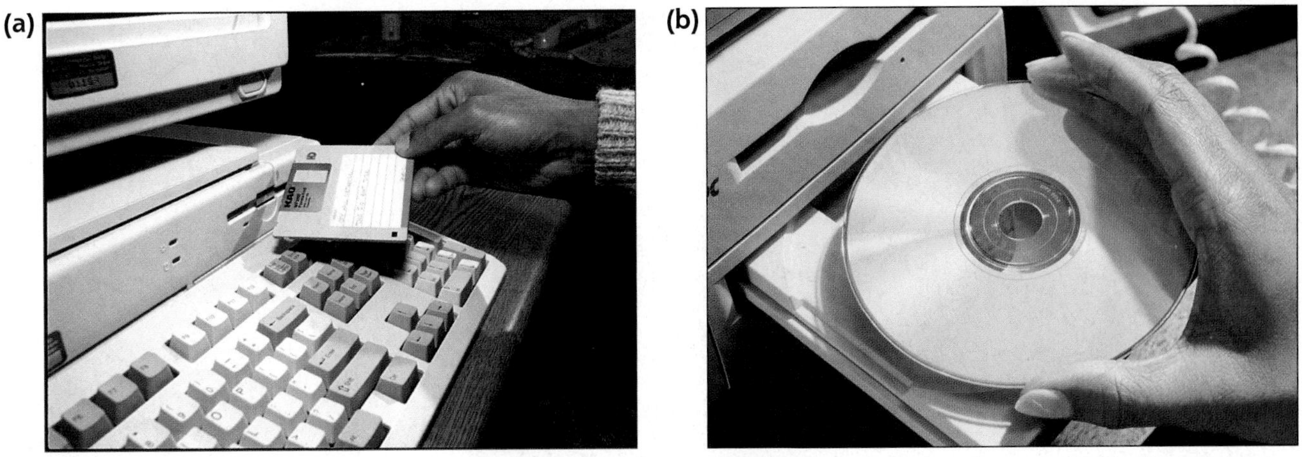

(a)

(b)

Secondary storage devices are used to store data for later use. Two examples are shown here: (a) A 3½-inch diskette is an example of magnetic media that can be used to store data. (b) A CD-R is an example of an optical media storage device.

direction or the other. Examples are a computer's main hard disk and removable floppy disks (see Figure 1.3a). It is common practice to use the term *disk* for magnetic media.

❱ *Optical media*—Data may be recorded in the form of small pits in a reflective surface on a disc. To read the data, a disc drive shines a beam of light on the surface, and a *sensor* picks up variations in the reflection. The flickering reflection is converted into a stream of data. The discs are called *compact discs*, or *CDs*. There are several distinctive types of CDs, which will be examined in detail in the chapter on hardware (see Figure 1.3b). It is common practice to use the term *disc* for optical media.

❱ *Flash memory*—Unlike magnetic or optical memory, flash memory has no moving parts. It is similar to RAM but does not require constant power to store data. It can be removed easily and is often used to transfer data between digital cameras and personal computers.

OUTPUT

The results of the processing—known as *output*—must be reported in some manner to the user. The monitor and printer are examples of output devices; so is the dashboard warning light that indicates it's time to service your car (see Figure 1.4).

FUNCTIONS AND DATA FLOW

The functions of a computer and their relationship to each other may be understood by following the flow of data as it moves through a computer. Data goes in, it gets processed according to a set of instructions, and information comes out. In order to produce organized and meaningful information, events occur in a particular order. The following sequence is typical of how data flows through the four main functions of a computer (see Figure 1.5):

❱ Input—The operator types words, numbers, or commands on the keyboard or uses the mouse to point to part of the screen and click.

❱ Primary Storage—The data, program, and commands are stored in RAM.

FIGURE 1.4

Forms of output

FIGURE 1.5

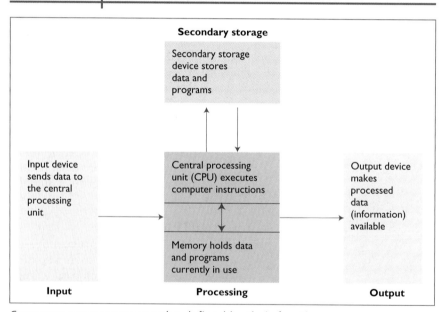

Computer components may be defined by their function.

> ❱ Processing—The processor manipulates the data according to a program and the commands provided by the operator.
> ❱ Primary storage—The results of the processing are stored in RAM.
> ❱ Output—The processed data is transferred from the memory to the monitor or printer.
> ❱ Secondary storage—The processed data or information is written to the hard disk, floppy disk, or optical disc.

Regardless of the shape or size of a computer component, you can categorize it by one of the four functions that make up a computer (see Figure 1.6).

FIGURE 1.6

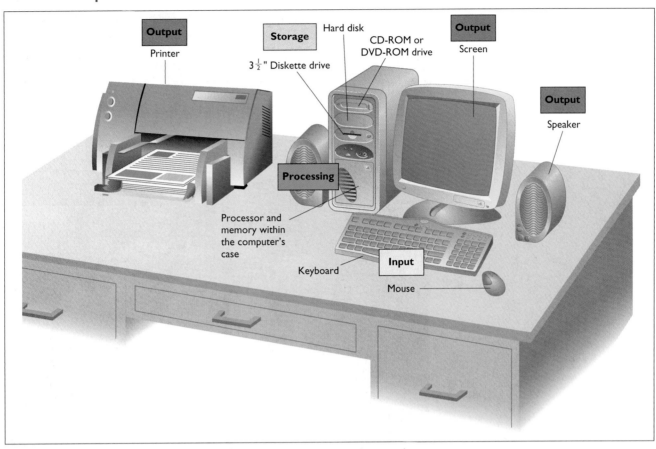

A computer is defined by its functions of input, storage, processing, and output.

AWARENESS OF COMPUTER INFLUENCE

Computers have enabled us to go to the moon, map the human genome, and track storm systems. The following are some examples of how computers are used in our lives or the lives of people we know. These examples are provided to help you become aware of the ubiquitous presence of computer technology in our world, but it is not a comprehensive list. You are encouraged to recognize computer applications in addition to those listed here.

BUSINESS AND GOVERNMENT

Organizations of all types use computers extensively to manage communication, finances, and projects, regardless of size. Here are some examples of how computers are used in business and in government agencies.

Documents

Businesses and government agencies use computers to create documents such as contracts, brochures, letters, annual reports, procedures manuals, and policy statements. These documents are stored, retrieved, edited, and distributed by computers using programs that are generically called *word processors*. Memoranda that were formerly written on paper and distributed by interoffice mail are now written on computers and distributed by electronic mail known as *e-mail*. Working with documents in paper or electronic form is a significant part of the workday for many people (see Figure 1.7).

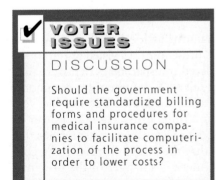

VOTER ISSUES

DISCUSSION

Should the government require standardized billing forms and procedures for medical insurance companies to facilitate computerization of the process in order to lower costs?

FIGURE 1.7

Computers are a primary tool used by workers in business and in government offices.

Finances

Computers are particularly good at working with numbers. One of the first uses of personal computers in business and government was to project the effect of changing interest rates over several years, a situation in which the values for a given year depend upon the preceding year and some basic assumptions about how the interest rates are likely to change. Computers can quickly and accurately recalculate hundreds of formulas to predict the effect of changing these assumptions. This ability allows organizations to make smart investment decisions. Programs designed for this type of work are generically known as *spreadsheets* (see Figure 1.8).

Presentations

When a person or group wants to communicate an idea to others, it is often effective to do so in a meeting where the presenter uses visual aids to make his or her point. In the past, people prepared transparencies that were projected onto a screen while the presenter talked. Computers are commonly used to organize pictures and text and project them onto a screen in a very similar process (see Figure 1.9). Presentations using computers can be assembled, edited, copied, and distributed far faster than presentations that use transparencies. Be aware, however, that they can still consume a considerable amount of time to create, and there is a danger of the presentation itself overshadowing the content.

FIGURE 1.8

	A	B	C	D	E	F	G	H
1		JAN	FEB	MAR	APR	TOTAL		
2	EXPENSES							
3	RENT	425.00	425.00	425.00	425.00	1700.00		
4	PHONE	22.50	31.25	17.00	35.75	106.50		
5	CLOTHES	110.00	135.00	156.00	91.00	492.00		
6	FOOD	280.00	250.00	250.00	300.00	1080.00		
7	HEAT	80.00	50.00	24.00	95.00	249.00		
8	ELECTRICITY	35.75	40.50	45.00	36.50	157.75		
9	WATER	10.00	11.00	11.00	10.50	42.50		
10	CAR INSURANCE	75.00	75.00	75.00	75.00	300.00		
11	ENTERTAINMENT	150.00	125.00	140.00	175.00	590.00		
12	TOTAL	1188.25	1142.75	1143.00	1243.75	4717.75		

Spreadsheet software is frequently used by businesses to track finances and project earnings.

FIGURE 1.9

Presentation software programs enable businesspeople to create effective presentations to communicate information to large groups.

Databases

Most businesses and government agencies maintain lists of people, as well as data regarding their interactions with them. These lists are usually organized in tables where each column is a category of data, such as name, address, or phone number, and each row is information about one person, event, or interaction. These tables of information are called *databases*. Databases that have several tables that are related to each other are called *relational databases*. Every time you make a purchase with a credit card

FIGURE 1.10

Whenever you make a purchase with a credit card, that transaction is recorded in a database, which is used to prepare a billing statement.

(see Figure 1.10), place a telephone call, or vote, the information is stored in a database.

Scheduling Meetings and Events

Group activities require coordination that often takes place in meetings. Finding times and places for meetings of more than a few people can be a daunting task if conducted by telephone. Organizations often use computer programs with a *calendar* feature where members of the group keep records of their activities (see Figure 1.11). If someone wants to set up a meeting, the program can first search the calendars of all the participants to find a time that is unscheduled for all, or most, of them. Then it checks a different calendar to find an available meeting room.

Project Management

Complex projects involve many different groups that must be coordinated and managed. Activities known as *tasks* often depend on each other, and delays or changes in one task affect the others. Key dates are called *milestones*, and changes that affect these dates must be identified. The relationships between parts of the project are often graphically represented by *Gantt* or *Pert* charts. Gantt charts use horizontal bars to represent the length of time a task will take, whereas Pert charts use boxes with connecting lines to show interactions. People and equipment are called *resources*, and their time may be allocated to different tasks. Computers may be used to automatically update the charts when the underlying data changes. They can also check the allocation of resources to identify times when people are overworked or underutilized.

EDUCATION

Most communities recognize the importance of computer access in the classroom for students. New uses of these computers and Internet connections go beyond student use. Computers and the Internet are also affecting higher education by allowing students to take classes online.

Parental Involvement

Many parents have computers and Internet connections. Some parents want to use them to see what's going on in the classroom, and some teachers are beginning to go online to communicate with parents.

Communication with parents   Teachers are increasingly called upon to comprehensively evaluate student development and report the results to parents. In the past, parents met the teacher once or twice a year during parent-teacher conferences, and most other communication went through the hands of the student in the form of report cards, permission slips, and notes. Teachers can keep parents informed of activities, required permissions, additional fees, and student progress directly using e-mail and class Web pages. Parents can provide the teacher with information about student illnesses and other situations using e-mail as well.

Monitoring classrooms   Some parents would like to take communication a step further and use *Webcams* to monitor classroom activity. Webcams are video cameras that are connected to a computer that is connected to the Internet. A parent with an appropriate password could log onto the class Web site and watch the class while at work or even while out of town. Noncustodial parents could observe the child's activities as well. Teachers have expressed concerns about the effect this could have on classroom behavior and about how brief observations could give the wrong impression (see the companion Web site **www.prenhall.com/preston** for a related article).

FIGURE 1.11

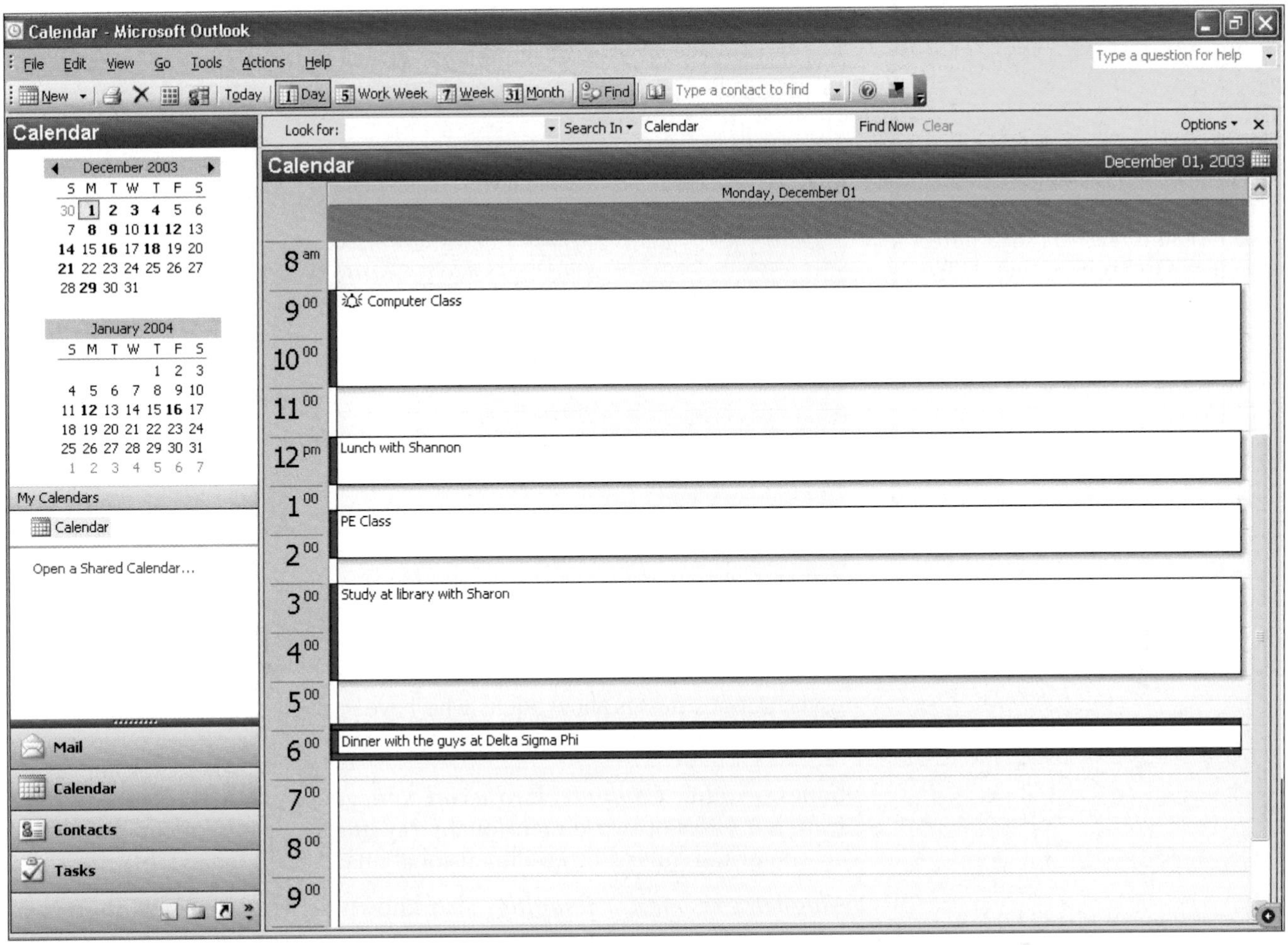

A calendar program can help you plan your day and can be used to schedule meetings for groups.

Distance Education

Higher education and adult education have been significantly affected by the use of computers to conduct classes remotely. If students and teachers use computers and the Internet to meet at the same time, it is called a *synchronous* class meeting. If students and teachers post messages and exchange views and information at different times, it is an *asynchronous* class. The term *distance education* is commonly used because this method became popular for teaching people in sparsely settled areas such as western Canada. However, it has also gained popularity among students who have irregular work and travel schedules (see Figure 1.12). It is very useful for students who cannot create a schedule of traditional classes without time conflicts or for students who have mobility limitations (see Figure 1.13).

HEALTH PROFESSIONS

The health-care industry uses computers as aids for diagnosis and treatment. It also uses them for the same functions as other businesses or government agencies.

Diagnostic Tools

Computers can be used to provide better images of the body. A traditional x-ray is a photographic technique that records two-dimensional shadows of

FIGURE 1.12

Asynchronous classes allow adults who have variable work hours or child-care responsibilities to go to class anytime.

CRITICAL THINKING

DISCUSSION

1. Should Webcams be installed in classrooms to allow parents to observe them from home or work via the Internet?

2. Should teachers send notes to parents by e-mail rather than give notes to students?

3. When you visit a doctor and he or she flips through a file of papers, do you think the doctor is familiar enough with your medical history?

4. Who owns your medical history? Do you have a copy of it? Are there any errors in your file that might affect treatment?

bones on film. *Computerized axial tomography*, also known as a *CAT scan*, is a series of two-dimensional x-ray images that are combined by the computer to render a three-dimensional image (see Figure 1.14).

Magnetic resonance imaging, also known as *MRI*, uses computers to analyze the electromagnetic waves given off by atoms in the fluids of body tissues when they are excited by magnetic waves. The method produces images of the soft tissues of the body.

Medical Records

Personal history   Every time we visit a doctor or hospital and every time we fill a prescription, information about our visits and the drugs we take becomes part of one or more databases that make up our personal medical history. In some doctors' offices, the diagnoses are kept on paper in file folders, whereas in others the records are kept on a computer.

Insurance   Most insurance offices use computers to handle billing and insurance claims (see Figure 1.15), but there is little standardization of claim forms and procedures among insurance providers in the United States, which limits the ability of computers to share information. Communication between computers requires compatibility of programs and systems, as well as forms and procedures.

MILITARY

The U.S. military relies on high technology to increase the effectiveness and safety of its troops. Computers are an important part of military activity.

Training

Computers are used to simulate the behavior of complex planes, vehicles, and weapons systems to provide trainees with practice and allow them to

FIGURE 1.13

Distance education allows people with mobility limitations to take part in classes more conveniently.

FIGURE 1.14 | FIGURE 1.15 |

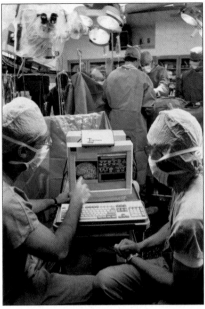

Computers can be linked to computer imaging devices to analyze problems without waiting for film to be developed.

Despite computerization of some databases, medical records are still often kept on paper.

learn from otherwise deadly mistakes. Computers can record a trainee's performance and replay it so the trainee can observe his or her own behavior and learn from it. Many military personnel enter combat with limited experience using live ammunition, but the simulations have been so realistic that they still perform well.

Advanced Weapons
Computers are used to identify targets and guide munitions to them. Individual soldiers, vehicles, or guided weapons may be equipped with *Global Positioning System* receivers that identify the exact locations of friendly and enemy positions. Weapons that can adjust to conditions automatically and hit their targets precisely are called *smart* weapons (see Figure 1.16). For example, bombs that can steer themselves to a target that is marked by a laser are called smart bombs.

Operations and Maintenance
Military equipment is often very advanced and complex. The paper manuals for systems on a naval cruiser used to weigh several tons. Computers are used to store, retrieve, and display technical manuals in digital form that takes far less space and weighs much less (see Figure 1.17).

TRANSPORTATION
Computers provide today's transportation industry with the ability to manage fleets of vehicles by tracking their location and utilization, to assist with maintenance and efficient engine operation, to control flow of traffic, and to take reservations.

Trucks and Cars
Cars and trucks have computers in them that maximize fuel efficiencies, report on maintenance problems, and communicate via satellite with information services or company headquarters.

Communication and emergency support   Computers make it possible to combine a Global Positioning System (GPS) with cell phone technology to provide constant communication between a driver and support providers who can give advice on navigation (see Figure 1.18) or send help in case of an accident. Locating devices can track stolen cars or cars in use by teenage drivers.

FIGURE 1.16 |

Computers identify and guide weapons to the target.

FIGURE 1.17

FIGURE 1.18

Complex military operations require advanced navigation and support systems.

Drivers can use computers for navigation and emergency support.

Engine control   A computer may be connected to sensors on the engine of your car to measure variables such as temperature and concentration of exhaust gases. It can control spark timing and fuel-air mixtures for optimum fuel efficiency and performance. Computers can control the car's suspension to match the speed and road condition to optimize control and comfort.

Maintenance   A car's computer stores information about engine and other systems' performance, as well as the date of the last service. It can alert the driver to scheduled maintenance needs and download engine performance history to the repair facility's diagnostic computer (see Figure 1.19).

FIGURE 1.19

Mechanics can use computers to download the car's history of maintenance and problems from onboard auto computers.

Traffic signals   Loops of wire may be installed in narrow cuts in the pavement near an intersection, or cameras may be installed above the intersection to detect the presence of cars waiting at a stop light. A computer can calculate the optimum timing of the traffic signals to facilitate traffic flow.

Airlines

Airlines were one of the first businesses to use computers to manage reservations, and today's airports could not function safely without using them to help track aircraft in the air and on the ground. Computers are also used to calculate fuel loads.

Reservations   The airline industry relies on computers to manage and control a large database of reservations. Electronic tickets are rapidly replacing paper tickets. Travelers may use their own computer connected to the Internet to make a reservation. Several airlines allow the traveler to go online within a day of their flight and print out a boarding pass.

Air traffic control   At any given time, there are thousands of airplanes in the air crisscrossing the country. Each large airplane has a transponder that broadcasts its identity. Computer systems at the airports track the planes and coordinate their movements in the air and on the ground (see Figure 1.20).

Fuel load calculations   The airline business is very competitive, and all airlines use computers to reduce unnecessary costs while maintaining an adequate margin of safety. Computers are used to calculate the amount of fuel each plane needs for a trip. The number of passengers, the weight of luggage and freight, and wind conditions are taken into account, and the fuel load is calculated. The computer that makes this determination may not even be in the same city as the airport.

FIGURE 1.20

Air traffic controllers use computers to coordinate use of busy airports.

FIGURE 1.21

Shipping by any mode uses computers to track items.

Ships

Large quantities of manufactured goods move from the Far East, South America, and Europe to the United States by way of container ships. Containers resemble truck trailers without wheels and may be stacked. Each one is marked with a *bar code*, which consists of vertical lines whose width and spacing are converted by a bar code reader to identification numbers that computers use to track their movement.

Trains

A computer system coordinates the use of railroad tracks to avoid collisions and to optimize traffic. Freight cars have bar codes that identify their owners. These freight cars can travel around the country and be used for many different tasks by different railroad companies. Computers collect information about the use of the freight cars, and the railroad companies pay each other for use of each other's freight cars regardless of where they are used in the country. Computers also track individual packages using bar codes (see Figure 1.21).

RECREATION

People use computers for fun as well as work. They may use them to simulate an opponent in a game or provide a game scenario for players who may be in the same room or anywhere in the world. They are also used extensively to aid vacation planning.

Gaming

Computers may be used for playing games in competition with the computer or with other players whose computers are connected via the Internet. One popular mode of gaming is a *Multi-user dungeon*, or *MUD*, in which users adopt a character that is represented by an animated figure or *avatar* (see Figure 1.22).

FIGURE 1.22

Players can use computers to interact with each other online.

Recreational Travel

Travelers can use their computers to make reservations for hotels, automobiles, airplanes, ships, and tours. They can view pictures of hotel rooms and destinations or check weather satellites for conditions.

PROTECTING YOUR PERSONAL HEALTH WHILE USING COMPUTERS

Computers have become part of our lives, and many people spend hours each day sitting at a desktop computer. When you perform a repetitive movement from the same physical position, parts of your body become fatigued. Incorrect positions can accelerate the onset of fatigue and even result in painful, chronic problems. The following tips may be effective at reducing fatigue but are not right for everyone. Seek professional medical advice if you have a health problem related to computer use.

ERGONOMICS

Ergonomics is the applied science of equipment design to reduce operator fatigue and discomfort. Computers are often added to a workspace with little regard for operator comfort or fatigue factors. Whether you work on a computer, or manage people who do, it is important to know some of the basics of ergonomic design.

HEALTHY PRACTICES

To maximize comfort and cause the least stress to your body while working at a computer, you need to have proper vertical and horizontal alignment between yourself and the computer. You also need to have proper lighting to avoid eye fatigue. Each of these aspects of a healthy ergonomic workstation is examined in detail.

Vertical Alignment

To achieve a comfortable and sustainable posture for working long hours at a desktop computer, you need to consider the effect of gravity and how to support important parts of your body. The key to success is to adjust your desk, chair, and computer components to promote good posture.

Minimize stress on your neck   Imaging holding a bowling ball above your head, at the end of your outstretched arm. If the center of the ball is directly in line with your forearm, it's not too hard. Imagine bending your wrist slightly so the weight of the ball is not directly above your forearm but is supported by your bent wrist. You can imagine how much harder this would be and how much more quickly your wrist would tire. Your head weighs about as much as a bowling ball, and it sits on top of your neck and spine. If you move your head forward so it is not directly above your spine, your neck muscles must work harder to support its weight, and the discs between the vertebrae in your spine will be compressed unevenly, which may result in disabling back pain. If you combine leaning forward with a twist to the right or left to look at a document lying on a desk, the stress and compression problems are even worse. It is important to choose a working position that keeps your head upright and above your spine.

The keyboard   Desktop computers usually consist of a monitor, keyboard, mouse, and a case. In some instances, the monitor and case are combined in a single unit. When the case is a separate unit, it can be placed under the desk and connected to the other components by wires that are several feet long so there is some flexibility regarding its placement. The monitor, keyboard, and mouse are the elements that must be aligned with the user. The keyboard sits

FIGURE 1.23

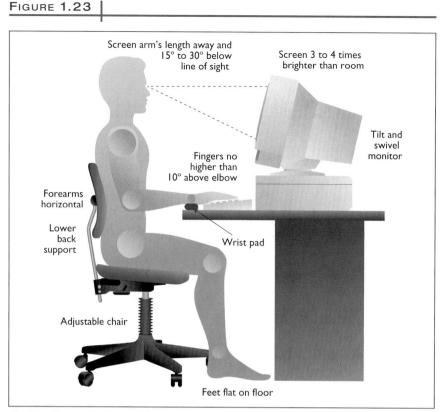

Screen arm's length away and 15° to 30° below line of sight

Screen 3 to 4 times brighter than room

Tilt and swivel monitor

Fingers no higher than 10° above elbow

Forearms horizontal

Lower back support

Wrist pad

Adjustable chair

Feet flat on floor

Chair adjustments and table heights are critical for good posture and support.

on the desk or on a special keyboard tray suspended below the desk. The keyboard is usually the least adjustable element of the computer and will serve as a starting point for adjusting the heights of the other elements. The height of your chair should be adjusted so your fingers rest comfortably on the keyboard with your forearms parallel to the floor, as shown in Figure 1.23. Pay particular attention to your wrists. They should not be twisted up or down for normal typing.

The monitor Older-model monitors can be quite large and deep, resembling a television. The depth of the monitor often leads the user to place it on a desk in the corner of the room. Newer monitors use *liquid crystal display (LCD)* technology like the display on a laptop, and they are much thinner, providing more choices for placement. The height of the monitor should allow you to look at the center of the screen without tilting your head up or down. Some people who wear bifocals or variable-focus lenses may need a special prescription that provides focus without necessitating tilting the head. If necessary, the monitor may be raised by placing it on a suitable support. It should also be tilted so the surface of the screen is perpendicular to your line of sight. If you work from paper documents, a stand or document attachment that holds the document in a vertical position to the side of the monitor minimizes your having to tilt your head down and to the side.

Chair selection and adjustments Many people spend a lot of money on an office desk and much less on a chair, but the chair is more important to your health and comfort. Choose a chair with an adjustable height and back. If the chair has armrests, they should be adjustable as well. The back of the chair should have a curved portion known as a *lumbar support* that supports your lower back. The seat of the chair should not be too deep for

FIGURE 1.24

Home office workstation designed for horizontal symmetry with monitors and document stand elevated to align with the user's eye level

your body. You should be able to sit on it with your back against the lumbar support, and your legs should be able to bend at the knee and go straight down. The front edge of the seat should curve downward without a sharp edge. If your chair has adjustable arm supports, they should be adjusted to take the weight of your arms off your shoulders and neck.

Footrest   Your feet should be flat on the floor, supporting the weight of your legs. If the weight of your legs is supported by the seat of the chair, the pressure on the backs of your legs will restrict circulation. If you cannot adjust the height of the chair to use the keyboard comfortably without raising your feet off the floor, then use a footrest that allows your feet to support the weight of your legs.

Mouse   The mouse should be at the same height as the keyboard or in a position where it can be used without requiring that the user's arm be unsupported.

Horizontal Alignment

The human body is bilateral, which means that there is a line of symmetry down the center, and the right and left sides of the body are mirror images of each other. This line of symmetry is called the *centerline*. To reduce stress on your neck and back, align your keyboard and mouse to minimize the time you spend in a twisted position. When you sit at your computer, the monitor should be directly in front of you. Imagine a vertical line directly in front of you. This line should pass through the center of your monitor.

Keyboard   Most keyboards used with desktop computers have groups of keys at the right for numbers, arrows, and special functions. When people center the keyboard in front of the monitor, it often places the center of the commonly used alphabet keys to the left of centerline. In order to type in this position, they twist their shoulders to the left. Consider moving the keyboard to the right so the centerline passes between the letters G and H on the keyboard (see Figure 1.24).

Mouse   Most people are right-handed, which means they commonly place the mouse to the right of the keyboard. If you move the keyboard to the right to get the alphabet keys centered, it requires an even greater reach to use the mouse. If you are left-handed, this works to your advantage. Right-handed people must compromise to use commonly available combinations of keyboard and mouse. One option is to learn to use the mouse left-handed on the left side of the keyboard. Another option is to learn keyboard shortcuts for most mouse operations to minimize the number of times you must take your hand from the keyboard and reach for the mouse.

Lighting

Another group of muscles that can be fatigued by improper conditions is those in the eye. When we change focus from nearby objects to those far away, muscles in the eyeball stretch the lens to make it flatter. When we change focus back to nearby objects, the muscles relax and the lens returns to its more curved state. If we look at brightly lit objects, muscles in the iris contract to shrink the opening, or pupil, to restrict the amount of light allowed into the eye. When we look at darker objects, the muscles relax and the iris expands to let in more light.

Monitors

Newer computers can manage several monitors at once, which reduces mouse movements or keystrokes necessary to switch between open documents and promotes moving the head side-to-side while working rather than maintaining a single head position for long periods of time (see Figure 1.25).

FIGURE 1.25

Use of more than one monitor at the same level promotes occasional head movement and reduces mouse movements or keystrokes necessary to switch between open documents.

Veiling reflections

If you look in a mirror, objects appear to be behind the mirror, not at its surface, and our eyes adjust focus accordingly. If there is a bright light source behind the computer operator, its reflection may be bright enough to be visible along with the document on the screen. This is called a *veiling reflection* (see Figure 1.26). Veiling reflections can fool the eye into changing focus from the surface of the monitor to the distant object reflected in it. This causes the eye muscles to contract. When we recognize that the document is going out of focus, the eye changes back to the nearby focus. This process can repeat itself, causing fatigue of the eye muscles. If you can see a window or bright light on the glass of your monitor, try to block the light or change the orientation of your desk. If that isn't practical, you can get an antireflection screen to place over your monitor to reduce reflections.

Contrast

If you work in a dark room, your iris will adjust to the brightness of the monitor but will have to readjust when you look at a document, the desktop, or some other darker object. If you have your desk in front of a window through which direct sunlight may enter, the light coming from the window may be brighter than your computer screen, making it difficult to see the dimmer monitor. To reduce muscle fatigue in the iris, your room and documents should be about as bright as the computer monitor. Most monitors have brightness adjustments so you can increase or decrease the brightness to obtain a better match with the surroundings.

FIGURE 1.26

Bright light sources that reflect off your screen can veil the screen's image.

Computers are an integral part of our lives and learning to use them is important to participating fully in today's society. However, everyone does not have the same opportunity to become familiar with computers.

THE "DIGITAL DIVIDE"

A large majority of students who attend college have computers in their homes, and virtually all of them have access to computers at school. It is easy for students to lose sight of the fact that many Americans and most of the other people in the world do not have computers or convenient access to them. The digital divide is a term that describes the separation of people into two groups: those who have technology and the ability to use it and those who don't. Discussion of this issue can be further separated into discussions about a digital divide within the United States and the divide between the United States and the rest of the world. Because the use of computers is so commonly associated with Internet use, studies about computer access also examine accessibility to the Internet.

United States

The U.S. Department of Commerce issued a report in February 2002 that shed light on America's use of the Internet. The report, *A Nation Online: How Americans Are Expanding Their Use of the Internet*, describes Internet use and breaks it down by demographic factors such as income, employment status, age, gender, education, urban or rural location, and race (see Figure 1.27). In the executive summary, the report provides several significant facts that describe the digital divide and how it is changing in the United States.

❱ Fifty-four percent of the nation is using the Internet, and 66 percent use computers.

❱ Ninety percent of children between five and 17 use computers.

❱ Computers at schools substantially narrow the gap in computer usage rates for children from high- and low-income families.

❱ Internet use among blacks and Hispanics is growing ten to thirteen percent faster than among whites and Asians.

❱ The highest rate of increase among different types of households, 29 percent, was among single mothers.

❱ Eighty percent of Americans who use the Internet access it through dial-up service.

❱ Residential use of high-speed, broadband service almost doubled from about 11 to 20 percent of Internet users.

❱ Forty-five percent of the population uses e-mail, up from 35 percent in 2000.

❱ Approximately one-third of Americans use the Internet to search for product and service information (36 percent, up from 26 percent in 2000).

❱ The presence in a household of someone who uses a computer or the Internet at work is associated with substantially higher computer ownership or Internet use for that household, by a margin of about 77 percent to 35 percent.

Other Developed Countries

The United States is far ahead of the rest of the world, especially developing nations, in the use of computers, and the gap seems to be getting

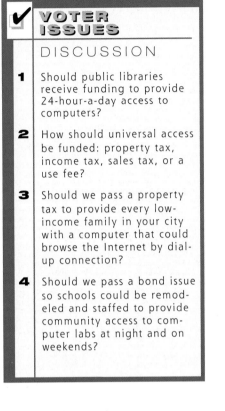

VOTER ISSUES

DISCUSSION

1 Should public libraries receive funding to provide 24-hour-a-day access to computers?

2 How should universal access be funded: property tax, income tax, sales tax, or a use fee?

3 Should we pass a property tax to provide every low-income family in your city with a computer that could browse the Internet by dial-up connection?

4 Should we pass a bond issue so schools could be remodeled and staffed to provide community access to computer labs at night and on weekends?

FIGURE 1.27

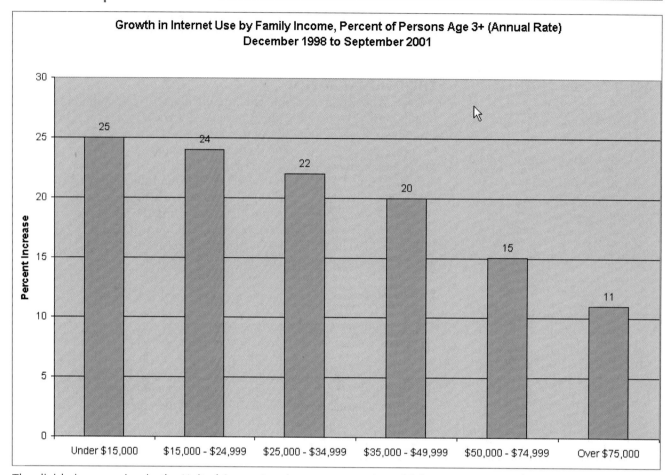

Growth in Internet Use by Family Income, Percent of Persons Age 3+ (Annual Rate) December 1998 to September 2001

The divide is narrowing in the United States: Low-income groups have higher percentages of growth in computer and Internet usage.

larger. A report from the Organization for Economic Co-operation and Development (OECD), a group of 30 countries that are mostly European and Asian, provides the following information:

❯ The penetration rate of Internet hosts for the United States is seven times that for the European Union, and just over eight times that for Japan.

❯ In March 2000, the United States added three times as many secure servers as did the rest of the OECD combined.

❯ Nations that charge by the minute for Internet access have much lower penetration rates than those that have flat fees for unlimited access.

❯ In the United States and in a small number of other countries with pricing structures favorable to Internet access, usage of the Internet is far higher than in other OECD countries, as reflected in average time spent online.

Developing Countries

Three main factors are responsible for the lack of access to and use of computers in poor, developing countries:

DIVERSITY ISSUES

DISCUSSION

1 How can distance education benefit people with disabilities?

2 What groups have less access to the Internet than others? Are they located in a particular geographic location?

3 If a child grows up in a home without a computer or Internet connection and does not have access to either at school, what effect will a very limited exposure to the Internet have on that child's future? Can you name five things that this child would not know how to do that most of his or her peers would know?

> ❯ lack of reliable electricity
> ❯ restricted access to telephone service
> ❯ general poverty

A computer that costs less than two percent of an American's annual income might cost more than someone in a poor country makes in an entire year. While the cost of computers is commonly found to be under $1,000, this amount exceeds the annual income of many people in third world countries.

USERS WITH SPECIAL NEEDS

Computer input and output devices are often designed assuming the user has full use of both hands and has good vision and hearing. The report from the Department of Commerce, *A Nation Online: How Americans Are Expanding Their Use of the Internet*, examined computer and Internet use among people with disabilities. The researchers gathered data on people who declared they had a physical condition that limited their hearing, vision, keyboard use, ability to walk, or ability to leave the home (see Figure 1.28). The results of that report give us insight into this accessibility problem.

> ❯ On average, 8.5 percent of the population reported at least one of these five disabilities.
> ❯ Only two percent of the population between ages 3 and 24 reported one of the disabilities.
> ❯ Almost 30 percent of the population aged 65 and older reported one of the disabilities.

FIGURE 1.28

	3-14	15-24	25-34	35-44	45-54	55-64	65 and Over
Multiple Disabilities	0.4	0.6	1.0	2.0	3.8	6.3	15.0
Blind or Severe Vision Impairment	0.3	0.4	0.4	0.5	0.6	0.7	1.4
Deaf or Severe Hearing Impairment	0.3	0.3	0.3	0.5	0.6	0.9	2.4
Difficulty Walking	0.2	0.4	1.0	1.9	2.7	5.7	7.1
Difficulty Typing	0.1	0.3	0.4	0.6	0.6	0.8	0.9
Difficulty Leaving Home	Not Asked	0.5	0.5	0.7	0.9	1.1	2.2
None of These Disabilities	98.7	97.6	96.4	93.8	90.7	84.6	71.1

Source: NTIA and ESA, U.S. Department of Commerce, using U.S. Census Bureau Current Population Survey Supplements

Age distribution of specific disabilities as a percent of population, 2001

USING FEATURES OF WINDOWS XP TO HELP THE VISUALLY IMPAIRED

The Windows and Macintosh operating systems have a group of accessibility features that allow users to modify the way the operating system interacts with them. There are options for those who have visual or hearing impairments and other options for those who have trouble using a mouse or keyboard. Elderly people are using computers to communicate with their children and grandchildren by e-mail, but many people in this age group have vision problems. Here are some tips for making changes to the Windows XP environment to assist someone who has some visual impairment or simply for customizing the visual environment to your own tastes. The Macintosh system has similar features.

Windows XP has a program that allows you to modify the font size, cursor width, color contrast, and mouse pointer to make them easier to see. It also can open a panel on the screen that acts like a magnifier to show details. If you are working in a computer laboratory, changes to the operating system may not be allowed. If they are, be sure to undo the changes to leave the computer the way you found it.

1. On the Windows task bar, click Start, All Programs, Accessories, Accessibility, and Accessibility Wizard. The Accessibility Wizard starts.
2. Click Next. Click Use Microsoft Magnifier, and large titles and menus.
3. Click Next. A panel opens at the top of your screen, and the font size increases in all the Windows dialog boxes. Three dialog boxes open that may overlap.
4. Click the Microsoft Magnifier dialog box to select it. Click OK to close the dialog box.
5. Click the Accessibility Wizard dialog box. Confirm that *Change the font size* and *Use Microsoft Magnifier* are both selected. Click Next.
6. Click *I am blind or have difficulty seeing things on screen*. Click Next.
7. Click one of the larger scroll bar options. Click Next.
8. Choose *Large* or *Extra Large* icons. Click Next.
9. Choose one of the high-contrast display color schemes. Click Next.
10. Choose a different mouse and cursor combination. Click Next.
11. Click the middle of the *Cursor Width* bar to select a wider cursor. Click Next.
12. If you are sharing a computer in a lab, click Cancel. Click *No* to undo the changes. Everything changes back to normal except the Magnifier.
13. Click the title bar of the Magnifier Settings dialog box. Click Exit. The magnifier pane closes.

If you want to change the settings, you can run the wizard again or choose Start, Control Panel, Display to change the settings individually.

TEST PREPARATION

The following section does not replace reading the text, nor does it contain all the information that will be tested. It is designed to provide examples and identify sections that need review.

summary by objective

WHAT IS A COMPUTER?

- Input
- Processing
- Storage
- Output

- **Identify the four main functions of a computer and give examples of each:**
  - Input—keyboard, mouse
  - Processing—central processing units like Intel's Pentium 4, AMD's Athalon, or Motorola's PowerPC
  - Storage—random access memory (RAM), magnetic media like the hard drive or floppy disk, optical media like CDs
  - Output—monitor, printer
- **Typical sequence—Input, primary storage, processing, primary storage, output, secondary storage**

AWARENESS OF COMPUTER INFLUENCE

- **Business and Government**
- **Education**
- **Health Professions**
- **Military**
- **Transportation**
- **Military**

- **Identify at least one way that computers are used in each of the following: business, education, health professions, the military, transportation, and recreation:**
  - Business—financial spreadsheets
  - Education—distance education
  - Health—diagnostic tools such as CAT scans and MRIs
  - Military—"smart" bombs
  - Transportation—bar codes on shipping containers and railroad cars, used for tracking
  - Recreation—airline, hotel, and car rental reservations

PROTECTING YOUR PERSONAL HEALTH WHILE USING COMPUTERS

- **Definition of Ergonomics**
- **Healthy Practices**

- **Define ergonomics—the applied science of equipment design to reduce operator fatigue and discomfort.**
- **Identify examples of proper alignment between the user and computer components such as the monitor, keyboard, and mouse—the top of the monitor's screen should be at eye level and the head should not be tilted or twisted while working.**
- **Identify key adjustment to chairs for proper posture—the chair height should be adjusted so the wrists are not bent up or down at the keyboard.**
- **Identify proper alignment of lighting sources—no bright light sources should be seen as reflections on the screen.**

UNIVERSAL ACCESS

- The "Digital Divide"
- Users with Special Needs

- **Define "Digital Divide"—a phrase that describes the separation of people into two groups: those who have technology and the ability to use it and those who don't.**
- **Cite statistics on computer and Internet use for the United States as a whole and for select groups such as children, blacks, Hispanics, whites, Asians, and single mothers. Example: 90% of children between 5 and 17 use computers.**
- **Compare Internet usage between developed countries that charge a flat fee for access and those that charge by the minute—countries that charge by the minute have significantly lower Internet usage.**
- **Identify three major factors that limit poor nations' access to the Internet—cost, reliable electric systems, and reliable telephone systems**
- **Cite statistics on the percentage of people in the United States, by age group, who report they have at least one disability that could affect computer use—8.5% of the population, 2% of the population aged 3 to 24, 30% aged 65 and older.**

1. ___ CD-R is a processor by AMD.

2. ___ A "smart bomb" is a computer-designed drug that targets specific tumors.

3. ___ Ergonomics is the applied science of design to reduce operator fatigue and discomfort.

4. ___ A veiling reflection causes eye fatigue because the muscles of the iris adjust constantly.

5. ___ The "digital divide" refers to the separation between the processor and RAM memory.

multiple choice

1. Which of the following is not one of the four functions that a computer performs?
   a) algorithm
   b) output
   c) storage
   d) processing

2. Which of the following uses of computers is mismatched with its area of application?
   a) Military—smart bombs, training, maintenance, GPS
   b) Business—documents, spreadsheets, project management
   c) Health—MRIs, CAT scans, insurance records
   d) Recreation—bar codes, fuel load, traffic control

3. Which of the following statements is least appropriate for ergonomic design of a computer workstation?
   a) Use bold, primary colors near the computer to reduce boredom.
   b) Your feet should be flat on the floor or on a footrest.
   c) Adjust the height of the chair to avoid bending your wrists while using the keyboard.
   d) The monitor should be placed where its screen does not reflect the light from a window to the operator's eye.

4. Which of the following is true about the digital divide?
   a) 75 percent of children between 5 and 17 use the computer.
   b) 50 percent of people older than 65 reported they had at least one disability that limited their use of a computer.
   c) Countries that charge a flat fee for Internet use have a lower rate of computer use than those countries that charge by the minute.
   d) One of the factors that limits Internet use in poor countries is the lack of reliable electricity.

5. Which of the following is not a storage device?
   a) MRI
   b) EPROM
   c) RAM
   d) CD

completion

1. If a distance education class is conducted online using live communication at the same time each week, it is using _____ communication.

2. A message like a memo or letter sent electronically is called _____.

3. The center of the monitor should align with the _____ of the body.

4. _____ is a type of display used in thin monitors.

5. A _____ database has two tables that have a field in common.

Match each term with its definition.

_____ **1.** asynchronous
_____ **2.** avatar
_____ **3.** bar code
_____ **4.** CAT scan
_____ **5.** CD
_____ **6.** centerline
_____ **7.** CPU
_____ **8.** database
_____ **9.** disc
_____ **10.** disk
_____ **11.** e-mail
_____ **12.** ergonomics
_____ **13.** flash memory
_____ **14.** Gantt
_____ **15.** GPS
_____ **16.** LCD
_____ **17.** lumbar support
_____ **18.** magnetic media
_____ **19.** optical media
_____ **20.** processing
_____ **21.** RAM
_____ **22.** secondary storage
_____ **23.** spreadsheet
_____ **24.** synchronous
_____ **25.** veiling reflection

a. a curved portion of the back of a chair that provides additional support for the lower part of the back
b. an image of a bright light source on a computer screen that partially obscures the object behind the reflective surface
c. a series of vertical bars and spaces that can be read by a computer
d. a type of chart that uses horizontal bars to represent tasks, the time they take, and their relationship to the start and end of other tasks
e. a general term for devices that are used to record information for later retrieval but do not require constant power to retain the information
f. an arrangement of cells in rows and columns that can be used to display and calculate numeric information, some of which is dependent on the results of calculations in other cells
g. an image that represents a person online
h. an imaginary line that bisects the human body vertically
i. at different times
j. at the same time
k. part of the computer that performs calculations
l. an optical memory device
m. an imaging system that uses x-rays and computers
n. mail exchanged between computers
o. a system that uses radio signals from satellites to accurately determine locations on earth
p. optical storage term that is similar to a term used for magnetic storage
q. magnetic media term that is similar to a term used for optical storage
r. a type of screen used in laptop computers and some desktop monitors that are typically much thinner than older-style monitors
s. lists of data organized in tables where each column is a type of information and each row is one person, event, or interaction
t. plastic or metal disks coated with a material usually containing iron used to store data
u. materials like reflective discs that can store data and retrieve it using light, usually in the form of a reflected laser beam
v. one of the four main functions of a computer—manipulating data according to a set of instructions to create information that can be stored
w. high-speed memory on computer chips
x. similar to RAM but does not require constant power
y. the applied science of equipment design to reduce operator fatigue and discomfort

beyond the facts

Factual knowledge provides the basis for higher levels of learning. In the following sections, you will work with the concepts and facts presented in the chapter to develop critical-thinking and problem-solving skills. You will practice research, analysis, and communication and become aware of diversity issues while exploring the impact of computer technology on career choices, social interactions, and home life. The Leadership section helps you identify ways in which you can lead others in organizing and implementing projects that meet worthwhile community needs. In the Lifelong Learning exercise, you build a set of learning resources that you can use after this course to continue learning.

objectives for beyond the facts

END OF CHAPTER EXERCISES	Achievement of the objectives for the end-of-chapter exercises requires evaluation of documents, class discussions, or presentations.
Critical Thinking–Research	1) Express an informed opinion on the digital divide 2) Demonstrate the following skills: locate relevant information online, analyze the information and form an opinion based on the research, consider diversity issues, work with others where appropriate, and communicate the results in writing or by public presentation
Problem Solving	1) Use Help to learn how to use the accessibility features if your mouse fails 2) If unsuccessful, write a detailed description of the process for seeking assistance 3) If successful, write a detailed description of the process for instructing others 4) Communicate the experience to the class
Anticipating Career Challenges and Opportunities	Demonstrate the following skills: 1) Teamwork: coordinate research on job postings with other students 2) Research: find job posting information online 3) Diversity: consider working abroad 4) Analysis: analyze the job postings and form an opinion about required computer skills 5) Communication: communicate the results in writing or by public presentation
Impact on the Workplace	Demonstrate the following skills: 1) Teamwork: ability to coordinate research on use of computers in the workplace with other students 2) Research: ability to identify use of computers at work by observation and interviews 3) Diversity: observe variations in computer use by age, race, and gender 4) Analysis: form an opinion about the degree to which the organization uses computers 5) Communication: communicate the results in writing or by public presentation
Impact on Social Interactions	Demonstrate the following skills: 1) Teamwork: allocate tasks for development of a survey with other students 2) Research: write survey questions that may be summarized numerically 3) Diversity: design questions that recognize and respect different priorities for social activity 4) Analysis: conduct and analyze the survey and summarize the results 5) Communication: communicate the results in writing or by public presentation
Impact on Home Life	Demonstrate the following skills: 1) Teamwork: allocate tasks for development of a survey with other students 2) Research: write survey questions that may be summarized numerically 3) Diversity: design questions that recognize and respect different priorities for social activity 4) Analysis: conduct and analyze the survey and summarize the results 5) Communication: communicate the results in writing or by public presentation
Leadership	Describe a plan to lead a group of people toward a worthy goal—in this case, a plan to distribute used computers to people who need them.
Lifelong Learning	Identify three or more online resources that may be used to learn more about the topics introduced in this chapter.

critical thinking–research

How does the digital divide within the United States compare with the digital divide between the United States and developing countries?

1. **Teamwork**—Join one to five other students. Decide how to divide up the work. Possible divisions could be: within the United States, between the United States and other countries, diversity issues, editing the group paper, and preparing the class presentation.

2. **Research**—Use a Web browser and go to the companion Web site at **http://www.prenhall. com/preston**. Use the resources provided for use with this book. Follow the links by clicking on the Web addresses that are highlighted and underlined. Read about the digital divide in the United States and between the United States and other countries. Use a Web search engine such as Google.com or Yahoo.com to search for keywords and phrases such as "digital divide." Make a list of the sources you find to be relevant that you may want to reference later. Include the title of the page or article, the name of the organization responsible for the Web page, the date the page or article was written, and the Web address. You may also go to the library and look

up books, articles, and news reports that are relevant to this topic. Many libraries have the full text of articles and news reports in proprietary databases that are not available to the public online.

3. **Diversity issues**—Look for differences based on race, geography, religion, and economic status.

4. **Analysis**—Write an essay that compares the digital divide within the United States to that between the United States and the rest of the world. Form and express an opinion. Go beyond simple reporting of the facts. Support your opinion with references to the articles you read. Ask your instructor for guidance regarding the required length of the essay.

5. **Communication**—Prepare a presentation in which you present your opinion and the supporting facts to the class. Depending on your computer skill, you could give the presentation using a program like PowerPoint and save it as a Web page or you could prepare a paper handout with your Web references for use while you talk to the class.

problem solving

The objective of this exercise is to learn valuable processes for solving computer problems, not just the solution to this particular problem.

Occasionally a component of your computer stops working. If the mouse stops working in the middle of an important document, you may need to know how to save the document and shut down your computer without a mouse. Operating a computer without a mouse is a situation that some people with mobility limitations face every day, and you can use the accessibility features provided for them to solve this problem.

1. **Search for help on the topic**—Use the extensive library of Help topics that is included with your computer's operating system. In Windows, click Start, Help, and Support. Look under the Accessibility section for help on using a computer if your mobility is limited. When you find a topic that appears to be appropriate for this problem, write down the sequence of choices that leads you back to it for future reference.

2. **Read the instructions and try it**—Attempt to follow the instructions for replacing your computer's mouse with keyboard functions. Write a description of the process. If you are not successful, describe what you tried and what did or did not happen. Be specific. If you were successful but found that the instructions were not clear at some point, write a description of the problematic instructions, and suggest improvements.

3. **Troubleshoot**—If your first attempt is unsuccessful, determine whether there are some alternative interpretations of the instructions that you can try. Record the results of these efforts.

4. **Communicate**—If you were unsuccessful, describe your attempt in step-by-step detail. This is necessary if you ask an expert for help.

   If you were successful, describe the process so it can be followed by others. Identify any instructions that you think could be improved, and provide a suggestion for improvement.

Illustrate your communication—in many cases, a screen capture is very useful when describing a problem or a procedure. In Windows, you can capture the computer screen by pressing the PrntScn button on the keyboard. Nothing seems to happen when you press that button, but if you open a Word processing document, you can paste the screen into the document to illustrate your point.

Present your findings to the class. Prepare a demonstration of how to use the keyboard to replace mouse functions.

anticipating career challenges and opportunities

Check job postings for your job or the job you want, and see what computer skills are expected.

1. **Teamwork**—Join one or two other students who have similar career plans. Decide how to divide up the work. Possible divisions could be: corporations, government, and other countries.

2. **Research**—Use a Web browser and go to the companion Web site at **http://www.prenhall.com/preston**. Use the resources provided for this book. Follow the links by clicking on the Web addresses that are highlighted and underlined. Search for jobs in your current career field or the field into which you would like to move. Make a list of the sources you find to be relevant that you may want to reference later. Include the title of the page or article, the name of the organization responsible for the Web page, the date the page or article was written, and the Web address. You may also go to the library and look up books, articles, and news reports that are relevant to this topic. Many libraries have the full text of articles and news reports in proprietary databases that are not available to the public online.

3. **Diversity issues**—Consider working in another country for a few years to expand your horizons and improve your résumé. Look for jobs in countries where English is commonly spoken and in countries where it isn't.

4. **Analysis**—Write an essay that describes the computer skills that are expected for your current career and for a possible alternate career. Form and express an opinion about the level of computer skills you need to keep your current job or to switch to another. Go beyond simple reporting of the facts. Support your opinion with references to the articles you read. Ask your instructor for guidance regarding the required length of the essay.

5. **Communication**—Prepare a presentation in which you present your opinion and the supporting facts to the class. Depending on your computer skill, you could give the presentation using a program like PowerPoint and save it as a Web page, or you could prepare a paper handout with your Web references for use while you talk to the class.

impact on the workplace

Identify where computers are used in your workplace.

1. **Teamwork**—Join one or two other students who work where you do or in a similar type of business or organization. Decide how to divide up the work. Possible divisions could be: financial records, customer relations, property management, and shipping and receiving.

2. **Research**—Do a survey of your place of employment or your college to identify where computers are used. Record specific information about what you observe. Refer to the examples given in the text, and also look for examples of the following:

- Property identification—Look for bar codes on computers and desks that may be used for tracking equipment and property. Look for bar codes on the doors to rooms that might be used for leasing or facility management purposes.
- Customer database—Talk to the information technology department, and ask what major functions of the business depend upon computers.
- Advertising—Talk to media relations, and find out how advertising materials are created and sent out for printing.

- Shipping and receiving—Talk to someone at the shipping dock to find out how shipments are tracked.
- Document management—Determine how interoffice memos, procedure manuals, and policy statements are written, distributed, and stored.
- Human resources—Determine whether computers are used to calculate and track employee benefits.
- Accounting and payroll—Find out if the computer work is done in-house or by a service, as well as how the data is transferred between the accounting and payroll functions. Find out whether direct deposit to employee checking accounts is allowed.

3. **Diversity issues**—Observe the age, gender, and race of the people who work with computers in your organization. Are there any obvious differences between the people who use computers most and the general population of your company or organization?

4. **Analysis**—Write an essay that describes how computers are used in your organization. Form and express an opinion about the degree to which your organization relies on computers to function and if you observed any differences based on age, gender, or race in the staff that uses computers most. Support your opinion with statistics based on your observations. Ask your instructor for guidance regarding the required length of the essay.

5. **Communication**—Prepare a presentation in which you present your opinion and the supporting facts to the class. Depending on your computer skill, you could create charts in application programs like PowerPoint or Excel to graphically communicate the data you recorded, or you could prepare a paper handout with data for use while you talk to the class.

impact on social interactions

Identify how computers impact the social lives of your friends and classmates.

1. **Teamwork**—Join two or three other students to devise a survey on how computers affect your social life. Decide how to divide up the work. Each student could write questions on topics such as the following: chat rooms, e-mail, dating, viewing sexually explicit Web sites, playing games against the computer, playing games with others in the same room, playing games with others remotely, and gambling.

2. **Research**
   a) Write questions that can be quantified. Here are some examples:
      (1) Measuring opinions—Make a strong positive statement, and ask responders if they strongly agree, mildly agree, mildly disagree, or strongly disagree. Notice there is no neutral response. For example: "I prefer using e-mail to writing and mailing letters."
      (2) Measuring time spent on an activity—Ask responders to estimate how many hours per week they spend on an activity. Provide ranges from which to choose.

   b) Check your college's policy on human subjects research.
      (1) Design your survey to protect the privacy of the responder.
      (2) Comply with any restrictions or requirements your college imposes on in-class surveys of this type.
   c) Review your questions for sensitivity to different lifestyle choices to avoid judgmental phrases.
   d) Use your survey on the class.

3. **Analysis**
   a) Compile the results of the survey.
   b) Prepare a summary report that includes the average score for each question.

4. **Communication**—Prepare a presentation in which you present your summary report to the class. Depending on your computer skill, you could create charts in application programs like PowerPoint or Excel to graphically communicate the data you recorded, or you could prepare a paper handout with data for use while you talk to the class.

impact on home life

Most offices have specific places for people to work with computers or paper documents. Few homes have a room designed to be a home office so most people either convert an unused bedroom or work at a small desk or kitchen table. Using a computer at home for schoolwork or to take work home from the office can have a significant impact on home life. Examine and analyze the impact of using a computer at home for schoolwork or as part of your job.

1. **Teamwork**—Join a large group of five to seven other students, at least half of whom have a computer at home that is used for schoolwork or office work. Decide how to divide up the work. Possible divisions could be: homes with children, homes without children, college dormitory rooms, and apartments shared by college students.

2. **Research**—Do a survey of your residence or that of a family member or friend who uses a computer at home. Record specific information about what you observe. Refer to the examples given in the text, and also look for examples of the following:
   • distractions due to location or time of use
   • limitations on location due to telephone or cable modem connections
   • differences in space utilization due to use of laptop versus desktop computers
   • the ergonomics of the home setup for using the computer

If you have permission from the people involved, take pictures that illustrate your observations.

3. **Diversity issues**—Observe the age and gender of the people who use the computer in the home. Are there any obvious differences between the way children use computers versus adults or adults over 65? Do homes with children have computers in different locations from those that do not?

4. **Analysis**—The size of your sample is too small to reach any conclusions about the way the population uses computers, but you can report how your sample used computers and how it may have differed from your expectations. Write an essay that describes how computers are used in the homes your group observed and how your observations differed from your expectations. Based on your observations, relate anecdotes that illustrate how observation differed from expectations. Ask your instructor for guidance regarding the required length of the essay.

5. **Communication**—Prepare a presentation in which you present your findings to the class. Depending on your computer skill, you could use a digital camera or ask for digital developing of regular film and include the pictures in a presentation or printed handouts.

leadership

Some people buy a new, faster computer before their old one stops working, and they end up with an extra computer they don't use. You can organize a group of students who could collect these computers and distribute them to people who are on the other side of the digital divide.

1. **Vision**—Write a vision statement that describes what you want your group to achieve. It should motivate people to volunteer to help.

2. **Research**—Don't reinvent the wheel. Do the following background research:
   a) Determine whether anyone is already doing this in your community. If so, contact them and describe their operation.
   b) Determine what groups do something like this with used clothes, eyeglasses, or other items, and interview someone from each group to see what they can tell you about running a volunteer operation like theirs.
   c) Determine which government or nonprofit agencies in your area know of people who do

not have computers because of cost, as well as who might help.
   d) Consider diversity issues. The digital divide is greater between the United States and other countries. Find out what it would cost to ship a computer to Eastern Europe, India, South America, or Africa.

3. **Plan of Action**—Write a simple plan of action. Test the plan by following it yourself on a small scale. Locate someone who agrees with your vision statement and who has a working computer they would like to donate, and then find someone who needs it and arrange to get it to them.

4. **Analysis**—Write up an analysis of what you learned by testing your plan.

5. **Communication**—Present your plan to the class. Describe what you learned by testing your plan and how you think it could be expanded if others joined you. Share your vision statement, and try to inspire others to join you in your worthwhile effort.

lifelong learning

Add links to your browser's favorites list.

1. Start your Web browser, and open the list of favorite sites. Create folders named *Digital Divide* and *Career*. (Look for Organize Favorites in Internet Explorer and Manage Bookmarks in Netscape.)

2. Go to the companion Web page **www.prenhall. com/preston** for this chapter, and select one of the Web links on the digital divide that you found useful.

3. Add this link to your browser's favorites list in the Digital Divide folder.

4. Repeat this process for other links in the companion Web page for this chapter, and add them to the appropriate folders.

Create a journal in a word processor to set learning goals.

1. Identify areas in which you feel you know the least. List three specific topics related to this chapter that you would like to learn more about in the future.

2. You will add to this journal after each chapter to compile a personal list of references and topics for future study.

chapter 2

The Internet Connects Us

outline & objectives

DEVELOPMENT OF THE INTERNET
- Match people with their contributions.
- Match key terms related to TCP/IP with definitions.
- Identify ARPANET applications that are still used on the Internet.
- Identify federal objectives that led to commercialization.
- Match the developers of the World Wide Web with their roles.
- Match key terms related to Web pages with definitions.

STRUCTURE OF THE INTERNET
- Match key elements of the Internet with their functions.
- Use the terms Internet and intranet to complete sentences correctly.

METHODS OF CONNECTION
- Match connection methods with their characteristics.
- Rank methods of connection by their speed from slowest to fastest.
- Identify features of virtual private networks.

INTERNET ADDRESSES
- Match address extensions to the type of organization.
- Identify the relationship between a domain name and an IP address.
- Identify the difference between a URL and an IP address.
- Identify the segments of a URL.
- Identify the functions of HTTP, FTP, and Telnet.
- Identify the function of domain name servers.

PERSONAL COMMUNICATIONS
- Identify parts of an e-mail address.
- Match e-mail terms with definitions.
- Identify rules of etiquette.
- Identify the role of file compression for attachments.
- Identify the differences between Web mail and mail clients that are installed on the user's computer.
- Match instant messaging terms with definitions, and use them in sentences.
- Identify the features of Web logs and personal Web pages.
- Identify features of Voice over IP and videoconferencing.

FINDING INFORMATION, WORKING, AND PLAYING

- Identify the function of a portal.
- Identify functions of applets and cookies.
- Identify common features of browsers.
- Identify popular Web browsers and the significant differences between them.
- Identify searching methods and tools.
- Identify resources found in libraries.
- Identify the objective for citing references.
- Match types of information available with example Web sites, for example, weather, news, maps, and events.
- Match types of commerce available with example Web sites.
- Identify issues related to using credit cards online.
- Identify terms used for types of commerce between business and customers.
- Identify types of online entertainment.
- Identify when Web-based training is appropriate.
- Identify features of online college courses.

The Internet plays an important role in our lives, and its use is increasing rapidly. We use it to communicate with each other in ways that are new and in ways that are adaptations of older technologies.

WHY DO I NEED TO KNOW THIS?

Many people buy a computer simply as a tool to get on the Internet to exchange e-mail. We send more personal mail as e-mail than by the U.S. Postal Service. Many people post personal Web pages to keep family and friends informed of developments in their lives, and since September 11, 2001, many people have started Web logs in which they share their daily experiences and thoughts. People can communicate directly with each other anywhere in the world even if their governments are not talking. Virtually all of the companies we deal with have Web sites where we can shop, receive product support, or ask questions. We can use computers and the Internet to find answers, or at least opinions, on any subject. Most people assume that any student who graduates from college today is familiar with using the Internet, but to understand the issues related to the Internet, you need to know how its structure is different from previous forms of communication. To do this, we start by looking at the origins of the Internet, its structure, and its organizations. Then we look at how individuals connect to the Internet and how Web addresses are structured and allocated. Next, we look at how people use the Internet to communicate with one another and enrich their lives on a daily basis.

The World Wide Web is just a part of the Internet. To understand how they relate to one another, it is necessary to examine how they came into being.

In the late 1950s and early 1960s, computers were large, expensive, and rare. The way they worked and stored data was not standardized, and they could not communicate with each other. If a researcher in New York wanted to run a particular program on a computer in California, he or she would have to travel across the country. A task that would take only hours if the computers could communicate directly would take weeks to accomplish.

Military Research and the Cold War

In 1962, at the height of the cold war between the United States and the Soviet Union, the United States had several research and command facilities around the country that used computers. At the time, differences in the computers slowed research, and there was a real fear that atomic war could break out and destroy large parts of the country. Government leaders wanted to speed up research by connecting the labs so they could share information, and they also wanted to establish a reliable system that would still function during a war when communication systems would be under attack. In August 1962, J. C. R. Licklider of the Massachusetts Institute of Technology (MIT) wrote a series of memos in which he described his concept of a "Galactic Network," which was a globally interconnected set of computers that could quickly access data and programs from each other. Licklider was the first head of a government agency named the *Advanced Research Projects Agency*, or *ARPA*, which later added Defense to its name and became known as *DARPA*. The U.S. government decided to build a network to connect the computers, and it wanted a reliable, decentralized system that could not easily be destroyed. In 1961, Leonard Kleinrock, also at MIT, published a paper on *packet switching*, which, along with later work by Bob Kahn and Vent Cerf, provided the method to fulfill Licklider's vision and the military's need for a reliable, decentralized system. ARPA used this method to create a network of computers named *ARPANET*.

To understand the concept of packet switching, we should compare it with the method most telephone systems use: *circuit switching*. When you place a telephone call, your call is completed by connecting a series of wires between you and the recipient of your call. If one of the connections between the two of you is broken, the call is interrupted. This method was too fragile for the military's needs.

If a message is sent using packet switching, the communication is translated into a sequence of numbers and then separated into thousands of small packets, which is easy for computers to do because they can perform millions of operations per second. Each packet is electronically addressed with the address of the recipient, the address of the sender, the sequence number of the packet, and a *checksum*. A checksum is the sum of numbers in the packet. These packets are sent out on the network using any available connection that happens to be unused at the moment. The computer at the destination checks each packet it receives to see if the checksum still matches the sum of the numbers inside the packet. If not, the computer determines the packet is flawed, and it requests a new one.

Eventually all the packets arrive at the destination computer, which reassembles them using the packets' sequence numbers. This method was refined by Bob Kahn and Vent Cerf in the early 1970s and called the *Transmission Control Protocol/Internet Protocol* or *TCP/IP*. Using this method, messages get through accurately even if large parts of the network are destroyed and some of the packets are lost or damaged. Both circuit switching and packet switching use the same wires, but packet switching with TCP/IP makes much more efficient use of the lines than circuit switching. The military adopted TCP/IP as its communication standard in 1980 because of its efficient use of transmission circuits and its reliability when parts of the system fail.

In the early days, ARPANET allowed people to exchange data and to run programs on computers from distant parts of the country. Two popular applications were **File Transfer Protocol**, or **FTP**, which allows users to transfer files between computers, and **Telnet**, which allows a user to log in to a remote computer as if he or she were at the facility. In 1972, ARPANET was demonstrated to the public with a new application, electronic mail, which changed the network into something that could be used by people to communicate directly with each other, and an important part of the Internet was added.

Commercialization of the Internet

The TCP/IP used by ARPANET is an **open architecture**, which means that anyone could use it to communicate with other computers even if the other computers didn't use the same internal communication methods. In the early 1980s, other networks such as USENET and BITNET existed to connect computers at colleges and universities, but they did not use TCP/IP and could not talk to each other. The federally funded National Science Foundation (NSF) supported **NSFNET** and announced it would use the TCP/IP method developed by ARPA. NSF also recognized the need for a widespread infrastructure to support the academic and research community that would initially rely on federal funding but would ultimately exist without it.

Important policy decisions were made that shaped the development of the Internet, as we now know it. Federal agencies would:

> help fund infrastructure such as transoceanic cables

> provide coordination

> encourage local academic networks to seek commercial customers and exploit the economies of scale to lower costs for all

> ban commercial users from the NSF backbone (major communication routes), thus encouraging creation of a separate commercial system (1988)

> drop federal funding for the NSF backbone and redistribute the money for buying access from the commercial system (1995)

In 1990, Tim Berners-Lee (see Figure 2.1), a programmer at the CERN (Conseil Europeen pour la Recherche Nucleaire) physics research facility in Switzerland, developed a way for computers to share text documents. The documents would be placed on computers that act as **servers**, and other computers could run programs called **clients** that could retrieve and display the documents. He used a **browser**, which is a client program that requests and displays Web pages, to display text. He envisioned a network of connected computers forming a World Wide Web. Many Web addresses today start with *www* to indicate they are part of the World Wide Web. The program was provided free to anyone on the Internet who wanted to use it.

In 1992, Marc Andreessen (see Figure 2.2) and several other students at the University of Illinois at Urbana-Champaign took the World Wide Web design of Berners-Lee and added the ability to work with graphic elements. They called their browser **Mosaic**. It was available as a free download from servers on the Internet, and by 1993 more than one million people were using

FIGURE 2.1

Tim Berners-Lee, the creator of the World Wide Web

FIGURE 2.2

Marc Andreessen, lead designer of Mosaic and Netscape

it. Andreessen and six of his fellow students went to work for Jim Clark, who assumed that the University of Illinois had the same policy as his alma mater, Stanford, which allowed students to own the ideas and software they developed as students. This was not the case. Andreessen and his six friends, known as "the gang of six," had to rewrite the code for the browser, which they privately called *Mozilla* but publicly named *Netscape*. Jim Clark gave the program away to individuals but charged businesses for its use. Within a year and a half, Netscape had 65 million users. When most people think of the Internet, they think of a graphic browser used to navigate the World Wide Web.

Graphical browsers like Mosaic and Netscape use *Hypertext Markup Language*, or *HTML*, to describe how text and figures in *Web pages* should be displayed. For example, when you download a Web page, the text and graphics you see on the screen are embedded between codes that tell the browser how the text should be displayed. If a word like "hello" is displayed in bold, the word is preceded by <b> and followed by </b>, as in this example; <b>hello</b>. The browser works with your computer's internal graphics system to display the word **hello** in bold. The method used to transfer Web pages written in html code is called *Hypertext Transfer Protocol*, or *HTTP*. Web pages can contain links to other Web pages, which are called *hyperlinks*. The links are typically identified with a different color font and underlining. They may also be attached to graphics. Hyperlinks are usually activated by a mouse click.

STRUCTURE OF THE INTERNET

The *backbone* of the Internet consists of major communication pathways connected to each other with routers and gateways. Organizations called Internet service providers (ISPs) provide connections to the backbone for smaller local area networks (LANs) or individuals.

Backbone

When we visualize a fishing net or a spiderweb, we see a network of lines of approximately equal size. The Internet is more like groups of small nets linked by large, thick ropes. To mix metaphors, the main connecting circuits between these smaller nets are like the backbone of an animal that supports and connects the various parts of the body. The long-distance, high-capacity communication links that consist of undersea cables, microwave antennas, satellite relays, and large bundles of traditional telephone lines are called the backbone (see Figure 2.3). Because NSFNET handed off responsibility for the backbone to private enterprise, individual companies such as regional telephone or cable companies own and operate different portions of the backbone. As the Internet grows in other countries, coordination between the providers of backbone services has become more difficult.

Gateways and Routers

Gateways and *routers* are computer devices at the junction of communication links that pass packets along to the next computer en route to their final destination. They are designed to do this quickly, and they do not examine the contents of the packets.

Internet Service Providers

Connection to the backbone is provided by *Internet service providers (ISPs)* like America Online (AOL) and Microsoft's MSN. A service provider like AOL rents local telephone numbers for individuals who use

FIGURE 2.3

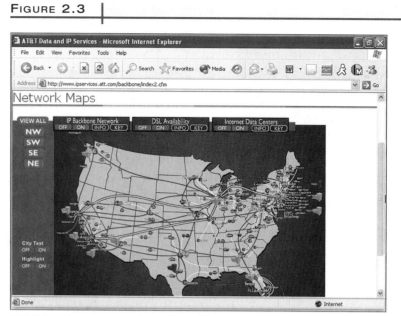

AT&T backbone network for IP traffic

telephone lines to connect. ISPs have the server software to connect to the backbone, and they provide the client software on CDs that individuals load onto their computers. Telephone companies and cable television companies that provide high-speed connections between the individual user and the company's computers are usually ISPs, as well. For example, if you pay extra for Internet service from Comcast, a cable television company, the company also serves as an ISP. Fast connections that are always on are often called *broadband* connections.

Local Area Networks and Intranets

A company or educational institution may have a network of computers that can communicate directly with each other through a server. This arrangement is called a *local area network*, or *LAN*. The company may connect its server to the Internet through an ISP, or it may not. Some large companies are concerned about privacy, security, and employee distraction if they connect their computers to the Internet, so they use TCP/IP software to simply connect their own servers to each other. They use browsers like Netscape to access Web pages, but they are not necessarily connected to the rest of the Internet. These networks are called *intranets*.

METHODS OF CONNECTION

To create a backbone, a company can build a few thousand miles of transmission equipment. The biggest problem is connecting the end user to this fast system. To connect the high-speed equipment at the ISP to individual users, we have to go *the last mile*. This phrase refers to the final connection to the user, and because there are millions of users, it requires millions of miles of connecting equipment. Methods of connection vary greatly in the speed at which they transmit data. For example, if you want a free copy of Netscape Communicator 7.02, you can request a CD and wait for it to come in the mail or you can choose to download a copy over the

Internet. The approximate time it would take to download a free copy of Communicator is shown in Figure 2.4.

DIAL-UP

Most people connect their home computer to their ISP through their existing telephone service. They may use the same line on which they talk, which can be inconvenient, or install a second telephone line for use with the computer. This system is slow, but it has the advantage of using existing wiring. To use a telephone line, the computer must have a device that changes electronic information into sounds that the telephone system can transmit. The device, called a *modem*, has a telephone jack in it that is the same size and shape as the one in the base of a telephone. A normal telephone extension line plugs into the modem in the computer and into a phone jack on the wall. To use a dial-up modem, you must have a telephone number provided by your ISP—preferably a local number so you can avoid paying long-distance charges to the telephone company. The ISP provides a list of telephone numbers it rents from the phone company, and when you install the client software, the setup program helps select a local number. When you connect to the ISP using a telephone modem, you may hear a dial tone and then a warbling sound. The computer is testing the quality of the telephone line to see how fast it can transmit data, and it is providing your personal user identification and password to the ISP server. Once the connection is established, you can download Web pages or you can use other Internet services like e-mail. Even if you have a faster connection, it is a good idea to establish a dial-up connection with a free ISP as a backup in case your other connection goes down. Some colleges provide a free dial-up ISP for students.

DIGITAL SUBSCRIBER LINE (DSL)

Some telephone companies have another option for customers who live within a mile or two of their high-speed equipment. It is possible to transmit data over existing telephone lines at significantly higher speeds for a few miles using *Digital Subscriber Line*, or *DSL*, technology. Use of this service does not interfere with normal telephone conversations so a second telephone line is unnecessary. The telephone company provides a DSL modem that connects to the computer or is installed inside the computer. A major advantage is that the computer is constantly connected to

FIGURE 2.4

Type of Connection	Approximate Time to Download a Copy of Netscape Communicator
Dial-up telephone	1 hour
Digital Subscriber Line (DSL)	4–13 minutes
Cable	4 minutes
Satellite	5 minutes
Cell phone	2 hours 20 min
Local area network with T1 connection	40 seconds

Comparison of approximate download times by connection method the Internet so there is no waiting to connect. This may save only a minute of time, but it tends to make a big difference in how often one uses the Internet.

CABLE

Cable television companies already have a high-speed connection into your home through which they transmit television signals. It was originally hoped that this system would quickly provide high-speed Internet service to everyone who already had cable television service. Unfortunately, the installed distribution equipment in the cable TV system was designed for one-way service, to deliver a television signal. It was not designed for signals to travel in the opposite direction. The system is being updated, and many cable television providers now offer two-way high-speed Internet connection as well. If you subscribe to Internet service through your cable television provider, a cable modem connects a branch of the cable television system to your computer.

SATELLITE

Another option for television reception, especially in areas without cable television systems, is satellite reception (see Figure 2.5). Advances in satellite receivers and the launching of more powerful broadcast satellites have reduced the size of a receiving dish to about two feet in diameter. Satellite television systems may be used to provide Internet connection. Subscribers can download Web pages and files at relatively high speed, but sending files is usually much slower or the system may require use of a dial-up telephone connection to send data.

CELL PHONE

Some cell phone companies provide connection to the Internet. Due to the small size of the screens on cell phones, the service is often limited to e-mail or Web pages designed for small screens. Higher-speed connections available in some areas make it possible to use a cell phone as a dial-up connection for a portable computer.

LOCAL AREA NETWORK

Most companies and organizations that have numerous networked computers use a computer called a server to coordinate communications and a device called a *router* to physically connect the computers. This configuration is called a local area network (LAN). The router may be connected to an ISP to provide all the computers on the LAN with Internet access. A company or ISP may rent a high-speed T1 connection from the telephone company to connect to the backbone. Many people who have two or three computers at home set up LANs to share Internet access. Short-range radio transmitters can be used for *wireless* connections between portable computers and a LAN.

VIRTUAL PRIVATE NETWORK

It is possible to use a connection like one of those listed above to connect to a company intranet from home or while traveling. A *virtual private network*, or *VPN*, uses a connection to an ISP to securely connect to a company intranet. To accomplish this, the client software on the employee's computer creates packets to be used on the company intranet and then places them within packets that are sent over the Internet. The packets meant to be read by the company's computer are encrypted to prevent anyone from reading them, but the exterior packets are easily read and routed by the computers on the Internet. This method allows the employee to work on the company intranet as if his or her computer were physically connected by a secure wire within the company's building.

INTERNET ADDRESSES

The Internet has hundreds of millions of users around the world and millions of computers connected to it. Delivering an e-mail message or locating one of the server computers requires a method of addressing that is easy to use and remember, but is also accurate and efficient.

DOMAIN NAMES

The server computers that handle e-mail and store Web pages have names called *domain names*, which are easy for people to understand and remember. They usually resemble the name of the organization: for example, Prentice Hall uses prenhall as part of its domain name, and Eastern Michigan University uses emich. Domain names often include www as a prefix, but www is no longer required to identify a Web server. Domain names have at least one extension to further identify the servers, such as www.prenhall.com and www.emich.edu. These extensions indicate the type of the organization (see Figure 2.5). Conventions used for domain names are managed by the *Internet Corporation for Assigned Names and Numbers (ICANN)* and are shown in the table in Figure 2.5.

FIGURE 2.5

Type of Organization	Extension
Air transportation	.aero
Business	.biz
Commercial (open to all)	.com
Cooperatives	.coop
Information	.info
Museums	.museum
Individuals	.name
General	.net
Noncommercial (open to all)	.org
Credentialed professionals (pending)	.pro
Education	.edu
Government	.gov
Military	.mil
Internet registration	.int

Domain name extensions used by ICANN

FIGURE 2.6

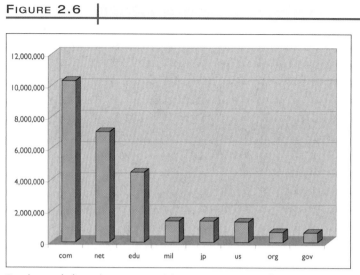

Registered domain names with common extensions

The first extensions used were .mil, .gov, .edu, and .com. The commercial extension, .com (pronounced dot com), is widely used (see Figure 2.6) and has become a term used to describe companies that do business on the Internet.

Because most computers are in the United States, no country designation is needed if the server is in the United States of America (see Figure 2.7). If the server is in another country, an extension is added to indicate the country. The extensions used in different countries do not all follow the same pattern. For example, the domain name for the government of British Columbia in Canada is www.gov.bc.ca, but the Ministry of Foreign Affairs in Japan is www.mofa.go.jp. See the table in Figure 2.8 for a partial table of country extensions that are recognized by ICANN. For a complete list, see the companion Web site at **www.prenhall.com/preston.**

UNIFORM RESOURCE LOCATOR

A server that provides Web pages for retrieval on the Internet is called a *host*. To retrieve a Web page from a host, the domain name is used along with other information according to the rules for a ***Uniform Resource Locator***, or ***URL*** (see Figure 2.9 on page 46). A URL describes:

❭ the mechanism used to access the resource

❭ the domain name of the server

❭ the resource's location and file name on the server

For example, the URL for the list of registrars that are accredited by ICANN is **http://www.icann.org/registrars/accredited-list.html.**

❭ **http://** indicates that the mechanism used to access the resource is the Hypertext Transfer Protocol.

❭ **www.icann.org** is the domain name of the server. Many servers that host Web pages are set to assume the www portion if you do not type it. Some domain names do not start with www and do not work if you add it.

❭ **/registrars/** is the name of a folder on the server where the Web page is stored.

FIGURE 2.7

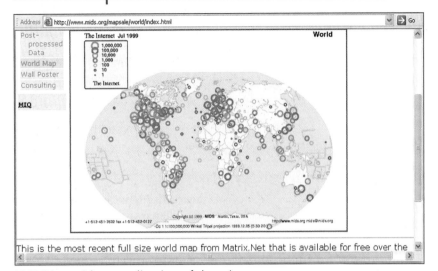

ICANN provides coordination of domain names.

FIGURE 2.8

Code	Country	Code	Country
.ac	Ascension Island	.it	Italy
.ae	United Arab Emirates	.jm	Jamaica
.af	Afghanistan	.jp	Japan
.aq	Antarctica	.ke	Kenya
.au	Australia	.kp	Korea, Democratic People's Republic of
.bb	Barbados		
.bm	Bermuda	.kr	Korea, Republic of
.ca	Canada	.mx	Mexico
.cg	Congo, Republic of	.ng	Nigeria
.cn	China	.nz	New Zealand
.cu	Cuba	.pk	Pakistan
.de	Germany	.th	Thailand
.eg	Egypt	.to	Tonga
.es	Spain	.tv	Tuvalu
.fi	Finland	.tw	Taiwan
.fj	Fiji	.uk	United Kingdom
.il	Israel	.us	United States
.in	India	.va	Holy See (City Vatican State)
.iq	Iraq		
.ir	Iran, Islamic Republic of	.ve	Venezuela

Domain name extensions used by ICANN

FIGURE 2.9

URL:
http://www.intel.com/pressroom/index.asp
Protocol · Host computer address (domain) · Path, directory, file name

Parts of a URL. Note the extension on the file name, .asp, stands for Active Server Page.

> **accredited-list.html** is the name of the Web page file. The name of the file has its own extension, .html, which indicates it is written in Hypertext Markup Language and identifies it as a Web page.

Some pages are created interactively based on information provided by the user and data drawn from the server's database. Pages of that sort are called **Active Server Pages** and are not stored. They have the extension .asp. Some of these pages cannot be accessed directly because they don't exist until you request the data. Examples are ticket or reservation confirmation pages.

IP ADDRESSES

Computers use numbers, not words, to identify servers that are connected to the Internet. The numbers are 32 digits long and consist of zeros and ones. This type of numbering system is called a **binary** numbering system because it has only two numbers, zero and one. For example, the address of the www.icann.org server is 11000000000000000010001010100011. This makes perfect sense to a computer, but to make these numbers more usable for people, they are separated into groups of eight digits called **octets** and converted to decimal numbers. The number for the ICANN server may be written as 192.0.34.163. The URL for the ICANN page could also be written as http://192.0.34.163/registrars/accredited-list.html, and it would work just as well. The numbers used to identify computers on the Internet are called **Internet Protocol addresses** or just **IP addresses**.

DOMAIN NAME SERVERS

The relationship between domain names and host servers is a **many-to-many relationship**. This means that a domain name could be assigned to several servers or a single server could be assigned to many domain names. If a domain name has a lot of traffic, it may use several host servers to share the workload. For example, the domain of the University of Michigan, **www.umich.edu**, is assigned to five different servers with five different IP addresses that all retrieve copies of the same Web page. Domains that have low traffic often share host computers or rent space on a server from a hosting service. For example, **www.indt.net**, **www.pctraining.net**, and **www.basicstudies.com** are all assigned to the pipeline.globalhost.com server, which is run by GlobalHost, a company that provides hosting services for a monthly fee. Network Solutions maintains a database of domain names and their assigned IP addresses on a special server called a **domain name server**, or **DNS**. When you type the URL in the address box of a browser, the browser program checks the DNS to find the IP address that is assigned to the domain name in the address, which it then uses to route the request to the correct server.

✳ DIVERSITY ISSUES

DISCUSSION

The country of Tuvalu sold the right to use its domain name extension, .tv, to commercial interests in the United States. Tuvalu still has use of the extension as well. If you were a citizen of Tuvalu, how would you feel about that? Use a Web browser and visit **http://www.tuvalu.tv** and learn more about this country to help form your answer.

- Search for domain names that are still available. Use a Web browser and go to **http://www.register.com**. See if a domain name that you would like to own is available. Use the View WHOIS links to see information about the owners of domain names.
- Download a free copy of IP Sniffer, and try it out. Go to **http://www.dandans.com** to download and install a free evaluation copy of IP Sniffer and Web Tracer. Look up the IP addresses of familiar Web sites. Make up an IP address and enter it to see whose domain name is associated with it.

PERSONAL COMMUNICATIONS

The Internet is used for a variety of communication tasks. This section looks at how the Internet is used and explores some of the issues that arise from its use.

E-MAIL

Electronic mail, or e-mail, has been around since the early days of ARPANET, and it is a fairly simple function for computers and the Internet to provide. E-mail provides a way for people to stay connected, whether they are employees at distant locations, or families or friends in the same town or across the world. It has replaced letter writing for some, and conversations via e-mail can replace phone calls. E-mail has also become a staple of business communications and has been used in court cases to fix responsibility in lawsuits and cases of criminal misconduct. All e-mail programs provide the same basic functions.

Functions

E-mail clients have four functions in common. They:

❱ show a list of messages waiting to be read in an in-box
❱ allow you to select one of the waiting messages and read it
❱ allow you to create new messages and send them
❱ allow you to attach files to the message

Other common features include the following:

❱ *CC* to send copies of a message to additional recipients
❱ *BCC* to send copies to additional recipients without the knowledge of the primary recipient
❱ subject line
❱ HTML formatting that allows formatting of text and figures within the message
❱ folders for sorting mail
❱ forwarding to other e-mail accounts

E-mail addresses consist of the recipient's user name followed by the @ symbol and the domain name of the computer that hosts the e-mail server program. An example is jpreston@emich.edu.

Two types of server programs are actually involved in processing mail: one for outgoing mail and another for incoming mail. The most commonly used server program for outgoing mail is called a *Simple Mail Transfer Protocol*, or *SMTP*. Incoming mail may be handled by *Post Office Protocol 3 (POP3)*, which downloads mail to the client computer for processing, or *Internet Message Access Protocol (IMAP)*, which allows the user to preview parts of e-mail messages while they are on the server and then decide which ones to download or delete.

Etiquette

Polite and considerate behavior is expected from well-educated people, and it is important that you know the rules of considerate e-mail use. Here are some guidelines that will be appreciated by those with whom you communicate:

> Clearly summarize the content of your message in the Subject line. It makes sorting and prioritizing much easier.

> Do not use the CC (courtesy copy) function too often. Sending e-mail to many people is easy and inexpensive because there is no physical letter to be carried and delivered, and it is tempting to send copies of messages to anyone who might possibly be affected or to cover ourselves just in case something goes wrong later. Unfortunately, the recipients receive more e-mail than they can reasonably read in a day so they must determine what to ignore. If you do this too often, they will start to ignore anything from you. Courtesy copies are intended to inform, not elicit a response.

> If you receive a message that was sent to a list of people, do not use the **Reply to All** feature if you intend to reply only to the sender.

> Use the BCC (blind courtesy copy) function when sending a message to a list of people who may not want the other people on the list to see their e-mail addresses, and to prevent people from accidentally using the Reply to All feature.

> Avoid using all capital letters. IT LOOKS LIKE YOU ARE SHOUTING.

> Use complete sentences, standard grammar, and punctuation in most business or school settings.

> Do not write anything you would be embarrassed to read later. It is easy to forward messages and store them.

> If you are angry when you write a message, save it and read it later before you send it. Better yet, have someone whose opinion you respect read it.

> Include your name at the bottom of the message. This is particularly important if your e-mail address does not have your name in it.

> Use emoticons to indicate emotions. Sarcasm or humor are easily misunderstood without visual cues from a person's face or body language (see "Emoticons," below).

Unsolicited E-mail

Unsolicited e-mail is similar to unsolicited mail, which is often referred to as *junk mail* by those who don't like it and as *direct mail advertising* by those who make a living sending it. The people who use the postal service for direct mail advertising have to pay the postal service to deliver the mail (but not the land-fill cost of disposing of it) and are restrained to some degree by this cost. The people who use e-mail for direct advertising do not incur the cost of delivery and are unrestrained in their use of this medium. The result is overwhelming. More than half of all e-mail is unsolicited advertising, and the people who are sending it are not paying for the resources used to deliver it. Some of it includes text or pictures that are unwelcome. The public's attitude toward this type of mail is reflected in a skit by *Monty Python's Flying Circus* in which a restaurant serves all its food with SPAM, a meat product. As part of the skit, the waitress keeps repeating the name and a chorus sings, "Spam, spam, spam, spam, spam, spam, spam, spam, lovely spam! Wonderful spam!" Thus, the term came to represent something repetitive and intrusive. When referring to junk e-mail, use the lowercase spelling *spam* rather than the trademarked name of the meat product from Hormel, SPAM™. In fairness to Hormel and in appreciation of diverse tastes, remember that SPAM is one of the most popular foods in Hawaii, where the residents eat 6.7 million cans a year.

Emoticons

It is important that the emotion we wish to convey in our e-mail messages not be misunderstood. This can happen when we rely on text messages and we cannot see the facial expressions of those with whom we are communicating. An early solution to this problem was to use keyboard characters to represent a facial expression. A smiling face, represented by three characters, a colon, a hyphen, and a right-parentheses, looks like :-) and is meant to be viewed sideways. Similarly, :-(represents a frown. With the advent of HTML mail, elaborate animated images can be used instead of simple keyboard characters.

These icons that indicate emotion are called *emoticons*. They are available as part of some e-mail clients, and they can be copied from Web sites. Refer to the references for this book at **http://www.prenhall.com/preston** for an example of such a site.

Web Mail

One of the drawbacks of the older server-client model of using e-mail is that you couldn't look at your mail if you were away from the computer that had your e-mail client on it. An example of an e-mail client is Microsoft Outlook. To solve this problem, another old feature of the Internet, Telnet, is combined with a Web browser. E-mail programs like Microsoft's Hotmail, AOL, and Yahoo.Mail! have mail client software that stays on the server, and you use a Web browser from any computer on the Internet to run the program and read your mail. Several Web sites offer this type of program for free to encourage people to visit the site often.

Compressing Attached Files

You may want to send a file or a photo to someone via e-mail by attaching the file to your e-mail message. Large file attachments can result in a slow transmission of the e-mail. You can reduce the size of a file to be sent by a factor of four or more by compressing the file. At the other end, it needs to be uncompressed. There are several methods for doing this, but the most popular in the Windows environment produces files with the file extension .zip. A compression program to zip files is included with Windows XP and may be activated by right-clicking on a file or folder name. Third-party software like *WinZip* is also commonly used to compress files. A program

FIGURE 2.10

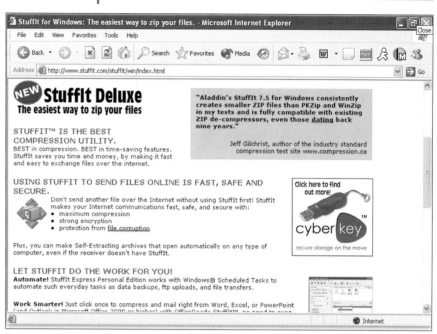

Compression programs can greatly reduce file size for faster transmission.

FIGURE 2.11

Instant messaging uses pop-up windows to display messages when they arrive.

named *StuffIt* provides a similar function on Macintosh and Linux, as well as Windows, computers (see Figure 2.10).

INSTANT MESSAGING AND CHAT

E-mail is a convenient way to exchange messages with people if you do not need an immediate response or if you want to choose when you wish to reply. Communication that does not take place immediately is asynchronous. A telephone conversation is an example of synchronous communication because the people on the call have to synchronize their listening and talking in real time. Two types of synchronous communication that use the Internet are *chat* and *instant messaging*, or *IM* (see Figures 2.11 and 2.12). Many Web sites offer chat rooms that are dedicated to a particular topic. Users log onto a chat room in which they see a list of participants and see the messages and responses. Simply watching without participating is called *lurking*. Most groups do not want to take time getting new participants up to speed on the topic so a list of *frequently asked questions*, or *FAQ*, is provided to allow a new participant to catch up quickly. Participation requires the use of a keyboard so some typing skills are valuable. Many acronyms used to reduce typing and speed response time, such as LOL (laugh out loud) and TTFN (ta-ta for now), are making their way into popular language.

Instant messaging is more like a private chat with your friends. If someone sends you a message, a window pops up on your screen to announce arrival of a message to which you can respond immediately. You choose the people with whom you participate by adding or removing their names from a list. IM can also include pictures and sounds from Web cameras and microphones. Some cell phone companies provide IM as well as normal telephone service. IM service providers include AOL, Yahoo!, and MSN. IM services often require that everyone on your list of approved partners use the same service. There is a free IM client provided by

FIGURE 2.12

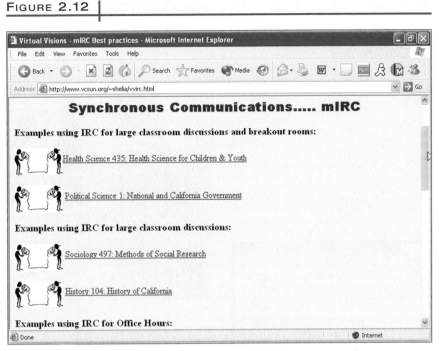

Chats are organized around topics and are open to many people at once.

Cerulean Studies named Trillian that allows users to connect across service providers.

PERSONAL INFORMATION
People make use of the Internet to share personal information with distant relatives, friends, and complete strangers.

Personal Web Pages
Many people create Web pages and post them to a server to provide information about themselves and what's going on in their lives. It's a convenient way to keep dispersed family members up-to-date and to share pictures of the family and pets. Web pages are easy to create. Many people buy special software to create pages with lots of special effects that take time to learn, but Microsoft's Office 2000 and Office XP products can create adequate Web pages. To create a Web page in Office, you can open a document in Word or a presentation in PowerPoint, choose a theme from the Format menu, insert the text and pictures, and then choose Save As Web Page. That's the easy part. The hard part is finding a server that will host your Web page and then uploading your Web pages. Many ISPs and colleges provide space on their Web servers for individuals' Web pages for no additional charge. Alternatively, you can rent space on a commercial Web server for a modest monthly fee.

Web Logs
Keeping personal journals online has become popular in the last few years. There are special sites where users can post their thoughts, opinions, events of the day, or anything else they choose to share. They can also read the logs of others. *Web logs* are popularly known as **blogs**.

CONFERENCING
The Internet can also be used for telephone conferences and videoconferences between businesspeople at distant locations. Telephone conference

FIGURE 2.13

Videoconferencing systems display video and documents while providing voice communication.

calls allow several people to share a connection and talk to each other at the same time. Videoconferencing includes a live image of the participants. Telephone and videoconferencing are relatively expensive using traditional circuit switched telephone networks. The same technology that made e-mail virtually free can have a similar effect on telephone calls and videoconferencing.

Voice over IP

Modern computers are fast enough to sample voices thousands of times per second and assign numbers to the volume and pitch. These numbers are enclosed in packets and sent to the other people using traditional Internet protocols, or TCP/IP. This technology is called *Voice over IP*, or *VoIP*. If some of the packets take too long to arrive at the destination, the quality suffers. Voice over IP is used on company intranets and is used to provide some low-cost calling card services (see the references for this book at **http://www.prenhall.com/preston** for more information).

Videoconferencing

Videoconferencing involves cameras, microphones, and computer technology to compress and process the signals at both ends of the conversation (see Figure 2.13). Traditional methods make this technology expensive. Using the Internet and IP, videoconferencing can be done on your desktop. The quality is not very good with slow connections, but it keeps getting better with fast connections. Microsoft includes a copy of NetMeeting with Windows. NetMeeting allows voice, video, chat, and applications sharing.

FINDING INFORMATION, WORKING, AND PLAYING

There is so much available on the Internet that finding it and deciding what you want to use are a challenge. Fortunately, there are options to help you make these decisions and then locate resources again quickly.

FIGURE 2.14

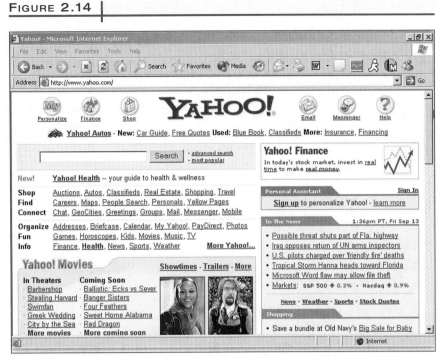

Portals provide searching and a host of other features and content.

PORTALS

Many Web sites make money through advertising or donations. In order to get as many people as possible to view the ads and information on their site, they provide free services such as searching, IM, chat, and information. They want to make their site the one that comes up when you open your browser and to which you go as often as possible for information. They want to be your *portal* to the Internet (see Figure 2.14). Some ISPs, like AOL or MSN, attempt to provide all the information you might want within their own service. At one time AOL described itself as "as a 'resort pool with lifeguards' next to the wild, untamed ocean of the Internet."

BROWSERS

Web browsers use a URL to request Web pages from a server. Different browsers have special features, some of which are incompatible with each other, which has been a source of controversy that will be discussed in a later chapter. The two most common browsers in use today are *Netscape Communicator* (see Figure 2.15 on page 54), which is owned by AOL, and *Internet Explorer (IE)* (see Figure 2.16 on page 55), which is owned by Microsoft. Netscape Communicator may be downloaded free, and IE is included with the Windows operating system that comes with most computers. Netscape Communicator and IE can store lists of Web pages the user would like to revisit. Netscape Communicator calls them *bookmarks*, and IE calls them *favorites*.

Stored Pages

Web pages can take time to download from a server. When you retrieve a Web page, a copy of the page is stored on your computer. This storage area is known as a *disk cache*. If you ask to see the same page again, the browser will recall it from the disk cache rather than take the time to download it

FIGURE 2.15

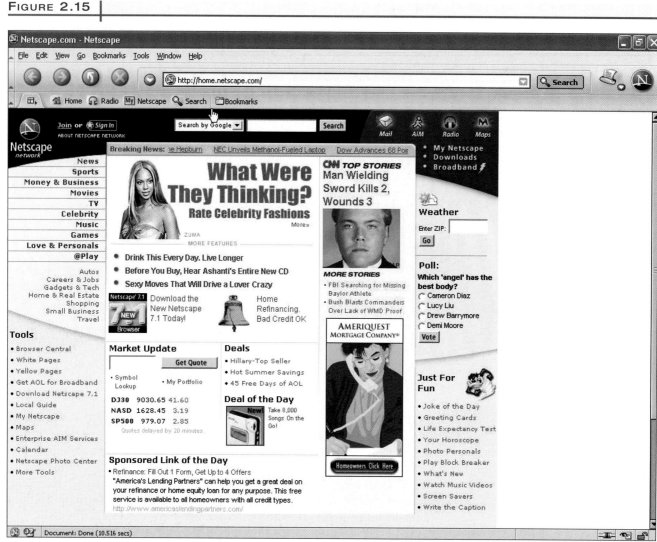

Netscape Communicator is one of the two most common browsers.

again from the server. If you browse the Internet a lot, the space required by the disk cache can become quite large. If it isn't managed properly, it can fill up enough of the storage space on the computer to affect its performance. Both Netscape Communicator and Internet Explorer provide the user with the option of limiting the amount of space used for this feature, as well as clearing the cache completely as needed. To force the download of a new copy of a Web page, use the Refresh button.

Applets

Small application programs, called *applets*, that run with a Web page can make Web use more convenient. For example, if you fill out a form that has several required boxes, an applet can check to make sure all the required boxes are filled in before it sends the form to the server for processing. This saves time and avoids errors. Applets can also provide animation for a Web page. Two competing technologies dominate this field. Microsoft uses *ActiveX controls* in IE, and Netscape uses applets written in the *Java* programming language. Internet Explorer can be modified to run Java applets as well by downloading and installing a special program. Applets are discussed in more detail in Chapter 4.

FIGURE 2.16

Internet Explorer: The URL goes in the Address box. The Refresh button forces the download of a new version of the page.

Cookies

Cookies are text files that are stored on your computer, usually in a folder such as c:\windows\cookies. Web servers can store these files on your computer and use them to identify you the next time you visit the site so you do not have to re-enter data such as shipping and credit card information that is already in the vendor's database. The first time you request a Web page from a server, it assigns an identification number and other facts about your visit, such as the date and time, and includes these facts in a hidden portion of the code for the Web page. The browser extracts that text from the incoming Web page code and stores it on your computer as a cookie. The next time you request information from the same Web server, the browser attaches the text in the cookie to the request. When the server receives the request with the user's ID and other information, it can look you up in its own database to see what you ordered the last time you visited and other information that you provided the first time you visited, like your credit card number and delivery address. This personal information is on the server's database, not in the cookie. The cookie is not an executable program that spies on the activity in your computer. It is a simple text file that you can open and read with a word processor.

SEARCH ENGINES AND DIRECTORIES

The Internet has hundreds of millions of Web pages available for download. The problem is finding the ones you want. Specialized programs that search the Web and organize indexes of the Web pages are called *search engines*. Some sites organize the pages by category and are called *directories*. Sites that use several other search engines and combine the results are called *metasearch sites* (see Figure 2.17). Choosing the right search engine

FIGURE 2.17

Directories		
About	About	Human experts, called Guides, compile directories organized around specific topics.
Yahoo!	Yahoo!	Well-organized categories let the user switch from browsing to searching in a certain area; but finds only keywords, not any word on a site
Search Engines		
alltheweb	AlltheWeb	Fast; supports a large number of languages; can limit results to specific domains
altavista	AltaVista	Very fast; indexes every word on every page of every site; searches Usenet too; excellent for custom searches
Google	Google	Results ranked by algorithm based on number of links from other pages
HotBot	HotBot	Fast; unique search options let you restrict searches; very comprehensive; excels at finding current news
Lycos	Lycos	Numerous search options, a comprehensive directory, and good returns on simple searches.
Metasearch Sites		
metacrawler	MetaCrawler	Accepts search terms and submits to several popular search engines; eliminates duplicates and ranks by relevancy
DOGPILE	Dogpile	Well-designed, easy-to-use interface; can search Usenet

A sample of the search tools available for finding Web pages

for the job and getting the results you want requires some knowledge of how search engines gather information about Web pages and learning a few simple searching techniques. Ideally, you should be able to describe what you want in a few words and have the Web page you need appear near the top in the list of pages found. Search engines are often built into other Web pages or portals such as AOL, Yahoo!, or MSN; alternatively, they can have their own Web sites like Google. Search engines like Google offer options for searching pictures, discussion groups, and Web pages that have text in other languages.

How Search Engines Find and Index Web Pages

Companies that sell search engine services must locate millions of Web pages and index the contents so your request can be quickly matched to a group of pages that satisfy it. This can be a difficult task, and search engines differ greatly in their methods of indexing Web pages and in the degree to which they succeed in locating what you want. However, before they can index the contents of a new Web page, they have to find it.

Following the metaphor of the Internet as a large spiderweb, programs that move from page to page searching for new pages are called *spiders*, and the process of searching is called *Web crawling*.

Most spiders start with servers that have a lot of traffic and look at the most commonly requested pages first. This process tends to reinforce the popularity of those sites. When a new Web page is found by the spider, the contents of the page must be summarized and indexed. Spiders look at the title and some hidden text called a *meta tag*, which is a list of key words provided by the author of the Web page to assist in indexing the contents of the site. Some spiders compare the words in the meta tag with the words on the page to determine if they are representative.

Querying

Search engines provide a box into which you type key words that indicate the most important and unique things about the information you want to find. You can improve the effectiveness of your searches by using the advanced search option available on most search engines.

Look for the following advanced search features to make your search more effective:

❱ Chose two or more key words, all of which must be matched, to reduce the search.

❱ Search for a phrase, if appropriate.

❱ Use the "at least one of these" option to widen the search and get more pages.

❱ If you know your pages are most likely to be in a particular domain, such as government or education, use the Domain option to restrict the search.

❱ If you are looking for pictures, news, or comments in discussion groups, consider using some search engines' special predefined categories to start your search.

❱ If you read more than one language, consider expanding the search to include pages in those languages, especially if the topic is international in nature.

Using the advanced search option improves the efficiency of your search. For example, if you wanted to know more about online voting for government elections and you are interested in official government sites, you could use the advanced search option in a search engine like Google (see Figure 2.18 on page 58). Notice the use of two key words and the exclusion of the word "school." Also note that the language is limited to English and the domain is limited to .gov.

RESEARCH AND CITING ELECTRONIC SOURCES

In the past, book and magazine publishers played a primary role in making documents widely available, and they usually edited the contents of articles for accuracy or, at minimum, lack of libelous statements. Today, anyone can put a Web page on an Internet server for worldwide distribution without any one else's input or control. It is up to the reader to determine whether the content is reliable or accurate. One way to do this is to consider the origin of the Web page. If it was posted by a well-known organization, the organization is responsible for its accuracy. If it is part of a professional journal, the editorial staff and reviewers are responsible for accuracy. The editing and reviewing of content either must be paid for or is performed by volunteers. Typically, edited content is found in online sources for which one pays a subscription fee. You can subscribe to various newspapers, magazines, and journals online.

Library Resources

If you are currently enrolled in college, there is a good chance that your college library subscribes to numerous magazines, news services, and factual databases, many of which you can access online. These services make

FIGURE 2.18

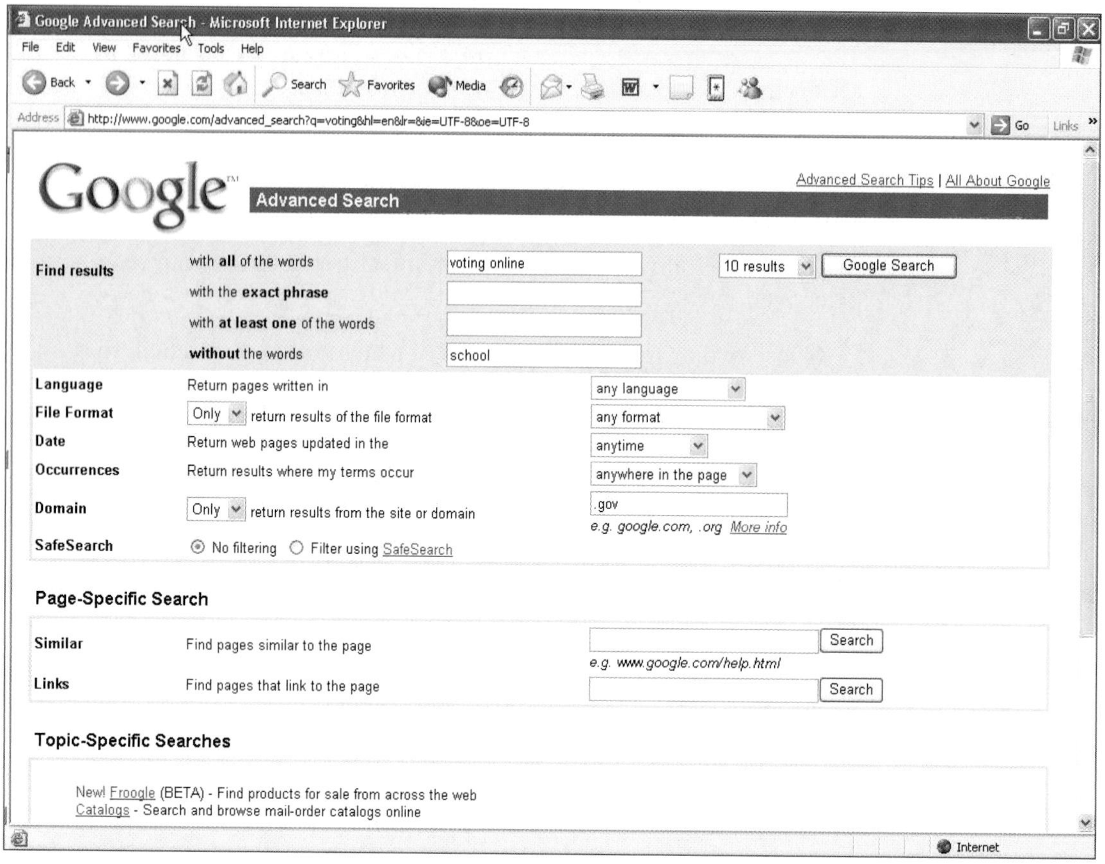

Use the advanced search option to focus your search.

available the full text of many journals and magazines, which is not available on the Internet. There are often search engines that are designed to search many of these documents. It is a good idea to use your browser and search engine to find the Web page for your local library or college library and see what subscriptions they already pay for that you can use.

Standards for Citing Sources

The difference between expressing your opinion in an essay and writing a research paper is that you are expected to support your opinion in the research paper by showing that you checked out what has already been written on the subject and that your opinions are based on facts and quality research. Readers of your research paper must be able to check your sources to see if your conclusions are warranted or to use the source in papers of their own. When you write a research paper, you *cite* the source when you use it in the paper, and you supply detailed information about the article so the reader can find it. This continuous thread of accurate references is at the heart of scholarly activity. Citing information taken from Web pages is relatively new, and standards are still being formulated. Refer to this book's companion Web site at **www.prenhall.com/ preston** for links to guidelines for writing references. In general, provide the title of the Web page, the author if one is identified, the date the Web page was written if one is given, the date the page was referenced, and the URL.

INFORMATION SERVICES

Many Web sites provide information services for free to bring customers to their sites. If you need to get driving directions, find a store in a nearby city, check the current weather, or find out if your relative's plane is on time before you leave for the airport, you can find the information faster online in most cases than by telephone, television, or print media.

Refer to the companion Web site for examples of the type of information you can get online faster than through traditional media, especially if you have a fast Internet connection that is always on.

The U.S. government makes extensive use of Web pages to provide information (see Figure 2.19).

COMMERCE

Some types of business can be done more quickly, safely, and cheaply on the Internet. You can also find uncommon items. Online commerce is a fast-growing segment of our economy, and you need to know its benefits and risks.

In his book, *Business at the Speed of Thought*, Bill Gates pointed out that most people think of using the phone or the car when it is time to buy something, but we are moving toward an era when the first thing we think of for these tasks is to use the Internet. Since that book was written in 1999, the Internet has become the first choice by many people for doing certain types of business.

Initially, many people were concerned about giving out their credit card numbers over the Internet, but now that millions of people have done it, we see that the security measures have been effective. A user's liability is limited when the card is used online in the same way it is limited when a waiter takes your card in a restaurant. If you see an incorrect charge on your statement, you contact the card issuing company and challenge it. If

FIGURE 2.19

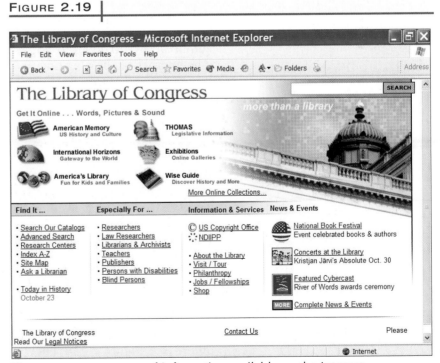

There are many sources of information available on the Internet.

FIGURE 2.20

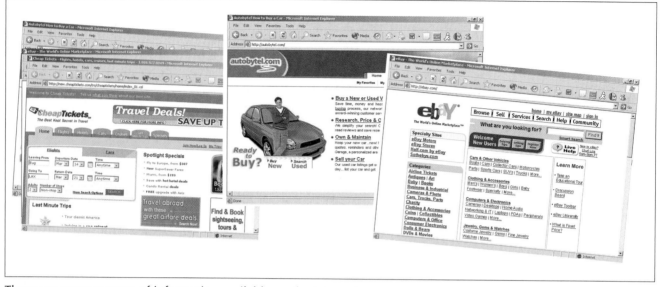

There are many sources of information available on the Internet.

you use your card online, it is important to check your monthly statement. It is also a good idea to print out order forms and e-mail sent from the company to confirm orders and use them to verify online charges because the cryptic name on the monthly statement from the credit card company may not resemble the name of the Web site from which you purchased your item.

Shopping on the Internet is easy, and products can be delivered to your doorstep or to the doorstep of a person to whom you are giving a gift. If you are searching for a store that is outside your immediate area, it will not be listed in your phone book, but you can use an expanded search on the Internet to find the type of store you want and sort the stores by distance from your location. Some sites create comparison tables for you automatically if you are trying to decide which brand or model to buy. The Internet can be a big time and money saver once you learn how to use it to shop (see Figure 2.20). Many people use the Internet for banking and investing, as well. If your employer offers direct deposit of your paycheck, you can handle almost all of your finances online without standing in a bank line again.

This type of commerce is called **business to consumer.**

Businesses can also use the Internet to buy and sell directly to each other. Dell owes much of its rapid growth to its strategy of selling directly to businesses by setting up a customized Web site for each major business customer that includes the customer's order forms. This type of commerce is called **business to business,** or **B to B.**

Consumers can sell to each other using an Internet broker. You can buy or sell used books or bid on items at auction sites. Individuals can set up their own Web pages and take orders directly for goods and services. This type of commerce is called **consumer to consumer.**

Here is a table of examples of the type of commerce you can take part in online (see Figure 2.21). They are provided as an example and not an endorsement of their quality.

FIGURE 2.21

Portals with multiple shopping options	Yahoo	http://www.yahoo.com/
	MSN	http://www.msn.com/
	AOL	http://www.aol.com/
	Netscape	http://www.netscape.com/
Search for stores with maps	SuperPages	http://www.superpages.com/
	Yellowpages.com	http://www.yellowpages.com/
Used books	Amazon.com	http://www.amazon.com/
Books	Amazon.com	http://www.amazon.com/
	Barnes & Noble	http://www.bn.com/
Specialty shopping	Computer Hardware	http://shopper.cnet.com/
Auctions	eBay	http://www.ebay.com/
	Yahoo! Shopping Auctions	http://auctions.shopping.yahoo.com/
	MSN uBid	http://eshop.msn.com/softcontent/ softcontent.aspx?scmId=978
Business services for businesses	EDS	http://www.eds.com/services_offerings/so_home.shtml
Automobile comparison shopping	Autobytel	http://www.autobytel.com/
	Consumer Reports	http://www.consumerreports.org/
	Edmunds	http://www.edmunds.com/
	MSN	http://autos.msn.com/
	Yahoo	http://autos.yahoo.com/
Travel: airline tickets, hotels, rental cars	Travelocity	http://www.travelocity.com/
	Northwest	http://www.nwa.com
	Southwest	http://www.southwest.com/
	Hotels.com	http://www.hotels.com/
Concert tickets	Ticketmaster	http://www.ticketmaster.com/

Examples of various commercial Web sites

ENTERTAINMENT

In addition to finding information about entertainment options or buying tickets or CDs online, you can use your computer to listen to music, watch movies, play games, chat with friends, or visit museums and art galleries (see Figure 2.22). To take advantage of your computer's capability to entertain you, it may be necessary to add or upgrade your peripherals. If you want to chat with friends, you may need to add a video camera and a microphone headset. If you want to listen to music online or play games with sound effects, you may want to upgrade your computer's speakers or subscribe to a faster Internet connection.

Some adult entertainment sites related to sex or gambling are the most advanced technologically, and they account for a large part of the Internet activity in the category of entertainment. The distributed nature of the Internet makes it hard to control by legislation. One effect that has been noted is that college students who did not formerly have easy access to professional gambling on college sports can now bet on games that their roommates and friends may be playing in. This topic will be revisited in the chapter on ethics.

FIGURE 2.22

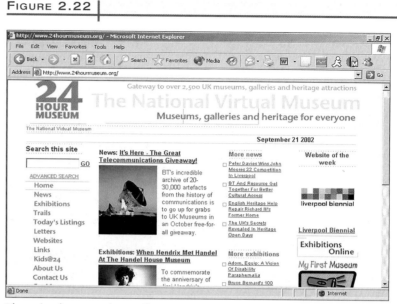

There is plenty to do on the Internet.

See Figure 2.23 for examples of entertainment you can take part in online or just on an unconnected computer. They are provided as an example and not an endorsement of their quality.

EDUCATION

Computers are common in schools, and they are also having an effect on education at the workplace through *Web-based training* and *online courses*.

Web-Based Training

Many companies are using the Internet to deliver training to small, widely separated groups that would be too expensive to bring together physically. Developing Web-based training is expensive due to the amount of time it

FIGURE 2.23

Activity	Examples	URL
Listen to music	Live radio from around the world	**http://windowsmedia.com/radiotuner/MyRadio.asp**
	Recorded music	**http://www.mp3.com/**
Chat with friends	Place calls to normal telephones from your computer at low cost	**http://web.net2phone.com/home_usen.asp**
	Videoconference with NetMeeting	**http://www.microsoft.com/windows/NetMeeting/default.ASP**
	Internet Relay Chat	**http://www.mirc.com/irc.html**
Watch movies	Preview Unreleased Movies	**http://www.ifilm.com/**
	Play DVD movies (requires a DVD drive in your computer)	**http://www.dvdtalk.com/**
Read books	Awe-Struck E-Books	**http://www.awe-struck.net/index.html**
Play games online	Yahoo! Games	**http://games.yahoo.com/**
	Games.com	**http://play.games.com/playgames/home.jsp**

Examples of various commercial Web sites

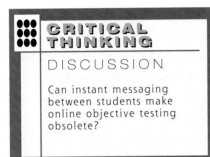
takes developers to create the content. It is most appropriate in the following circumstances:

❱ The content is stable and not subject to frequent revision.

❱ A large number of people need to be trained.

❱ It would be expensive or detrimental to the business to gather people together for training.

❱ The subject matter can be tested using the online training.

Online Courses

Most colleges offer some of their courses via the Internet (see Figure 2.24). Some classroom methods translate effectively, but others do not. Online courses use programs that provide the following synchronous and asynchronous features:

1. Synchronous
   a. Chat—live discussions, often used for office hours
   b. Streaming video—a one-way distribution of video and audio to the students that may be used for showing a recorded video.

2. Asynchronous
   a. *Threaded discussions*—conversations in which participants can track comments and responses
   b. *Document sharing*—a place where documents may be uploaded or downloaded for transmission between students and the instructor. This feature uses FTP, but the users don't see the details.
   c. Grade book—a record of grades that students can see at any time
   d. Drop box—a feature that is similar to document sharing but is associated with specific assignments. It is used to hand in and return assignments.
   e. E-mail
   f. Objective exams

FIGURE 2.24

Computers make training, taking classes, and working from home possible.

- **Delete stored Web pages from the IE cache:** If you use Internet Explorer, choose Tools, Internet Options, General, Delete Files. If it takes a long time to delete all the Web pages stored on your computer, you may see a significant improvement in the performance of your machine. In the dialog box, click Settings to choose how much space to allow for these files.

- **Look up cookies and read one:** Open a word processing program and set it to view files that end in **.txt**. Search for a folder named **Cookies** on the C: drive of your computer. Open some of the cookies to read what is in them.

TEST PREPARATION

The following section does not replace reading the text, nor does it contain all the information that will be tested. It is designed to provide examples and identify sections that need review.

summary by objective

DEVELOPMENT OF THE INTERNET

- **Match people with their contributions:**
  - Licklider envisioned a "Galactic Network" and headed ARPA in 1962
  - Kleinrock described concept of packet switching in 1961
  - Kahn and Cerf developed TCP/IP in early 1970s; it was adopted by the military in 1980
- **E-mail demonstrated on ARPA in 1972**
- **Match key terms related to TCP/IP with definitions (see glossary).**
- **Identify ARPANET applications that are still used on the Internet: e-mail, FTP, Telnet.**

COMMERCIALIZATION OF THE INTERNET

- **Identify federal objectives that led to commercialization:**
  - Design TCP/IP as open architecture
  - Fund infrastructure such as oceanic cables
  - Coordinate
  - Encourage academic networks to seek commercial customers for local use of Internet
  - Ban commercial customers from NSFNET backbone but encourage them to develop their own
  - Turn over backbone services to private enterprise
- **Match the developers of the World Wide Web with their roles:**
  - Berners-Lee created a text-based World Wide Web in 1990
  - Andreessen wrote Mosaic in 1992, then rewrote it as Netscape
- **Match key terms related to Web pages (see glossary).**

STRUCTURE OF THE INTERNET

- **Match key elements of the Internet with their functions:**
  - Backbone—long-distance, high-capacity communication links
  - Gateways and routers—devices at the nodes of communication links that pass on the packets
  - ISP—provide connection between the end user and the Internet
  - LAN—local area network, groups of computers connected to each other
- **Use the terms Internet and intranet to complete sentences correctly—an intranet uses TCP/IP and browsers like the Internet but is separate from it, usually for security and privacy reasons.**

METHODS OF CONNECTION

- **Match connection methods with their characteristics:**
  - Dial-up—uses normal telephone lines and a modem to convert computer signals into sounds
  - DSL—Digital Subscriber Line; uses normal telephone lines for Internet connection over a distance of a few miles
  - Cable—uses the television cable system and a cable modem
  - Satellite—uses the same equipment as the satellite television signal to access the Internet, but needs a dial-up connection for outgoing transmission
  - Cell phone—used for text and simplified Web pages or as a dial-up connection for portable computers
  - LAN—local area network; may be connected via a modem or T1 line
- **Rank methods of connection by their speed from slowest to fastest:**
  - Cell phone, dial-up, DSL, cable, satellite (download), LAN with T1
- **Identify features of virtual private networks—use Internet to send encrypted TCP/IP packets to a company intranet.**

INTERNET ADDRESSES

- **Match address extensions to the type of organization (see table of extensions).**
- **Identify the relationship between a domain name and an IP address—many-to-many.**
- **Identify the difference between a URL and an IP address—an IP address is a 32-bit binary number that identifies a specific location on the Internet; a URL is the address of a particular file and the method used to deal with the file.**
- **Identify the segments of a URL:**
  - Method, such as http:// or ftp://
  - Domain name
  - Folder
  - File name with extension
- **Identify the functions of HTTP, FTP, and Telnet:**

- HTTP is used for retrieving Web pages written in HTML
- FTP is used for transferring files
- Telnet is used for running programs on a remote computer
- **Identify the function of domain name servers—to store and serve up Web pages upon request.**

E-MAIL

- **Identify parts of an e-mail address:**
  - To—addresses of the recipients
  - CC—carbon copy; addresses of recipients who receive copies (seen by all recipients)
  - BCC—blind carbon copy; addresses of additional recipients (not seen by the other recipients)
- **Match e-mail terms with definitions (see glossary).**
- **Identify rules of etiquette:**
  - Be polite and considerate
  - Summarize clearly in the subject line
  - Limit use of copies
  - Use Reply to All feature only when appropriate
  - Don't use all capital letters
  - Use complete sentences, standard grammar, and punctuation in most business or school settings
  - Don't write anything you would be embarrassed to read later
  - Don't send mail that you wrote while you were angry
  - Include your name at the bottom
- **Identify the role of file compression for attachments—compression programs can reduce file sizes by approximately a factor of four to speed up transmission of attachments.**
- **Identify the differences between Web mail and mail clients that are installed on a user's computer—the Web server and client are both on the server in Web mail; the user accesses the client via a Web browser. In standard e-mail programs like Microsoft Outlook, the mail client is on the user's computer.**

INSTANT MESSAGING

- **Match terms with definitions, and use them in sentences (see glossary).**

PERSONAL INFORMATION

- **Identify the features of Web logs and personal Web pages—Web logs, or blogs, are dated journal entries posted on the Internet for others to read. A personal Web page contains pictures and information about the owner of the page.**

CONFERENCING

- **Identify features of Voice over IP and videoconferencing:**
  - VoIP uses TCP/IP packets to transmit voice at lower cost than circuit switched networks typically used by telephone companies
  - Videoconferencing may use TCP/IP to send video and voice simultaneously for the purpose of seeing people while conversing with them

BROWSERS

- **Identify the function of a portal—provides a variety of information and services to retain the user's attention.**
- **Identify functions of applets and cookies:**
  - Applets are small programs that accompany a Web page to perform functions like checking forms for completion or animating part of the page
  - Cookies are text files that contain user ID numbers
- **Identify common features of browsers:**
  - Address box for URL
  - List of Web sites to revisit
- **Identify popular Web browsers and the significant differences between them—Netscape uses Java applets and other third-party software like RealPlayer; IE uses Microsoft software.**

SEARCH ENGINES

- **Identify searching methods and tools:**
  - Advanced search options using AND, OR, NOT
  - Options to search for pictures and comments in group discussions

RESEARCH

- **Identify resources found in libraries—subscription services to the full text of books, magazines, and journals.**
- **Identify the objective for citing references—provide enough information for the reader to find and read the source.**

INFORMATION SERVICES

- **Match types of information available with example Web sites. AOL-portal; Amazon-books; auctions-ebay**

COMMERCE

- Match types of commerce available with example Web sites (see Figure 2.22).
- Identify issues related to using credit cards online—liability of user limited.
- Identify terms used for types of commerce between business and customers:
  - B to B—business to business
  - B to C—business to customer
  - C to C—customer to customer

ENTERTAINMENT

- **Identify types of online entertainment.**
  - Listen to music
  - Chat with friends
  - Watch movies
  - Read books
  - Play games

EDUCATION

- **Identify when Web-based training is appropriate:**
  - Stable content
  - Large audience
  - Expensive to bring people together for traditional training
- **Identify features of online college courses:**
  - Synchronous—chat, streaming video
  - Asynchronous—threaded discussion, drop box, grade book, e-mail, objective tests

true/false questions

1. ___ Intranet is another term for backbone.

2. ___ VoIP has been around since the early days of ARPANET.

3. ___ The government encouraged academic networks to seek commercial customers to expand the use of the Internet.

4. ___ A LAN with a T1 line is a faster connection to the Internet than a cable modem.

5. ___ A domain name can have only one IP address.

multiple choice

1. Which of the following is not a function of e-mail?
   a) posting daily thoughts for anyone on the Internet to read
   b) CC
   c) BCC
   d) Reply to All

2. Web-based training is not appropriate under which of the following conditions?
   a) geographically dispersed workforce
   b) workforce dispersed among different shift schedules
   c) high travel costs to assemble workforce
   d) content of training changes often and requires regular updates

3. Which of the following is not a method or device used to connect to the Internet?
   a) cell phone
   b) CD-RW
   c) satellite television dish
   d) modem

4. Which of the following people was not directly involved in creating or developing important products for use on the Internet or World Wide Web?
   a) Tim Berners-Lee
   b) Mark Andreessen
   c) J. C. R. Licklider
   d) Leslie Groves

5. Which of the following is the best ranking of connection speed from slowest to fastest?
   a) dial-up, LAN with T1, cable
   b) LAN, satellite, DSL
   c) DSL, cable, cell phone
   d) dial-up, DSL, LAN with T1

completion

1. An IP address is 32 binary digits long. It is divided into four groups called _____, which are represented as decimal numbers separated by periods.

2. The abbreviation CC in an e-mail message stands for _____ _____ (two words).

3. The new domain name extension for museums is _____ .

4. Icons used to show emotion are called _____ .

5. The acronym HTML stands for _____ _____ _____ (three words).

matching key terms/definitions

Match each term with its definition.

_____ **1.** blog
_____ **2.** checksum
_____ **3.** client
_____ **4.** disk cache
_____ **5.** DNS
_____ **6.** domain name
_____ **7.** DSL
_____ **8.** FAQ
_____ **9.** FTP
_____ **10.** HTML
_____ **11.** HTTP
_____ **12.** IM
_____ **13.** ISP
_____ **14.** Java
_____ **15.** LAN
_____ **16.** POP3
_____ **17.** SMTP
_____ **18.** spam
_____ **19.** spider
_____ **20.** T1
_____ **21.** TCP/IP
_____ **22.** Telnet
_____ **23.** URL
_____ **24.** VoIP
_____ **25.** VPN

a. method of transferring files on the Internet
b. a group of connected computers
c. a high-speed connection to the Internet from a company or ISP
d. a method used to retrieve Web pages from a server
e. a name that often resembles the name of the organization and is easier to remember than a number; it often includes www as a prefix and always has an extension to indicate the category
f. a program that searches the Web for Web pages and indexes them for use by a search engine
g. a series of dated journal entries available online
h. a programming language used to write applets
i. area of the computer where recently visited Web pages are stored for quick retrieval
j. computer with a database of domain names and IP addresses and the relationships between them
k. company or group that provides a connection to the Internet backbone
l. direct communication between users with windows that display text or video
m. encrypts packets within packets that are sent to an intranet via the Internet
n. high-speed connection technology that uses existing telephone lines over distances of a few miles
o. identifies the method of interaction with the server, a domain name or IP address, the local folder, and file name
p. language used to create Web pages that can be displayed on any computer
q. method of running programs on a remote computer
r. method of sending telephone conversations using TCP/IP packets
s. method of transmitting packets on the Internet
t. program to handle mail being received by the user
u. program to handle mail being sent from the user
v. program that communicates with the server and usually resides on the user's computer
w. questions and answers posted so new participants can catch up
x. sum of numbers within a packet
y. term used to describe unsolicited e-mail

beyond the facts

Factual knowledge provides the basis for higher levels of learning. In the following sections, you will work with the concepts and facts presented in the chapter to develop critical-thinking and problem-solving skills. You practice research, analysis, and communication and become aware of diversity issues while exploring the impact of computer technology on career choices, social interactions, and home life. The Leadership section helps you identify ways in which you can lead others in organizing and implementing projects that meet worthwhile community needs. In the Lifelong Learning exercise, you build a set of learning resources that you can use after this course to continue learning.

objectives for beyond the facts

END OF CHAPTER EXERCISES	Achievement of the objectives for the end-of-chapter exercises requires evaluation of documents, class discussions, or presentations.
Critical Thinking—Research	Express an informed opinion about the issues facing ICANN over maintaining common domain names as other countries like China become large Internet users.
Problem Solving	1) Use Help features to learn how to test your Internet connection using IPCONFIG and PING. 2) Write a detailed process description for seeking assistance if unsuccessful. 3) Write a detailed process description, if successful, for instructing others. 4) Communicate the experience to the class.
Anticipating Career Challenges and Opportunities	Demonstrate the following skills: 1) Teamwork: coordinate research 2) Research: find information about disintermediation and your career 3) Diversity: consider direct marketing from other countries to your customers and vice versa 4) Analysis: analyze the impact of direct Internet contact on your career and determine whether your job adds value 5) Communication: communicate the results in writing or by public presentation
Impact on the Workplace	Demonstrate the following skills: 1) Teamwork: coordinate research on the use of e-mail in the workplace with other students 2) Research: identify the use of e-mail at work by observation and interviews 3) Diversity: observe variations in e-mail use by age, race, and gender 4) Analysis: form an opinion about how workers manage e-mail in your organization 5) Communication: communicate the results in writing or by public presentation
Impact on Social Interactions	Demonstrate the following skills: 1) Teamwork: allocate tasks for research 2) Research: determine e-mail addresses and Web sites for elected officials at local, state, and national levels 3) Diversity: see how interest groups encourage their members to use the Internet to contact legislators 4) Analysis: form an opinion on the usefulness of this method of communication with elected officials based on your research 5) Communication: communicate the results in writing or by public presentation
Impact on Home Life	Demonstrate the following skills: 1) Teamwork and research: work with family members to design a personal Web page 2) Research and diversity: find out how age influences your family members' attitudes toward the project 4) Analysis: form an opinion based on your experience 5) Communication: communicate the results in writing or by public presentation
Leadership	Describe a plan to lead a group of people toward a worthy goal—in this case, development of a customer-to-customer Web site for artisans in developing countries to sell direct.
Lifelong Learning	Identify three or more online resources that may be used to learn more about the topics introduced in this chapter.

critical thinking-research

How should ICANN interact with emerging Internet users in Asia such as China and India?

1. **Teamwork**—Join one to four other students. Decide how to divide up the work. Possible divisions could be: China's position, India's position, search newsgroups using Google's Groups feature, search newspapers from other countries for articles, and search the library's LexisNexis database for articles.

2. **Research**—Use a Web browser and go to the companion Web site at **http://www.prenhall.com/preston**. Follow the links by clicking on the Web addresses that are highlighted and underlined. Read the articles about ICANN to familiarize yourself with the issue. Use a search engine and the features discussed in this chapter to look for more information about control of Internet domain names and IP addresses. Make a list of the sources you find to be relevant that you may want to reference later. Include the title of the page or article, the name of the organization responsible for the Web page, the date the page or article was written, and the Web address. You may also go to the library and look up books,

articles, and news reports that are relevant to this topic. Many libraries have the full text of articles and news reports online in proprietary databases that are not available to the public.

3. **Diversity issues**—Look for articles that express views from China and India.

4. **Analysis**—Write an essay that discusses some of the problems ICANN faces due to growing Internet use in China and India and one or two options for resolving the problems. Form and express an opinion. Go beyond simple reporting of the facts. Support your opinion with references to the articles you read. Ask your instructor for guidance regarding the required length of the essay.

5. **Communication**—Prepare a presentation in which you present your opinion and the supporting facts to the class. Depending on your computer skill, you could give the presentation using a program like PowerPoint and save it as a Web page, or you could prepare a paper handout with your Web references for use while you talk to the class.

problem solving

The objective of this exercise is to learn valuable processes for solving computer problems, not just the solution to this particular problem.

If at work you use a LAN or one of the continuously connected services like cable, DSL, or satellite, you have no doubt become accustomed to using the Internet for many of your daily functions. Interruption of your connection can be frustrating. You can solve many problems quickly if you know a few basic procedures. Even if these don't work, your repair technician will start with them so you can save time when you call for help.

1. **Search for help on the topic**—Use the extensive library of Help topics that is included with your computer's operating system. In Windows XP, click Start, Help, and Support. Look under Networking and the Web, Fixing networking or Web problems, Test a TCP/IP configuration using the ping command. If you are using a different operating system, search help for the terms IPCONFIG and PING. When you find a topic that appears to be appropriate for this

problem, write down the sequence of choices that leads you back to it for future reference.

2. **Read the instructions and try it**—Attempt to follow the instructions for determining your computer's IP address and connection using the IPCONFIG and PING commands. Try using PING to test the connection to a known Web site. You can addthe switch **-t** to the command to watch the process for a while to see if you have intermittent conection. Use CTRL + C to stop the process. Write a description of your efforts. If you are not uccessful, describe what you tried and what did or did not happen. Be specific. If you were successful but found that the instructions were not clear at some point, write a description of the problematic instructions, and suggest improvements.

3. **Troubleshoot**—If your first attempt is unsuccessful, determine whether there are some alternative interpretations of the instructions that you can try. Record the results of these efforts.

4. Communicate—

   a. If you were unsuccessful, describe your attempt in step-by-step detail. This is necessary if you ask for help from an expert.

   b. If you were successful, describe the process so it can be followed by others. Identify any instructions that you think could be improved, and provide a suggestion for improvement.

   c. Illustrate your communication. In many cases, a screen capture is very useful when describing a problem or a procedure. In Windows, you can capture the computer screen by pressing the PrntScn button (the spelling on this key varies) on the keyboard or capture just the active window by pressing and holding Alt and pressing PrntScn. Nothing seems to happen, but if you open a word processing document you can paste the screen into the document to illustrate your point.

   d. Present your findings to the class. Prepare a demonstration of how to determine your computer's IP address and how to test your Internet connection using PING.

anticipating career challenges and opportunities

Companies can do business directly with their customers through Web sites at tremendous savings. For example, it costs a bank $1.07 per teller transaction but $0.01 per transaction at the bank's Web site. It costs an airline more than $5.00 for an agent to sell a ticket but less than $1.00 to sell one online. It costs a company between $1.65 and $2.70 to send out and process bills but only $0.05 to $0.10 to do it online. In 1999, Bill Gates predicted in his book *Business at the Speed of Thought* that the Internet would drastically change the way customers relate to businesses. He used the term **disintermediation** to describe the process of removing the layers of distribution and salespeople between the company and the customer. Jobs in which the worker passes information or goods without adding value would disappear. Jobs that will grow in number are those in which the worker adds value to the information or service. Evaluate your current career or the one you want to go into, and determine whether expanded use of the Internet for business-to-customer sales or service will reduce the number of jobs in that field. Look for related jobs that add value to the information or services that won't be readily replaced by direct contact with the customer through Web pages.

1. **Teamwork**—Join one or two other students who have similar career plans. Decide how to divide up the work. Possible divisions could be: employment trends in your specific job versus the economy as a whole, and related careers that add value for the customer.

2. **Research**—Use a Web browser to search for articles on your career. Use key words like **trend** and **Internet**. Use the Groups and News options in search engines like Google.com. Make a list of the sources you find to be relevant that you may want to reference later. Include the title of the page or article, the name of the organization responsible for the Web page, the date the page or article was written, and the Web address. You may also go to the library and look up books, articles, and news reports that are relevant to this topic. Many libraries have the full text of articles and news reports online in proprietary databases that are not available to the public.

3. **Diversity issues**—Consider expanding what you do to other countries using the Internet. Check to see if other countries are competing for the same customers with better service and price and reaching them through their Internet presence.

4. **Analysis**—Write an essay that describes the trend in employment in your career or your chosen career. Form and express an opinion about the future of your career as it relates to disintermediation. Go beyond simple reporting of the facts. Support your opinion with references to the articles you read. Ask your instructor for guidance regarding the required length of the essay.

5. **Communication**—Prepare a presentation in which you present your opinion and the supporting facts to the class. Depending on your computer skill, you could give the presentation using a program like PowerPoint and save it as a Web page, or you could prepare a paper handout with your Web references for use while you talk to the class.

impact on the workplace

E-mail has replaced many other forms of communication in the workplace. Many people find themselves overwhelmed with incoming messages. Survey some of your coworkers to find out how they manage their e-mail.

1. **Teamwork**—Join one or two other students who work where you do or in a similar type of business or organization. Decide how to divide the work.

2. **Research**—Do a survey of your place of employment or your college to identify how people manage their e-mail. Record specific information about what you observe. Look for examples of the following:
   - Junk mail filters—do workers use the filters available in their e-mail clients to block or divert mail from their normal in-box?
   - Multiple e-mail addresses—do workers have more than one e-mail address and give out one of them only to trusted individuals?
   - Presorting—do the workers who use Microsoft Outlook use the Rules Wizard to sort incoming mail into folders by sender?
   - Deleting based on the subject line—do workers delete messages without reading them based on the subject line?

   - Attachments—are people afraid that attachments contain viruses to the point that they simply do not open any attachment?

3. **Diversity issues**—Observe the age, gender, and ethnicity of the people who work with computers in your organization. Are there any obvious differences in the use of e-mail based on one of these factors?

4. **Analysis**—Write an essay that describes how e-mail is managed by workers in your organization. Form and express an opinion, bearing in mind that your small sample is not large enough to establish any statistically valid relationships. Support your opinion with statistics based on your observations. Ask your instructor for guidance regarding the required length of the essay.

5. **Communication**—Prepare a presentation in which you present your opinion and the results of your observations. Depending on your computer skill, you could create charts in application programs like PowerPoint or Excel to graphically communicate the data you recorded, or you could prepare a paper handout with data for use while you talk to the class.

impact on social interactions

E-mail and the Internet make it easy to communicate with our elected officials. Determine how to monitor the activity of elected officials and how to communicate your opinion on issues to them.

1. **Teamwork and Research**—Join two or three other students to research this topic. Find Web pages and e-mail addresses for elected officials that represent you at each of the following levels:
   - local elected officials, for example, school board, county commissioners, city officials
   - state elected officials
   - national elected officials

2. **Diversity issues**—Look for Web pages by organizations that represent special interest groups that are defined by issues related to age, race, gender, or ethnicity. See if they provide legisla-

tors' e-mail addresses to facilitate contact and expression of views.

3. **Analysis**—Write an essay that describes how e-mail and Web pages are used to communicate with your elected officials. Form and express an opinion. Support your opinion with statistics based on your observations. Ask your instructor for guidance regarding the required length of the essay.

4. **Communication**—Prepare a presentation in which you present your opinion and the results of your observations. Prepare a handout of the information you compiled. If you have the computer skill, create a Web page with this information, and post it to a server.

impact on home life

Create a personal Web page, and post it on a Web server. Use a program that creates Web pages, such as Microsoft Word or PowerPoint, to create your page. Include information about your hobbies and activities, as well as pictures.

Obtain permission from your ISP or college to post your Web page, or rent space on a commercial service. To upload your files to a Web server, you usually need a user name and password. You also need to know where you are allowed to place your page on the server. This information must be supplied by the server's administrator. To get your files from your computer to the server, you use a feature of the Internet that has been around since its inception, FTP. There are free FTP programs that you can download from the Internet. The FTP software is already built into Internet Explorer. In the address box of IE, you use the following format, **ftp:// <Username>:<password>@<URL of the server>**, for example, ftp://TheBoss:0001@www.pctraining.net.

Most Web servers have a folder named *httpdocs* where you place Web pages. You can use the copy and paste method to move copies of your files.

1. **Teamwork and research**—Involve your family members in designing the Web page and determining what should be included. Get permission to use pictures or provide personal information.

2. **Diversity issues**—Consider the implications for any children and older adults. Ask them how this would affect them.

3. **Analysis**—Write a report on this process and what you discovered about your family's willingness to participate. If grandparents are involved, report their interest in the project.

4. **Communication**—Prepare a presentation in which you show your Web page to the class and report on the reactions of family members.

leadership

A recent article in a U.S. newspaper described the efforts of a South American village to sell its blankets and other woven textiles directly to customers in the United States via a Web site. The locals got five times as much for their products and the customers got them at half the price they would have paid had they used a middleman. You and a few associates could use your knowledge of computers and the Internet to help a group in a developing country sell its products directly to customers in the developed world over the Internet.

1. **Vision**—Write a vision statement that describes what you want your group to achieve. It should motivate people to volunteer to help.

2. **Research**—Don't reinvent the wheel. Do the following background research:
   - Determine whether anyone is already doing this. If so, contact them and describe their operation.
   - Consider diversity issues. The digital divide is great between the United States and other countries. Find out what it takes to provide a reliable Internet connection to the location in the developing country. What kind of connection would they use? Do they have a reliable method of shipping their products out of the country?

3. **Plan of Action**—Write a simple plan of action. Test the plan by following it yourself on a small scale. Locate someone nearby who makes a product that might have national or worldwide appeal and sells it locally. Create a Web page or use a prepackaged store-in-a-box software to advertise the product and take orders.

4. **Analysis**—Write up an analysis of what you learned by testing your plan.

5. **Communication**—Present your plan to the class. Describe what you learned by testing your plan and how you think it could be expanded to developing countries. Share your vision statement, and try to inspire others to join you in your worthwhile effort.

lifelong learning

Add links to your browser's favorites list.

1. Start your Web browser, and open the list of favorite sites. Create folders named Research, Information, Commerce, and Entertainment.

2. Go to the companion Web page for this chapter **www.prenhall.com/preston,** and select one of the Web links on research that you found useful.

3. Add this link to your browser's favorites list in the Research folder.

4. Repeat this process for other links on the companion Web page for this chapter, and add them to the appropriate folders.

Add learning goals to your journals.

1. Identify areas in which you feel you know the least. List three specific topics related to this chapter that you would like to learn more about in the future.

2. You will add to this journal after each chapter to compile a personal list of references and topics for future study.

Understanding Hardware and Its Function

outline & objectives

PERSONAL COMPUTERS

- Identify the differences among a desktop, laptop or notebook, and a personal digital assistant.

COMPUTERS FOR ORGANIZATIONS

- Identify the differences among categories of computers by their relative capacity and by their function.

SUPERCOMPUTERS

- Identify the types of problems that require a supercomputer.

DISTRIBUTED PROCESSING AND DATABASES

- Identify the types of problems that are suitable for distributed processing.
- Identify examples of distributed databases.

NUMBERING SYSTEMS

- Identify the relationship between characters and bytes.
- Identify the role of ASCII and Unicode standards.

PICTURES

- Identify the relationship between pixels and visible details.

ANALOG AND DIGITAL

- Identify the types of information that change smoothly with time and which representation method is most suitable for them.
- Identify the function of A-D and D-A converters and how they are used.

POWER CONTROL SYMBOLS

- Match power control symbols with their associated meanings.

KEYBOARDS

- Identify examples of function keys.

POINTING DEVICES

- Identify features and maintenance issues for mice and trackballs.

SCANNERS

- Identify types of scanners and how they convert paper documents and pictures into digital files.

DIGITAL CAMERAS AND VIDEO

- Identify how digital cameras connect to computers.

MICROPHONES

- Identify uses for microphones.
- Identify appropriate placement for microphones when using voice recognition software.

CENTRAL PROCESSING UNIT

- Identify measurements used to rate CPU performance.

PRIMARY AND SECONDARY STORAGE

- Identify the difference between memory and virtual memory.
- Compare storage methods by speed and typical capacities.
- Distinguish between disks and discs.
- Identify the different types of optical storage methods.

MONITORS AND PROJECTORS

- Identify the difference between CRT and LCD monitors.
- Identify the different methods of measuring the size of monitors.
- Identify the difference between flat-screen and flat-panel monitors.
- Compare brightness of projectors.

PRINTERS

- Identify types of printers, and match them with the type of ink delivery system.

INDICATOR LIGHTS

- Identify the function of indicator lights on the case.

SPEAKERS

- Identify functions of speakers.

PORTS AND PLUGS

- Identify types of USB plugs.
- Compare speeds of USB 1.1 and USB 2.0 connections.
- Identify common use of FireWire connections.
- Distinguish between an RJ-11 and RJ-45 connector and their functions.
- Identify the most likely problems when connecting the parts of a computer to the case.

SURGE SUPPRESSORS AND UPS

- Identify the functions of a surge suppressor and how it differs from a circuit breaker.
- Describe the function of an uninterruptible power supply.

WHY DO I NEED TO KNOW THIS?

When you sit down in front of most desktop personal computers, you see a display device called a *monitor* that looks like a television screen and a case, or *system unit*, with slots in the front and numerous holes in the back. You also notice a keyboard, a mouse, speakers, and a printer, all connected by a maze of wires. Some people enjoy understanding how things work, and others consider the devices as means to an end. In either case, there are basics that you need to know about a computer in order to buy it, use it, or move it. You also need to know something about the more powerful computers used by schools, hospitals, banks, the government, and other organizations. The operation of these computers is necessary to the functioning of the organization, and a little knowledge about the power, cooling, physical security, and location of these systems helps the average person understand how these computers affect the workplace.

Computers vary in their size, capacity, and cost, so we must use modifiers to categorize them. The traditional categories—*supercomputer*, *mainframe*, *midrange*, *minicomputer*, and *microcomputer*—refer to their relative capabilities from highest to lowest. Their actual capabilities change with time so that today's microcomputer has more computing power than a supercomputer did 40 years ago, and the average automobile today has more computing power in it than the Apollo 11 lunar module. Another way to categorize computers is by the way they are used and who uses them. From an individual's point of view, types of computers may be separated into two broad categories: personal computers and computers shared by people within an organization.

PERSONAL COMPUTERS

Microcomputers are similar to larger computers but are intended for use by one person and are usually called *personal computers*.

Desktop

A *desktop computer* is a personal computer that is too big to carry around but is still intended for use by one person at a time. It has a keyboard, a mouse, speakers, a monitor, and a case (see Figure 3.1). Some companies, like Apple, combine the monitor, speakers, and case into a single unit.

Laptop and Notebook

Notebook computers, also called *laptop computers*, are personal computers that are portable and fit on your lap or in a briefcase and have batteries (see Figure 3.2). The monitor is a flat-panel liquid crystal display, or LCD, and the mouse is often replaced by a *touch pad*, *track ball*, or very small *pointing stick* embedded in the keyboard. The screen and case are connected by a hinge, and the unit closes to protect the LCD screen and keyboard during transport. Some units have a screen that pivots from its regular position and becomes a tablet that recognizes handwriting.

FIGURE 3.1

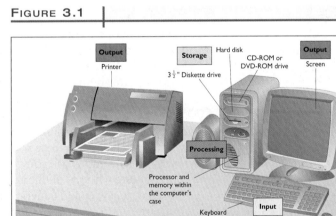

Desktop computer systems typically consist of several components.

FIGURE 3.2

Portable computers are often called laptop or notebook computers.

FIGURE 3.3

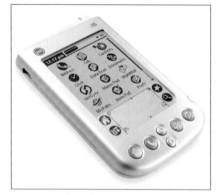

A personal digital assistant fits in one hand and manages daily tasks.

Personal Digital Assistant, Appliances, and Mobile Communication Devices

A *personal digital assistant*, or *PDA*, is small enough to fit in your hand or pocket (see Figure 3.3). It has less memory and a smaller screen than a laptop and uses software specifically designed to accommodate these limitations. A PDA is most often used to manage appointments, tasks, lists of phone numbers, and e-mail. It can also run limited versions of desktop software such as word processors. Palm Inc. popularized this form of computer with its Palm Pilot.

Appliances are computers that are dedicated to one task, such as browsing the Internet, word processing, recording television programs, or playing games.

PDA and cell phone technology are merging into a class called *mobile communication devices*. Manufacturers of PDAs add cell phone technology to provide e-mail, Web browsing, and instant messaging capabilities. Cell phone manufacturers are adding larger screens and contact management software.

COMPUTERS FOR ORGANIZATIONS

Organizations have numerous employees who must communicate with each other. They also have a database of customer, employee, or member information. Many organizations use computers to conduct business on the Internet and communicate with the public through Web pages and e-mail. Computers consume electric power and generate heat; numerous or large computers used by organizations use a lot of power and generate a lot of heat. Wiring, air conditioning, and physical security all become important issues for organizational computing—issues that affect all of an organization's employees.

Workstations

An individual employee usually has a desktop computer that is similar to a home computer, except it is connected to other computers and shared printers on a *local area network (LAN)*. Some of the desktop computers in an organization such as a design firm have more than usual speed, larger monitors, and special attached devices. These high-performance desktop computers are called *workstations*. Many organizations have a computer for each employee, which can cause problems with temperature control and wiring. If a building's cooling system was designed before workstations became common, it may be inadequate. Providing LAN connections to workstations is a challenging problem in older buildings, where the wiring may run through ceilings, walls, and floors that were not designed for easy access. Some organizations use *wireless* connections to the LAN that use radio signals. This solves the problem of running wires, but the radio signals can be received outside the building, which makes this type of connection vulnerable to eavesdropping (security is addressed in Chapter 6).

Network Servers

Workplaces with many computers enhance productivity by sharing resources and information on a local area network, or LAN. A computer called a *network server* coordinates traffic among the computers and printers on the LAN, communicates with other LANs, and provides Web page and e-mail functions on the Internet or company intranet. The network server may be similar to a desktop computer, but it is usually faster and has more memory than most desktop computers. Servers that handle network activity between hundreds of employee computers and the Web are the size of file cabinets. They are often placed in closets or in a back room where wiring for the LAN converges with wiring from the telephone company. Physical security is often accomplished by locking the door to the room or closet. In many cases the value of the server to the organization is not reflected in the effort made to secure it from malicious activity. For example, during an inspection of a bank, the manager showed off the vault, which contained hundreds of thousands of dollars and had a steel door a foot thick. He also said the bank handled millions of dollars of business electronically but upon inspection, it was pointed out to him that the door to the server closet was wood and was only two inches thick.

Mini, Midrange, and Mainframe File Servers

An organization's records are critical to its existence. Billing, sales, accounting, and customer information is kept in a database on a computer that is more powerful than a typical workstation or network server. These computers vary in capability depending on the size of the organization and the size of the data files they manage. The terms *mini*, *midrange*, and *mainframe* are used to describe their relative capabilities. They are also known by their function of managing database files and are called *file servers*. Users often communicate directly with these file servers via a *dumb terminal* or a *point-of-sale (POS) terminal*. When you check out at a supermarket, order a burger at a major chain, or buy clothing, the transaction is handled by a POS terminal (see Figure 3.4). POS terminals look like computers, but they don't have storage and are useless if disconnected from the file server. Midrange computers are used in midsize companies with thousands of customers, and mainframes are used in large companies with millions of customers. Both produce enough heat to warrant special air conditioning systems and dedicated space in the building. These computer rooms are secured with special locks on the doors and are often in the basement where there are no windows. They have raised floors to facilitate wiring and the flow of cold air through the computers to remove the heat. They often have backup electrical power systems and a staff of

FIGURE 3.4

Point-of-sale (POS) terminals record sales data.

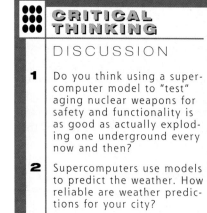
professionals to run them. Many organizations have duplicate equipment at other locations that can take over in case of an emergency.

Supercomputers

The midrange and mainframe computers used by businesses are characterized by their ability to manage large databases with many individual records, such as a customer database for a utility or bank. The individual records in these databases seldom interact with each other. Supercomputers are characterized by their ability to evaluate complex interactions quickly. One use of supercomputers is *modeling* using *finite element analysis*. For example, supercomputers are used to design airplanes. A design drawing of an airplane is divided into very small pieces (finite elements) and formulas are provided that determine how each part of the plane reacts to air flow and stress and how movement or stress on each part affects the parts next to it. The interaction of these elements is evaluated thousands of times each second to simulate how the plane will perform. Designers can simulate many different maneuvers with this type of model to evaluate and modify a new design before they ever build the plane. Supercomputers can evaluate millions of these complex interaction formulas each second to simulate the behavior of an airplane in a reasonable amount of time, where a mainframe might take weeks. Rapid evaluation also allows designers to test the formulas and assumptions they use to gain better understanding of how the elements affect each other. Supercomputers are found at national research laboratories, large research universities, government facilities, and military research facilities (see Figure 3.5). They are the most expensive computers.

DISTRIBUTED PROCESSING AND DISTRIBUTED DATABASES

An alternative to large, expensive, centralized computing is appropriate for some tasks. Some large computing problems can be solved by breaking them into smaller parts that can be solved individually on several different computers and then reassembled into an integrated solution. This

FIGURE 3.5

Supercomputers often require special facilities with raised floors to accommodate wiring and cooling air.

process is called *distributed processing*. For example, a company may own hundreds of powerful workstations connected by a LAN that are idle at night or on weekends. Instead of buying a supercomputer, the company could use its mainframe to assign parts of a large problem to these workstations when they are idle at night and then integrate the results in the morning. Computers that are continuously connected to the Internet may be used for distributed processing. One creative example is the SETI@home project. SETI stands for Search for Extraterrestrial Intelligence. We have radio telescopes that receive radio signals from outer space, and we have programs that can analyze a radio signal to see if it contains patterns that might indicate in intelligent source. The telescopes receive far more data than can be analyzed by a single computer. The solution used by SETI@home is to distribute the processing to personal computers. Volunteers leave their personal computers on at night, connected to the Internet, and allow SETI@home to download some of the data onto the PCs for analysis and then upload the results in the morning. SETI@home coordinates 1.85 million personal computers around the world to process more data than is possible with the most powerful supercomputer.

It is also possible to store a large database on several smaller computers, resulting in a *distributed database*. A database of customer accounts could be separated into sections, each of which would be stored on a different computer. A coordinating computer would keep track of the location of the files, and users would not see the difference.

The Internet may also be used to manage a distributed database. Digital recordings of music and videos may be stored on thousands of different personal computers and shared over high-speed connections. The location of files could be coordinated by a central computer, or the individual computers could communicate file locations to each other via *peer-to-peer* communication (see Chapter 5 to learn about the ethical use of computers).

Words, pictures, and sounds may be represented by numbers, which a computer can manipulate to perform valuable services such as checking for incorrectly spelled words, changing contrast in pictures, and removing static in audio recordings.

NUMBERS AND TEXT

We are familiar with the *decimal numbering system*, which use ten digits from zero to nine. Early computer designers found that mechanical or electrical devices like switches could represent digits using a simple numbering system with only two digits, 0 and 1, known as the *binary* number system. Electrical devices were eventually replaced by electronic switches called *transistors*, but the simple binary numbering system is still in use. For comparison of decimal and binary numbers, see Figure 3.6.

Computers that interact with us by representing our world using the digits of binary numbers are called *digital computers*.

In order for computers to communicate with each other, a standard was developed. The *American Standard Code for Information Interchange (ASCII)* is a standard that began by assigning a binary number to each capital and lowercase letter in the alphabet and to the ten decimal digits, as well as to other commonly used function keys such as the Enter and Backspace keys. The early ASCII code used seven-digit binary numbers and was limited to only 128 different characters. The code was later expanded to eight-digit binary numbers to provide an additional 128 binary numbers, for a total of 256, to represent additional computer functions and keys. IBM was already using a different standard for its mainframe computer, the IBM 360, named *Extended Binary Coded Decimal Interchange Code (EBCDIC)* (see Figure 3.7). This system is still in use on the IBM S/390 mainframe computer. A newer code, *Unicode*, has been developed that uses 32-digit binary numbers and includes codes for characters in many languages besides English.

Each digit in a binary number is called a *bit*. An eight-digit binary number, such as one used by the ASCII code, is called a byte. Data transmission rates are often given in bits per second, and data storage is usually given in bytes.

PICTURES

The most common way that computers communicate with us is visually, either on paper or on a computer screen. To convert binary numbers into letters on the screen or on paper, computers display patterns of individual dots. If the dots are close enough and small enough, they look like continuous lines. If you take a close look at your computer screen, you will see that the screen is made up of many small elements that can turn on (bright) or off (dark). These picture elements are called *pixels* (see Figure 3.8). The more pixels into which your screen is divided, the finer the detail that can be represented. For example, if a monitor is set to display images that are 800 pixels wide by 600 pixels high, it may not display small fonts as well as a monitor set to 1024 by 768. There are three different color elements in each pixel that can be turned on or off or set to a given brightness to produce a variety of colors.

SOUND

Using computers to communicate and manipulate sound is a bigger challenge because sound waves are not static like a page of text or a picture.

FIGURE 3.6

Counting with Binary, Decimal, and Hexadecimal Numbers

Decimal Number	Binary Number	Hexadecimal Number
0	0	0
1	1	1
2	10	2
3	11	3
4	100	4
5	101	5
6	110	6
7	111	7
8	1000	8
9	1001	9
10	1010	A
11	1011	B
12	1100	C
13	1101	D
14	1110	E
15	1111	F

Binary numbers use zero and one.

FIGURE 3.7

ASCII and EBCDIC Character Codes

Character	ASCII Representation	EBCDIC Representation
0	00110000	11110000
1	00110001	11110001
2	00110010	11110010
3	00110011	11110011
4	00110100	11110100
5	00110101	11110101
6	00110110	11110110
7	00110111	11110111
8	00111000	11111000
9	00111001	11111001
A	01000001	11000001
B	01000010	11000010
C	01000011	11000011
D	01000100	11000100
E	01000101	11000101
F	01000110	11000110
G	01000111	11000111
H	01001000	11001000
I	01001001	11001001
J	01001010	11010001
K	01001011	11010010
L	01001100	11010011
M	01001101	11010100
N	01001110	11010101
O	01001111	11010110
P	01010000	11010111
Q	01010001	11011000
R	01010010	11011001
S	01010011	11100010
T	01010100	11100011
U	01010101	11100100
V	01010101	11100101
W	01010101	11100110
X	01011001	11100111
Y	01011001	11101000
Z	01011010	111010011

ASCII and EBCDIC codes in binary form for some of the characters they represent.

Everything about music or speech, such as the volume and pitch, varies with time. Before the use of digital computers, music was converted with a microphone into electrical signals that varied in a way that was analogous to the way the volume and pitch varied. This type of signal is called an *analog* because it behaves in a way that is analogous—similar to the thing it represents. These signals were transmitted, received, amplified, and sent to a speaker that converted the electrical signals back into sound waves.

A digital computer takes the analog signal from the microphone and samples the signal thousands of times each second. Each time it samples the signal, it assigns numbers to the volume and pitch, converting the analog signal into a series of binary numbers. The specialized integrated circuit that converts analog signals to a series of digital numbers is called an *A to D converter*, or *analog to digital converter*. A digital computer is so fast at this task that it can sample music thousands of times each second, compare the volume and pitch of each individual sample with the ones that come before and after it, and fix problems if the values of the numbers vary too much from the ones that come before and after. This is why you can play a music CD that has many small scratches in it without hearing any static. It is also how telephone conversations can be transmitted thousands of miles and sound like the people are next door to each other. The digital signal, which consists of a series of numbers, can be changed back into an analog electrical signal by a *D to A converter*. The analog electric signal moves the cone of the speaker, producing the sound waves we hear. Whenever a digital computer works with something that varies continuously with time, it uses this process of converting from analog to digital and back.

Digital computers are good at manipulating numbers and communicating through mechanical devices, sound, and images. They have not yet been developed to the point where they are good at communicating with us through our senses of touch, smell, and taste.

FIGURE 3.8

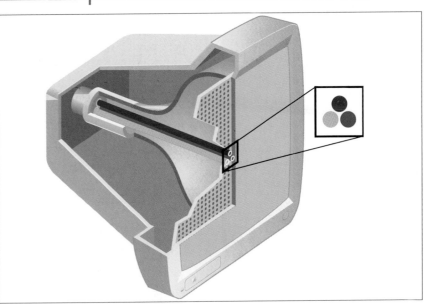

A range of colors is produced by the relative brightness of three color elements in each pixel.

The physical components of a computer are called *hardware*, and the instructions that direct the activity of the computer are called *software*. In this section, you learn about personal computer hardware.

Your first interaction with a computer's hardware may be turning on the computer. Now that you know something about binary numbers, you can use this knowledge to interpret symbols used on the power control buttons. You may see one of these symbols on a button or switch that controls the power to the hardware (see Figure 3.9).

The symbol on the left is a 1 inside a 0. This type of switch turns the power on or off. The next symbol shows a 1 overlapping the 0, which indicates the power may be on or partially off. This partially powered state is known as *standby* or *sleep mode*. Some desktop computers with a standby button on the front also have a power switch on the back that is labeled with a simple 1 and 0 that may be used to turn the power completely off like the third switch in Figure 3.9. Some laptop computers use a combination of symbols like the one at the right to indicate the button can turn the computer on or bring it back from standby.

After you have turned on the computer, you will want to communicate with it in some fashion. As you will recall from Chapter 1, a computer is a system that includes input, processing, storage, and output. In this section, you will learn about the hardware devices that control these computer functions in the order in which they are used.

INPUT DEVICES

When you turn the computer on, it runs some specialized software that will be described in the next chapter. In this section, we look at the various pieces of hardware you might use to enter data or commands into the computer.

Keyboard

The most commonly used piece of input hardware is the keyboard. Each keystroke is converted into a binary number the computer understands. Keyboards have function keys at the top that can be programmed to perform special functions. Laptop users often plug a monitor or projection device into their computers and switch it on using the special function keys, which vary by model. There are other special function keys on some keyboards that start a browser or open the Start menu in Windows. Some keys are intended for use with other keys. The *Control (Ctrl)* and *Alternate (Alt)* keys, and occasionally the *Shift* key, may be used in combination with other keys for special commands (see Figure 3.10). Macintosh keyboards have similar keys called the Option key and the Command key.

Instruction manuals indicate this use of combinations of keys by writing a plus sign between them, for instance, Ctrl+C, which means press and hold

FIGURE 3.9

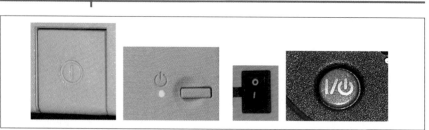

Symbols on power control buttons indicate what the buttons do.

FIGURE 3.10

QWERTY
These are the keys that identify the most common keyboard layout

function keys
These keys have different functions, depending on the program being used

num lock
Switch the keypad between a number entry and cursor movement

status indicators
These light up to inform you whether a toggle key's function is on or off

escape
Generally used to cancel or interrupt an operation

tab
Enables you to indent text

caps lock
Switches the keyboard between all-caps and normal modes

Alt and Ctrl
Pressed together with other keys gives commands to the program in use

shift
Allows you to enter a capital letter or punctuation mark

arrow keys
These move the cursor around the screen

numeric keypad
Designed for users to enter numbers quickly

Ctrl, Alt, and Shift keys may be used in combination with other keys. The Num Lock key in the upper left corner of the numeric keypad toggles the numeric keys' function between the navigation arrows and numbers.

FIGURE 3.11

On an Apple keyboard, the key with the apple on it is the Command key, which may be used in combination with other keys or mouse clicks to provide alternative functions and screen menus.

the Ctrl key, then press the C key. Since there is a key with a plus sign on it, this instruction is easily misinterpreted. If a program stops responding and you are running Windows, you can press and hold both the Ctrl and the Alt keys and then press the Delete key to bring up a dialog box that lets you close the unresponsive program and continue working. Similarly, if a program stops responding and you are running a Macintosh computer, hold both the Command and Option keys, and press the Esc key. Most laptop computers have a *function (Fn)* key that provides another possible combination of keys. Most desktop computer keyboards have a numeric keypad at the right that can double as navigation keys; these keys are labeled with a number and an arrow or a navigation term. There is a *Num Lock* key that switches the function of the keypad back and forth. There is usually a status light on the keyboard that comes on to indicate when the keypad is in numeric mode. If a program ever freezes and pressing Ctrl+Alt+Delete doesn't bring up a dialog box in Windows, you can check to see if the computer is still communicating with the keyboard. To find out if the keyboard is being recognized by the computer, press the Num Lock key a few times to see if the indicator light goes on and off. If not, the keyboard isn't recognized, and you will have to turn the computer off using the power button.

Apple computers use the Control key in combination with a mouse click to emulate a right-click of the mouse (see Figure 3.11).

Mouse, Trackball, Touch Pad, and Joystick

Most systems use a device that controls a pointer on the screen. The pointer can move up and down, left and right, or any combination of the two, and so must the device used to control it. There are several variations of devices. They are not all shown here, but they all convert a motion or touch by the user into motion of a pointer on the screen. The most common of these devices is the *mouse*. Mathematicians, scientists, and

FIGURE 3.12

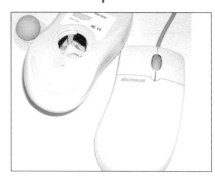

A rubber ball rolls against two perpendicular rollers.

FIGURE 3.13

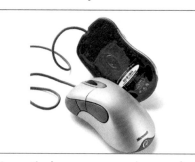

An optical mouse uses a beam of light that reflects off the desktop to sense motion.

FIGURE 3.14

The ball in a trackball is manipulated directly by the user while the rest of the device remains stationary.

FIGURE 3.15

Joysticks are often used by gamers and may have elaborate additional controls.

FIGURE 3.16

Pointing sticks are used in some laptop computers to save space.

engineers use a coordinate method to locate positions on a flat surface using two numbers. One number indicates the left-to-right position (the X direction) and the other number indicates the up-and-down position (the Y direction). Most mice hold a rubber ball that rolls on the desk or a *mouse pad*. Inside the mouse, the rubber ball presses against two rollers that are perpendicular to each other (see Figure 3.12). The motion of the rolling ball is converted into two separate rolling motions that indicate motion in the X or Y direction. The computer uses an A-D converter to turn this continuous motion into series of binary numbers the computer uses to control the position of the pointer on the screen.

The rollers inside a mouse often get lint or fibers wrapped around them, which causes the pointer to behave erratically. Some mice use reflected light beams instead of rollers to eliminate this problem. Such a mouse is called an *optical mouse*. It does not need a mouse pad for traction (see Figure 3.13).

A similar pointing device is the *trackball* (see Figure 3.14). It's like a mouse turned upside down, and you move the ball directly. Some people prefer trackballs because you control them using just your fingers, not your arm.

A *joystick* (see Figure 3.15) uses the same technology as a mouse or trackball, but the rotating ball is inside the case and the user moves an attached rod. The term *joystick* is more common for game controllers, and the stick often has a button attached near the top for controlling game action.

A *pointing stick* (see Figure 3.16) is a small knob in some laptop keyboards that responds to sideways pressure.

A *touch pad* (see Figure 3.17) is a small rectangle of glass below the spacebar on many laptop computers. It senses the position of your finger when you touch it, and it can be set to interpret a brief touch as a mouse click. Care must be taken not to accidentally touch this pad while typing.

Scanner

The process of converting an image into digital data a row at a time is called *scanning*, and a device that does this is a *scanner*. Using a scanner is a great way to input pictures into a computer or to convert printed documents into text documents online. Scanner prices have fallen drastically in the last few years, and they are relatively easy to use. Scanners that work with individual sheets of paper or books are called *flatbed scanners*. They have a pane of glass and a bright fluorescent lamp that travels the length of the glass (see Figure 3.18). The light reflected from the picture or document as the lamp travels the length of the glass is detected and converted to

FIGURE 3.17

Touch pads are common on portable devices and are usually placed below the space bar on the keyboard.

FIGURE 3.18

Flatbed scanners can scan pages of bulky books as well as individual pictures or pages of text.

numbers using an A-D converter. These numbers are assigned to pixels. Most scanners are rated using a measurement that is common in the graphic reproduction industry, ***dots per inch (dpi)***. The higher the number of dots per inch, the smaller the pixels and the more detailed the image. Generally, images require more storage space than text files.

In some devices such as all-in-one machines (see Figure 3.19) that print, fax, copy, and scan, the lamp is stationary, and the paper moves past it. This type of machine can scan several sheets of paper at a time, which can be very convenient if you are scanning multi-page documents, but it cannot scan books or small pieces of paper like receipts.

If you want to convert printed documents into text that your word processor can use, you need a computer program that can recognize the image of a character and convert it to its ASCII or Unicode number. Programs that do this are called ***optical character recognition (OCR)*** programs. Some companies bundle an OCR program with the scanner. Look for this feature when you purchase a scanner, because the OCR program can cost as much as the scanner if purchased separately.

Digital and Video Cameras

In a digital camera, a lens focuses an image on an array of light-sensitive detectors that convert the image into electrical signals that are analogous to

FIGURE 3.19

Multifunction office machines often have a scanner built in that can scan several sheets of documents sequentially.

FIGURE 3.20

Flash cards come in different formats and store data from digital cameras and PDAs.

the brightness of the light at each detector. These signals are fed into an A-D converter that produces a number that represents the brightness of the image for each detector. The digital numbers are recorded on a removable storage medium like flash memory. There are several options for transferring the image files into your computer. Some cameras use wires, and some use a ***docking station*** where the camera sits. Most digital cameras use flash memory on small ***compact flash cards*** (see Figure 3.20) that may be removed from the camera and placed in a card reader that is connected to the computer by a wire.

Digital video cameras are like digital cameras, except they take several pictures each second. The number of pictures they take each second is measured in ***frames per second***. It takes 30 frames per second to simulate smooth motion. Most video cameras that are attached to computers are used for videoconferencing or monitoring a scene. If the video is intended for transmission over the Internet, a rate of 30 full-screen images per second is more than most connections can handle. In that case, most video cameras use 15 frames per second, and the picture does not have enough pixels to fill the screen so it shows in a small window. Video cameras that are attached to a computer and intended for videoconferencing or monitoring are called ***Web cams***. Handheld digital video cameras are typically more expensive than Web cams and are capable of recording full-screen motion at 30 frames per second with sound.

Microphones

Microphones pick up sounds such as our voice and convert them into analog signals. The computer uses an A-D converter to change the sounds into binary numbers. You can use computer programs that recognize voice commands to control the computer. Other programs translate what you say into text for use in a document or e-mail. This process is called ***voice recognition***. You can also use a microphone for online conference calls or to record comments that can be attached to an e-mail. Microphones used for voice recognition should be placed within a few inches of the speaker's mouth and off to one side for best results.

PROCESSING

Transistors were invented in the 1950s, and they replaced the vacuum tubes and mechanical switches used in early computers. In the mid 1970s, individual transistors were replaced by ***integrated circuits (ICs)*** that contained thousands of transistors on a wafer of silicon smaller than a fingernail. Integrated circuits are also called ***chips***, and they now have millions of transistors. ICs can be designed to perform specific tasks such as analog and digital signal conversion, or they may be designed to perform a variety of tasks according to instructions provided by the user. Performing mathematical or logical operations on data is called ***processing***. An integrated circuit designed for this purpose is a ***microprocessor***, which is also known as the central processing unit (CPU). A microprocessor has the ability to accept an instruction, retrieve data from specified memory locations, perform a mathematical or logical operation with the data as specified by the instruction, and then place the results of the operation in a different memory location. Early CPUs worked with eight-digit binary numbers, also called eight-bit numbers. Most modern personal computers use CPUs that work with 32-digit binary numbers and some that work with 64-digit numbers.

The CPU uses a special-purpose IC called a ***clock*** to coordinate its activities. The clock emits electrical pulses that are used to coordinate the functions within the CPU and with the other ICs in the computer. The rate at which the clock emits pulses is measured in ***megahertz*** (millions of pulses per second) or ***gigahertz*** (billions of pulses per second). The clock speed may be used as one indicator of how quickly the CPU processes data. CPUs are often rated by the clock speed at which they operate and the size of the numbers they work with. For example, the Power Mac G5 from Apple has a CPU that processes 64-bit numbers at a clock speed of 2 gigahertz.

The earliest personal computers used eight-bit processors running at 4.7 megahertz. This was ample power for simple text applications like word processing. Applications that work with pictures, video, sound, or voice recognition require high-speed processors. Computer manufacturers often compete with each other on the basis of processor speed. In many cases, the processor speed is not the limiting factor of performance. The size of the computer's memory or the speed of its Internet connection may be more important than processor speed.

The CPU communicates with other special-purpose ICs and devices via a ***data bus***. A bus in this context is like a multilane highway with a lane for each digit of the binary numbers that travel on it. A 32-bit data bus has 32 separate pathways, one for each digit of the binary numbers used by the CPU and the devices with which it exchanges data. The data bus is part of the ***motherboard***, which connects the integrated circuits to each other and to slots into which additional devices may be connected (see Figure 3.21).

PRIMARY STORAGE

The CPU processes data that is stored in some form of ***memory***. An ideal form of computer memory would store enormous amounts of data at very low cost, read and write that data very quickly, and remember the data indefinitely when the computer power is turned off. Unfortunately, that ideal memory does not exist yet. Memory that is fast enough to keep up with the CPU cannot use moving mechanical parts, and individual pieces of data must be available without reading all the data in the memory. Random access memory (RAM) is a form of memory that uses a special-purpose integrated circuit—also called ***physical memory***—that is fast enough to keep up with the processor. The memory ICs are mounted on small circuit boards (see Figure 3.22) that can plug into sockets on the motherboard. Unfortunately, current technology for making RAM ICs

☑ **VOTER ISSUES**

DISCUSSION

Key computer parts, such as RAM, are made in countries such as Korea or China. Some people are concerned that this gives those countries too much control over an important sector of our economy. Should laws be passed to protect companies that make key computer components from foreign competition?

FIGURE 3.21

(a)

(b)

Intel and AMD are the two leading manufacturers of processors for personal computers. IBM now makes the processors for Apple's newest computers. (a) Intel brand microprocessor, (b) motherboard.

FIGURE 3.22

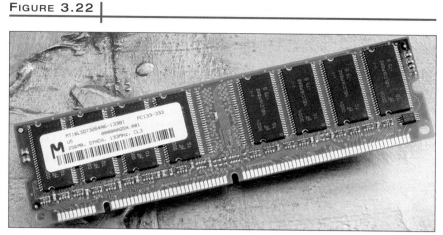

A RAM module plugs into the motherboard.

requires that they have continuous power and they are more expensive than other kinds of memory.

If a computer does not have enough RAM for a task, the computer will use its disk storage system, which is much slower. Using the disk in place of RAM is called ***virtual memory***. If the computer takes a long time to switch between programs running in separate windows, it may have too little RAM.

RAM is measured in megabytes, where one byte is enough to store one character. When purchasing software, look at the side of the application's box to see how much RAM is required to run the software. These estimates are low-end. Assume you need at least twice as much RAM as the minimum. If you run several programs at once, it takes more RAM to switch back and forth between them quickly.

SECONDARY STORAGE

Storage uses low-cost methods to store large quantities of data, but its speed is much slower than that of RAM. Storage methods do not require continuous power. Storage is measured in kilobytes (thousands of bytes), megabytes (millions of bytes), or gigabytes (billions of bytes). In the front of the case are slots, or ***drives***, where you can insert portable data storage devices such as floppy disks, Zip® disks, CD-ROMs, CD-Rs, CD-RWs, and USB drives. Inside the case is the hard drive.

Floppy disks and ***Zip disks*** both use plastic disks with a magnetic material on them. Information is recorded on the disks as binary numbers by magnetizing very small areas of the disk. The drive has a motor that turns the disk and a set of tiny coils that can read or write data on the disk. As the disk turns, the tiny coils can either magnetize the area of the disk below them or sense the direction of the magnetization already on the disk. The floppy disk drive on most personal computers other than Macintoshes is generally referred to as drive A, but it is not labeled as such on the drive. Older computers often had two floppy disk drives, and the second one was called drive B. It is rare now to find a computer with two floppy disk drives so the drive letter B is seldom used. Floppy disks hold 1.44 megabytes of data (see Figure 3.23).

The proprietary Zip disk is less common and can hold 250 megabytes of data (see Figure 3.24). Floppy disks and Zip disks are commonly replaced by other types of storage, such as CD-ROMs, and many new laptop computers do not have a floppy disk drive. Floppy disks are not included on many new

FIGURE 3.23

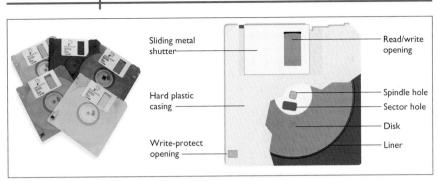

Floppy disks have a hard plastic case with a flexible plastic disk inside.

FIGURE 3.24

Zip disks are similar to floppy disks but require a proprietary drive.

desktop computers either, so if you have data stored on them, you may have to transfer it to another storage medium such as a CD.

Keep the disks away from magnets, which could erase them. Do not store floppy disks on top of your stereo speakers. The speakers have strong magnets that move the speaker cone, which could degrade the data on the disks.

The ***hard drive*** also stores data in magnetic form on a disk called a ***hard disk***. The hard drive (see Figure 3.25) is a stack of thin, rigid metal disks—hence the name hard disk. Because the metal disks flex less than plastic disks, the data tracks can be placed much closer together. A typical hard drive holds more than 20 gigabytes, which is equivalent to 20,000 megabytes. The hard drive is usually referred to as drive C, but there are no external labels.

Devices that store information using magnetic methods are called disks, whereas devices that store data using optical methods are called discs. Compact discs, or CDs, store information as binary numbers by making very small pits that absorb light in the shiny layer of the disc (see Figure 3.26). A laser beam scans the disk as it turns, and the reflection is picked up by a sensor that converts the flickering reflection into binary numbers.

FIGURE 3.25

Hard drives comprise a stack of hard disks.

FIGURE 3.26

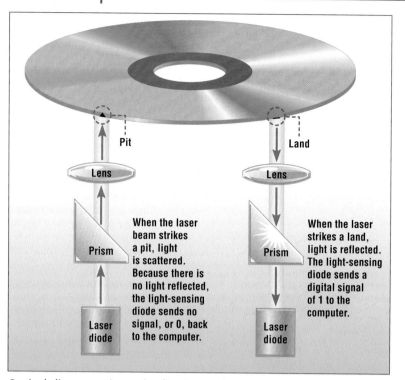

Optical discs use pits and reflective surfaces to represent data.

There are three types of discs:

❯ The oldest and most common is the **CD-ROM**. ROM stands for read-only memory. This type of disc comes with information already written on it, and the CD-ROM drive only reads the data. Newer CD drives can record as well as read.

❯ If your CD drive can write as well as read, you can use **CD-R** discs on which you can record data one time and read it many times. These disks are comparable in price to a floppy disk but hold approximately 400 times as much data. Many people simply keep recording onto an unused part of a CD-R instead of using a floppy disk that can be erased and rewritten.

❯ A **CD-RW** is like a floppy disk in that it is rewritable. A CD-RW is about twice as expensive as a CD-R and is becoming common on new computers. CD-Rs and CD-RWs hold about 650 megabytes of data.

Two patterns are used to write data onto discs. If the data is intended to be played in a continuous stream, like music or video, the data is written in a **continuous spiral**. If the data will be retrieved in pieces from different parts of the disk depending on the program in use by the computer, the data is written in **concentric circles**, where a piece of data has a location given by the distance of its track from the edge and the angle of rotation of the disk. The location of data is kept in a **file allocation table (FAT)** that is also recorded on the disc. Floppy and hard disks also use file allocation tables to locate data.

Another optical method of recording data on a disc for continuous replay is called **digital versatile disc (DVD)**. DVDs also use spiral tracks, but data can be recorded on two different layers and on both sides of the disc. DVDs can hold approximately 4.7 gigabytes, or 4,700 megabytes on a single-sided single layer and up to 17 gigabytes on a double-sided double layer disc. A

DVD can hold up to 133 minutes of 30-frames-per-second, full-screen video. Some computers come with drives that can write DVDs. DVDs may be used for working with video or as data backups for hard drives.

Discs work with reflected light so if they get too dirty they do not work. To clean a music CD or video DVD, wipe toward or away from the center of the disc. If you scratch across a data track, the computer can guess what the missing data might be from the data next to it and calculate a replacement. If you scratch along a data track, too much data is lost to calculate a replacement. CDs and DVDs are made of are tough plastic, but do not store them in the sun or leave them on the dashboard of a car in the summer.

Many computers have a small rectangular hole in the front called a **Universal Serial Bus (USB)** port (this type of port is covered in more detail in the section on connecting devices). Small devices that could hang from a key chain and contain flash memory, like that used with digital cameras, can be plugged into a USB port. They can store the data without a power source if they are removed from the USB port. Names for these devices vary. Some are called **disk-on-key**, **USB drives**, or **thumb drives** (see Figure 3.27). When you plug one into a USB port, the computer treats it as if it were a hard disk drive. They are very convenient to use and provide a good alternative to floppy disks. Capacities vary from 64 megabytes to 1 gigabyte.

OUTPUT DEVICES

The result of processing data is information that must be communicated to the user. This is usually done visually using a monitor or printer or with sounds through speakers.

Monitors and Projectors

Most computers use a display called a **monitor** that uses a glass picture tube, called a **cathode ray tube (CRT)**, that is similar to those used in televisions. Most of these tubes have a convex front surface, but some of them are flat and are called **flat screens**, which can cause confusion with LCD monitors, described below (see Figure 3.28a). CRT monitors are measured

FIGURE 3.27

Flash memory plugs into a USB port and emulates a hard drive.

FIGURE 3.28

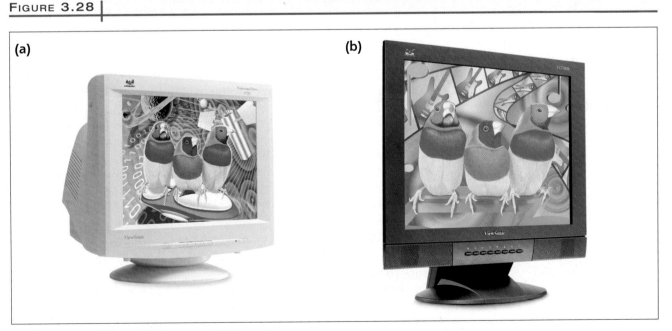

(a) Flat-screen CRT and (b) flat-panel LCD monitor

diagonally across the face of the tube, but the viewable picture is smaller than the size of the tube. Consequently, a 17-inch CRT displays a viewable picture that is only 15½ inches from corner to corner. CRTs use a large glass tube in which an electron beam starts at the small end and strikes the phosphors at the wide end. The great weight and depth of a CRT monitor are due to the heavy, long glass picture tube.

The development of portable computers depended on using a different display technology, called *liquid crystal display (LCD)*. An LCD uses a fluorescent light behind a flat panel. The fluorescent light is called a *backlight*. The panel has small elements that change from transparent to opaque depending on an electric charge applied to them. Filters are used to produce different colors. The computer controls the electric charges applied to the elements to make picture elements, or pixels. The LCD technology of laptop computers (see Figure 3.28b) is available for desktop computer monitors as well. They are often called *flat-panel* monitors. Since this term resembles *flat-screen*, used to describe some CRTs, confusion is possible. LCD monitors are measured diagonally, but the measurement is of the viewable screen area. A 15-inch LCD monitor is actually 15 inches from corner to corner. If you try to compare costs of CRTs and LCDs, it's important to remember that the viewable screen area of a 15-inch LCD is only a half-inch smaller than a 17-inch CRT.

Computers are often used to create presentations that are projected on a screen for group viewing (see Figure 3.29). *Projectors* that work with computers are really monitors that are designed to project images. The projectors have a very bright lamp, and the brightness of the light coming from the projector is rated in *lumens*. To show a computer slide show to a group of 20 people in a classroom or conference room with some of the lights on, the projector should have a rating of at least 600 lumens. Brighter lamps can project pictures on larger screens or in brighter rooms. The most common projectors use three LCD screens, one for each color, through which the light passes. Another technology, developed by Texas Instruments, uses thousands of tiny mirrors that are controlled by the computer. The mirrors do not absorb light as the LCDs do, so this technology can produce brighter images from similar lamps. Most computer projectors accept inputs from a VCR and may also project video or television signals.

Printers

Printers place ink on paper in patterns that resemble text or pictures. Early printers employed typewriter technology in which a metal rod struck an ink-impregnated ribbon and the impact transferred the ink to the paper to make a dot. Printers that use this method are called *impact printers*. A group of tiny rods are arranged in a rectangular bundle, or matrix, and the computer activates selected rods to produce patterns of dots that looked like text characters. This type of printer is called a *dot-matrix* printer. Impact printers are rarely used with personal computers now, but businesses may need them to print duplicate copies using older, multilayer forms.

The copying industry developed a method of transferring powdered ink to paper in the shape of text or pictures and then heating the ink to make it stick to the paper. This technology was adapted for use in computer printers called *laser printers* (see Figure 3.30). In a laser printer, a laser beam traces the shapes to be printed, producing an electrostatic charge on the paper. The powdered ink, known as *toner*, is attracted to the static electricity, and then a hot drum melts the ink into the paper. Most laser printers

FIGURE 3.29

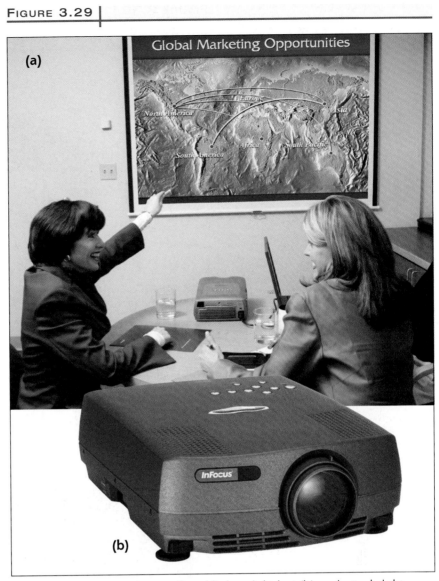

(a) LCD projectors can be small and lightweight but (b) project a bright image in a lighted room.

print only in black and white, but some offices are installing color laser printers that can be shared by many employees.

A cheaper method of producing high-quality printouts uses liquid ink that is fed through a special device that separates the flow of ink into separate tiny droplets that can be directed to the paper using electric fields. This type of printer is called an ***ink-jet*** printer (see Figure 3.31). Ink-jet printers usually have four colors of ink: black, magenta, cyan, and yellow. The magenta, cyan, and yellow inks are used in combination to produce all the other colors.

Indicator Lights

On the front of a computer's case, there are usually several colored lights that indicate various activities. A green light near the power button indicates the computer is on. A red light near an icon that looks like a drum indicates when the hard disk is being accessed. The floppy drive and CD drive also have lights to indicate when they are in use.

FIGURE 3.30 |

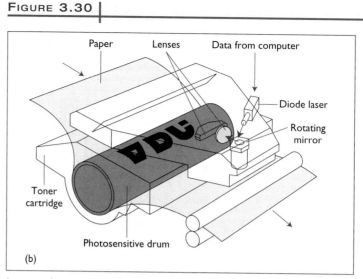

Laser printers use a focused beam of light and ink powder to form an image electrostatically.

FIGURE 3.31 |

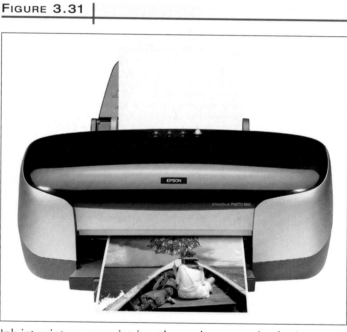

Ink-jet printers can print in color and are popular for home use.

Speakers

Computers are capable of playing music, producing sound effects with games, or speaking the content of documents. A pair of external speakers is provided with many computers, and some monitors have built-in speakers. More expensive systems include a larger speaker called a ***subwoofer*** to play low base notes. Most computers have a small speaker inside the case that is used when the dial-up modem connects. When there is a significant hardware problem with the computer that may prevent the monitor from working, this speaker beeps several times in a code that can inform a technician of the nature of the problem.

The mouse needs periodic maintenance because the rubber ball picks up lint from the desk or mouse pad that becomes wrapped around the two rollers inside. If your mouse is not responding properly, turn it over and look at the rubber ball. It is probably retained by a ring with arrows on it to indicate how to twist it for removal. Remove the retaining ring, and the ball will drop out. Look for two thin rollers that may have lint or fibers wrapped around them. Scrape the lint or fibers off these rollers, then replace the ball and retaining ring. The mouse should work more smoothly.

CONNECTING PARTS OF A DESKTOP COMPUTER

Most computers consist of a system unit with several other devices connected to it. These devices are called **peripherals**, and most of them connect through **ports** at the back of the system unit. If you set up a new desktop computer or have to move an existing one, you need to know something about the connectors and the ports. *Ports* is a general term for male or female connectors into which wires are plugged. Ports come in a variety of shapes. Most shapes are unique to a particular peripheral and only accept a plug from that type of device. For example, the monitor has a cord that terminates in a plug that is wider at the top than at the bottom and has three rows of small pins. No other type of port at the back of the computer will accept this plug. Many computer manufacturers use color coding to make it more apparent which ports go with which wires, but manufacturers haven't standardized this practice. Some ports are round but have a small slot that ensures the plug fits in only one position. The corresponding plastic projection in the plug is called a **key**. Ports use shape and keys to prevent a peripheral's accidental use of the wrong port.

USB PORT

To reduce the number of different ports on the system unit, the Universal Serial Bus (USB) port is designed to accept a variety of devices. USB ports may be used to attach the keyboard, mouse, printer, scanner, video camera, speakers, and other devices like docking cradles for PDAs, cameras, and flash memory modules. It also provides a small amount of electrical power so that some small peripheral devices do not need their own power supplies. This connection method facilitates assembling and moving a computer, because it provides one type of port that works for many different peripherals.

Most computers come with two USB ports at the back and one or two at the front of the case. New computers come with **USB 2.0** ports, which are the same shape and size as older USB 1.1 ports but which transfer data 40 times as fast. Older **USB 1.1** devices work with the new ports.

Some devices, such as a mouse, that plug into a USB port have a wire extending from them that terminates in a **type A USB** plug that fits the port in the computer. The connection uses a key to ensure that the plug fits in only one orientation. Other devices, such as a digital camera, do not have a connecting wire permanently attached. These devices have a **type B USB** port in them. USB cords usually have a type A USB plug on one end for plugging into the computer and a type B USB plug on the other end for plugging into a peripheral device to connect it. A type B USB plug is smaller than a type A and has a rectangular shape with two angled corners (see Figure 3.32).

Connection devices called **hubs** can be used to provide multiple USB ports. Up to 127 devices may be connected to a computer using a USB hub. USB

FIGURE 3.32

USB ports are type A on the host computer and type B on a device.

devices are **hot-swappable**, which means you can safely plug them in or remove them without shutting down the host computer.

SERIAL PORT

Serial ports were originally designed to work with telephone modems when they were external devices. They are often labeled with a series of zeros and ones to indicate data moving serially, one bit at a time. They are used to send and receive data sequentially like a USB, but they have additional wires that were used to control and communicate with an external modem.

A serial connector has nine pins in two rows, and it is one of the few male connector ports with pins. The serial port can be used to connect a mouse or keyboard, and some keyboards and mice come with adapters for that purpose. Telephone modems are all internal on newer computers so this port will probably be discontinued in the future as more devices use USB. Serial ports typically have a top speed of 115 kilobits per second, which is about one-hundredth the speed of a USB 1.1 connection. The plug that fits into a serial port has a pair of threaded rods that screw into nuts on either side of the port (see "VGA connector," below).

PARALLEL PRINTER PORT

Parallel ports also date back to the early days of personal computer design (see Figure 3.33). The old serial ports were too slow to send large amounts of data to a printer, so a faster port was needed. A parallel connection has eight pairs of wires used for transmitting data and is about eight times as fast as a serial connection from the same era. New printers may be connected with a USB connector or with a parallel connector.

Newer printers can sense low ink levels and empty paper trays and send this information back to the computer. These printers require newer parallel cables that use some of the wires to support two-way communication between the printer and the computer. If you try to use an older printer cable with a new printer, some of these new features do not work.

PS/2 PORT

Most keyboards and mice connect to the computer at a **PS/2** port, which is a round serial connector with a key that fits in only one orientation. The PS/2 ports for the keyboard and mouse are usually next to each other on the back of the computer. It is possible to plug the keyboard into the mouse port and the mouse into the keyboard port. This is one of the few connectors that will fit in the wrong place. Many computers use color coding or label the ports with pictures of a mouse or keyboard to make it easier to distinguish between them. It does not damage the equipment if you make this mistake, but the mouse or keyboard may not work if they are plugged into the wrong port. This type of serial port is also being replaced by USB ports, and many mice and keyboards come with an adapter that converts the male PS/2 plug into a male USB plug.

WIRELESS MOUSE OR KEYBOARD

Some keyboards and mice are wireless, which means they do not connect by wire. Most wireless mice and keyboards use radio waves to bridge the gap between the keyboard or mouse and a receiver. The receiver is plugged into the computer using a PS/2 plug or a USB plug. Wireless keyboards and mice require batteries that need to be replaced periodically.

FIREWIRE AND SCSI

USB has become the new standard for connecting peripherals, but two competing connection methods are still available. Some computers use a connection system called **FireWire**, which is Apple Computer's version of the Institute of Electrical and Electronics Engineers (IEEE) standard 1394

FIGURE 3.33

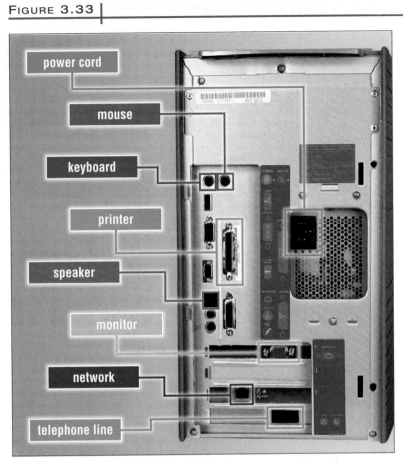

power cord

mouse

keyboard

printer

speaker

monitor

network

telephone line

Ports are a variety of shapes to match the corresponding plugs.

for a high-performance serial bus. FireWire is very similar to USB, but it has some advantages for use with devices that require very high rates of data transfer or for enabling devices to communicate directly with each other without a host computer. A FireWire connection is most commonly found where people want to work with digital video cameras. It has a data transfer rate of 400 megabits per second, which was a big advantage over USB 1.1, but USB 2.0 has a similar data transfer rate. The next version of FireWire will reach 800 megabits per second, and a connection is planned that will go up to 3.2 gigabits per second.

An older connection method uses a *Small Computer System Interface (SCSI)* bus, pronounced "scuzzy." It has been around since 1986 and may be used to connect to some older scanners or external hard drives. Recent versions have speeds of 1280 megabits per second. There are several variations of SCSI connectors. A SCSI bus needs a device called a *terminator* at the end of the bus.

RJ-11
Telephone connectors are often called *jacks*. In the United States, the Federal Communications Commission (FCC) sets standards for telephone connection devices. The jack used to connect telephones is *Registered Jack 11*, or *RJ-11*. The term *jack* refers to both the receptacle and plug or sometimes just the plug. It connects a cable with six wires. Dial-up modems have two RJ-11 receptacles (see Figure 3.33). One of the two receptacles connects the modem to the telephone service and is often labeled *wall*. The other, often labeled *phone*, connects to a normal phone, which allows the phone to be used when the modem is not in use.

FIGURE 3.34

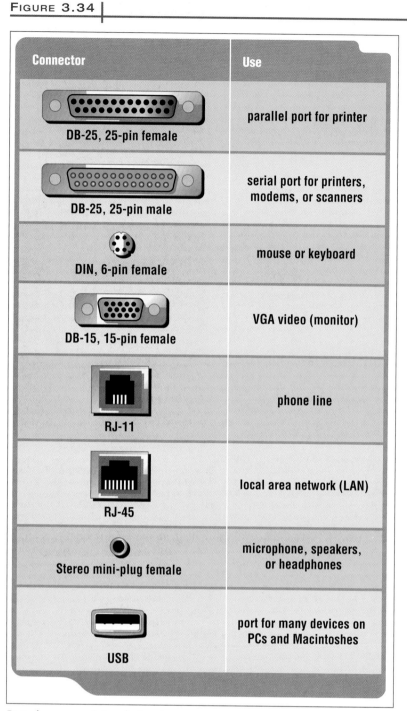

Connector	Use
DB-25, 25-pin female	parallel port for printer
DB-25, 25-pin male	serial port for printers, modems, or scanners
DIN, 6-pin female	mouse or keyboard
DB-15, 15-pin female	VGA video (monitor)
RJ-11	phone line
RJ-45	local area network (LAN)
Stereo mini-plug female	microphone, speakers, or headphones
USB	port for many devices on PCs and Macintoshes

Ports have a variety of pin placements.

RJ-45

A similar but larger jack, *RJ-45*, is used for network connections. The RJ-45 jack is in a *network interface card (NIC)*. RJ-45 plugs also snap into the receptacle, and a small tab must be depressed to withdraw the plug.

VGA CONNECTOR

The *video graphics adapter (VGA)* port is wider at the top than at the bottom and has three rows of holes. This port and plug arrangement dates back to the early IBM PC in the 1980s and is the standard connector for monitors and projectors. The port is the same size and shape as the serial port, which can cause confusion. The serial port has two rows of pins, and the VGA port has three rows of holes so the plugs are not interchangeable. Some computers have more than one VGA port to run one or two extra monitors, but this is uncommon.

SPEAKER AND MICROPHONE

Microphones and speakers connect using 2.5-millimeter stereo plugs that are standard size for small music devices. Icons that resemble a microphone and speaker are often found next to the sockets, but they can be difficult to see. The plugs may fit in the wrong sockets, so colors are often used to match the plugs and sockets, in which case, red is often used for the microphone socket (see Figure 3.34). Damage can be done to some types of microphones if they are plugged into the speaker socket so care needs to be taken when connecting the microphone.

POWER CORDS

The power cord of a computer, unlike that of most appliances, detaches. The connector is recessed and has three large pins. Power cords for computer devices are similar and are usually interchangeable. They have a normal three-pronged plug that goes in a wall outlet and a female plug that goes in the connection at the computer. Some computers also have a switch to adapt to 115 volt power, which is common in the United States, or 220 volt, which is common in Europe (see Figure 3.35).

SURGE SUPPRESSORS AND UNINTERRUPTIBLE POWER SUPPLIES

Most computer systems have several devices that require power from a wall outlet. Because most outlets have only two receptacles, an extension cord with a box of additional receptacles called a *plug strip* is often used. Many of these plug strips have a small red button on the side that indicates the presence of a *circuit breaker*. A circuit breaker protects the house from fire if an appliance shorts out. Computers need protection that is more sophisticated. The electronic parts of a computer are so small and close together that a sudden surge of voltage in the building can damage the circuits. Lightning can also induce very short but high voltage pulses that travel along the power lines for miles and can damage a computer. These surges and pulses are not stopped by a simple plug strip with a circuit breaker.

Many plug strips also include devices that limit the relatively slow surges of power that may be visible to the eye when lights dim and also block the lightning-induced spikes of transient voltage. These types of plug strips are *surge suppressors* (see Figure 3.36). Many surge suppressors offer guarantees against lighting damage. If you use a dial-up modem, be sure to get a surge suppressor that also has receptacles for RJ-11 jacks to block lighting-induced pulses from entering the computer via the telephone lines.

A lighting strike can cause the safety equipment in the power lines to shut off for a moment, or electric motors starting up on the same circuit can cause the voltage to drop below the minimum required by the computer. In either case, there may be too little power to run the computer, causing it to freeze up or lose information stored in RAM. Units with batteries provide temporary power during brief power shortages or give you enough time to save your work and shut down your computer if the power goes out for longer periods. This type of unit is an *uninterruptible power supply (UPS)* (see Figure 3.37). A good UPS includes the functions of a plug strip with surge suppression in one set of outlets for noncritical devices, and provides another set of receptacles with continuous power for critical devices like the monitor and the system unit.

FIGURE 3.35

The power cord plugs into a three-pin male connector.

FIGURE 3.36

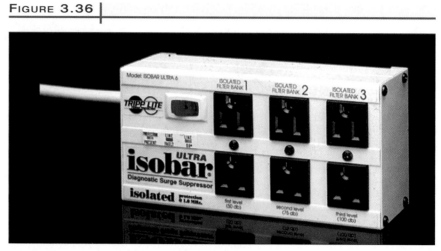

Surge suppressors also function as plug strips.

FIGURE 3.37

UPS provides temporary battery power.

SUMMARY

You do not have to remember all of these details to install or move a computer. A few tips will suffice:

> It's highly unlikely that you could damage the computer by accidentally connecting the wrong plug to the wrong port.

> The parallel, serial, and VGA connectors are slightly wider at one side so you may have to turn the plug halfway around to align it.

> The VGA port for the monitor is the same shape as the serial port, but the VGA port has three rows of holes, whereas the serial port has two rows of pins.

> The PS/2 ports are round with a plastic key. Look at the end of the plug to see where the key is to align it with the hole in the port. If the keyboard and mouse use PS/2 connectors, be sure to check the colors or labels to get them into the correct ports.

> USB ports are interchangeable, but if you connect several USB devices that depend on the USB for power, use a hub with its own power supply.

TEST PREPARATION

The following section does not replace reading the text, nor does it contain all the information that will be tested. It is designed to provide examples and identify sections that need review.

summary by objective

PERSONAL COMPUTERS

- Identify the difference among a desktop, laptop or notebook, and a personal digital assistant—a desktop computer is designed for individual use but isn't portable, laptop and notebook are synonyms for portable computers that have the same functions as a desktop, and a PDA is dedicated to performing certain functions such as managing calendar and contact lists.

COMPUTERS FOR ORGANIZATIONS

- Identify the differences among categories of computers by their relative capacity and by their function:
  - Supercomputers are the most powerful. They model systems using finite element analysis.
  - Mainframes are larger than midrange computers, but both are used to manage databases as well as provide Web server functions. They are often called file servers because their main function is to look up database files.
  - Network servers provide coordination of other computers on a local area network.
- Personal computers or workstations are used by one person at a time.

SUPERCOMPUTERS

- Identify the types of problems that require a supercomputer:
  - Modeling complex systems where the parts require interaction and complex calculations

DISTRIBUTED PROCESSING AND DATABASES

- Identify the types of problems that are suitable for distributed processing:
  - Sections of the problem may be solved without interaction with other parts of the problem
- Identify examples of distributed databases:
  - Customer records
  - Music and video files

NUMBERING SYSTEMS

- Identify the relationship between characters and bytes—a byte of binary digits represents each character.
- Identify the role of ASCII and Unicode standards—ASCII uses eight-bit numbers for 256 possible characters. Unicode uses 32-bit binary numbers and has codes for characters in many different languages.

PICTURES

- Identify the relationship between pixels and visible details—more pixels per screen means finer details may be seen.

ANALOG AND DIGITAL

- Identify the types of information that change smoothly with time and which representation method is most suitable for them: sounds, water pressure, automobile speed, etc.—analog.
- Identify the function of A-D and D-A converters and how they are used—A-D converters change analog signals to digital by sampling and assigning numbers. D-A converters reverse the process.

POWER CONTROL SYMBOLS

- Match power control symbols with their associated meanings:
  - Single vertical line, a one, represents on
  - Single circle, a zero, represents off
  - A vertical line inside a circle indicates a button that can turn the power on or completely off
  - A broken circle with a vertical line indicates a button that can turn power on but only partially off, sometimes called a standby position.

KEYBOARDS

- Identify examples of function keys—Ctrl, Alt, Shift, Fn, (Apple—Command, Option).

POINTING DEVICES

- Identify features and maintenance issues for mice and trackballs—lint can get wrapped around the rollers inside the device and must be removed periodically.

SCANNERS

- Identify types of scanners and how they convert paper documents and pictures into digital files—flatbed scanners shine a bright light at the document a line at a time and convert the reflection into digital data. Some scanners are built into printers, and the paper moves past the lamp.

DIGITAL CAMERAS AND VIDEO

- Identify how digital cameras connect to computers:
  - A USB connection may be used, or a flash memory card may be removed from the camera and placed in a device that is attached to the computer via a USB or serial port
  - FireWire or SCSI connections may be used to transfer digital video files.

MICROPHONES

- Identify uses for microphones—recording voices, entering commands, dictating text.
- Identify appropriate placement for microphones when using voice recognition software—the microphone should be placed within a few inches of the speaker's mouth.

CENTRAL PROCESSING UNIT

- Identify measurements used to rate CPU performance—clock speed in megahertz and size of the numbers that can be processed.

MEMORY AND STORAGE

- Identify the difference between memory and virtual memory—memory is RAM, which resides on integrated circuits, whereas virtual memory uses space on a storage device like a hard disk.
- Compare storage methods by speed and typical capacities—the hard disk is the largest and fastest with sizes from 20 gigabytes to over 100 gigabytes, DVDs store approximately 1.2 gigabytes, CDs store around 600 megabytes, Zip disks store up to 250 megabytes, floppy disks store 1.44 megabytes.
- Distinguish between disks and discs—magnetic media use disks and optical media use discs.
- Identify the different types of optical storage methods—DVD: multiple layers and two sided; CD-ROM: read-only; CD-R: recordable, CD-RW: recordable and rewritable.

MONITORS AND PROJECTORS

- Identify the difference between CRT and LCD monitors—CRTs use a large glass tube in which an electron beam starts at the small end and strikes the phosphors at the wide end. LCDs use a backlight and small elements of liquid that are transparent or opaque depending on an applied electric current.
- Identify the different methods of measuring the size of monitors—both LCDs and CRTs are measured diagonally, but LCDs measure viewable screen area, whereas CRTs measure to the edge of the tube, which is hidden behind the edge of the case.
- Identify the difference between flat-screen and flat-panel monitors—flat-screen is a CRT with a flat front on the tube; flat-panel is a thin monitor.
- Compare brightness of projectors—projectors with higher lumen ratings are brighter and may be used with larger screens in brighter rooms.

PRINTERS

- Identify types of printers, and match them with the type of ink delivery system—impact printers use devices that hit an inked ribbon to transfer ink to paper, laser printers use toner like a copier, ink-jet printers use a spray of ink droplets.

INDICATOR LIGHTS

- Identify the function of indicator lights on the case—show when a device, such as a floppy disk drive or the hard disk, is in use.

SPEAKERS

- Identify functions of speakers—music, audio cues, and trouble codes.

PORTS AND PLUGS

- Identify types of USB plugs—type A is rectangular, type B is smaller with two angled corners.
- Compare speeds of USB 1.1 and USB 2.0 connections—USB 2.0 is 40 times faster, at 480 megabits per second.
- Identify common use of FireWire connections—connection to digital video cameras.
- Distinguish between an RJ-11 and RJ-45 connector and their functions—RJ-11 is a typical telephone jack and RJ-45 is a typical Ethernet jack.
- Identify the most likely problems when connecting the parts of a computer to the case—PS/2 plugs for keyboard and mouse can fit in the wrong port, the VGA and serial ports are the same size and shape but have different numbers of pins.

SURGE SUPPRESSORS AND UPS

- Identify the functions of a surge suppressor and how it differs from a circuit breaker—a surge suppressor protects against fluctuations in power such as surges in voltage due to operating large motors on the same circuits or against pulses caused by lightning.
- Describe the function of an uninterruptible power supply—provide backup power for a short time to allow orderly shutdown.

true/false questions

1. ____ Computer applications such as simulating the behavior of an airplane are good candidates for distributed processing.

2. ____ A byte is eight bits.

3. ____ An A-D converter changes continuously varying signals into a stream of numbers.

4. ____ A circle that is open at the top with a vertical line through the opening is a symbol used on power buttons to indicate that this button does not turn the power completely off.

5. ____ OCR programs are used with scanners to convert images of documents into editable text.

multiple choice

1. Which of the following is not a device that can use a USB port?
   a) mouse
   b) monitor
   c) printer
   d) keyboard

2. Which of the following storage devices can use both sides of the disc?
   a) CD-R
   b) DVD
   c) CD-ROM
   d) CD-RW

3. Which of the following is not a keyboard key that is commonly used in combination with other keys to perform functions?
   a) Alt
   b) Num Lock
   c) Ctrl
   d) Fn

4. An eight-bit binary number can represent how many different numbers or characters?
   a) 64
   b) 128
   c) 256
   d) 512

5. Which of the following is the slowest connection?
   a) SCSI
   b) USB 1.1
   c) FireWire
   d) serial port

completion

1. A device that converts a series of numbers into smooth variations in an electrical signal is a(n) _____ to _____ converter.

2. The _____ standard expands upon the ASCII standard to provide codes for letters and symbols in many other languages.

3. A round, flat piece of plastic used to record data optically is called a _____ .

4. A round, flat piece of plastic or metal used to record data magnetically is a _____ .

5. A USB 2.0 connection is about _____ times as fast as a USB 1.1 connection.

Match each term with its definition.

____ **1.** A to D converter
____ **2.** Unicode
____ **3.** liquid crystal display (LCD)
____ **4.** voice recognition
____ **5.** dumb terminal
____ **6.** flat screen
____ **7.** network interface card (NIC)
____ **8.** PS/2
____ **9.** hub
____ **10.** byte
____ **11.** random access memory (RAM)
____ **12.** CD-RW
____ **13.** CD-R
____ **14.** digital versatile disc (DVD)
____ **15.** key
____ **16.** flash memory
____ **17.** USB drive
____ **18.** clock
____ **19.** virtual memory
____ **20.** ASCII
____ **21.** RJ-45
____ **22.** RJ-11
____ **23.** flat panel
____ **24.** SCSI
____ **25.** sleep

a. ability to convert speech into digital files or commands
b. Removable electronic memory
c. communication device with a keyboard and monitor that depends on another computer for processing and storage
d. optical storage that can record in layers on both sides
e. device that converts analog electric signals to a series of numbers
f. projection that requires the proper orientation of plug and receptacle
g. round connector used for mice and keyboards
h. code that uses 64-bit numbers to represent characters from numerous languages
i. group of eight bits used to represent characters, decimal numbers, and other special characters
j. integrated circuits that work with the CPU
k. standard telephone connector
l. optical disc to which data may be written
m. CRT with a less curved screen
n. device used to connect a computer to other computers
o. thin display that often uses LCD technology
p. used to provide additional USB connections
q. device that sends out pulses used to coordinate computer component activity
r. similar to Standby on Apple computers
s. type of bus connection for high-speed data transfer between devices and the computer
t. standard Ethernet connector
u. optical disc from which data may be read and to which data may be written, erased, and rewritten
v. remembers data even when disconnected from a power source; used with electronic devices like cameras
w. code for assigning eight-bit numbers to characters and commands
x. type of display the uses electric fields to change the transparency of liquids cells
y. space on a hard disk used to supplement physical memory

beyond the facts

Factual knowledge provides the basis for higher levels of learning. In the following sections, you will work with the concepts and facts presented in the chapter to develop critical-thinking and problem-solving skills. You practice research, analysis, and communication and become aware of diversity issues while exploring the impact of computer technology on career choices, the workplace, social interactions, and home life. The Leadership section helps you identify ways in which you can lead others in organizing and implementing projects that meet worthwhile community needs. In the Lifelong Learning exercise, you build a set of learning resources that you can use after this course to continue learning.

objectives for beyond the facts

END OF CHAPTER EXERCISES	Achievement of the objectives for the end-of-chapter exercises requires evaluation of documents, class discussions, or presentations.
Critical Thinking–Research	Understand the challenges of developing Unicode to work with many different languages.
Problem Solving	Find out what you would need to do to add RAM to a computer, and communicate the terms, steps, and risks to the class.
Anticipating Career Challenges and Opportunities	Demonstrate the following skills: 1) Teamwork: coordinate research 2) Research: find information about component manufacturing in other countries 3) Diversity: find out about the language and culture of countries whose hardware you may use 4) Analysis: analyze the impact of foreign manufacturing of components on your career 5) Communication: communicate the results in writing or by public presentation
Impact on the Workplace	Demonstrate the following skills: 1) Teamwork: coordinate research on the impact of heat and wiring in the workplace 2) Research: through observation and interviews, identify heating and wiring problems due to computers at work 3) Analysis: form an opinion about how your organization has handled the extra heat and wiring problems 4) Communication: communicate the results in writing or by public presentation
Impact on Social Interactions	Demonstrate the following skills: 1) Teamwork: allocate tasks for research 2) Research: determine how distributed databases for sharing music and videos work 3) Diversity: observe any relationships in age, gender, or economic status in people who use distributed databases of music or videos 4) Analysis: form an opinion on the effectiveness (not the legal or moral issues) of this method of file sharing 5) Communication: communicate the results in writing or by public presentation
Impact on Home Life	Demonstrate the following skills: 1) Teamwork: allocate tasks for research 2) Research: find studies on home offices 3) Diversity: find out how working at home influences your family members' attitudes towards computers 4) Analysis: form an opinion based on your experience 5) Communication: communicate the results in writing or by public presentation
Leadership	Describe a plan to lead a group of people toward a worthy goal—in this case, installation of pointing devices or wireless networks for people with special needs.
Lifelong Learning	Identify three or more online resources that may be used to learn more about the topics introduced in this chapter.

107

How does Unicode work? How does it represent languages that don't use individual characters to spell words? How does it represent languages that write from right to left? How widespread is its use?

1. **Teamwork**—Join one to four other students. Decide how to divide up the work. A possible division could be having one person address each of the questions asked above. Search newsgroups using Google's Groups feature, search newspapers from other countries for articles, and search the library's database of journals for articles.

2. **Research**—Use a Web browser and go to the companion Web site at http://www.prenhall.com/preston. Follow the links by clicking on the Web addresses that are highlighted and underlined. Read the articles about Unicode to familiarize yourself with issues related to it. Use a search engine to look for more information about Unicode. Make a list of relevant sources that you may want to reference later. Include the title of the page or article, the name of the organization responsible for the Web page, the date the page or article was written, and the Web address. You may also go to the library and look up books, articles, and news reports that are relevant to this topic. Many libraries have the full text of articles and news reports online in proprietary databases that are not available to the public.

3. **Diversity issues**—Look for articles that express views from other countries on the use of Unicode.

4. **Analysis**—Write an essay that explains what Unicode is and gives some examples. Comment on how other countries view it. Form and express an opinion. Go beyond simple reporting of the facts. Support your opinion with references to the articles you read. Ask your instructor for guidance regarding the required length of the essay.

5. **Communication**—Prepare a presentation in which you present your opinion and supporting facts to the class. Depending on your computer skill, you could give the presentation using a program like PowerPoint and save it as a Web page, or you could prepare a paper handout with your Web references for use while you talk to the class.

Assume that you need to install more RAM in a Windows-based personal computer to run a new software package or to speed up performance and that you want to do it yourself to save money. Find out what you need to know to buy additional RAM, and share this process with the class. You do not have to attempt to add RAM to complete this assignment successfully.

Find out how much RAM is in your computer. If you have a computer that uses the Windows operating system, choose Start, All Programs, Accessories, System Tools, System Information. Print the System Summary that shows the total physical memory.

1. **Ask for professional help**—Take the system printout to a local office-supply store that sells RAM modules, and ask for assistance.

- Ask the salesperson or technician to describe the issues that must be considered when matching RAM to a computer.
- Include information about access time in nanoseconds and the number of connectors.
- Find out the full meanings of any acronyms used, such as DRAM and DIMM.
- Ask for advice on installing the RAM module.
- Determine the price for a module of RAM.
- Find out how much it would cost to have someone else install the RAM for you.
- Determine the risks to your computer if you open the system case and try this yourself.

2. **Communicate**—Present your findings to the class.

anticipating career challenges and opportunities

The cost of computer hardware decreases dramatically every year. Some of this decrease is due to the efficiencies of a global economy in which many components are manufactured outside the United States. This shift to overseas manufacturing may have a significant impact on your career or the career you have chosen. If the company you work for manufactures electronics or buys electronic components to put in its products, look into the effect of competition from other countries. If your company uses components from other countries, find out which countries and something about their culture to be ready to work with people from those countries.

1. **Teamwork**—Join one or two other students who have similar career plans. Decide how to divide up the work. Possible divisions could be: manufacturing and foreign competition trends in your specific job, and language and cultural skills needed to communicate with representatives from foreign companies.

2. **Research**—Use a Web browser and search for articles on your career. Use key words like "outsourcing" and "imports," along with key words for your business. Use the Groups and News options in search engines like Google. Make a list of relevant sources that you may want to reference later. Include the title of the page or article, the name of the organization responsible for the Web page, the date the page or article was written, and the Web address. You may also go to the library and look up books, articles, and news reports that are relevant to this topic. Many libraries have the full text of articles and news reports online in proprietary databases that are not available to the public.

3. **Diversity issues**—If your company imports hardware from other countries, the user manuals may need editing due to translation problems, or you may need to visit the other countries to work on joint projects. Find out about the language and culture of one of these countries. Learn some basic phrases for greeting people politely in their language.

4. **Analysis**—Write an essay that describes the trend in using hardware from other countries in your career or your chosen career. Form and express an opinion about the future of your career as it relates to hardware imports. Go beyond simple reporting of the facts. Support your opinion with references to the articles you read. Ask your instructor for guidance regarding the required length of the essay.

5. **Communication**—Prepare a presentation in which you present your opinion and supporting facts to the class. Depending on your computer skill, you could give the presentation using a program like PowerPoint and save it as a Web page, or you could prepare a paper handout with your Web references for use while you talk to the class.

impact on the workplace

Computer hardware is on most desks and in most back rooms of today's workplace. If the building where you work is more than 25 years old, it is likely that the building's designers never had this use in mind. Consequently, the air conditioning system may be overloaded by the heat from computers, and the wiring that provides power and LAN connections may be in people's way.

1. **Teamwork**—Join one or two other students who work where you do or in a similar type of business or organization. Decide how to divide the work. Possible divisions could be: effect of heat from computers on the cooling system, and how LAN wiring affects the placement of workstations.

2. **Research**—Ask the facility manager of your building what effects the heat from computers has on the air conditioning system and what costs it adds to the annual operation. Talk to the LAN administrator and ask him or her about the problems he or she has with running wires to all the workstations.

3. **Analysis**—Write an essay that describes how computer hardware affects your workplace with regard to heat and wiring issues. Form and express an opinion. Support your opinion with your observations. Ask your instructor for guidance regarding the required length of the essay.

4. **Communication**—Prepare a presentation in which you present your opinion and the results of your observations. Depending on your computer skill, you could take digital photos to graphically communicate your observations, or you could prepare a paper handout with data for use while you talk to the class.

impact on social interactions

The Internet can be used to connect individual computers into a massive peer-to-peer network for sharing files. Music can be reduced to a digital file that can be stored, copied, and distributed (copyright violations and associated legal problems will be discussed in Chapter 5). This technology has great potential to change how entertainment is distributed.

1. **Teamwork and Research**—Join two or three other students to research this topic. Find Web pages, discussions, and technical descriptions on the following topics:
   • how Napster worked
   • what its successors are
   • file sharing methods of successors that are different from Napster's

2. **Diversity issues**—Does age, gender, or income affect the use of this file sharing system?

3. **Analysis**—Write an essay that describes how music and video file sharing is done. Form and express an opinion without dealing with the legal or ethical issues at this time. Support your opinion based on research and observation. Ask your instructor for guidance regarding the required length of the essay.

4. **Communication**—Prepare a presentation in which you present your opinion and the results of your observations. Prepare a handout of the information you compiled. If you have the computer skill, create a Web page with this information, and post it to a server.

impact on home life

The decreased cost of computer and networking hardware has resulted in many people having better computer systems at home than they do at work. Many people prefer to work in home offices at least part of the time. What effect does working at home have on a person's home life? If you work at home part of the time, survey your family and at least one other family in which one of the adults works at home.

1. **Teamwork**—Join one or two other students who have an interest in working at home. Decide how to divide up the work. Possible divisions could be: finding articles and research on home offices and effects on the family, and designing a set of survey questions to ask family members.

2. **Research**—Use a Web browser and search for articles on home offices. Use key word phrases like "home office" and key words like "family." Use the Groups and News options in search engines like Google. Make a list of relevant sources that you may want to reference later. Include the title of the page or article, the name of the organization responsible for the Web page, the date the page or article was written, and the Web address. You may also go to the library and look up books, articles, and news reports that are relevant to this topic. Many libraries have the full text of articles and news reports online in proprietary databases that are not available to the public.

3. **Diversity issues**—Observe how children's and adults' opinions differ.

4. **Analysis**—Write an essay that summarizes the literature on the subject, and compare it with what you observed. Form and express an opinion on how the articles written on the subject relate to your situation or the one you observed. Support your opinion based on research and observation. Ask your instructor for guidance regarding the required length of the essay.

5. **Communication**—Prepare a presentation in which you present your opinion and the results of your observations. Prepare a handout of the information you compiled. If you have the computer skill, create a Web page with this information, and post it to a server.

leadership

Some people with mobility or other physical limitations could benefit from using improved pointing and control devices or from wireless network connections. You could put together a team of students who learn how to install a wireless network or specialized control hardware and offer your services to local nonprofit organizations that have members who need this service.

1. **Vision**—Write a vision statement that describes what you want your group to achieve. It should motivate people to volunteer to help.

2. **Research**—Don't reinvent the wheel. Do the following background research:
   a. Determine whether anyone is already doing this in your community. If so, contact them and describe their operation.
   b. Determine what groups specialize in teaching members to use computer control devices.

   c. Determine which government or nonprofit agencies in your area know of people who could use this type of help.
   d. Consider diversity issues. Determine what type of devices are suitable for different physical challenges.

4. **Plan of Action**—Write a simple plan of action. Test the plan by following it yourself on a small scale. Locate someone who could use help with his or her computer system's accessibility.

5. **Analysis**—Write up an analysis of what you learned by testing your plan.

6. **Communication**—Present your plan to the class. Describe what you learned by testing your plan and how you think it could be expanded if others joined you. Share your vision statement, and try to inspire others to join you in your worthwhile effort.

lifelong learning

Add links to your browser's favorites list.

1. Start your Web browser, and open the list of favorite sites. Create a folder called Hardware.

2. Go to the companion Web page for this chapter at **www.prenhall.com/preston**, and select one of the Web links on research that you found useful.

3. Add this link to your browser's favorites list in the Research folder.

4. Repeat this process for other links on the companion Web page for this chapter, and add them to the appropriate folders.

Add learning goals to your journals.

1. Identify areas in which you feel you know the least. List three specific topics related to this chapter that you would like to learn more about in the future.

2. You will add to this journal after each chapter to compile a personal list of references and topics for future study.

Using Software: Standing on the Shoulders of Giants

outline & objectives

CATEGORIES OF COMPUTER LANGUAGES

- Match key terms such as source code, machine code, and compiler with their definitions.
- Name three early 3GLs still in use that used GOTO statements.
- Identify the slang term for code written in languages that use GOTO statements.
- Identify the programming solution to branching problems.
- Identify the features of modular programming.
- Identify the relationship between C and operating systems.
- Identify characteristics of a 4GL.
- Give an example of a 4GL language.
- Identify definitions and examples of event-driven languages.
- Identify the characteristics of object-oriented programming.
- Identify languages that use OOP.
- Identify characteristics of a 5GL.
- Give an example of a 5GL language.

APPLICATIONS

- Identify what the acronym BIOS stands for.
- Identify the functions of BIOS.
- Identify the functions of an operating system.
- Name four common operating systems.
- Identify functions of server applications.
- Define GUI.
- Name three IBM mainframe operating systems.
- Identify the characteristics of Linux.
- Identify four productivity application suites.
- Identify types of utility programs.

LANGUAGES AND APPLICATIONS FOR THE INTERNET

- Identify the relationships among applications, browsers, and operating systems.
- Identify the relationships among Java, byte code, and Java virtual machine.
- Identify Microsoft applications that compete with Java.
- Identify the role of CGI.
- Identify at least four script languages.
- Identify two types of Web pages created by scripts in response to user input.

A computer's physical equipment is known as hardware. In contrast, the programs that instruct computers on how to accomplish tasks are **software**. Writing software is programming, and the people who do it are programmers.

One of the greatest scientists of all time, Isaac Newton, wrote in 1676, "If I have seen farther than others, it is because I was standing on the shoulders of giants." We all stand on the shoulders of giants today by using the creative product of dozens of geniuses and thousands of talented programmers when we use the software they have written to work, create, and play using computers.

WHY DO I NEED TO KNOW THIS?

Programming and careers related to software development are growth areas. Students from around the world come to the United States to learn how to write software because of the available expertise, plentiful supply of computer hardware, and available jobs. If you like working with computers and solving problems, a career as a programmer, systems analyst, or system administrator may be for you. This chapter gives you some idea of what languages programmers use and the types of software they write (see Figure 4.1).

Even if you do not choose a career writing software, you will still be faced with software-related decisions in your job or home. Some different types of software exchange files easily, and some are incompatible. Expertise in one type of software does not necessarily transfer to others. Your choices of which software you use will determine the groups of people with whom you can most conveniently exchange information or from whom you can seek help. Many of these choices are made for you or are determined by your choice of hardware, but it is important that you be aware of the ramifications of these choices.

FIGURE 4.1

DAY IN THE LIFE **Delphine Corbin, Java Programmer**

Originally from France, Delphine now works as a programmer for a cellular phone company. Specifically, she programs Java applications for use with digital cellular phones. Not surprisingly, programming for a mobile platform is nothing like programming for the desktop computer. "Working with the small resources available to a cellular phone is extremely challenging," She explains. "It's like you've suddenly gone back in time ten years and have to work with the same tools they had back then." She laughs. "I didn't even know how to use a computer ten years ago!"

What's worse is that the technology keeps changing. "You have to be extremely focused when you program," Delphine points out. "You can't release a project too late, because by the time it's available to the public, the hardware they're using may already have advanced sufficiently to allow even more new features. If you keep waiting to incorporate new functionality, you'll never get done. You just have to know when to draw the line. And, you have to get it right the first time!"

Delphine Corbin, originally from France, is a Java programmer.

On the Internet, Web pages are becoming increasingly interactive because there are programs embedded in these pages that your Web browser uses. Understanding this use of Web pages helps you make decisions about ways you can communicate with your customers or how you can communicate your needs to a business.

In this chapter, you learn about how software is written and you become familiar with some of the tools used to write it. You learn what jobs are related to these skills. You also learn about the competing visions for software development and how they affect you.

CATEGORIES OF COMPUTER LANGUAGES

When we speak to each other in a particular language like English, we assign certain meaning to words. Some of the words are nouns, others are verbs, and there are rules for using them together in sentences. The rules for using words in a language are called its *syntax*. A computer's microprocessor can perform logical and mathematical operations on data if the data and the instructions use binary numbers and follow a set of rules like the syntax of a human language. We say that instructions in this format are in *machine language*. The problem with communicating with a microprocessor is translating data and instructions from a language we understand into machine language. The first step is translating individual characters and numbers. In Chapter 3, you learned about the ASCII standard that is used to translate individual characters and decimal numbers into binary numbers. A machine language also assigns binary numbers to specific memory locations and different mathematical and logical operations. These numbers are used like nouns and verbs, and the rules for constructing instructions the microprocessor can follow is the syntax of the machine language.

Translating individual letters and numbers into machine language is easy compared to translating a sentence like "Get me the Thompson contract." Human languages have complex syntaxes and assume a lot of unstated facts and cultural knowledge that do not translate easily into machine language. Special-purpose programming languages were created with simple syntaxes that use specific terms like save, print, add, and subtract. These programming languages could be understood by humans and easily translated into machine language. Programmers use these languages to write instructions that can be interpreted by the computer's microprocessor.

One way to categorize programming languages is to group them by their similarity to human languages, ranging from most machinelike to most humanlike. The most machinelike are called *first-generation languages (1GLs)*, and the most humanlike are *fifth-generation languages (5GLs)*. Another way to categorize them is to group them by the increasingly sophisticated methods used to organize instructions. Examples of sophisticated language groups are *procedural* and *object-oriented programming (OOP)*. These two categorization methods are often mixed together when discussing computer languages because the more sophisticated methods result in more humanlike languages. The following discussion organizes the languages by generation, and then within a particular generation the programming methods are discussed as subcategories. In general, first- and second-generation languages are procedural, and fourth- and fifth-generation languages use object-oriented programming. Third-generation languages are mixed.

FIRST-GENERATION LANGUAGE

Machine language is a first-generation language (1GL) and is the language the computer processor understands. Electrical engineers work with instructions at this level when they design integrated circuits and connections between parts of the computer. The first computers were programmed using machine language, but the programmer had to know a great deal about the binary numbers used for specific memory addresses, processor characteristics, input devices, and output devices to work with this language. A sequence of instructions written in machine language is called *machine code*. Some examples of machine code and their corresponding instructions are shown in Figure 4.2. One great advantage of a program written in machine language is that it can execute very quickly because no translation or interpretation is needed. A program in machine language is a series of zeros and ones, which is very tedious to work with and difficult for anyone to read.

SECOND-GENERATION LANGUAGE

Programmers realized that they needed to do something to make it easier to program computers, so they created a slightly more convenient language called *assembly language*, which is a *second-generation language (2GL)*. Assembly language allows the use of command words and decimal numbers. For example, a 2GL statement might look like this:

PORTDLC: EQU $00FE + REGBASE

An assembler is a program that takes assembly language statements like this one and converts them into a series of machine language instructions. In this case, the computer is told to load the contents of memory location 3000 into the eighth holding place (called a *register*) in the processor. All of these instructions in machine language would be groups of zeros and ones, and they would be unique to a particular processor and memory circuit. An instruction like this example is *source code*, and the translated binary instructions are machine code. Assembly language is the closest language to machine language that programmers use, and they use it only when

FIGURE 4.2

Operation Code	Instruction
00000001	Load: copy the value of the word addressed into the accumulator register
00000011	Add: replace the present value of the accumulator register with the sum of its present value and value of the word addressed
00000100	Subtract: replace the present value of the accumulator register with the result obtained by subtracting from its present value the value of the word addressed
00000101	Branch: jump to the instruction at the word addressed
00000010	Store: copy the value of the accumulator register into the word addressed
00000111	Halt: terminate execution

Examples of machine codes and the instructions they provide to the microprocessor.

FIGURE 4.3

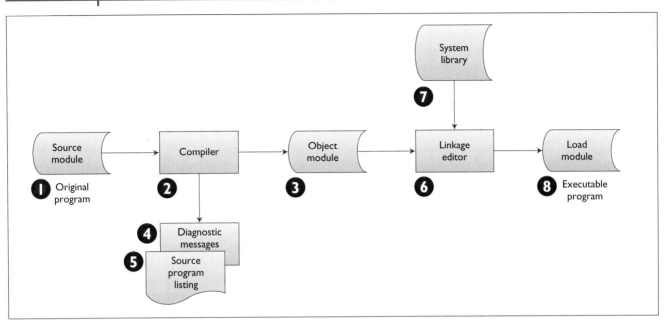

Source code (1) goes to the compiler (2), which produces diagnostic messages if it finds syntax errors (4) and a list of the source code (5). If the source code compiles correctly (3), it goes to a linkage editor (6), which plugs in modules of standard code from the system library (7) to produce an executable program in machine language (8).

speed is at a premium or processor power is very limited. Gaming programs that interact with the user must process data very quickly to respond realistically so some games are written in assembly language to take advantage of characteristics of a particular processor. Assembly language source code is specific to a particular hardware, which limits its use.

THIRD-GENERATION LANGUAGES

Third-generation languages (3GLs) use commands that are not specific to a particular processor. The source code is sent to a *compiler*, which converts it into machine code for a particular processor (see Figure 4.3). This separation of programming and machine-specific instructions allows programs to run on different computers as long as there is a compiler that can convert the language into machine code for that computer. First- and second-generation languages are considered *low-level* languages. Third-, fourth-, and fifth-generation languages are considered *high-level* languages.

Each language has very specific rules governing it called syntax. Spelling and punctuation must be correct, and commands are limited to a given set of words. If any of the syntax rules are violated, the compiler issues an error report. Errors are called *bugs*, and fixing errors is *debugging* (see Figure 4.4). Third-generation languages are procedural languages in which the programmer gives a specific set of instructions on how to handle the data and processing (see Figure 4.5). There are many different third-generation languages, and they can be further divided into subcategories based on the methods they use.

Early Languages with GOTO Instructions

Three of the early 3GLs were *FORTRAN*, *COBOL*, and *BASIC*. FORTRAN, which stands for FORmula TRANslation, is very good at working with formulas. COBOL, which stands for COmmon Business Oriented Language, is used for business functions like payroll and accounting.

FIGURE 4.4

Calling a computer problem a "bug" dates back to 1945 when Grace Hopper, a computer pioneer working for the Navy, was trying to find a problem with the Mark I computer. A moth was attracted to the lights and heat of the computer and had jammed an electrical relay. She taped the dead moth to her logbook, and the term "bug" became synonymous with computer program errors.

BASIC is a general-purpose language created to help students learn programming. BASIC was adapted by Bill Gates and Paul Allen to run on the first personal computer.

A significant feature of a program is its ability to perform different operations based on certain conditions. This is called **branching**. Early third-generation languages in the 1950s and 1960s used conditional IF operations combined with GOTO commands that transferred control to a different part of the program. For example, if a program were written to calculate an individual's income tax, it could evaluate a condition like marital status (IF operation) and then transfer control (GOTO command) to the appropriate section of program instructions to deal with that status. As programs became more complex, this method was very difficult to follow because you did not know when a particular part of the program was in use and where control had originated. It was difficult to fix a program if there were an error in its logic. Programs using the GOTO statement that were hard to follow were often called **spaghetti code** by frustrated programmers because following their logic was like tracing an individual noodle in a plate of spaghetti. Early versions of FORTRAN, COBOL, and BASIC used GOTO statements.

FIGURE 4.5

```
'BASIC PROGRAM
'AVERAGING INTEGERS ENTERED THROUGH THE KEYBOARD
CLS
PRINT "THIS PROGRAM WILL FIND THE AVERAGE OF INTEGERS YOU ENTER"
PRINT "THROUGH THE KEYBOARD. TYPE 999 TO INDICATE END OF DATA."
PRINT
SUM=0
COUNTER=0
PRINT "PLEASE ENTER A NUMBER"
INPUT NUMBER
DO WHILE NUMBER <> 999
      SUM=SUM+NUMBER
      COUNTER=COUNTER+1
      PRINT "PLEASE ENTER THE NEXT NUMBER"
      INPUT NUMBER
LOOP
AVERAGE=SUM/COUNTER
PRINT "THE AVERAGE OF THE NUMBERS IS"; AVERAGE
END
```
(a)

```
THIS PROGRAM WILL FIND THE AVERAGE OF INTEGERS YOU ENTER
THROUGH THE KEYBOARD. TYPE 999 TO INDICATE END OF DATA.

PLEASE ENTER A NUMBER
?6
PLEASE ENTER THE NEXT NUMBER
?4
PLEASE ENTER THE NEXT NUMBER
?11
PLEASE ENTER THE NEXT NUMBER
?999
THE AVERAGE OF THE NUMBERS IS    7
```
(b)

A program written in BASIC that uses the DO-WHILE loop form of structured programming

DIVERSITY ISSUES

DISCUSSION

Some of the pioneers of programming, like Augusta Ada Byron and Grace Hopper, were women. Do you know many women from the United States who plan to be programmers? If you don't know of any, speculate on why that is. Do you know any women from India studying to be programmers? Consider finding out more about this topic by doing the "Impact on Social Interactions" exercise at the end of this chapter.

Structured Programming Languages

In the late 1960s, programmers agreed to drop GOTO statements and use blocks of commands like IF-THEN-ELSE or DO-WHILE, which could handle different conditions in one location in the program. This method is called ***structured programming***. See Figure 4.5 for an example written in BASIC, using a DO-WHILE loop.

Modular Programming

As programs continued to develop, it became clear that code to perform certain procedures could be used repeatedly. Programmers learned to create blocks of code to handle standard procedures and keep them in a separate file from which they could be copied when needed rather than written again. This practice evolved into a method called ***modular programming***. The programmer supplied information, and an answer or command came out. The programmer did not care what went on inside that block of code. This feature is called ***information hiding***. Input and output were standardized so programmers could share modules, which significantly increased programmer productivity and reduced errors. ***Ada*** is an example of a modularized language that uses information hiding. Ada is a language used by the Defense Department of the U.S. government and is named after Augusta Ada Byron, Countess of Lovelace, who is considered to be the first programmer.

Languages Used to Write Application Programs

Instead of writing programs that worked directly with the computer to solve specific problems, programmers could write programs that coordinated modules of code to provide a complete set of tools that could be used by other programs. In 1972, the ***C*** language was created. It allowed programmers to specify manipulation of bits within the processor like a 2GL program but had the high-level language features of a 3GL. As a result, programs written in C ran faster than those written in other 3GLs. C and its successors, C+ and C++ (see Figure 4.6), are used to write ***operating systems***. An operating system is a special class of software that provides standard tools for communicating with particular types of processors. Operating systems will be discussed in more detail in a later section.

FIGURE 4.6

```
// C++ PROGRAM
// AVERAGING INTEGERS ENTERED THROUGH THE KEYBOARD

#include <iostream.h>
main ()
{
  float average;
  int number, counter = 0; int sum = 0;
  cout << "THIS PROGRAM WILL FIND THE AVERAGE OF INTEGERS YOU ENTER \ n";
  cout << "THROUGH THE KEYBOARD.  TYPE 999 TO INDICATE END OF DATA. \ n";
  cout << "PLEASE ENTER A NUMBER";
  cin >> number;
  while (number !=999)
    {
      sum + = number;
      counter ++;
      cout << "\nPLEASE ENTER THE NEXT NUMBER";
      cin >> number;
    }
  average = sum / counter;
  cout << "\nTHE AVERAGE OF THE NUMBERS IS " << average
}
```

(a)

A program written in C++

Special-Purpose Languages for the Web

The Internet spawned a variety of special-purpose languages that work with operating systems, including Java and C#. These languages are discussed in a later section, following the discussion of operating systems (see Languages and Applications for the Internet).

FOURTH-GENERATION LANGUAGES

Fourth-generation languages (4GLs) may be used by nonexpert programmers as well as experts for working with specific applications like databases. They are closer to normal human language than 3GLs, but they still require a strict syntax. They are *nonprocedural*—meaning detailed instructions on how to accomplish the task are not included—and, therefore, much less code is required to accomplish the same task. A request for information from a database is called a *query*, and the standard language for writing queries is *Structured Query Language (SQL)*. For example, if you wanted to know which department had the highest average worker salaries, such a request in SQL would look like this:

SELECT MAX(AVG(salary))
FROM employee_salary_table
GROUP BY department_number;

The programmer does not have to provide a procedure for retrieving each employee record and calculating the average by department. This request would take a far more complex program in a 3GL such as COBOL, but it still has a strict syntax. SQL is used with a 3GL that handles other tasks. For example, Oracle Corporation, a major database software company, uses PL/SQL (Programming Language/Structured Query Language) to create a 4GL. 4GLs have some or all of the following properties:

❯ They work with database structures and programming.

❯ A centralized data dictionary holds information about system components.

❯ They offer visual programming using icons positioned with a pointing device like a mouse.

❯ Novices as well as experts can use them.

❯ They offer an interactive and multifunction programming environment.

The term 4GL is not strictly defined; it is also used to describe languages that are event driven or that use a new system called object-oriented programming (OOP), which is described below.

Event Driven

Visual Basic (VB) was introduced in 1987 to make it easy for developers to use standard Windows features like buttons, dialog boxes, scroll bars, and menus. Each of these items could contain hundreds of lines of code, but the developer could incorporate them by simply dragging an icon onto the screen in the desired location and then describing the desired results of using that feature. In previous procedural programs, the structure of the program determined when a user could enter data or perform an action. The user of a VB program can choose to click buttons or input data in a dialog box when he or she chooses. Choosing an object like a button or dialog box is an *event*, and the program is *event driven*. For example, in Figure 4.7 the *cmdAccept_Click( )*, *cmdCompute_Click( )* and *cmdExit_Click( )* commands are activated by clicking the associated button on the screen. Visual Basic works with Microsoft Office applications, which are

FIGURE 4.7

```
'Visual Basic Program
'Averaging integers entered through the keyboard
Option Explicit
Dim intNumber As Integer
Dim intSum As Integer
Dim intCounter As Integer
Dim sngAverage As Single

Private Sub cmdAccept_Click()
    intNumber = Val(txtNum.Text)
    intSum = intSum + intNumber
    intCounter = intCounter + 1
    txtNum.Text = ""
    txtNum.SetFocus
End Sub

Private Sub cmdCompute_Click()
    sngAverage = intSum / intCounter
    lblResults.Caption = Format(sngAverage, "fixed")
    intSum = 0
    intCounter = 0
    txtNum.Text = ""
    txtNum.SetFocus
End Sub

Private Sub cmdExit_Click()
    End
End Sub
```

(a)

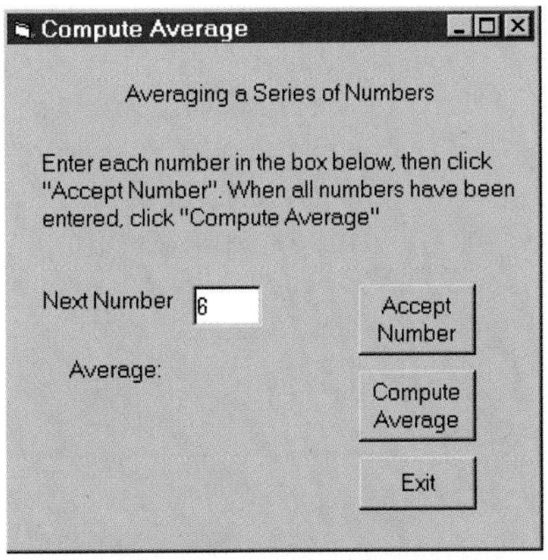

(b)

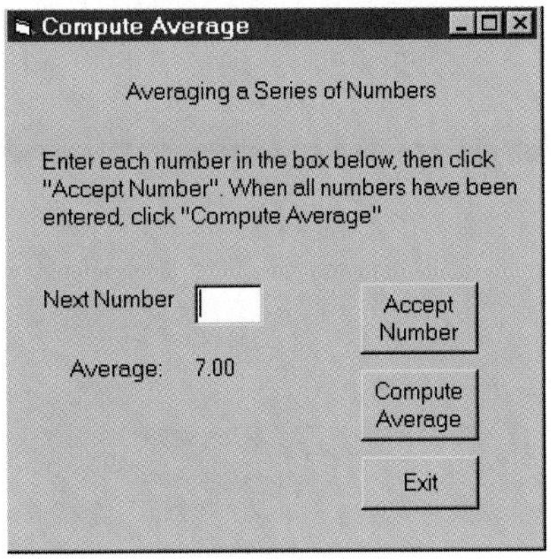

(c)

Visual Basic gives control of the program's execution to the user by using event-driven programming.

described later, and can run on Windows or Macintosh computers. Buttons and dialog boxes are often called objects in event-driven programs, which may cause confusion with object-oriented programs (see the next topic).

Object-Oriented Programming

Most programs consist of a set of procedural instructions that are separate from the data they work on. An error in one part of the program could corrupt data used by another part of the program. Another problem occurs in large organizations. A programmer can write instructions for certain types of operations, but cannot anticipate all the individual applications that might be included in a program or how they might interact with each other. A completely new way of dealing with data and programming, called object-oriented programming (OOP), has emerged. It is similar to modular programming but goes beyond it by including data as well as instructions. These self-contained modules of data and instructions are called **objects**. An object contains facts that describe the object called **attributes** and programmed instructions called **methods** or **operations**. Objects can belong to a **class**, and one class can **inherit** attributes from another class.

For example, consider a class of objects called Boat. Facts that describe boats could be length and location, and methods could be move and change direction. Within the class are subclasses for sailboat, powerboat, and canoe (see Figure 4.8). Because these three subclasses are members of the boat class, they inherit the attributes length and location (not particular values, just the ability to specify values for length and location) and the methods move and change direction. In addition to the attributes and methods inherited from the class, each subclass has its own unique attributes and methods. If you were in command of this small flotilla, you could issue the order, called a **message**, to "go East" and each of the objects would use the change direction and move methods of the class, along with any of its own methods that comply with the message, to accomplish the goal. The ability of each object to determine how to use variables to accomplish the goal of the message based on the context is called **polymorphism**. Inheritance and

FIGURE 4.8

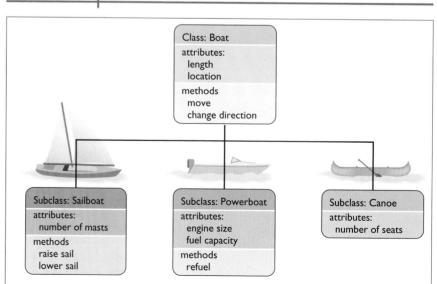

Object-oriented programming identifies attributes and methods of a class that are shared by objects in the class.

polymorphism are two characteristics of OOP that distinguish it from event-driven programming.

Object-oriented programming features have been added to some languages; other languages only use OOP. The C+ and Visual Basic languages were updated to include OOP and renamed **C++** and **VB.NET**. C++ can be used to write traditional procedural code as well as OOP. The original OOP language is **Smalltalk**, which is still in use. Two new languages use OOP exclusively. They are Java from Sun Microsystems and **C#**, pronounced "C sharp," from Microsoft.

FIFTH-GENERATION LANGUAGES

A fifth-generation language (5GL) is similar to a 4GL that uses a **knowledge-based system** that can interpret instructions in a more humanlike manner. Like the term 4GL, 5GL is loosely defined. In general, 5GLs have the following properties:

- ❭ All computer code is generated automatically.
- ❭ The created code can be compiled by a 3GL or 4GL compiler.
- ❭ Programs are modified and maintained working with the 5GL statements or icons, not the underlying 3GL or 4GL code.

Examples of languages that use graphical interfaces to generate OOP programs that are considered by many to be 5GL are JBuilder by Borland and JDeveloper by Oracle.

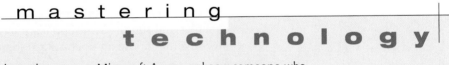

mastering technology

Look at SQL in Access. If you know how to use Microsoft Access or know someone who does, open one of the queries. From the View menu, choose SQL View to see the Structured Query Language that Access queries use.

APPLICATIONS

Programming languages are used to create special sets of instructions to accomplish specific tasks that are called **application programs** or simply **applications**. The instructions are usually written in a third-generation language and are called the **source code**. The source code is compiled for use on different computer systems and distributed on CD or by download from the Internet.

BIOS

When you turn on your computer, the first program it runs is stored in special memory on the motherboard. This program is called the **Basic Input/Output System**, or **BIOS**. It checks the connections to each of the major components such as the monitor, keyboard, mouse, RAM, CPU, and ports. If a component is unplugged or faulty, a message appears on the screen or a series of beeps are sounded. The pattern of beeps indicates the type of problem and is called the **beep code**. Once the BIOS confirms that the components are working properly, it copies the operating system instructions from the hard disk into RAM and hands off control of the computer to the operating system. While the BIOS is starting up the computer, you see a display of text providing the status of different components.

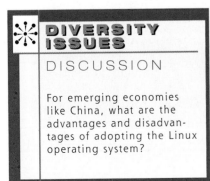

DIVERSITY ISSUES

DISCUSSION

For emerging economies like China, what are the advantages and disadvantages of adopting the Linux operating system?

OPERATING SYSTEMS

When the BIOS has finished checking the computer, it loads a program from disk storage called the operating system (OS), which controls the computer once it is running. The OS determines the way information is displayed on the screen, how it is printed, and how the mouse works. It also provides a group of common functions that other programs can utilize and controls how data is written on disks. Manufacturers of peripherals like printers provide small programs called *drivers* that are used by the operating system to manage communications between the computer and the component.

In the early days of personal computing, the **Microsoft Disk Operating System**, or **MS-DOS**, became popular when IBM adopted it for the IBM PC. MS-DOS represented numbers and letters on the screen and on paper with an array of simple dots.

Windows operating systems still support MS-DOS commands. If you choose Start, Run, then type cmd and press Enter, you can run MS-DOS commands like DIR to list the contents of a directory (see Figure 4.9).

Apple Computer popularized the **graphical user interface**, or **GUI** (see Figure 4.10). The Apple operating system that ran on the Apple Macintosh computer used icons and a mouse pointer to drag, select, and draw elements on the screen. The characters were drawn with scalable curves that made it possible to display letters in different fonts and in different sizes. Microsoft adopted the GUI approach several years later and incorporated it into Windows (see Figure 4.11).

If two computers use the same operating system, they can easily exchange data files and run the same application programs. This fact provides strong incentive to choose an operating system that is the same as on most other

FIGURE 4.9

```
C:\WINDOWS\System32\cmd.exe                              _ □ X

C:\>DIR E:
 Volume in drive E has no label.
 Volume Serial Number is F80D-C42F

 Directory of E:\

06/20/2003  04:28 PM    <DIR>          John
06/18/2003  09:34 AM    <DIR>          My Documents
10/13/2001  06:59 PM    <DIR>          Program Files
06/25/2003  08:02 PM    <DIR>          Waterslide pics
08/17/2001  01:33 PM            20,992 ~WRD0623.tmp
               1 File(s)         20,992 bytes
               4 Dir(s)   1,215,524,864 bytes free

C:\>_
```

MS-DOS is still available from Windows XP through the Run option.

FIGURE 4.10

Mac OS X is an Apple operating system that is strong in multimedia operations.

FIGURE 4.11

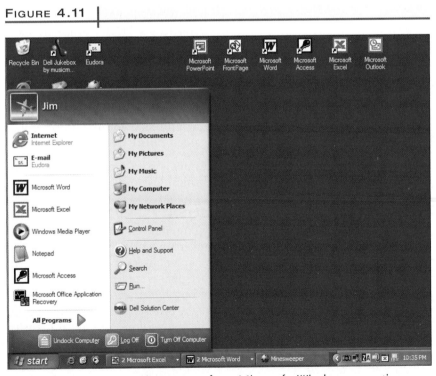

Windows XP is an operating system from Microsoft. Windows operating systems are the most common on personal computers by a wide margin.

FIGURE 4.12

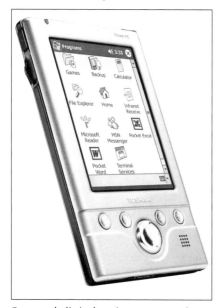

Personal digital assistants are miniature computers that fit in your hand and use a special OS for small-format computing.

computers. Due to the early popularity of the IBM PC, and DOS's availability on other computers besides IBM PCs, MS-DOS was more commonly used than Apple OS, which was available only on Apple computers. When Microsoft introduced the Windows operating system, Windows could run the older application software that used MS-DOS, and it provided the ease of use of the GUI. As a result, Windows grew in popularity, and today is found on over 90 percent of the personal computers in use, whereas about 5 percent use Apple OS. The Apple OS has much greater market share among graphic communication professionals and educators.

Operating systems work with specific types of microprocessors. Together, an operating system and type of processor are a *platform*. A common combination is the Windows operating system and an Intel microprocessor. Computers that use this platform are often referred to as *wintel* machines. There are significant advantages to using the same operating system as the people with whom you intend to communicate most often. Choosing an operating system will have a direct effect on what application software you buy.

Personal digital assistants (PDAs) and multifunction cell phones also use operating systems that must run on small amounts of RAM and manage small screens. PDAs were popularized by *Palm Pilot*, which uses the *Palm OS*. Other PDAs use a special version of Windows called *Windows CE* (see Figure 4.12).

Large computers or mainframes found in companies and big organizations use a variety of operating systems. IBM mainframe computers use *MVS* or newer operating systems named *OS/390* or *Z/OS*. *UNIX* is an operating system written in the C language that is popular on other brands of mainframe computers and at universities. UNIX was the first widely used open-source operating system written in a standard language that could be used by anyone. It has evolved into several versions that are not completely compatible. UNIX originated at Bell Labs in 1969, but the intellectual property rights to the code are currently owned by SCO Group (see Chapter 5). Microsoft is also offering *Windows 2000 Datacenter*, which is designed to compete for mainframe applications. With the rise of popularity of the Internet, medium-size computers are commonly used by smaller companies to host Web pages and connect them to databases. These medium-size computers often use UNIX or a similar operating system named *Linux* (see Figure 4.13).

Linux is free and may be downloaded from the Internet (see Chapter 5, Ethical Use of Computers).

CLIENT/SERVER APPLICATIONS

Computers connected to LANs or to the Internet can be far more productive than isolated systems. The software used to provide services to multiple computers is called *server software*. Software that resides on the user's personal computer or workstation, called *client software*, requests files or Web pages from server software on an organization's computer. There are many different combinations of operating systems and server software. See the companion Web site at **http://www.prenhall.com/preston** for links to sites that show various combinations.

Web Servers

Servers that provide Web pages are called *Web servers*, and there is a variety of software available to provide this service. One of the popular programs for low-cost Web server systems is *Apache*, which is an open-source

Figure 4.13

Linux has a graphical user interface similar to Mac OS or Windows.

software that runs on UNIX or Linux operating systems. The combination of free operating system—Linux—and free server software—Apache—makes this combination attractive. Apple offers Mac OS X Server, and Windows has Windows Server 2003, which includes Internet Information Server (IIS), which can serve Web pages as well as LAN services. Browsers like Netscape and Internet Explorer are client programs that work with Web servers.

Messaging and Collaboration Applications

Local area networks use server software to coordinate communication with computers. Additional services like coordinating calendars and scheduling meetings may be handled by additional software like Microsoft's Exchange Server. Microsoft Outlook is an example of client software that works with Microsoft Exchange Server. Lotus Notes is used on IBM mainframe systems for these services (see Figure 4.14). Programs that coordinate groups are often called *groupware*.

PRODUCTIVITY APPLICATIONS FOR PERSONAL COMPUTERS

Productivity applications are programs that help users perform a function such as word processing or preparing presentations. In the early days of computing, there were many competing products for each type of application. The drawback to using applications from a variety of different vendors is that each one had a different way of performing basic functions like inserting text, saving files, and printing. The user had to spend considerable time learning how to perform basic functions whenever he or she used a new application. Microsoft took advantage of users' familiarity with the Windows operating system and incorporated a uniform method of doing things into its word processing and financial software, Word and Excel. This method was very attractive to businesses, and Microsoft added presentation (PowerPoint), database (Access), Web browser (Internet Explorer), and personal information (Outlook) software to its offerings and grouped them into a *suite* named

FIGURE 4.14

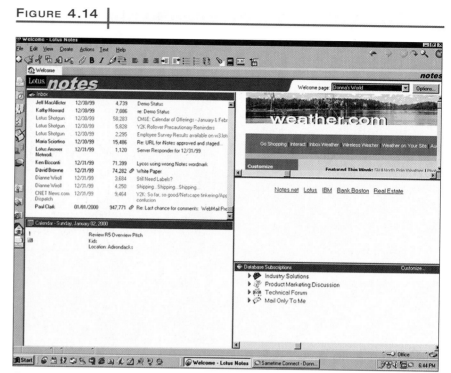

Groupware programs like Lotus Notes coordinate employee activities.

Microsoft Office. This suite became the dominant applications suite with over 90 percent market share in most business markets (see the companion Web site at **http://www.prenhall.com/preston).** Microsoft has another suite named *Microsoft Works*, which often comes bundled with new computers. Microsoft Works is a different set of programs from those in Microsoft Office and is intended for home use.

Microsoft's competitors for productivity applications went out of business, banded together, or acquired each other to create their own suites of applications. The main productivity suites that remain to compete with Microsoft Office are *Corel WordPerfect Office* and *Lotus SmartSuite* (see Figure 4.15). These suites are less expensive than Microsoft Office, but the convenience of sharing files and the advantage of widespread expertise with MS Office makes it difficult for competitors to gain market share.

FIGURE 4.15

Office Suites (Microsoft Windows)			
	Microsoft Office	**WordPerfect Office 2002**	**Lotus SmartSuite**
Word Processing	Microsoft Word	WordPerfect	Word Pro
Spreadsheet	Microsoft Excel	Quattro Pro	Lotus 1-2-3
Database	Microsoft Access	Paradox	Lotus Approach
Presentation Graphics	Microsoft PowerPoint	Corel Presentations 10	Freelance Graphics
Person Information Managers (PIMs)	Microsoft Outlook	Corel Central	Lotus Organizer

Suites package individual applications into an integrated package.

All the major suites run on the Windows operating system, and some of them have versions for Mac OS. Because the code is specific to the platform, it has to be rewritten for Mac OS so the Mac versions usually come out a year or more after the Windows versions.

A notable newcomer is *OpenOffice*. OpenOffice runs on the Linux operating system. A commercial version, *StarOffice*, is available on CD for approximately $50 and runs on Linux, Windows, and Solaris. OpenOffice is a free suite of productivity applications that runs on a free operating system and has gained the backing of some powerful companies like IBM, which competes with Microsoft. Emerging economies like China's are attracted to this low-cost option. Some units of government are required to buy the lowest-priced product that meets their specifications, which makes the Linux/OpenOffice combination a viable competitor. Hardware has fallen in price faster than software. It is now possible to pay more for a Windows operating system and MS Office productivity software than for the computer itself. However, the advantage of using software that is already well known by most office workers is significant.

There are numerous other programs that perform valuable functions. Some of these, like file management and disk maintenance, are bundled with the operating system, whereas others, like antivirus programs, are sold separately.

UTILITIES
Managing Files
Productivity software helps the user create files like documents, financial spreadsheets, presentations, and databases. Storing and retrieving these files becomes problematic when you have thousands of them. Applications written for Windows use a set of *file name extensions* to help identify files (see Figure 4.16). A file name extension is a three-letter code at the end of a file name following a period. For example, a document created in WordPerfect, SalesContract.wpd, has the file name extension .wpd, and a similar file created in Microsoft Word, SalesContract.doc, has the file

FIGURE 4.16

Commonly Used Extensions	
Extension	File Type
.exe	Application
.doc	Microsoft Word
.xls	Microsoft Excel
.ppt	Microsoft Power Point
.mbd	Microsoft Access
.pdf	Adobe
.txt	SimpleText
.htm or .html	Web pages
.rtf	Files in Rich Text Format

Common extensions for several file types

FIGURE 4.17

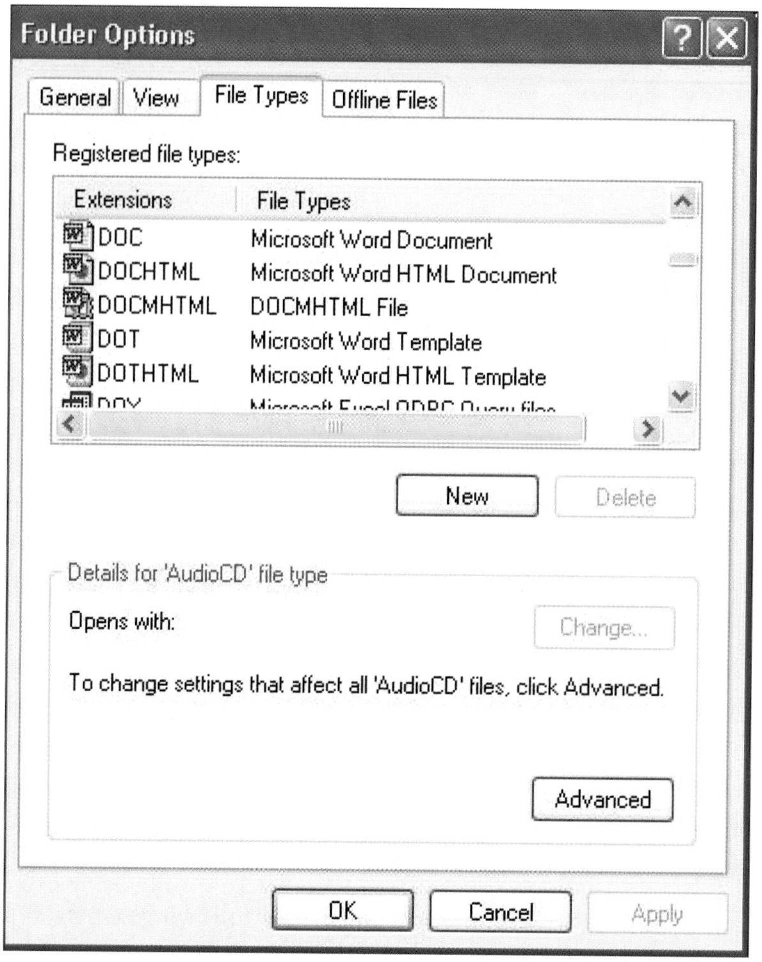

Extensions may identify file types. One example is .doc, which is registered as a Microsoft Word Document.

name extension .doc, which identifies it as a file created by Microsoft Word.

These file name extensions are recorded in the operating system's registry (see Figure 4.17). If you double-click a file name that has an extension, the Windows operating system looks up the extension in the registry and starts the related program automatically.

Windows represents the location of a file on one of the drives using a filing system metaphor of folders and subfolders in which the folder names are separated by a *backslash* (\). For example, the files for the fourth chapter of a book on computer concepts could be stored on partition E: on the hard disk. The shorthand notation for that location is:

E:\John\Books\Concepts\Ch04\Manuscripts

The name of the file may be appended to this location for a full description (see Figure 4.18):

E:\John\Books\Concepts\Ch04\Manuscripts\Manuscript for Chapter 4.doc

The Windows and Macintosh operating systems allow spaces in file names such as Manuscript for Chapter 4.doc, but UNIX and Linux do not. Some

FIGURE 4.18

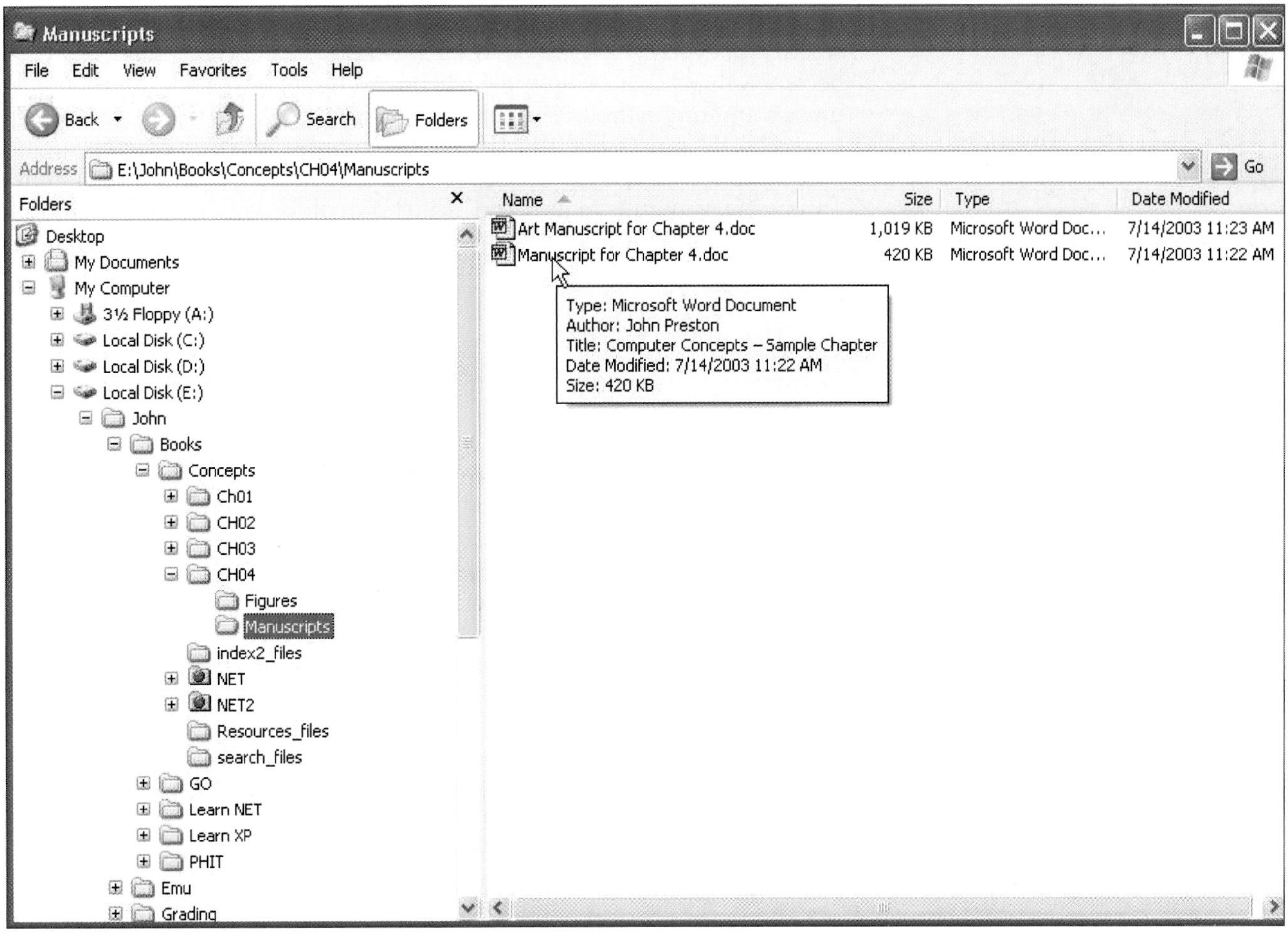

Windows Explorer uses a folder metaphor with icons and file extensions to show file types.

users replace spaces with underscore characters to give the appearance of spaces, as in this example: Manuscript_for_Chapter_4.doc. This convention works for most file names except the names of Web page files. Hyperlinks are references to Web pages and are normally underlined. If the name of the Web page file is used as a hyperlink, the underline overlays the underscore characters as in this example; Resources_for_Chapter_4.htm. If you use an application that creates Web pages, it is best to avoid using underscore characters or blanks in file names to avoid confusion and problems with operating systems that do not use blanks. Another difference to watch for is capitalization. Windows and Macintosh operating systems usually ignore differences in capitalization in a folder or file name, but UNIX and Linux treat capital and lowercase letters as entirely different characters.

File Compression

Most files contain words, phrases, or commands that are repeated. Utility programs are available that use some form of logic to reduce the size of the file. One method replaces the repeated words with a reference number and supplies a conversion table where the number can be converted back into the word or phrase.

This type of process is called *file compression*. It is common for a file compressor to reduce the size of a word processing document by a factor of four. The compressed version of the file is not usable by the application program, and the utility must be used again to *decompress* the file to return it to its usable form. This utility was created when hard disk space was scarce and expensive. That is no longer the case, but file compression has become valuable for saving time when sending files over the Internet. The most common method used for compression produces files with the .zip extension. Compressing a file is also commonly known as *zipping* it, and decompression is known as *unzipping*. This feature is built into Windows XP and is available as an extra utility for older versions of Windows, Macintosh, and UNIX operating systems (see Figure 4.19 and the companion Web site at **http://www.prenhall.com/preston.**).

Disk Use and Maintenance

Formatting   Operating systems manage space on rewritable disks by dividing the disk into *tracks* and *sectors*. Tracks are concentric circles of rewritable space on the disk. These circular tracks are divided into pie-shaped sections called sectors. Two or more adjacent sectors are a *cluster* (see Figure 4.20). Setting up the locations of these tracks and sectors is called *formatting*. A formatting utility is provided by the operating system and does not need to be purchased separately. The size and spacing of tracks and sectors varies by operating system, which is why a Windows computer does not recognize data on a disk that was formatted on a Macintosh computer even though the disk fits into the floppy disk drive. Macintosh computers include utilities that read floppy disks that have been formatted on Windows computers. The hard disk is already formatted when you purchase a computer. You can purchase preformatted floppy disks, or you can use your computer's formatting utility to reformat a floppy disk. When you reformat a disk, new tracks and sectors are marked on the disk, and data written on the old tracks and sectors is lost.

Scanning   Some magnetic disks have flaws in the magnetic coating rendering small parts of the disk unusable or unreliable. A utility is available that tests or *scans* the disk to find and mark any unusable sectors in any of the tracks. These "bad sectors" are marked as such and are not used.

FIGURE 4.19

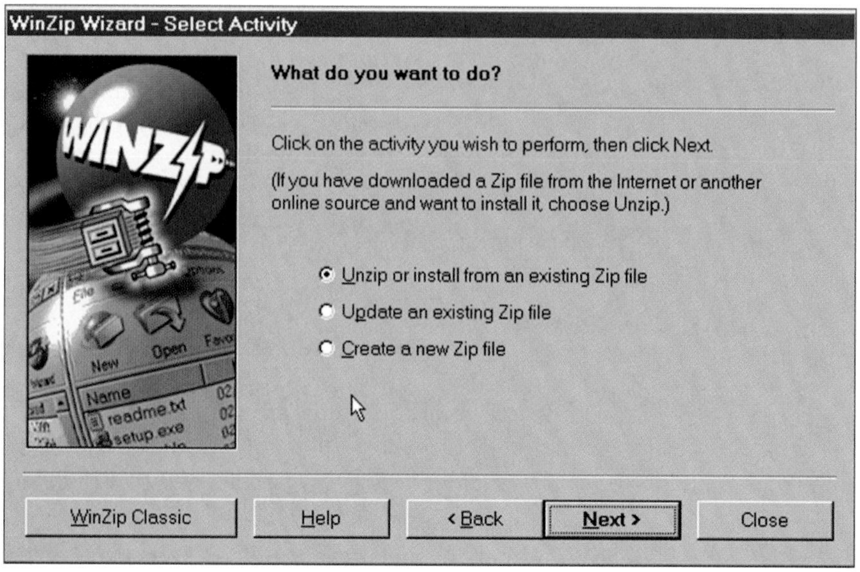

WinZip is a popular compression program.

FIGURE 4.20

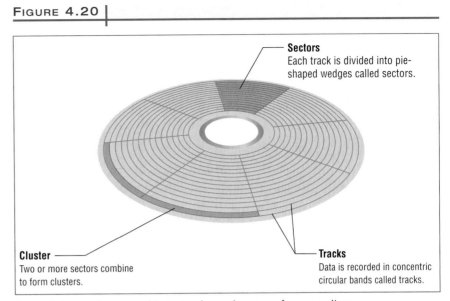

Sectors
Each track is divided into pie-shaped wedges called sectors.

Cluster
Two or more sectors combine to form clusters.

Tracks
Data is recorded in concentric circular bands called tracks.

Data disks are formatted into tracks and sectors for recording.

Erasing   When a file is written to a disk, the operating system records the location of the data in a file allocation table (FAT). If a file requires more than one sector of one track, the various track sectors and their sequence are recorded in the FAT. If a file is deleted from the disk, those sectors are listed in the FAT as available for use; they are not actually erased. When the computer records the next file, it may overwrite the previous data. Until then, the data is still on the disk and may be recovered. If you accidentally delete a file from your hard drive, the file may be listed in the operating system's wastebasket or recycle bin and may be restored to active use. Utilities are available that go through the disk and overwrite all the unused sectors to ensure that the data is not recoverable. They also reformat the disk to change the location of the sectors and reset the FAT. It is very important to use this type of utility when selling or giving away an old computer to prevent the new owner from recovering sensitive information on the hard disk.

Defragmenting   When a file is deleted, the sectors where it was stored are available for reuse. If the next file to be written is larger than the file that was deleted, the operating system places parts of the file in whatever sectors are available. The file in not written in contiguous sectors but is scattered around the disk (see Figure 4.21). After months of writing and erasing files, the files may be broken into many pieces that take more time to retrieve than if they were recorded in adjacent sectors. Utilities are available for moving the file fragments back together to make reading existing files faster. This process is called *defragmenting* and may take hours for a large hard disk. Defragmentation programs are often provided as a utility with the operating system or may be provided by independent vendors.

Antivirus, Web Security, and Spam Blocking Utilities
Viruses are a serious threat to your computer, and protecting against them is necessary (see Chapter 6). Antivirus utility programs scan files for the presence of viruses and delete or isolate them. A good antivirus program updates its list of known viruses regularly, usually over the Internet. Some antivirus programs charge an initial fee and a subscription fee for updates,

FIGURE 4.21

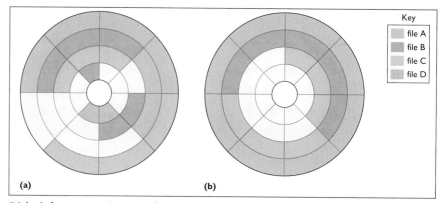

Key
file A
file B
file C
file D

(a)   (b)

Disk defragmentation: (a) fragmented files are stored in non-adjacent sectors, slowing retrieval; (b) defragmented files are rewritten to adjacent sectors.

whereas others are free to individual users (see the companion Web site at **http://www.prenhall.com/preston** for links).

If your computer is connected to the Internet, programs may be downloaded to your computer without your knowledge. These programs can steal information from your contacts files or track and report your Internet browsing. Most major antivirus program vendors also sell products to block unwanted access to your computer and unwanted e-mail (see Chapter 6 for more details on security). Unsolicited e-mail is called spam. Your e-mail program may divert suspected messages into a separate folder, or you can use utility programs that block most of these messages at the mail server. Programs that prevent spam from reaching your mail program's in-box are called *spam blockers*.

Viewing Documents

In many cases, people want to share documents without losing control of the contents. Sharing an original file allows others to change it. Adobe Acrobat is a program that captures documents along with their images and formatting in a way that they cannot be changed. Adobe Acrobat produces files with the .pdf extension, often referred to as PDF files (see Figure 4.22). If you get a PDF file as an e-mail attachment, you can easily download and install a PDF viewer from the Internet.

m a s t e r i n g
t e c h n o l o g y

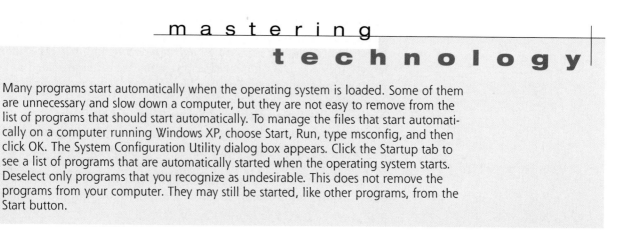

Many programs start automatically when the operating system is loaded. Some of them are unnecessary and slow down a computer, but they are not easy to remove from the list of programs that should start automatically. To manage the files that start automatically on a computer running Windows XP, choose Start, Run, type msconfig, and then click OK. The System Configuration Utility dialog box appears. Click the Startup tab to see a list of programs that are automatically started when the operating system starts. Deselect only programs that you recognize as undesirable. This does not remove the programs from your computer. They may still be started, like other programs, from the Start button.

FIGURE 4.22

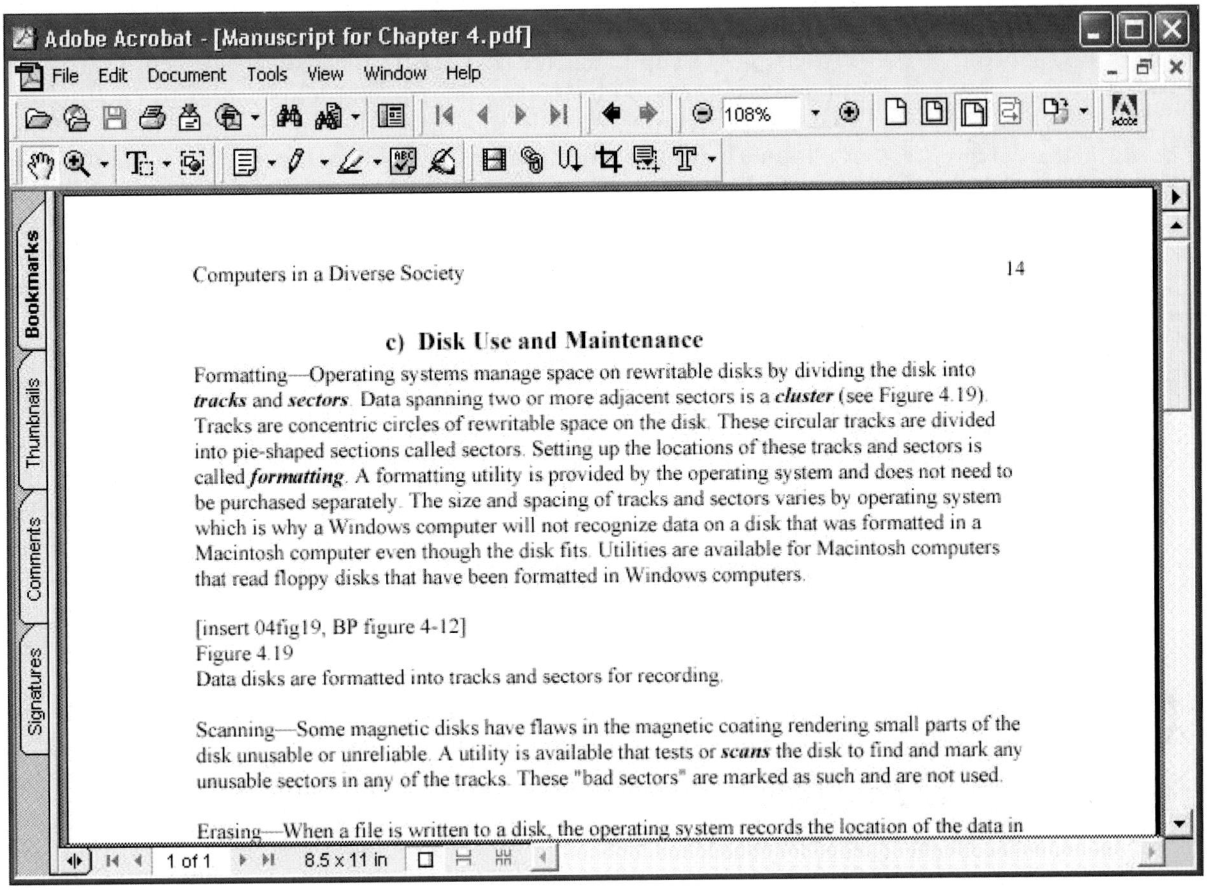

A PDF version of a Word document

CUSTOM SOFTWARE

Horizontal software is applications like word processing that may be used by many different types of organizations. *Vertical software* is applications written for specific market segments such as medical offices, restaurants, supermarkets, manufacturers, or tax return preparers. Horizontal and vertical software may be combined by service providers in an *enterprise resource package (ERP)*. Companies like SAP, PeopleSoft, Oracle, and Microsoft provide solutions of this type. For example, a university may need a database program for tracking student records that also works with an accounting program, a class scheduling program, and a distance learning program. Programs of this sort are often customized to fit the needs of a particular company or organization. There are more than 350,000 different application programs available for specific purposes. These programs may be free, or they may cost much more than general-purpose productivity software.

LANGUAGES AND APPLICATIONS FOR THE INTERNET

Most of the languages covered earlier in this chapter were designed for writing applications like operating systems, productivity software, utility programs, and custom software. These programs were compiled and the machine code distributed for use under a *licensing agreement*. Extensive use of the Internet produced a different type of language.

> **CRITICAL THINKING**
>
> DISCUSSION
>
> Would you prefer to subscribe to a service that downloads the part of an application you need or to buy and install the whole application on your computer?

LANGUAGES FOR CREATING WEB PAGES

The Internet consists of a web of computers connected to each other. It became the World Wide Web when Tim Berners-Lee developed the Hypertext Markup Language (HTML), which could represent Web pages on any computer. HTML uses pairs of predefined ***tags*** to enclose text that tell the computer how to display the information. For example, <b>John</b> displays **John** in boldface. HTML is used to write the code for a Web page (see Figure 4.23). The file is stored on a Web server and transmitted to the client computer upon request. HTML files have file extensions of .html or .htm. The client computer has a browser and operating system that interpret the HTML code and display the Web page.

A Web browser is a program that can interpret HTML code for display on a given platform.

As more people started using Web pages to place orders for goods, it became necessary for the pages to become more interactive with the user on the client computer and then manage the data when it returned to the server. The solution to this problem is to include programming code with the HTML code to run small application programs called applets. These applets could check forms for completeness and accuracy, calculate shipping charges, or animate weather radar images. The problem with embedding programming code in a Web page is that the browser is not equipped

FIGURE 4.23

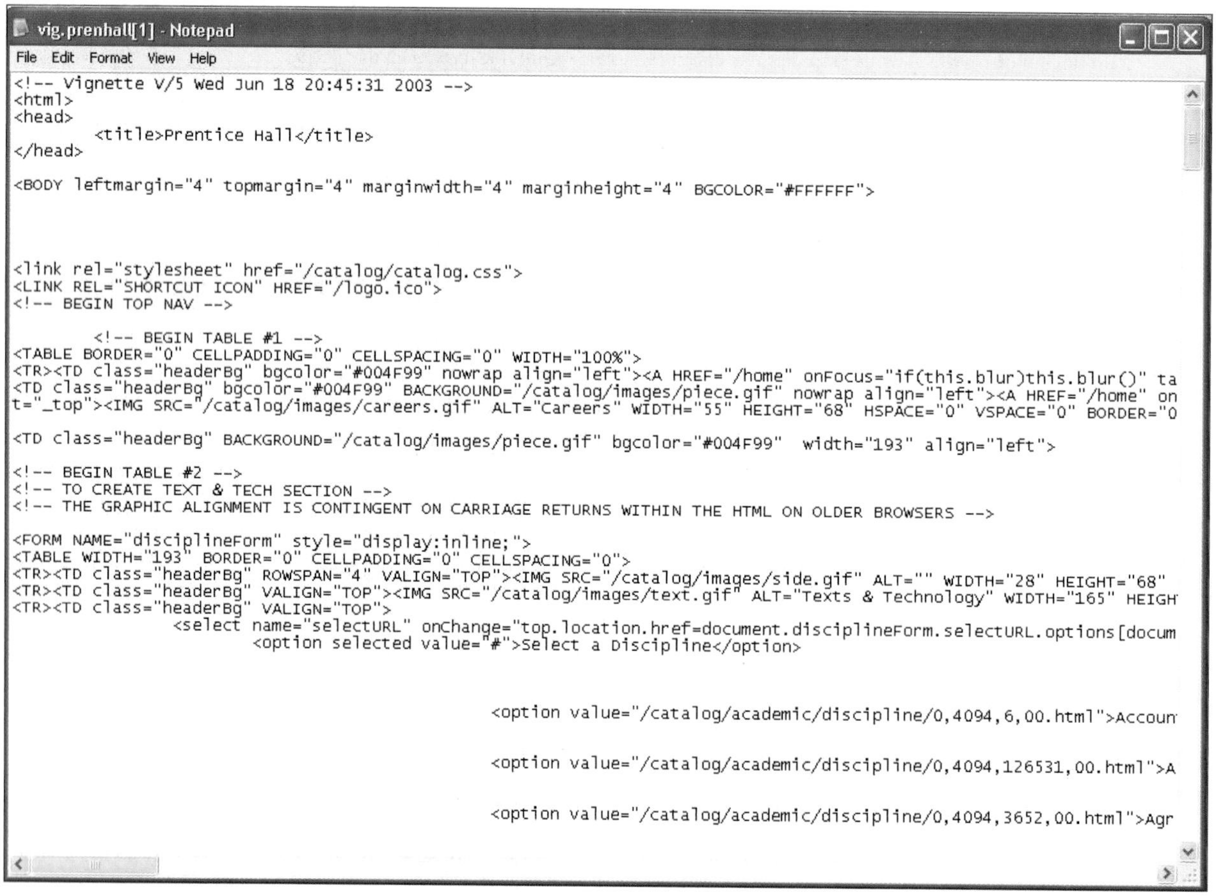

```
vig.prenhall[1] - Notepad
File Edit Format View Help
<!-- Vignette V/5 Wed Jun 18 20:45:31 2003 -->
<html>
<head>
        <title>Prentice Hall</title>
</head>

<BODY leftmargin="4" topmargin="4" marginwidth="4" marginheight="4" BGCOLOR="#FFFFFF">



<link rel="stylesheet" href="/catalog/catalog.css">
<LINK REL="SHORTCUT ICON" HREF="/logo.ico">
<!-- BEGIN TOP NAV -->

        <!-- BEGIN TABLE #1 -->
<TABLE BORDER="0" CELLPADDING="0" CELLSPACING="0" WIDTH="100%">
<TR><TD class="headerBg" bgcolor="#004F99" nowrap align="left"><A HREF="/home" onFocus="if(this.blur)this.blur()" ta
<TD class="headerBg" bgcolor="#004F99" BACKGROUND="/catalog/images/piece.gif" nowrap align="left"><A HREF="/home" on
t="_top"><IMG SRC="/catalog/images/careers.gif" ALT="Careers" WIDTH="55" HEIGHT="68" HSPACE="0" VSPACE="0" BORDER="0

<TD class="headerBg" BACKGROUND="/catalog/images/piece.gif" bgcolor="#004F99"  width="193" align="left">

<!-- BEGIN TABLE #2 -->
<!-- TO CREATE TEXT & TECH SECTION -->
<!-- THE GRAPHIC ALIGNMENT IS CONTINGENT ON CARRIAGE RETURNS WITHIN THE HTML ON OLDER BROWSERS -->

<FORM NAME="disciplineForm" style="display:inline;">
<TABLE WIDTH="193" BORDER="0" CELLPADDING="0" CELLSPACING="0">
<TR><TD class="headerBg" ROWSPAN="4" VALIGN="TOP"><IMG SRC="/catalog/images/side.gif" ALT="" WIDTH="28" HEIGHT="68"
<TR><TD class="headerBg" VALIGN="TOP"><IMG SRC="/catalog/images/text.gif" ALT="Texts & Technology" WIDTH="165" HEIGH
<TR><TD class="headerBg" VALIGN="TOP">
                <select name="selectURL" onChange="top.location.href=document.disciplineForm.selectURL.options[docum
                        <option selected value="#">Select a Discipline</option>


                                        <option value="/catalog/academic/discipline/0,4094,6,00.html">Accoun

                                        <option value="/catalog/academic/discipline/0,4094,126531,00.html">A

                                        <option value="/catalog/academic/discipline/0,4094,3652,00.html">Agr
```

HTML source code for the Prentice Hall home page

FIGURE 4.24

```
(a) // Java Program
    // Averaging integers entered through the keyboard
    public class SumNumbers {
      public static void main(Stringt args[]) {
        int number, counter = 0, sum = 0;
        System.out.prntln("This program will find the average of integers you enter");
        System.out.println("through the keyboard. Type 999 to indicate end of data.");
        System.out.print("Please enter a number ");
        number = VCCinput.getInteger();
        while (entered !=999) {
          sum += number;
          counter++;
          System.out.print("Please enter the next number ");
          number = VCCinput.getInteger();
        }
        System.out.println("The average of the numbers is " + (double) sum / counter);
      } // end main method

    } // end class SumNumbers
```

Sample of a Java program

to compile programming code for its platform. The answer to the client-side problem came from Sun Microsystems. Sun's Java language took a unique approach (see Figure 4.24). A programmer writes a program in Java and then partially compiles it into an intermediate form called *byte code*. This code is included with a Web page and sent to the client computer. On the client computer, a program called a *Java virtual machine (JVM)* converts the byte code into machine language compatible with the platform. Java virtual machines have been written for all the major platforms. JVMs are included in Netscape Communicator and may be downloaded for Windows/Intel platforms if they are not included in Microsoft's Internet Explorer. The advantage of this system is that the program embedded in the Web page works on any computer that also runs Netscape Communicator or has downloaded and installed the JVM for that platform. Microsoft has a competing product named *C#* (pronounced C sharp) that is designed to run on Windows platforms using the Internet Explorer (IE) browser. If you use IE and find that embedded programs in some Web pages do not work properly, you can download a Java virtual machine for your Windows platform to get them to work. If you use Netscape Communicator, some embedded programming intended for Windows systems may not work properly. Microsoft's version of a Java applet is *ActiveX*.

HTML has also been extended to make it more compatible with applets. The *Extensible Markup Language (XML)* allows programmers to attach tags that describe what the text is. For example, <firstName>John</firstName> identifies John as a particular type of data that can be sorted, filtered, or manipulated based on what type of data it is. Applets can manipulate the data on a Web page using this information.

Software is emerging that is designed to communicate between different types of software and provide an environment where programmers who are adept at different languages can work together. The two leading contenders are *Java 2 Platform Enterprise Edition (J2EE)*, which uses Java tools, and *Microsoft.NET*, which uses XML and *Simple Object Access Protocol (SOAP)*. Microsoft has a strategy for using the .NET environment that allows vendors to write programs in their favorite languages and then sell the use of them as services from links within Web pages or Office applications. For example, if you get an e-mail message from someone that is written in a foreign language, you could choose to have it translated into English for a fee by choosing a link from within the e-mail program. The J2EE environment is less proprietary and may be incorporated into a variety of organizational strategies.

WEB SERVER LANGUAGES

Applets and HTML run on the client software after a Web page has been delivered by the server. Web pages that allow the user to interact with a database on the server require more programming on the Web server side. Instead of simply serving up Web pages on demand, the server must record transactions in a database or assemble a custom Web page from a database. The standard method of handling requests for programmed actions on the server by applets within the Web page is called the *common gateway interface (CGI)*. Small programs called *scripts* reside on the server and are used by the applets within the Web page. Several languages are available for writing scripts, some of which are common on servers that run the UNIX or Linux operating system and some of which are common on Windows servers.

- *Perl* is used extensively on Web servers running UNIX or Linux. Programs written in Perl may be compiled for use on the Web server or partially compiled into byte code to be used by a JVM on the client's computer.

- *ECMAScript*, created by Netscape, is a standard script language like Perl. Netscape called it *JavaScript*, which was confusing because it was not developed by Sun; therefore, its name was changed to ECMAScript. It was standardized to work with Netscape and Internet Explorer under the auspices of the *European Computer Manufacturers Association (ECMA)*.

- *Jscript* is a script language from Microsoft that adheres to the ECMA standard for a script language.

- *TCL* is a script language developed by Sun Laboratories.

- *Rexx* is an IBM script language designed for ease of use by nonprogrammers.

- *Hypertext Preprocessor (PHP)* is an open-source software commonly used with Apache Web Server. It can be used to create custom Web pages from information in a database. Custom Web pages created by PHP have file extensions like .php, .php3, or .phtml.

- *VBScript* is a subset of the Visual Basic language used for writing scripts.

A customized Web page that is created upon request by a user is called an Active Server Page (ASP).

1. Look at source code in a browser. Start a browser, and open a Web page of your choice. Pick a word on the page. From the View menu, choose Source (Page Source in Netscape Communicator). The HTML code for that page is displayed. Choose Edit, Find, and look for the word you chose. Look to the left to find codes within angle brackets (<code>), and look to the right of the word for similar codes with a back-slash (<\code>). These pairs of codes control the appearance of the word you chose.

2. Look up registered file types in Windows. In Windows, start Windows Explorer and from the menu choose Tools, Folder Options, and then click the File Types tab. Scroll through the registered file types. If the wrong program starts when you double-click a file name, you can change that in this dialog box.

3. Turn on file extensions in Windows Explorer. Windows hides file extensions for registered file types and displays unknown extensions by default. You can force the display of all the file extensions by making a change in Windows Explorer. Start Windows Explorer and from the menu choose Tools, Folder Options, and then click the View tab. Deselect the "Hide extensions for known file types" option, and click OK. Use Windows Explorer to display a list of files. From the menu choose View, Details to show the file names with extensions.

TEST PREPARATION

The following section does not replace reading the text, nor does it contain all the information that will be tested. It is designed to provide examples and identify sections that need review.

summary by objective

CATEGORIES OF COMPUTER LANGUAGES

- **Match key terms such as source code, machine code, and compiler with their definitions:**
  - Source code—written by a programmer
  - Machine code—consists of binary numbers and is used by a processor
  - Compiler—converts source code into machine code
- **Name three early 3GLs still in use that used GOTO statements:**
  - FORTRAN
  - COBOL
  - BASIC
- **Identify the slang term for code written in languages that use GOTO statements—spaghetti code.**
- **Identify the programming solution to branching problems—structured programming using IF-THEN-ELSE or DO-WHILE statements.**
- **Identify the features of modular programming:**
  - Information hiding
  - Standardized input and output
  - Sharing and reusing
- **Identify the relationship between C and operating systems—C, a language that combines high-level programming features with the ability to use specific features of a processor, is used to write operating systems.**
- **Identify characteristics of a 4GL:**
  - Nonprocedural
  - Works with databases
  - Uses visual programming
  - Useful for novices and experts
  - interactive and multifunction programming environment
- **Give an example of a 4GL language—SQL.**
- **Identify definitions and examples of event-driven languages—events like clicking buttons activate parts of the code.**
- **Identify the characteristics of object-oriented programming:**
  - Objects have attributes and methods and are grouped in classes.
  - An object can inherit attributes and methods of its class.
  - Commands are called messages, and the ability to act on the message independently is called polymorphism
- **Identify languages that use OOP:**
  - C++
  - VB.NET
  - Smalltalk
  - Java
  - C#
- **Identify characteristics of a 5GL—all code is generated automatically and can be compiled by a 3GL compiler.**
- **Give an example of a 5GL language:**
  - Jbuilder
  - JDeveloper

APPLICATIONS

- **Identify what the acronym BIOS stands for—Basic Input/Output System.**
- **Identify the functions of BIOS—Boot up the computer and check components.**
- **Identify the functions of an operating system:**
  - Manage communication between applications and the processor
  - Manage storage systems
  - Manage peripherals
  - Provide tools for applications to use
- **Name four common operating systems:**
  - Windows
  - Mac OS
  - UNIX
  - Linux
- **Identify functions of server applications—find and deliver data or Web pages.**
- **Define GUI—graphical user interface.**
- **Name three IBM mainframe operating systems:**
  - MVS
  - S/390
  - Z/OS
- **Identify the characteristics of Linux—similar to UNIX but open source and free.**
- **Identify four productivity application suites:**
  - MS Office
  - Star Office
  - Corel WordPerfect Office
  - Lotus SmartSuite
- **Identify types of utility programs:**
  - File management
  - Disk maintenance
  - Antivirus
  - Viewing documents

LANGUAGES AND APPLICATIONS FOR THE INTERNET

- **Identify the relationships among Web applications, browsers, and operating systems—Web applications use browsers, which in turn use the operating system to display Web pages.**
- **Identify the relationships among Java, byte code, and Java virtual machine—Java is a programming language. Its programs are converted to byte code, which can be executed by a Java virtual machine on the client computer.**
- **Identify Microsoft applications that compete with Java—C# is a programming language, and ActiveX is similar to Java applets.**
- **Identify the role of CGI—The common gateway interface handles requests for scripts by Web pages and locates the scripts in a directory on the server.**
- **Identify at least four script languages:**
  - Perl
  - ECMAScript
  - Jscript
  - PHP
  - TCL
  - Rexx
  - VBScript
- **Identify two types of Web pages created by scripts in response to user input:**
  - Active Server Pages (ASPs)
  - Hypertext Preprocessor pages

true/false questions

1. ____ First-generation languages use hexadecimal numbers and command codes.

2. ____ BIOS is an operating system designed to work with medical research devices and programs.

3. ____ Script languages are simpler than most 3GLs.

4. ____ CGI is a script language.

5. ____ Fifth-generation languages may be compiled by 3GL or 4GL compilers.

multiple choice

1. Which of the following is not a characteristic of OOP?
   a) methods
   b) messages
   c) operations
   d) structured queries

2. Which of the following applications is the first to run when you turn on a computer?
   a) Microsoft Office
   b) operating system
   c) BIOS
   d) HTML

3. What term describes the development of programming that eliminated use of the GOTO branching method and replaced it with IF-THEN-ELSE statements?
   a) structured code
   b) procedural code
   c) spaghetti code
   d) logical synchronicity

4. Which of the following is a characteristic of object-oriented programming that is not a feature of event-driven programming?
   a) uses graphic elements
   b) polymorphism
   c) may be compiled by a 3GL compiler
   d) higher level than 2GL

5. Which of the following is not an operating system?
   a) MVS
   b) LINUX
   c) C++
   d) Mac OS X

completion

1. A programming method that reuses blocks of code using standardized inputs and outputs is _____ programming.

2. The _____ language was named in honor of an early programming pioneer and adopted by the military.

3. The first program a computer runs when it is turned on is the _____.

4. The _____ converts source code to machine code.

5. Reorganizing the data on a disk to place data from the same file in adjacent sectors is called _____ the disk.

Match each term with its definition.

_____ **1.** applets
_____ **2.** assembler
_____ **3.** attributes
_____ **4.** byte code
_____ **5.** C#
_____ **6.** class
_____ **7.** Common gateway interface (CGI)
_____ **8.** compiler
_____ **9.** drivers
_____ **10.** event
_____ **11.** event driven
_____ **12.** Extensible Markup Language (XML)
_____ **13.** information hiding
_____ **14.** Java
_____ **15.** Java virtual machine (JVM)
_____ **16.** Linux
_____ **17.** machine language
_____ **18.** message
_____ **19.** methods
_____ **20.** object-oriented programming (OOP)
_____ **21.** objects
_____ **22.** polymorphism
_____ **23.** scripts
_____ **24.** Structured Query Language (SQL)
_____ **25.** syntax

a. a 2GL language one step higher than machine language

b. a fourth-generation language that is used for extracting specific sets of data from a database

c. a group of objects with common attributes and methods

d. a partially compiled program that can be run by a Java virtual machine

e. a program on a Web server that handles requests for scripts

f. a program that converts higher-level programs into machine language

g. an action by the user such as clicking a button on the screen

h. characteristic of modular programming

i. characteristic of object-oriented program in which objects can accomplish a stated message independently

j. characteristics of an object

k. compiles byte code for execution on a particular platform

l. derivative of UNIX that is free and open source

m. instruction in object-oriented programming

n. language that is in written in binary code that a computer processor can interpret directly

o. language that uses byte code and a virtual machine to create interactive Web pages

p. method of attaching additional information to text or pictures on a Web page

q. Microsoft's version of Java

r. nonprocedural method that uses attributes, methods, classes, and messages

s. programming entity with attributes and methods that belongs to a class

t. characteristic of programs that are executed when the user chooses an option

u. rules for a software language that must be followed when writing code

v. sets of instructions on how to accomplish a task in OOP

w. short programs that reside on the Web server that are used with Web pages

x. small application programs included with Web pages

y. small programs that provide communication instructions between a peripheral and the operating system

beyond the facts

Factual knowledge provides the basis for higher levels of learning. In the following sections, you work with the concepts and facts presented in the chapter to develop critical-thinking and problem-solving skills. You practice research, analysis, and communication and become aware of diversity issues while exploring the impact of computer technology on career choices, the workplace, social interactions, and home life. The Leadership section helps you identify ways in which you can lead others in organizing and implementing projects that meet worthwhile community needs. In the Lifelong Learning exercise, you build a set of learning resources that you can use after this course to continue learning.

objectives for beyond the facts

END OF CHAPTER EXERCISES	Achievement of the objectives for the end-of-chapter exercises requires evaluation of documents, class discussions, or presentations.
Critical Thinking–Research	Describe how BIOS uses beep codes to solve hardware problems.
Problem Solving	1) Use Help to learn about BIOS beep codes and how they are used to troubleshoot a problem 2) Try to find the beep code that indicates an unplugged keyboard on your computer. 3) Communicate the experience to the class.
Anticipating Career Challenges and Opportunities	Demonstrate the following skills: 1) Teamwork: coordinate research 2) Research: conduct interviews, investigate programming languages used, and determine career opportunities as a programmer 3) Diversity: interview programmers with different backgrounds 4) Analysis: analyze the benefits of a career in programming and the aptitudes, education, and certifications that are required to be successful 5) Communication: communicate the results in writing or by public presentation
Impact on the Workplace	Demonstrate the following skills: 1) Teamwork: coordinate research on use of interactive Web pages in the workplace with other students 2) Research: identify use of interactive Web pages on your company's Web site by observation and interviews 3) Analysis: form an opinion about how interactive Web pages are used in your organization and whether they could be designed better 4) Communication: communicate the results in writing or by public presentation
Impact on Social Interactions	Demonstrate the following skills: 1) Teamwork: allocate tasks for research 2) Research: find Web sites and blogs related to women in the programming professions 3) Diversity: see how the cultures in which Augusta Byron and Grace Hopper found themselves compare with today's society 4) Analysis: based on your research, form an opinion about the influence of culture on women's choices to become programmers 5) Communication: communicate the results in writing or by public presentation
Impact on Home Life	Demonstrate the following skills: 1) Teamwork: work with classmates 2) Research and diversity: find out how low-cost computers compare to others on the market and what free software runs on them for home use by family members of different ages. 3) Analysis: form an opinion based on your experience 4) Communication: communicate the results in writing or by public presentation
Leadership	Describe a plan to lead a group of people toward a worthy goal. In this case, research the availability of free software that could be used by nonprofit groups to lower their costs.
Lifelong Learning	Identify three or more online resources that may be used to learn more about the topics introduced in this chapter.

critical thinking–research

Some programmers hide small programs called Easter eggs in the applications they write, even though it could cost them their jobs if they are discovered. Find a few of them, and read some articles about them. Form an opinion about why programmers do this.

1. **Teamwork**—Join one to three other students. Decide how to divide up the work. Possible divisions could be: eggs in operating systems, eggs in hardware, eggs in games, and eggs in applications; or search newsgroups using Google's Groups feature, search newspapers from other countries for articles, and search the library's database of journals for articles.

2. **Research**—Use a Web browser and go to the companion Web site at **http://www.prenhall. com/preston**. Follow the links by clicking on the Web addresses that are highlighted and underlined. Read the articles about Easter eggs to familiarize yourself with the issue. Use a search engine to look for more information about Easter eggs. Make a list of relevant sources you find that you may want to reference later. Include the title of the page or article, the name of the organization responsible for the Web page, the

date the page or article was written, and the Web address. You may also go to the library and look up books, articles, and news reports that are relevant to this topic. Many libraries have the full text of articles and news reports online in proprietary databases that are not available to the public.

3. **Diversity issues**—Consider how your friends and classmates react to the idea of Easter eggs. Do you observe any differences by gender or culture?

4. **Analysis**—Write an essay that explains what Easter eggs are, and give some examples. Form and express an opinion about why programmers create them. Go beyond simple reporting of the facts. Support your opinion with references to the articles you read. Ask your instructor for guidance regarding the required length of the essay.

5. **Communication**—Prepare a presentation in which you present your opinion and supporting facts to the class. Depending on your computer skill, you could demonstrate some Easter eggs to the class.

problem solving

If the BIOS discovers a problem during start-up, it displays a message on the screen describing the problem. However, if the problem occurs before the video drivers are loaded, the BIOS cannot display an error message. To give you some idea of what may be wrong, the BIOS can use the small speaker inside the system unit to indicate the problem with beep codes, which are a series of beeps and silences. These codes vary from one BIOS program to another. Find out what BIOS you have and what some of the beep codes mean.

1. **Search for help on the topic**—If you use Windows, click Start, Programs, Accessories, System Tools, System Information to find out what BIOS you have. Use your Web browser and a search engine to find the beep codes for your BIOS.

2. **Read the instructions and try it**—Shut down your computer, and unplug the keyboard. Turn on the computer, and listen for a beep code.

Removing the keyboard may or may not produce a beep code, depending on your BIOS. Other problems that produce beep codes are too serious to attempt to simulate. Shut down your computer using your mouse, reconnect the keyboard, and start the computer again.

3. **Troubleshoot**—Make a copy of the beep codes for your computer's BIOS, and print them out. Save the printout in a location where you can find it. If your computer fails to start in the future, one of your circuit boards may be loose, or your motherboard could have a serious problem. If that ever happens, listen for a beep code to find out if it is a simple problem like an unplugged keyboard or something that may require replacement of the whole system unit.

4. **Communicate**—Present your findings to the class. Provide tips to help classmates determine whether they have a simple or severe problem.

anticipating career challenges and opportunities

Companies who utilize large databases and mainframe computers to track customer, inventory, or accounting records often employ programmers to keep the software current, write new programs for specific tasks, or troubleshoot existing programs. Explore the opportunities for a career in programming.

1. **Teamwork**—Join one or two other students who have similar career plans. Decide how to divide up the work. Possible divisions could be: design an interview questionnaire, interview programmers at your company or school, and investigate coursework available.

2. **Research**—Use a Web browser to research the programming languages that are in current use. Look at a local newspaper and on the Internet to determine the programmer skills that are in demand, the pay ranges, the career paths, and the educational and certification requirements to get and retain a job. Interview programmers at your company or school, and find out what programming languages they use. Find out if the skills of the programming staff affect the decision-making process when new software packages are purchased. If possible, find out your company or school's pay ranges for programmers, career path, and educational requirements. Determine the courses that are available in your area for learning programming languages and what kind of certification might be required. Talk with your school counseling staff to learn if your school administers aptitude tests to screen for basic skills that are well suited to programming.

3. **Diversity issues**—Look at the diversity of the staff of programmers and other computer technicians at your company or school. If possible, interview programmers with different backgrounds to determine what led them to a career in programming. Do you see a cultural bias here? Find out what they like and dislike about their jobs, what they find interesting, and what they find tedious.

4. **Analysis**—Write an essay that describes the types of programming jobs that are available in your area. Include an analysis of career opportunities, career paths, pay rates, skill sets required, and ongoing educational expectations. Form and express an opinion about the future of a career in programming. Go beyond simple reporting of the facts. Support your opinion with references to the articles you read or interviews you conducted. Ask your instructor for guidance regarding the required length of the essay.

5. **Communication**—Prepare a presentation in which you present your opinion and supporting facts to the class. Depending on your computer skill, you could give the presentation using a program like PowerPoint and save it as a Web page, or you could prepare a paper handout with your Web references for use while you talk to the class.

impact on the workplace

How do interactive Web pages with scripting affect your job?

1. **Teamwork**—Join one or two other students who work where you do or in a similar type of business or organization. Decide how to divide up the work. Possible divisions could be: retraining programmers to work with Java or C#, retraining programmers to think in terms of object-oriented programming instead of procedural programming, and applets that could enhance your company's Web page.

2. **Research**—Ask the computer information systems manager of your company what languages your programmers use. Ask whether they use OOP. Look at your company's Web site. Does it use interactive Web pages? Interview programmers about how they create interactive pages.

3. **Analysis**—Write an essay that describes how OOP and script languages are used at your company. Form and express an opinion about the impact of applets on your company's Web page. Support your opinion with your observations. Ask your instructor for guidance regarding the required length of the essay.

4. **Communication**—Prepare a presentation in which you present your opinion and the results of your observations. If your company's Web page uses applets, demonstrate it to the class. You could also prepare a paper handout with data for use while you talk to the class.

impact on social interactions

Programming is a growth area for well-paid jobs. Find out if women are going into this field in numbers proportional to men. Some of the pioneers of programming included women such as Augusta Ada Byron and Grace Hopper. How did the cultures in which they grew up differ from that of the United States today, and did it support or discourage their career choice?

1. **Teamwork**—Join two or three other students to research this topic. Decide how to divide up the work. Possible divisions could be along the lines of the research questions below.

2. **Research**—Find Web pages, discussions, and technical descriptions on the following topics:
   - What percentage of programmers are women?
   - What were the circumstances of Augusta Ada Byron's life that helped or hindered her career as the first programmer?
   - What were the circumstances of Grace Hopper's life that helped or hindered her career as a programmer?

3. **Diversity issues**—Ask women in your class or other women you know if they considered computer programming as a career. Ask if they were encouraged or discouraged from considering it. Look for blogs by female programmers in which they talk about being a female in this profession.

4. **Analysis**—Write an essay that describes how women you know were encouraged or discouraged from pursuing programming as a career. Compare their environments with those of Augusta Byron and Grace Hopper. Form and express an opinion about the comparison. Support your opinion based on research and observation. Ask your instructor for guidance regarding the required length of the essay.

5. **Communication**—Prepare a presentation in which you present your opinion and the results of your observations. Prepare a handout of the information you compiled. If you have the computer skill, create a Web page with this information, and post it to a server.

impact on home life

Wal-Mart has offered a desktop computer, without monitor, that uses the Linux operating system and includes the Mozilla Web browser and e-mail client for under $200. Would you buy this low-cost computer with Linux and use it in your home? Would your favorite programs work, or could you replace them with equivalent applications?

1. **Teamwork**—Join one or two other students who have an interest in buying a low-cost computer for home use. Decide how to divide up the work. Possible divisions could be: What hardware components are in the PC, and how do they compare in quality and power with other PCs? What software do you use at home, and does it run on Linux? What free programs are available that run on Linux and do the same things as the software you run now?

2. **Research**—Use a Web browser and search for articles on Linux for home use. Use key word phrases like "home office" and key words like "Linux." Use the Groups and News options in search engines like Google. Make a list of relevant sources that you may want to reference later. Include the title of the page or article, the name of the organization responsible for the Web page, the date the page or article was written, and the Web address. You may also go to the library and look up books, articles, and news reports that are relevant to this topic. Many libraries have the full text of articles and news reports online in proprietary databases that are not available to the public.

3. **Diversity issues**—Are there many children's games or entertainment programs that run on Linux?

4. **Analysis**—Write an essay that summarizes the literature on the subject. Form and express an opinion on how the articles written on the subject relate to what you would do. Support your opinion based on research and observation. Ask your instructor for guidance regarding the required length of the essay.

5. **Communication**—Prepare a presentation in which you present your opinion and the results of your observations. Prepare a handout of the information you compiled. If you have the computer skill, create a Web page with this information, and post it to a server.

leadership

Your school, church, or local nonprofit organization could save considerable money if low-cost or free software were available that could do the job of software they pay for now. Examine a local nonprofit group and the software they use; then gather information on free alternatives.

1. **Vision**—Write a vision statement that describes what you want your group to achieve. It should motivate people to volunteer to help.

2. **Research**—Choose a local group that uses computers that may be faced with increased fees for software. If another group of students in your class is working on the impact of Microsoft's .NET strategy, ask them for references to determine the cost of licensing software from Microsoft. Determine the software used by the group, and determine whether free software exists that uses the same file formats and would require minimal training to switch to. Determine whether the free software runs on Windows, Mac OS, or Linux.

3. **Plan of Action**—Write a simple plan of action. Test the plan by following it yourself on a small scale. Download and try some of the free software that could replace software used by the organization.

4. **Analysis**—Write up an analysis of what you learned by testing your plan.

5. **Communication**—Present your plan to the class. Describe what you learned by testing your plan and how you think it could be expanded if others joined you. Share your vision statement, and try to inspire others to join you in your worthwhile effort.

lifelong learning

Add links to your browser's favorites list.

1. Start your Web browser, and open the list of favorite sites. Create a folder named Software.

2. Go to the companion Web page for this chapter at **http://www.prenhall.com/preston**, and select one of the Web links on software that you found useful.

3. Add this link to your browser's favorites list in the Software folder.

4. Repeat this process for other links in the companion Web page for this chapter, and add them to the appropriate folders.

Add learning goals to your journal.

1. Identify areas in which you feel you know the least. List three specific topics related to this chapter that you would like to learn more about in the future.

2. You will add to this journal after each chapter to compile a personal list of references and topics for future study.

chapter 5

Ethical Use of Computers

Computers are seldom used in isolation. We use them to collaborate and interact with people socially and professionally. Our behavior affects those people, and their behavior affects us. Societies have developed rules of behavior that allow them to function and help define their values. Those rules must be interpreted and applied to the use of computers. This is particularly important because computers allow us to interact with many people in a variety of cultures. In this chapter, you learn about the laws that apply to computer use, codes of conduct developed by organizations, and guidelines for making personal decisions. You then look at how these laws, codes, and guidelines apply to situations at school, at work, in social interactions, and at home. In the next chapter, you apply this knowledge to the issues of privacy and security.

WHY DO I NEED TO KNOW THIS?

Behavior that is accepted among a group of friends or acquaintances might result in a failed course or expulsion from college. Practices allowed in the classroom may get you fired from a job at a corporation or barred from your profession. You need to know what behaviors violate the laws of the country, and you need to know what types of behavior are encouraged and what behaviors are prohibited by each group of which you are a member. You also need to consider and refine your own code of behavior to help you make difficult choices when they arise.

LAWS, CODES OF ETHICAL CONDUCT, AND PERSONAL ETHICS

Philosophy is the critical analysis of fundamental assumptions or beliefs. From this analysis, standards of right and wrong behavior are derived. *Moral behavior* is concerned with making judgments about conforming to standards of right and wrong. For example, being loyal to friends and obeying the law are both moral behaviors. When two moral behaviors conflict, such as in the case where a friend is doing something illegal, we have a *moral dilemma*. To determine how to resolve a moral dilemma in the context of our job, organization, or profession, we use *ethical principles*. Most companies, colleges, and professional societies have a formal *code of ethics* that describes ethical behavior in that group. Societies formalize certain codes of behavior as *laws*, which often include penalties that society imposes through courts and a police force.

FIGURE 5.1

Societies develop laws over time to protect the rights of individuals and limit some types of behavior.

In the following sections, you learn about some of the laws that govern the use of computers and then look at codes of ethical behavior that are representative of several types of organizations. You also examine and discuss ethical codes for personal behavior related to computer use.

LAWS
The legal system has evolved to settle disputes and protect the rights of groups and individuals (see Figure 5.1). If someone violates a law, the individual or the organization he or she works for may be subject to severe penalties. The following sections use U.S. laws as examples. See the companion Web site at **www.prenhall.com/preston** for references to U.S. laws and similar laws from other countries and the World Intellectual Property Organization. Laws that relate to the ethical use of computers may be grouped into four categories—intellectual property rights, decency, taxation, and criminal behavior. Decency laws will be discussed in the next chapter and taxation laws will be considered from a voter's perspective.

VOTER ISSUES

DISCUSSION

Have you used Amazon's 1-Click ordering system? Do you think it is a unique business method that deserves a patent?

Intellectual Property Rights

Many people dream of becoming rich and famous by writing a best-selling novel, popular song, or computer game. Some dream of inventing a new device and starting a successful company. They work many hours on unsuccessful attempts and fail many times, but they continue because of the hope that one day they will get it right and hit it big. This dream is possible because our society protects these people with laws that give them rights to their work and the money they can earn from it. These rights are protected by ***intellectual property laws***.

Copyright ***Copyright*** is the legal right of the artist, author, composer, or playwright to exclusive publication and sale of artistic, literary, musical, or dramatic work. A copyright may belong to an employer if the work was done as part of person's job or if a person is hired to create the work, which is known as a ***work for hire***.

For example, if someone writes song lyrics, someone else cannot simply use those lyrics without permission, and if they do so, they may be sued for whatever money they made from their version of the song.

If you buy a print of a painting, some of the purchase price goes to the artist. You may hang the print wherever you like, but you do not have the right to make copies of the print to give away to your friends or to sell. When you buy a copy of a computer program, you do not buy the original program; you buy the right to use a copy of it. Just like in the case of the print, you do not have the right to make copies to give to your friends or to sell. When you install a copy of the software, you must agree to the ***end user license agreement (EULA)***, which is a legal agreement between the manufacturer of the software and the purchaser that explains rights and limitations (see Figure 5.2). Some agreements allow you to install the software on two

FIGURE 5.2

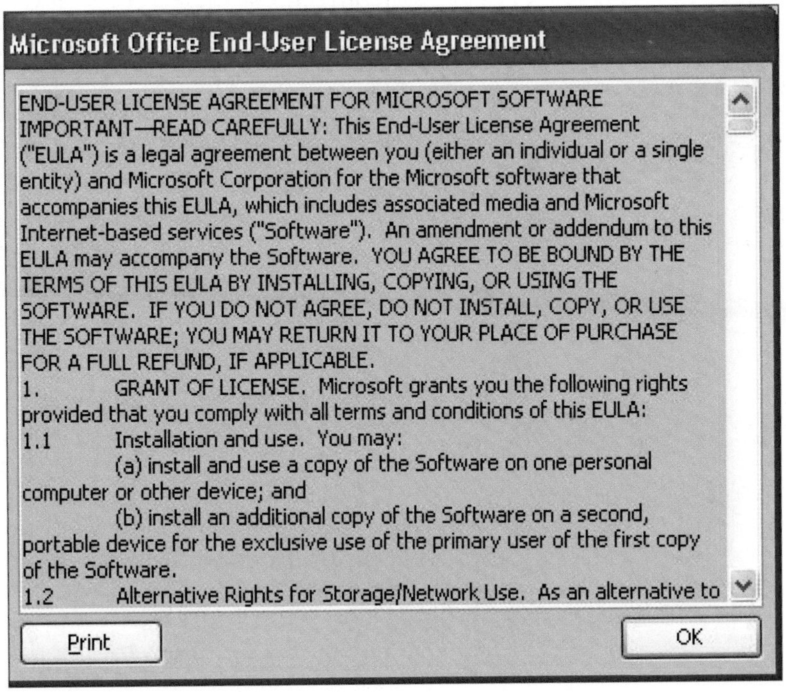
Microsoft Office End-User License Agreement

END-USER LICENSE AGREEMENT FOR MICROSOFT SOFTWARE
IMPORTANT—READ CAREFULLY: This End-User License Agreement ("EULA") is a legal agreement between you (either an individual or a single entity) and Microsoft Corporation for the Microsoft software that accompanies this EULA, which includes associated media and Microsoft Internet-based services ("Software"). An amendment or addendum to this EULA may accompany the Software. YOU AGREE TO BE BOUND BY THE TERMS OF THIS EULA BY INSTALLING, COPYING, OR USING THE SOFTWARE. IF YOU DO NOT AGREE, DO NOT INSTALL, COPY, OR USE THE SOFTWARE; YOU MAY RETURN IT TO YOUR PLACE OF PURCHASE FOR A FULL REFUND, IF APPLICABLE.
1. GRANT OF LICENSE. Microsoft grants you the following rights provided that you comply with all terms and conditions of this EULA:
1.1 Installation and use. You may:
(a) install and use a copy of the Software on one personal computer or other device; and
(b) install an additional copy of the Software on a second, portable device for the exclusive use of the primary user of the first copy of the Software.
1.2 Alternative Rights for Storage/Network Use. As an alternative to

Print OK

Microsoft's end user license agreement

computers for use at work and home with the understanding that only one copy will be used at a time. Organizations may purchase **site licenses** that allow the organization to install copies on any computer they choose within the organization as long as the total number does not exceed the agreed-upon quantity.

If no part of a copyrighted work could be reproduced without permission of the author or artist, it would be difficult to comment on it in a newspaper or teach students about it in a classroom. Parts of a copyrighted work may be reproduced for the purpose of criticism, comment, news reporting, teaching, scholarship, or research without violating the copyright. This policy is called **fair use**, and its application requires judgment. The law provides the following points to consider when determining whether this exception to the copyright protection is allowed:

- the purpose and character of the use, including whether such use is of a commercial nature or is for nonprofit educational purposes
- the nature of the copyrighted work
- the amount and substantiality of the portion used in relation to the copyrighted work as a whole
- the effect of the use upon the potential market for or value of the copyrighted work

If authors of printed works wish to make it clear that they claim a copyright, they include a notice. Copyright notices include the symbol © or the word Copyright, the year, and the name of the copyright owner—for example, © 2004 John Doe. Works published before January 1, 1978, that do not have a valid copyright notice may be considered to be in the public domain. Work published after 1978 without this type of notice may still be copyrighted, but when you see this notice, you know specifically that the owner of the copyright does not want it used without permission beyond the limits of fair use. Copyright was intended to protect the work during the lifetime of the author or artist. Copyright expires after 95 years (see the companion Web site for links to the U.S. Copyright Office for details).

Work that is in the **public domain** is not copyrighted and may be duplicated and freely distributed. All work authored by the federal government is in the public domain. Works may also be in the public domain if the copyright has expired.

Sometimes the owners of copyrighted software do not charge for its use. This type of software is called **freeware**. Freeware may be copied and distributed, but it may not be revised or sold to a third party. The compiled machine code is usually distributed instead of the source code.

Some freeware is also available as source code, known as open-source software. Linux, an operating system similar to UNIX, is open-source freeware. People around the world write extensions and improvements to the software. They submit their code to a coordinating group that coordinates and issues revisions of the software. The open-source initiative has members worldwide who share resources and work together on projects (see Figure 5.3).

Trademark   A **trademark** is a name or symbol used to identify a product (see Figure 5.4). Companies spend a great deal of money on advertising to make a trademark familiar to the public. People are most familiar with trademarks that are symbols or product names like Coca-Cola®. If someone

FIGURE 5.3

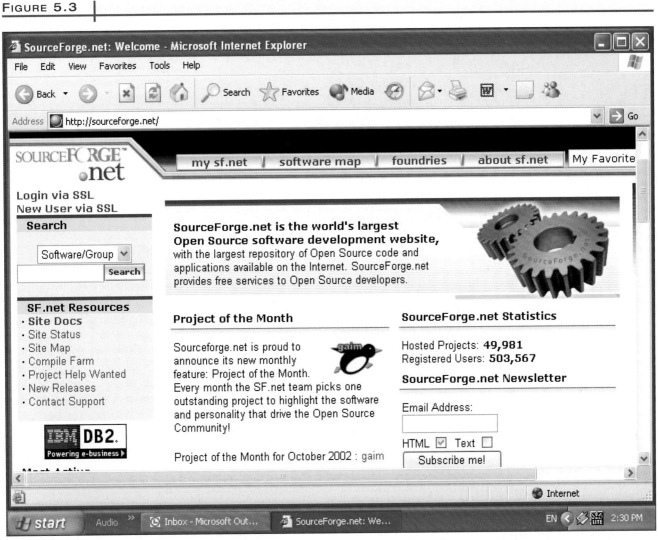

Open-source software provides a valuable alternative to typical commercial software.

FIGURE 5.4

Trademarks are easily recognized symbols or logos.

claims that name or symbol is a trademark, they include the abbreviation TM. If the trademark is officially recognized and registered by the U.S. Patent and Trademark Office, the name or symbol has the ® symbol. Many established companies did not immediately recognize the importance of reserving domain names on the Internet that matched their company or product names. In some cases, competitors paid for rights to use those domain names and diverted visitors to the site to other products. Some people simply paid the small registration fee and then offered to resell the domain name to the company for a large fee. Attempting to profit from someone else's trademark is called *cybersquatting*. This practice was outlawed by the Anticybersquatting Consumer Protection Act of 1999.

Patents *Patents* are granted to protect the rights of the inventor of a physical device. In July 1998, the U.S. courts affirmed that business method–related software may be patented, as well. In 1999, in a very controversial move, Amazon, an online book retail company, applied for and received a patent on its 1-Click ordering business method that many consider too obvious to be patented. However, the patent has survived competitor's challenges. The U.S. Patent Office has improved the review process for this type of patent in an effort to keep up with emerging technology. If a business method–related software is patented, programmers must obtain permission to use the method (see the companion Web site at **http://www.prenhall.com/preston** for more information).

Computer Crime

Computers may be involved in various types of illegal behavior, such as theft and fraud, that have been around for a long time; but the power of a computer, its Internet connection, and user anonymity give criminals new tools. Protecting yourself from criminals who use computers is discussed in the next chapter, but you should be aware that the ability of computers and users' apparent anonymity may tempt people who would not normally break the law to commit illegal acts. The areas described below represent types of illegal behavior that have increased among otherwise law-abiding people due to the nature of computers.

Communication over the Internet may appear to be anonymous. Users can elect to use a false name when they interact on the Internet, and some are tempted by the cloak of anonymity to be inconsiderate or even insulting if they feel that the object of their comments cannot retaliate because their identity is unknown. This sense of anonymity can lead to criminal behavior such as cyberstalking or cybersmearing. *Cyberstalking* includes the use of the Internet, e-mail, and chat rooms to harass someone. *Cybersmearing* is a campaign of false information used to ruin the reputation of a person or company. Existing laws that apply to stalking and slander apply to the Internet, and law enforcement authorities may obtain a user's identity with a court order. *Identity theft* involves obtaining key pieces of information to impersonate someone, to gain access to bank accounts, or to request expensive services in their name. Some people who go through disputed divorces or breakups are tempted to use their knowledge of the other person's identification numbers and accounts to harm them or take money they think belongs to them.

Many state and local governments have laws that regulate activities like retail sales and gambling. They license establishments and practitioners to protect the consumer, and they often require the establishment to collect taxes on their activities. However, the Internet makes it easy to do business anywhere. In some cases, this violates state and local laws because the user avoids paying required taxes. For example, most states restrict gambling to establishments that are closely regulated and heavily taxed. The Internet makes it possible to gamble online in other countries without paying taxes.

Computers are also very good at making high-quality digital copies and sharing them electronically. This makes it easy to violate copyright laws and license agreements. The prospect of getting free music, videos, and software without paying royalties to the authors and artists is attractive to many people. This illegal behavior is called software *piracy* (see Figure 5.5).

Criminal behavior that involves the use of computers may be easy to undertake and hard for law enforcement officials to detect, but it is still illegal and unethical. The debate on how to adapt our laws and enforcement methods to computer capabilities is an important one that will reflect the ethics of our society.

ORGANIZATIONAL CODES OF ETHICS

Most organizations provide a code of ethics that members are expected to follow. If you are a member of a group such as a college, business, or profes-

FIGURE 5.5

The Software Publisher's Association (SPA) raises awareness of software piracy.

If you spent two years creating a computer game or other piece of software and offered it for sale, how would you feel if it became popular but you earned very little in royalties due to copying?

Does not having enough money to buy software or music justify using a copy because the author would not have made a sale anyway?

If a machine were invented that could be placed next to a new car and convert scrap metal into an exact copy of the car, would it be ethical to use it? Who is harmed? Does it violate the rights of the designer or manufacturer?

sional organization, you should know what behavior is expected of you as a member. Refer to the companion Web site at **http://www.prenhall.com/preston** for links to examples.

Colleges

Schools provide students with a code of conduct that describes prohibited behaviors. These codes reflect the ethical standards of the school, and chief among them is a standard for academic honesty (see links to codes of conduct on the companion Web site at **http://www.prenhall.com/preston**). An important function of higher education is to develop critical-thinking and analysis skills in students, as well as to impart factual knowledge. This process often takes the form of researching and writing papers or taking tests. Trying to shortcut this process by representing someone else's research, analysis, or writing as your own is called *plagiarism* and is specifically disallowed. Other acts designed to achieve higher grades than are deserved are generally known as *cheating*. In some institutions, it is considered cheating to submit the same paper for two different classes, even if you wrote the paper yourself. In other institutions, it is considered cheating simply to know that someone else has done this and not report it. Computers facilitate plagiarism and cheating because it is very easy to copy text and share it with others.

Because colleges have a concentration of computers, they often have specific codes of conduct for computer use that prohibit peer-to-peer file sharing of music and videos using campus networks. They also prohibit installing unlicensed software on school computers.

If you plan to write software, a children's story, or a musical score using the school's computers, you should check to see whether the college claims ownership of your work. Most colleges make their codes of conduct available online or in the college catalog.

Companies

Companies have codes of conduct that reflect their priorities. They do not want their employees to engage in illegal activities for which the company could be sued. Fines for installing unlicensed copies of software can be up to $10,000 per computer. To protect themselves, most companies make such illegal activity grounds for dismissal. Companies also do not want employees using company time to do personal work, especially if it ties up the company's computer resources. Consequently, they may consider it ethical to monitor employee e-mail and computer use. They may also search an employee's hard disk for unlicensed software. Companies are also concerned with sexual harassment lawsuits that can arise from employees using Internet connections to view sexually explicit images in the workplace where they may be seen by other employees. The company's code of conduct and its computer use policy are usually available from the human resources department.

Computer Professionals

If you decide to become a computer professional, you will learn how to use computers more effectively than most people. With that ability comes a responsibility to use that knowledge ethically. Companies who hire professionals expect a high level of ethical behavior in safeguarding a company's secrets and the integrity of their computer systems. Computer professionals specifically do not write programs intended to do harm, such as computer viruses (see the link to the ACM code of ethics on the companion Web site at **http://www.prenhall.com/preston**).

Chat Groups

You may join a group like a chat group or a role-playing game for only a short time, but it is still important to be familiar with the group's code of conduct. Most of its items deal with polite behavior, whereas some are specific to the group. If you are new to a group, other members will expect you to read the frequently asked questions (FAQ) so you do not waste other members' time by asking questions they have already answered for other new members.

PERSONAL ETHICS

It is important to know what laws and codes of ethics apply within a specific group or context, such as your company, your school, or the laws of your country. An external group does not always define standards of behavior, however. As you encounter decisions, you will find some choices are easy to make, whereas others are difficult, such as the moral dilemma of what to do if you find a friend is doing something illegal. To deal with moral dilemmas, you must develop your own personal ethics. This is easier if you choose *ethical principles*, which are basic rules that may be applied to specific situations. Philosophers have debated the issue of ethical principles for centuries, and they have produced a number of different sets of principles from which you can choose. Here are a few that may be applied to the ethical use of computers, as well as to many other areas of your life (see Figure 5.6).

These three principles help you determine whether an act is ethical.

> *If everyone acted the same way, society as a whole would benefit.* This principle is useful when deciding issues related to software piracy. If everyone used music, video, or software without paying royalties, there would be far fewer new creative works.

> *Do not treat people as a means to an end.* This principle is useful for choosing your behavior in chat rooms or other types of interaction. Being cruel to or abusive of others to make yourself feel more important would be unethical according to this principle.

FIGURE 5.6

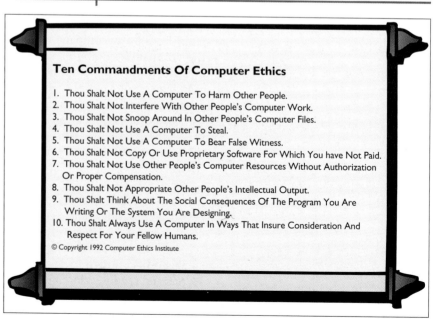

The Computer Ethics Institute provides a simple list of commandments.

> *An impartial observer would judge that you have been fair to all parties concerned.* Applying this principle helps you look at a decision from several points of view and consider the effect on all parties.

Another approach is to apply the principle of respect.

> *Respect yourself*—Do not do anything you would be ashamed of, even if others do not know your true identity. Do not give out your user accounts and passwords to people who may use them in a way that harms your reputation.

> *Respect others*—Do not use more than your share of computer resources. Leave laboratory computers in good working condition.

> *Respect your school*—Do not use computers to cheat or plagiarize the work of others. Do not use school computers to perform illegal acts that will get your school into trouble or cause it embarrassment. Your school's reputation for integrity adds value to your degree.

> *Respect your company and your profession*—Do not use your company's computers in ways that may embarrass the company or cause it legal problems. Conduct yourself in a way that makes you and others proud to be associated with your company and your profession. Give good value for the pay you receive.

You can also ask yourself questions on how others would view your actions if they knew about them.

> Would you be proud to tell your friends, neighbors, and parents about your decision or read about it in the local paper?

> If your action involves your place of employment, would your boss or the company's customers agree with what you have done?

> If the people affected by your decision knew all the details, would they think they had been treated fairly?

If you are a computer professional, you may ask yourself these questions:

> Did you provide the high level of skill and knowledge expected of someone in your profession?

> Did you respect the customer's privacy? Would the customer be angry to know what you have said about his or her company?

> Did you take reasonable steps to safeguard the customer's secrets and the integrity of the customer's computer system?

mastering
technology

- Read several end user license agreements (EULAs). During installation of most software, a window appears that requires users to agree to the EULA before installation can proceed. Many people do not take the time to read the contract they are entering into. You can find a copy of the EULA on the company's Web site or within the software itself. To read various sections of Microsoft's EULA, open a Microsoft application program like Microsoft Word and search for EULA in the Help menu. If you use Word 2002, choose Help, then click the Contents tab, select End-user license agreement (Retail), and click Questions about the End-user license agreement. Click Can I make a second copy for my portable computer?

- Read the content of this dialog box and answer the question, "If I buy an upgrade, can I give away my old version to a friend?"

In the following sections, we examine how laws, organizational codes of conduct, and personal ethics apply to specific computer-related situations at school, at work, socially, and at home. The author is not a lawyer, and discussion of legal issues in this chapter should not be construed as legal advice. If you decide to take legal action based on any of the items discussed in this book, you should seek professional legal counsel.

SCHOOL

A college education culminates in a degree that represents to the world that the holder of the degree has a mastery of required facts and writing skills and is also capable of critical thinking, analysis, and cogent argument. These skills are developed through a process of study, reading, discourse, and writing papers that are reviewed and corrected by qualified faculty. Bypassing this process by substituting the finished work of another results in the granting of a degree to someone who has not developed these skills, but who has instead developed skills of deceit and dishonesty. When the degree has been obtained under false pretenses, presenting oneself as a legitimate graduate who has the skills and morals of an educated person is to commit fraud upon the public and future employers.

College Papers

Academic writing at the undergraduate level is a process that seeks to acquaint students with research in a subject and analysis by authorities in the field. Students may compare differing opinions of experts to develop their own analytical and argumentative skills. For research papers, students begin by acquainting themselves with the facts and then read analysis and opinion articles. When writing a paper on the research subject, the student must provide sources as citations in the text, footnotes, or endnotes. Any quotations must be within quotation marks or in a block of indented single-spaced text. The rest of the paper must be the student's own original writing and thinking. Learning to write well takes time and practice. You will find there is no easy shortcut, but once attained, the skill will be yours for a lifetime.

Some students attempt to bypass the process by buying research papers online. Papers on common subjects are available for a fee of about $9 per page, or writers can be hired to write a customized paper for about $19 a page. These services claim to provide the paper as an example that you can use when you write your own paper; however, it is not credible that students would spend that much money for an example. It is important to recognize that the purpose of the exercise is not to provide the professor with another student paper to grade, but to build skills within the student. Buying a paper written by someone else and then representing it as your own work is plagiarism. Plagiarism is not an illegal act, but it is prohibited by the code of conduct of all accredited academic institutions and may be cause for failing a course or dismissal from the school. If you consider the principles for personal ethics, this act fails several tests:

❱ If all students did this, a degree would be worthless.

❱ Having a professor take the time to give advice on improving the content or style of a paper that you did not write is using that profes-

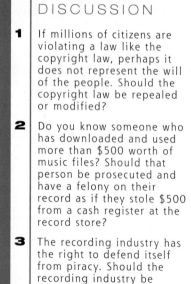

VOTER ISSUES

DISCUSSION

1 If millions of citizens are violating a law like the copyright law, perhaps it does not represent the will of the people. Should the copyright law be repealed or modified?

2 Do you know someone who has downloaded and used more than $500 worth of music files? Should that person be prosecuted and have a felony on their record as if they stole $500 from a cash register at the record store?

3 The recording industry has the right to defend itself from piracy. Should the recording industry be allowed to place viruslike code in its music files that allows it to trace a file if it is copied and transmitted over the Internet?

sor as a means to an end. An impartial observer would not consider that you have acted fairly.

❭ The act does not show respect for yourself, others, or your school.

❭ It is unlikely you would want your parents and neighbors to know about it.

Honor Codes

Some schools rely on students to police themselves. They have an *honor code* that students sign in which the students pledge to behave according to a specific code of conduct. Some honor codes stipulate that students are expected to report other students who break the code, and there is often a student disciplinary committee that decides individual cases.

Vetting

Acts of academic dishonesty committed in college can affect a person's career or tarnish his or her later achievements. If you ever run for office, request a security clearance, or become famous, your background may be investigated for clues to your character. This process is called *vetting*. A famous example is the case of Senator Joe Biden, who was seeking the Democratic presidential nomination in 1987. He was accused of plagiarizing parts of his speeches from a British politician, Neil Kinnock, and from Robert Kennedy. His candidacy might have survived this charge if he had blamed his speechwriters, but it was discovered that he received a failing grade for plagiarism in a law school course 20 years earlier. The disciplinary action for plagiarism in college persuaded the public that the current charges were true. His campaign collapsed, and he withdrew from the race (see the companion Web site). Senator Biden was reelected to his Senate seat and remains a strong congressional leader. He declined to join the presidential campaign for 2004.

The papers you write in college and the grades you receive are part of your permanent record, and you do not want errors of judgment to affect your future.

Software

Some software companies sign contracts with schools to provide software at a reduced rate. Typically, the schools agree to limit sales to students, and the students pay a reduced price. Students are required to show identification and proof of student status to buy the software. The difference between retail price and the student discount price may be hundreds of dollars on a software suite like Microsoft Office or CadCam. Friends or relatives may ask you to use your status as a student to buy a copy of the software for them at the reduced price. This would violate the agreement between the school and the software company, and you would have to violate the end user license agreement in which you agree to the terms of the license. In this case, your friend has created a moral dilemma for you. On the one hand, you want to help your friend, but on the other, you prefer not to perform an illegal act that also violates the code of conduct of the school. To decide how to act, consider the guidelines for personal ethics. If all the students did this, would the deal be canceled? Would an impartial observer judge that you have been fair to all parties concerned? Is this an act that you would be proud of or would respect yourself for doing? Dealing with moral dilemmas is not easy and often requires tact. You may decide to ask your friend or relative not to put you in this type of uncomfortable situation.

Computer Labs

Your school probably has computer labs where students use personal computers. These computers are shared, and the software on them is set up for general use. These labs usually have their own code of conduct that is designed to keep the computers configured in a uniform manner. Downloading and installing software is either prevented by security settings or disallowed by the code. Software for personal computers is customizable for personal preferences, but it is inappropriate to customize the software in a lab and then leave it that way for the next person. For example, it is possible to set a financial software program like Excel to display figures in euros rather than dollars. If you made such a change, it would be disrespectful of others to leave it that way for the next person to use.

FAIR USE OF COPYRIGHTED MATERIALS

One of the most controversial and confusing ethical problems that is specific to schools is applying the policy of fair use. The fair use policy allows limited reproduction of copyrighted works for the purpose of instruction if it does not harm the market for the work. Instructors often collect and reproduce articles from various copyrighted sources that are printed by a local copy shop and sold as **course packs** (see Figure 5.7). Kinko's, a major copy shop chain, was sued in 1991 for copyright violation for reproducing copyrighted works in the course packs it prepared for college courses. Since this ruling, copy shops require permission from the copyright holder to reproduce the work, and they collect royalty fees that are included in the price of the course pack. The ruling was challenged in 1996 by Michigan Document Services, which won an early decision that was overruled later that year. The court found that copy services that were collecting and paying the royalties were demonstrating that this system could work and that sums collected were substantial, demonstrating that allowing copy services to reproduce the works without collecting royalties

FIGURE 5.7

Course packs are commonly used to provide students with a variety of articles related to the course.

would harm the market value of the work. The key to this case is the development of online clearinghouses that make it practical to obtain permission and pay royalties for individual articles or book excerpts (see the companion Web site).

This raises the question about fair use for other purposes, such as classroom presentations by students. According to the fair use policy, you may copy portions of copyrighted works such as text and pictures for use in classroom presentations or papers if it does not harm the market value of the work. Because there is no convenient way to pay for the use of a single picture or article if you copy it from a Web page, the market value of the work is not harmed, so this practice is allowed (you still must cite the source). This could change in the near future. New software technologies like Microsoft's .NET strategy may make it possible to collect a small fee each time you use a picture or article from a Web page. If that ability becomes available, one could argue that using copyrighted material for classroom presentations without paying royalties would harm the market value of the work just as it did for course packs. At the time of writing, student presentations are included in the fair use policy, but this could change in a few years.

WORK

Companies must be careful to abide by the law to avoid costly lawsuits. Companies are responsible for the actions of their employees, and they are careful to provide codes of conduct that exclude illegal behavior. They may dismiss an employee for illegal conduct if it exposes the company to a lawsuit. The pressures of competition and desire for increased profits may result in a company or one of your bosses ordering you to commit an illegal or unethical act, which requires you to make some difficult decisions. In this section, we look at some examples of ethical problems related to computers that could arise at work.

Using Company Resources for Private Purposes

An Internet connection at work is often much faster than a dial-up connection from home. Some people find this a compelling reason to use the Internet for personal tasks while at work. In addition, the distinction between the workplace and home is blurred. If the company expects you to use your home computer to do company work in the evenings and on weekends, you may reason that it is all right to use company time and equipment to do some personal tasks like shopping or answering personal e-mail. Refer to the company policy on using company computers and equipment for personal activities. Many company policies do not reflect the blended nature of today's work and home environments and strictly prohibit use of company resources for any personal activity. In cases like this, your activity may be ethical but still contrary to company policy. You may wish to try to change the company's policy. The company may decline to change its policy because some workers who do not work at home use their Internet connection at work for entertainment, detracting from their job performance. In cases like this, the unethical behavior by fellow workers limits how you can use the company's computer resources.

Intellectual Property

The fair use policy that applies to schools does not apply to companies. A practice that was common at college may be a serious violation at work. If

FIGURE 5.8

Retail software is a major business that is threatened by software piracy.

you intend to use copyrighted work in a company publication, you must obtain permission, which often requires payment of a royalty. Several online services can assist in this process (see the companion Web site at **http://www.prenhall.com/preston**).

Software

In a company, there must be a legal license for each installation of software (see Figure 5.8). This may take the form of an individual license for each computer or a site license. In either case, records must be available to prove that all the installations are legally licensed. The Business Software Alliance (BSA) is a group supported by software manufacturers that is dedicated to enforcement of copyright laws. It takes reports of illegal software installations or illegal manufacture and sale of pirated CDs and works with law enforcement agencies to prosecute the violators. Some companies or organizations ask employees to sign statements that there is no unlicensed software on the computer they use. Be careful about signing such a document if you share the computer, do not control access to it, or do not know if the installed software is licensed. The company may be setting you up to take the blame if it is sued. Be aware that the computer you use at work is not your computer; it belongs to the company and the company has the right to search it or to monitor activity. If you are responsible for several other employees, you may be asked to search their computer hard drives for unlicensed software. You may feel this is an unethical invasion of their privacy. It is probably not illegal or against company policy. To decide this ethical issue, ask yourself how to be fair to all the parties involved and how to respect them. You could resolve this dilemma by posting a notice in advance that all company computers are subject to monitoring for unlicensed software before you search them. Similarly, some companies use software that records every keystroke at each computer (see Chapter 6, Protecting Our Security and Privacy). If you are asked to review records from this type of monitoring, consider the principles for ethical behavior to help you decide how to act.

FIGURE 5.9

Digital alteration can change the impression made by a picture.

Unethical and Illegal Behavior by the Company

In some cases, company executives may direct you to act in a manner that is unethical, against company policy, or illegal, which produces a moral dilemma. Some of these dilemmas may be resolved internally, and others may require reporting the illegal behavior or quitting the job.

Computers are capable of manipulating images to give a false impression. Tabloids often show a picture of two celebrities next to each other that is a composite of two separate photos to give the impression that they are together. A famous instance of digital manipulation of a photo occurred during the trial of O. J. Simpson. *Time* magazine altered a police photo to darken it, which made him seem sinister (see Figure 5.9). If you work with digital images as part of your job, you may be asked to use a computer to change the original image. Changes of this type are seldom illegal and are not usually against company policy, but they may be unethical. In the case of O. J. Simpson's picture, the people who made the alteration did not show respect to Mr. Simpson or themselves, and it is unlikely that they were proud of what they did when it became widely known. In this example, Mr. Simpson was treated as a means to an end. Other cases are much less clear. It is commonplace to improve the contrast or color density of images to make products look better, and few people consider this practice to be unethical. However, if you are asked to alter a photo that may be used as evidence in a trial, it is likely that the act is illegal.

Ethical dilemmas occur when you are asked to change a photo to give a false impression. For example, you may be asked to make a person look thinner in the "after" photo in an advertisement for a weight-loss product by digitally reducing the size of their stomach and thighs.

Companies maintain databases of customer and/or employee records that contain private information and data that is valuable to marketers. If you are a computer professional, your ethical duty is to safeguard that information from people who are trying to steal identities. In some cases, companies sell part of this information, such as the name, address, phone, e-mail address, and salary range, to marketers without divulging Social Security numbers, medical histories, or specific salaries. This makes money for the

DISCUSSION

1 Do you use unlicensed copies of software? If so, how do you rationalize breaking the law? How does this differ from rationalizations of other forms of illegal behavior?

2 If television is responding to personal video recorders (PRVs) by embedding advertising in the shows themselves, for instance, displaying certain brands of products in the background or in use by the actors, how might the music industry do this? Give some examples. Would you rather pay for music than see this happen?

3 In 1999, Jeffrey Levy, a 22-year-old student, pleaded guilty to illegally distributing thousands of MP3 files, movie clips, and software, including Adobe Photoshop. Prosecutors estimated the value of the files distributed illegally to be approximately $70,000. Tests performed during his pretrial supervision were positive for marijuana. His punishment was two years of probation, periodic urine tests, and limits to his use of the Internet. He was caught because the network administrators at his university noticed an unusually high volume of data transfer on his account and reported him. Do you think the punishment fits the crime? Do you think he acted ethically? Do you think the university acted ethically?

4 Your babysitter used your computer while you were out. She downloaded and installed chat software so she could converse with her friends. The next day, several software programs, including your financial management software, did not function, and you spent four hours recovering data and reinstalling programs. Did the babysitter behave ethically? What should you do?

company but results in additional unsolicited mail and telephone calls. This practice treats people as a means to an end, and a detached observer would be unlikely to consider that all parties have been treated fairly.

If you find yourself in a job in which you are routinely asked to do jobs that you consider unethical but that are not illegal, you may need to change jobs if continuing in it results in a loss of self-respect.

Some companies commit illegal acts that are not specifically related to computers, such as using illegal accounting practices, but which impact computer use. An investigation into the activities of corporate executives may involve a review of all e-mail and computer records. It is important to know that e-mail is not necessarily erased when you delete it from your mail program. A copy of it is often kept on the company's mail server, which may be opened by court order. In one ironic case, the software installed by a company's executives to monitor every keystroke of employee activity provided proof to investigators of accounting fraud, which convicted those executives. Even if you did not play any part in a particular crime, an investigation can uncover embarrassing e-mail or unauthorized computer use. If the company for which you work is engaged in illegal activity, you have a serious moral dilemma. The consequences of your action, or inaction, can be significant. Calling attention to illegal activities is called ***whistle-blowing***, and there are several Web sites that discuss the ethics and implications of taking this action (see the companion Web site at **http://www.prenhall.com/preston**).

SOCIALLY AND AT HOME

In our personal interactions and with our friends and families, we have more control over our actions and fewer formalized guidelines to direct our behavior. In these situations, individual ethics play their most important role.

Entertainment

The entertainment industry historically makes money in three basic ways: by selling tickets to performances, by selling recordings of performances on physical media, or by selling advertising mixed in with the entertainment. Advances in computer technology that allow individuals to make high-quality copies of recordings, videos, and TV shows; edit out the advertising; and distribute copies worldwide are threatening to change this model dramatically. Entertainment companies are concerned they will lose control of their product and profits will plunge. The future of the entertainment industry will be decided by how they adapt their economic model to new technologies, what laws can be passed to protect their rights, and how ethically their customers behave.

Copying music and videos   When the video tape recorder was introduced, the motion picture industry opposed its use. Jack Valenti, the head of the Motion Picture Association of America, testified before Congress in 1982 and said, "I say to you that the VCR is to the American film producer and the American public as the Boston Strangler is to the women home alone." The Congress did not ban the video tape recorder, and the industry adapted to the new technology. Now video rentals of movies provide significant profits.

The music industry reacted in a similar fashion when cassette tapes and recordable CDs were introduced. These recording devices share the same restriction—the average person can make only one copy at a time. Piracy by organized groups with manufacturing facilities was a problem but was manageable. It did not matter very much if customers respected the copy-

FIGURE 5.10

The band Metallica sued Napster to ban illegal downloads from the Internet.

right of the work or not; the harm they could do as individuals was limited. This changed when four new technologies were combined:

》 digital recordings, which may be copied many times without losing quality
》 high-speed broadband Internet connections
》 computers that were powerful enough to run the **MP3** compression program that is similar to zipping software files
》 peer-to-peer (P2P) distributed file management

Using these four technologies, Napster provided a service that allowed individuals to form a distributed file management system through which individuals could exchange MP3 files. To enable users to retrieve music files from other users' computers, the Napster service provided a database of users and the files they had available to share. Napster's activities were ruled illegal in 2000, and the site was shut down (see Figure 5.10).

Napster has been replaced by several other systems that decentralize the database of users and available files. The providers of the software attempt to avoid charges of copyright infringement by declaring themselves ignorant of how their software is being used. Control of the distributed networks is now in the hands of individuals and is limited only by their personal ethics and actions that can be taken against individuals.

In 2003, the Recording Industry Association of America (RIAA) announced that it would sue individuals for copyright infringement and filed several hundred lawsuits against individuals seeking financial damages of up to $150,000 per song. One of the popular P2P sites reported that activity on the site decreased for about 10 hours after the announcement and then returned to normal.

Using these sites to copy, distribute, and listen to songs without paying royalties to the copyright holder is illegal and unethical. Several sites are adapting to the new technology by offering individual songs for less than a dollar and the option of mixing your own CDs. If you want to have the convenience and availability of hundreds of thousands of titles online and are willing to pay a small but reasonable amount for music, these sites offer an ethical choice (see the companion Web site at **http://www.prenhall. com/preston**).

The television industry is likely to be the next entertainment medium to undergo this type of change. It relies on advertising, intermixed with its shows, for revenue. The *personal video recorder (PVR)* is a dedicated computer that can digitize television signals and save them on a large hard disk. PVRs are connected via a telephone or broadband connection to the Internet. They download weekly program listings and allow the user to search for programs by title, subject, stars, and key words. Viewers can watch previously recorded shows while recording currently playing shows. An attractive feature of a PVR is that it can skip commercials at the touch of a button. Commercial television shows contain up to 10 minutes of commercials per half-hour that can be skipped using a PVR. Advertisers are concerned that widespread adoption of PVRs will result in fewer viewers seeing their commercials, and they are responding by embedding more of their products in the shows.

A more significant concern for the future is the ability of a PVR to record television shows and then transmit them over the Internet. Current technology restricts this type of file sharing due to the file size. Recorded video files may take hours to transmit over broadband connections in their current file format. However, *MP4* file compression for video has already reduced an hour of video to about 350 megabytes, which is only six times as large as an hour of music compressed with MP3. It is likely that the television industry will have to deal with P2P file sharing of programs that have been stripped of their advertising in the next few years, and users will have to make ethical decisions about paying for the shows or watching them with commercials.

Radio is another medium that is affected by advances in computer technology. Radio stations normally broadcast their signal from a central location, and the size of the potential audience for the station depends on the location of the transmitter, the power of the signal, and the number of people who live in that area. The size of the potential audience is used to calculate how much they can charge advertisers for commercial time and how much they have to pay in royalties to music copyright holders. Laws that govern radio stations and the long-term contracts they have with each other and content providers like sports teams are also based on these geographical limitations. These limitations are removed by using *streaming audio* technology, which allows the user to listen to stations anywhere in the world over the Internet. Internet radio stations that were playing copyrighted music were sued by RIAA for infringement. As a result, some streaming audio providers such as Yahoo!, a popular Internet portal, are now offering pay radio service (see the companion Web site at **http://www.prenhall.com/preston**).

Computer technology is drastically changing the way entertainment is delivered, and companies, government officials, and concerned individuals are examining new ways to pay for it. If unethical copying becomes so excessive it threatens the viability of some entertainment formats, those formats will wither away and be replaced by forms that make money. Television is already countering the new technologies by embedding commercial products in shows themselves. The extent to which this type of commercialization of the entertainment performances increases is directly related to the ethical practices of the customers.

Social Interaction

The Internet provides methods of communication that are not restricted by geography or time zone. It also allows us to assume new identities and role play in ways that we could not do in a community where we are well known. When you use a chat room, a dating service, a group game, or other service that lets you interact with other people, the code of conduct of the group and your personal ethics are your guide. To determine your personal behavior in these situations, refer to some of the guidelines for personal ethics: respect yourself and others, and treat people as an end in themselves rather than as a means to an end.

Children

Parents have a moral obligation to guide and protect their children (see Figure 5.11). New computer technologies make that task harder and easier, depending on the situation. The Internet is a portal to the world, which

FIGURE 5.11

Children need guidance to learn ethical computer practices.

can be a great learning tool, but it can also expose children to vile criminals (see Chapter 6 for a discussion about protecting children). Children need guidance in ethical behavior in their social interactions online. If you have children, you can use the guidelines for making personal ethical choices provided above to discuss how they should behave in chats and interactive games.

Monitoring a child's behavior is possible in new ways with Web cameras. *Web cameras* are small, inexpensive video cameras that connect to the computer and the Internet that may be accessed from another computer on the Internet using a password. Some parents place Web cameras in their home to monitor the behavior of children and babysitters while they are away, which may violate the rights of the babysitter if he or she is not informed. Some parents request that Web cameras be placed in classrooms so parents can monitor their child's behavior from work. It is possible to use satellite and computer technology to track the movements of the family automobile while it is in use by a teenage driver. Deciding how to use this type of monitoring technology ethically requires that you consider issues of respect and how an impartial observer would judge the fairness of your actions.

Shopping

Shopping on the Internet has become big business that, unlike the entertainment industry, has an established, effective economic model of ordering, shipping, and payment. Still, some ethical problems arise. At the time of this writing, the moratorium on sales tax collection is still in effect. Under the terms of this moratorium, when you buy an item online from a retailer in another state, you do not have to pay sales tax in that state. However, you are supposed to declare these purchases when you fill out your annual state income tax return and pay the sales tax to the state where you reside. This method of self-reporting requires you to make an ethical decision about reporting your purchases (see Figure 5.12).

Another problem with shopping online is that computer monitors do not represent colors accurately and reliably. This limits purchases of items for which exact color matching is important. Some online retailers suggest you go to a local store that has the same brand and write down the color codes you like and then order from the online retailer for a lower price. An impartial judge would consider this strategy unfair to the local retailer who has to pay for the facility that made it possible for you to compare the colors on physical samples.

Software

Several software options available for home use help you reduce costs ethically. If you want to work at home on the same software you use at work, check the licensing agreement to see if you are allowed to install the software on two computers as long as they will not be in use at the same time. Many programmers write software, called freeware, which they copyright but make available to the public. There are thousands of freeware programs available that may be used ethically at no cost. Some software is available for a free trial period after which you are asked to pay a modest fee. In some cases, the software ceases to function at the end of that time, but in many others it still works. This type of software is called *shareware*. The copyright holders rely on the ethical behavior of users to pay for the software if they like it and plan to use it. Shareware is often of higher quality than freeware.

FIGURE 5.12

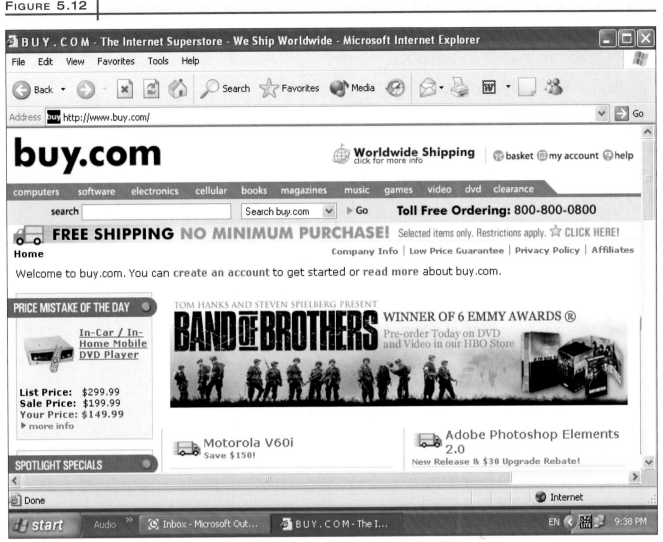

You may be expected to pay state sales tax for online purchases.

One of the challenges to ethical behavior arises in homes where there is more than one computer. Current license agreements require separate purchases for each computer. Several editorials in prominent computer magazines have called for site licenses for homes, in which someone could buy a license for two or three machines in the same residence or using the same Internet service provider. These types of licenses are not available at this time so buying one copy of software and installing it on two or three machines in the home is prohibited by license agreements.

TEST PREPARATION

The following section does not replace reading the text, nor does it contain all the information that will be tested. It is designed to provide examples and identify sections that need review.

summary by objective

LAWS, CODES OF ETHICAL CONDUCT, AND PERSONAL ETHICS

- **Distinguish among laws, codes of conduct, and ethical principles:**
  - Laws are passed by the government and enforced by the police and courts
  - Codes of conduct are provided by organizations
  - Ethical principles are guidelines for choosing between morals when they conflict

LAWS

- **Define copyright—ownership of intellectual property.**
- **Identify the conditions of fair use:**
  - The purpose of the work
  - The nature of the work
  - The amount copied
  - The effect on the market value of the work
- **Identify the copyright symbol and the three elements required of a copyright notice—© symbol, name, year.**
- **Distinguish among public domain software, freeware, and shareware:**
  - Public domain software—no restriction on copying
  - Freeware—copyrighted but no charge for use
  - Shareware—copyrighted but may be used for a limited time for free
- **Describe how cybersquatting affects trademarks—by using another's trademark as a domain name, cybersquatters profit and compromise the value of the trademark.**
- **Identify an example of a business method patent in computer software—1-Click ordering by Amazon.**

ORGANIZATIONAL CODES OF ETHICS

- **Identify the important ethical considerations at colleges, at companies, and by computer professionals:**
  - Colleges care about plagiarism, cheating, and reputation
  - Companies care about profits and lawsuits
  - Computer professionals care about reputation
- **Define plagiarism—using the work of someone else without informing the reader or viewer that the work is not original work of the purported author.**

PERSONAL ETHICS

- **Identify principles used to make ethical decisions.**
  - If everyone acted the same way, society as a whole would benefit
  - Do not treat people as a means to an end
  - An impartial observer would judge that you have been fair to all parties concerned
- **Identify different points of view in ethical guidelines. List of commandments, respect, opinion of others, consideration of the customer.**

ETHICAL USE OF COMPUTERS

Name reasons why plagiarism and cheating are unethical and unwise:
  - Plagiarism treats people as a means to an end
  - Cheating shows lack of respect for oneself and others
- **Describe ethical considerations at school when using software, computer labs, and course packs and when making presentations:**
  - Software—consider what would happen if everyone bought discount software for friends
  - Labs—respect others
  - Course packs and presentations—be fair to all parties concerned
- **Describe ethical considerations at work when using company resources, intellectual property, and software:**
  - Resources: consider judgment by an impartial observer
  - Intellectual property and software: respect others
- **Describe ethical considerations when a company is acting illegally or unethically:**
  - Consider what the community would think
  - Respect yourself
- **Describe ethical considerations when consuming entertainment products, interacting socially, guiding and protecting children, shopping, and installing software:**
  - Fairness to all parties
  - Respect for others

true/false questions

1. ___ A copyright is in effect only if the author provides a notice.

2. ___ Patents are issued only to protect the design of physical objects.

3. ___ Cybersquatting involves using a company's trademark as part of a domain name.

4. ___ Plagiarism is the use of a trademark without permission.

5. ___ Downloading and playing copyrighted music from file-sharing sites without paying a royalty is like listening to music on the radio. Both are legal.

multiple choice

1. Which of the principles does not belong with the others in this group?
   a) respect yourself
   b) respect your school
   c) respect your profession
   d) respect your self-interest

2. Which of the questions used to determine ethical behavior does not belong with the others in this group?
   a) Would you be proud to have your parents and neighbors know?
   b) Do most of your friends do it?
   c) If the people affected by your decision knew all the details, would they think they had been treated fairly?
   d) If your action involves your place of employment, would your boss or the company's customers agree with what you have done?

3. Which of the following is not considered plagiarism?
   a) quoting something from a government publication without using quotation marks or an indented block of single-spaced text
   b) copying text from a Web page without indicating the source
   c) writing your own opinion that is based on a variety of facts and readings
   d) writing down what your roommate dictates while you type and then turning in the paper with only your name on it

4. Which of the following is true about using course packs in college classes?
   a) Royalties do not have to be collected or paid, regardless of the amount of text copied, because it is for educational purposes.
   b) Web sites exist that make it much easier than it used to be for people to pay to use excerpts of articles and books.
   c) Determining fair use is a simple matter of applying the standards set forth in the copyright laws.
   d) Reproducing copyrighted material for use in classes is permitted if the people doing the reproduction do not profit from including the copyrighted material.

5. Which of the following is true about most end user license agreements, excluding those for freeware and shareware?
   a) You are allowed to deconstruct the machine code and use up to 49 percent of the program in other programs.
   b) You are allowed to make and distribute copies on the Internet.
   c) You are allowed to install the software on one computer.
   d) You are allowed to install the software on all the computers you personally own.

completion

1. Reporting an illegal activity is called _____.

2. A difficult choice between two moral behaviors is called a moral _____.

3. A person owns the copyright on his or her writing unless it is done as a _____ _____ _____ (three words).

4. An agreement that covers software installations on all the computers at a particular location is called a _____ _____ (two words).

5. Parts of copyrighted works may be used for criticism, commentary, news reporting, teaching, scholarship, or research without paying a royalty under certain conditions. This policy is called _____ _____ (two words).

Match each term with its definition.

_____ **1.** course packs
_____ **2.** cybersmearing
_____ **3.** cybersquatting
_____ **4.** cyberstalking
_____ **5.** end user license agreement (EULA)
_____ **6.** fair use
_____ **7.** freeware
_____ **8.** frequently asked questions (FAQ)
_____ **9.** honor code
_____ **10.** identity theft
_____ **11.** moral dilemma
_____ **12.** MP3
_____ **13.** MP4
_____ **14.** open source
_____ **15.** personal video recorder (PVR)
_____ **16.** philosophy
_____ **17.** plagiarism
_____ **18.** public domain
_____ **19.** site license
_____ **20.** software piracy
_____ **21.** sreaming audio
_____ **22.** trademark
_____ **23.** vetting
_____ **24.** whistle-blowing
_____ **25.** work for hire

a. agreement to allow installation of software on all the computers at one location
b. checking someone's background for indications of character
c. collections of copied works
d. compression technique for video
e. compression technique used with music files
f. contract between the software copyright holder and the user
g. copyrighted work that is available without charge
h. creative product for which the copyright is owned by the company that paid for the creator's services
i. creative work that is not copyrighted
j. critical analysis of fundamental assumptions and beliefs
k. device that records television programs and can share them over the Internet
l. ethical conduct agreed to by a group's members
m. lists of questions and answers that help a new user take part in a group rapidly
n. policy that allows use of copyrighted works without permission or payment under certain circumstances
o. profiting from a trademark as part of a domain name without permission
p. reporting illegal activity
q. representing the work of others as one's own
r. sound delivered over the Internet
s. programming code that is available to the public
t. symbol or logo used to identify a product
u. two conflicting moral behaviors
v. using copyrighted software without permission
w. using private facts to impersonate
x. using the Internet to defame
y. using the Internet to harass

beyond the facts

Factual knowledge provides the basis for higher levels of learning. In the following sections, you work with the concepts and facts presented in the chapter to develop critical-thinking and problem-solving skills. You practice research, analysis, and communication and become aware of diversity issues while exploring the impact of computer technology on career choices, the workplace, social interactions, and home life. The Leadership section helps you identify ways in which you can lead others in organizing and implementing projects that meet worthwhile community needs. In the Lifelong Learning exercise, you build a set of learning resources that you can use after this course to continue learning.

objectives for beyond the facts

END OF CHAPTER EXERCISES	Achievement of the objectives for the end-of-chapter exercises requires evaluation of documents, class discussions, or presentations.
Critical Thinking–Research	Compare software piracy rates in different regions of the world and examine trends in those rates. Demonstrate the following skills: ability to locate relevant information online, analyze the information and form an opinion based on the research, consider diversity issues, work with others where appropriate, and communicate the results in writing or by public presentation.
Problem Solving	1) Ask for permission to reproduce pictures and lyrics as if you were going to set up a fan site for a music group. 2) Write a detailed process description for seeking permission to use lyrics, music, photos, and other copyrighted materials. Describe the responses from the copyright holders or Web sites that broker use of those materials. 3) Communicate the experience to the class.
Anticipating Career Challenges and Opportunities	Demonstrate the following skills: 1) Teamwork: coordinate research on types of jobs affected by the advertising and distribution changes in the entertainment industry 2) Research: find articles related to the topic 3) Diversity: consider the potential for new markets abroad 4) Analysis: analyze the change in the way music and video entertainment is sold, and predict new job opportunities and which types of jobs will be diminished 5) Communication: communicate the results in writing or by public presentation
Impact on the Workplace	Demonstrate the following skills: 1) Teamwork: coordinate research on the use of computers in the workplace with other students 2) Research: identify company policies toward whistle-blowing 3) Diversity: compare men's and women's opinions on whistle-blowing 4) Analysis: form an opinion about the degree to which your organization wants its employees to report illegal activity 5) Communication: communicate the results in writing or by public presentation
Impact on Social Interactions	Demonstrate the following skills: 1) Teamwork: allocate tasks for research on online dating services 2) Research: review at least five online dating services 3) Diversity: look for proportional representation of racial groups and age groups 4) Analysis: compare codes of conduct and relate them to the ethical behavior guidelines provided in this chapter. 5) Communication: communicate the results in writing or by public presentation
Impact on Home Life	Demonstrate the following skills: 1) Teamwork: allocate tasks for surveying a friend's home for unlicensed software 2) Research: conduct the survey 3) Analysis: prepare a summary table of freeware or shareware alternatives and costs 4) Communication: communicate the results in writing or by public presentation
Leadership	Describe a plan to lead a group of people toward a worthy goal—in this case, offering nonprofit organizations the service of writing computer use guidelines.
Lifelong Learning	Identify three or more online resources that may be used to learn more about the topics introduced in this chapter.

critical thinking–research

According to the BSA, the rate of software piracy in the United States is 24 percent, which is the lowest in the world. What are piracy rates in other regions? Are the rates changing? Do people on the other side of the digital divide claim they are acting ethically when they use pirated software?

1. **Teamwork**—Join one to three other students. Decide how to divide up the work. Possible divisions could be: research, editing the group paper, and preparing the class presentation.

2. **Research**—Use a Web browser and go to the companion Web site at **http://www.prenhall.com/preston**. Follow the links by clicking on the Web addresses that are highlighted and underlined. Read about the trends in software piracy, starting with the link to the BSA Web site. Use a Web search engine such as Google.com or Yahoo.com to search for key words and phrases such as "software piracy" and "trend." Make a list of relevant sources that you may want to reference later. Include the title of the page or article, the name of the organization responsible for the Web page, the date the page or article was written, and the Web address. You may also go to the library and look up books, articles, and news

reports that are relevant to this topic. Many libraries have the full text of articles and news reports online in proprietary databases that are not available to the public.

3. **Diversity issues**—Look for differences based on culture, politics, geography, religion, and economic status.

4. **Analysis**—Write an essay that compares the rate of software piracy within the United States with that of the rest of the world. Form and express an opinion. Go beyond simple reporting of the facts. Support your opinion with references to the articles you read. Ask your instructor for guidance regarding the required length of the essay.

5. **Communication**—Prepare a presentation in which you present your opinion and supporting facts to the class. Depending on your computer skill, you could give the presentation using a program like PowerPoint and save it as a Web page, or you could prepare a paper handout with your Web references for use while you talk to the class.

problem solving

The objective of this exercise is to learn valuable processes for solving computer-related problems, not just the solution to this particular problem.

Ask for permission to reproduce pictures and lyrics as if you were going to set up a fan site for a music group.

1. **Search for help on the topic**—Use the links on the companion Web site to the Copyright Clearance Center and the Copyright Permissions Office. Read the guidelines, and follow links to related informational sites.

2. **Read the instructions and try it**—Follow the instructions for requesting permission to use pictures, lyrics, or other copyrighted materials that would go in a fan Web site.

3. **Troubleshoot**—If your early attempts are unsuccessful, search for another service and try it.

4. **Communicate**—Describe your experience. Were you able to get permission? Who holds the copyright to the photos and lyrics for your favorite group? Did they give you a reason for their decision or ask for royalties? Prepare a presentation for the class that describes what you learned through this experience.

anticipating career challenges and opportunities

A dramatic change in business models often results in established careers disappearing and new ones taking their place. It is a time when someone who guesses the new direction of the marketplace can greatly benefit. It is also a time when those who do not anticipate the change can be suddenly out of a job. The change in the way music and video entertainment are sold or advertised will be dramatic. What careers are likely to have fewer jobs because of the changes in entertainment technology, and what are some new jobs that might appear or old ones that might grow?

1. **Teamwork**—Join one to three other students who have similar interests. Decide how to divide up the work. Possible divisions could be: music, television, movies, and Internet radio.

2. **Research**—Use a Web browser and search for articles on methods of making money from music and video file sharing. Look at P2P file-sharing sites that are making it easy to copy music files without paying. How do those sites make money? Do they have EULAs?

3. **Diversity issues**—Consider how other countries pay for television, music, and video entertainment. Would those models work well in this new environment?

4. **Analysis**—Write an essay that describes the future of the electronic entertainment industry as you see it. Describe how artists will be paid and who will make money and how. Go beyond simple reporting of your opinion. Support your opinion with references to the articles you read. Ask your instructor for guidance regarding the required length of the essay.

5. **Communication**—Prepare a presentation in which you present your opinion and supporting facts to the class. Depending on your computer skill, you could give the presentation using a program like PowerPoint and save it as a Web page, or you could prepare a paper handout with your Web references for use while you talk to the class.

impact on the workplace

Does your organization have a policy about whistle-blowing related to computer use such as the installation of unlicensed software, copyright violation, or unethical use of computers to manipulate images? How is this act viewed by workers in your organization? What are some examples?

1. **Teamwork**—Join one or two other students who work where you do or in a similar type of business or organization. Decide how to divide up the work. Possible divisions could be: company policy statements, and examples from the past in your company or in your industry.

2. **Research**—Talk to someone in human resources about company policy. Be sure to explain that your inquiry is part of a class project, not a real concern.

3. **Diversity issues**—In the three largest corporate scandals in 2002, the whistle-blowers were all

women. Ask some women and some men how they feel about this topic to see if you detect a difference. Recognize that a small sample provides too little information to form a statistically valid conclusion.

4. **Analysis**—Write an essay that describes how violations of software licenses and copyrights are reported in your company. Form and express an opinion about the degree to which your organization relies on computers to function and whether you observed any differences based on age, gender, or race in the staff that uses computers most. Support your opinion with statistics based on your observations. Ask your instructor for guidance regarding the required length of the essay.

5. **Communication**—Prepare a presentation in which you present your opinion and supporting facts to the class.

impact on social interactions

Online dating services have flourished. Find out what codes of ethical conduct they use and what they have in common. Compare them with the guidelines for personal ethical behavior.

1. **Teamwork**—Join one or two other students to find out about online dating services.

2. **Research**—Check at least five dating services and find out what their rules are for accurate disclosure of personal information and photos.

3. **Diversity**—Determine what age groups typically use the service. Do the number of people who appear to be African-American or Hispanic appear in numbers that are representative of their percentage of the population? Are there more postings for men or women?

4. **Analysis**—Compare codes of conduct and determine what they have in common. Compare them with the ethical behavior guidelines provided in this chapter. Comment on any findings related to diversity.

5. **Communication**—Prepare a presentation in which you present your findings to the class.

impact on home life

Survey the computers in the home of an anonymous friend. Compile a list of any unlicensed software that is installed. Determine whether the software could be replaced by freeware or shareware products. Determine how much it would cost to license all the software.

1. **Teamwork**—Join one or two other students. Decide how to divide up the work. Possible divisions could be: survey the computers, search for replacement freeware or shareware, and find prices for licenses.

2. **Research**—Conduct a survey of a friend's home computers. Record specific information about what you software you find.

3. **Analysis**—Match up software with alternative freeware or shareware. Determine licensing fees to bring any unlicensed software up to legal status. Prepare a table to show the options and the cost.

4. **Communication**—Prepare a presentation in which you present your findings to the class. Depending on your computer skill, you could use a financial spreadsheet program to chart the figures.

leadership

Nonprofit organizations often use personal computers and the Internet, and they may need to develop guidelines for ethical computer use to avoid lawsuits or embarrassment. They may not have the time or familiarity with computer issues to prepare such a policy. Contact a local nonprofit organization, and ask if they need such a policy statement.

1. **Vision**—Write a vision statement that describes what you want your group to achieve. It should motivate people to volunteer to help.

2. **Research**—Do not reinvent the wheel. Do the following background research:
   a) Determine whether any similar organizations have policies you can use with their permission.
   b) Determine which government funding agencies your nonprofit works with and whether they have requirements regarding computer use policies for groups they support.

3. **Plan of Action**—Write a simple plan of action. Test the plan by following it yourself on a small scale. Locate a small nonprofit, and search for information that would help you write a policy for it.

4. **Analysis**—Write up an analysis of what you learned by testing your plan.

5. **Communication**—Present your plan to the class. Describe what you learned by testing your plan and how you think it could be expanded if others joined you. Share your vision statement, and try to inspire others to join you in your worthwhile effort.

lifelong learning

Add links to your browser's favorites list.

1. Start your Web browser, and open the list of favorite sites. Create a folder named *Ethics*. (Look for Organize Favorites in Internet Explorer and Manage Bookmarks in Netscape.)

2. Go to the companion Web page for this chapter, and select one of the Web links on ethics that you found useful.

3. Add this link to your browser's favorites list in the ethics folder.

4. Repeat this process for other links on the companion Web page for this chapter, and add them to the ethics folder.

Add learning goals to your journal.

1. Identify areas in which you feel you know the least. List three specific topics related to this chapter that you would like to learn more about in the future.

2. You will add to this journal after each chapter to compile a personal list of references and topics for future study.

6

Protecting Our Security and Privacy

outline & objectives

PHYSICAL SECURITY

- Know methods used to identify and secure computer equipment.
- Understand how to back up data.
- Understand how to choose secure passwords.
- Identify types of biometric identification.
- Give examples of types of possessed objects.

SECURE CONNECTIONS TO OTHER COMPUTERS

- List types of software used for secure Internet connections.
- Define types of attacks and countermeasures.

ENCRYPTED COMMUNICATIONS

- Explain how encryption works.
- Explain how encryption is used to protect communications.

INDIVIDUAL PRIVACY

- Use online sources to find personal information about individuals.
- Minimize availability of your own personal information to other individuals.

BUSINESS PRIVACY

- Explain how databases are compiled for targeted advertising.
- Understand how spam works and how to reduce it.
- Explain how cookies are used.
- Understand how to block cookies and Web bugs.
- Be aware of spyware and how to block it.
- Describe how presence technologies determine your location.
- Know what privacy to expect while using computers at work.
- Be aware of problems managing health records.

GOVERNMENT PRIVACY

- Understand the risks of government officials gaining access to private information.
- List tools used by security agencies and law enforcement that look at personal information.

While most of us share a common set of morals and respect the rights of others, there are some who do not. Those people may attempt to break into your computer to do harm or just for the fun of it. To protect yourself from them, you must expend time and resources that could be put to better use.

Fortunately, there are effective measures you can take to make your computer secure from break-ins. Another problem is protecting your privacy. Some people who want to know about your personal life are just nosy; others are well meaning and feel it's necessary for the common good. Choosing how much privacy to give up for national security, more efficient health care, and better police protection may pose moral dilemmas that are difficult to resolve.

In this chapter, we consider threats to your computer security and look at how to protect computers from physical and electronic break-ins. Next, we discuss how to protect interactions over the Internet from criminal behavior. Finally, we consider computer-related privacy issues and methods to prevent unauthorized prying into your personal life.

WHY DO I NEED TO KNOW THIS?

You need to protect your work from attack, theft, and malicious destruction of data. Some attacks are familiar, like stealing a laptop while you stand in line at an airport. Other attacks are subtle, and you need knowledge of your computer and the available countermeasures to protect yourself. Computers are an important part of our personal lives as well as our business lives. They are used to convey your private thoughts to friends and loved ones, as well as store medical and financial records. To protect your privacy, you need to know what you can do to prevent other people from looking at your personal files or compiling a detailed profile of your behavior. You also need to know when it is unreasonable to expect privacy so you can avoid inappropriate behavior.

SECURITY

To secure your computer, start with protecting it from theft, from physical damage, or from someone who has stolen it. Next, learn how to prevent others from breaking into it electronically and how to protect your communications while they are moving between your computer and others.

PHYSICAL SECURITY

If someone stole your computer or it was damaged by fire or a natural disaster, what effect would it have on you? The cost of replacing the computer might be much less than the value of the time it would take to recreate the files on the computer. To secure your computer and its files from theft or disaster, you need to consider the physical security of the system unit and the files in it.

Protecting Computer Hardware

To help deter theft, especially in a lab environment, special antitheft devices such as cables with locks can secure the computer to its physical location (see Figure 6.1). Companies or educational institutions may have a policy that requires locked doors and limited access to rooms containing computer equipment. If a computer is stolen and then recovered by the police, you must be able to identify it as your property. One way to do this is to have a unique identifying tag affixed to the computer or a number inscribed into the metal of the case. Another option is to record the serial number of the system unit in another location. Portable computers make a

FIGURE 6.1

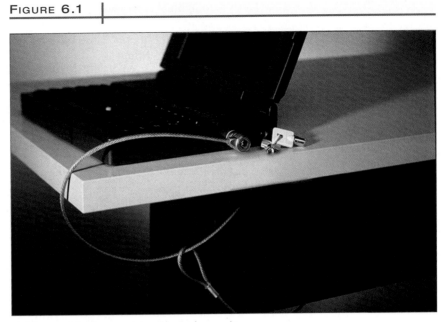

Cables and locks provide physical security.

convenient target for theft. In 2001, 591,000 laptops were reported stolen, so vigilance is required when traveling to prevent simple theft, particularly at airports. Another option is to install tracking software from a security service on your computer. When the computer is used on the Internet, it will send the IP address of the user to the service's Web site, which may be used to identify whoever is using the stolen computer (see the companion Web site at **http://www.prenhall.com/preston** for more information).

Creating Backup Files

The files on your computer may have no value to a thief, but they would take many hours to replace. Making backup copies and updating them frequently will reduce the time it takes to replace the original files, minimizing the impact of theft, natural disaster, equipment failure, or accidental erasure. Computers with CD-R drives can write approximately 600 megabytes of files on each CD-R disc so this is a low-cost solution. Tape backup drives can store up to 10 gigabytes (see Figure 6.2). Computers that are connected to a network can back files up on another computer. Businesses have standardized backup procedures for their large databases that require them to make daily copies. Some businesses also require employees to back up their individual work files regularly. Many businesses transfer backup files to an off-site or secure location. If you have files on your home computer that you cannot afford to lose, you need to establish the habit of backing up your files regularly.

Controlling Access

An unauthorized person can gain physical access to your computer files by stealing the computer, walking into your office while you are not there, or obtaining your old computer from the dumpster or surplus equipment sale. To prevent this type of access, several methods are used to identify someone as an authorized user before allowing access to files.

The most common method of protection is a combination of ***user name*** and ***password***. A user name, sometimes referred to as the a user ID or login ID, is usually a variation or abbreviation of the person's name, and it establishes that

FIGURE 6.2

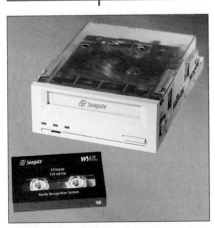

Small tape cartridges provide low-cost backup for large quantities of data.

individual as someone who is authorized to use the system. The password is a set of letters and numbers, known only to the user, which is used in combination with the user name to complete the login process. The user name is not a secret, but the password should remain secret. When you provide both to a computer, it compares them with its database of user names and passwords and then grants access to the user if they match. If someone else knows your user name and obtains your password, he or she can impersonate you and gain access to the computer. To reduce the risk of impersonation, you must choose a password that is easy to remember but difficult to guess. Avoid simple dates, names, or words found in the dictionary. Use a mix of upper- and lowercase letters with numbers and symbols. Your password should be at least eight characters long, and you should not write it down. A good method for creating a memorable password that is hard to guess is to think of a saying or rhyme and then use the first letter of each word in the saying and combine it with a memorable number. For example, Tqbfjotld+48104, stands for: The quick brown fox jumped over the lazy dog plus a local zip code, 48104. Instead of writing down the password, write a hint that would remind you of the password. For example, this password hint would be "first exercise in Mrs. White's 9th-grade class plus college girlfriend's home zip code." Such a password is easier to remember than a string of random numbers and letters, and the hint would be useless to anyone but a family member or close friend (see the companion Web site at **http://www.prenhall.com/preston** for more information about strong passwords). Most operating systems, including Windows XP, can be set to require a password to log in, and they can also log the user off if the computer has been left on and unused for a set period of time. It is also a good idea to change your password regularly.

Even memorized passwords may be stolen by analyzing a video of someone's typing or by intercepting the keystrokes between the keyboard and the system unit. In an incident at the University of Michigan computing lab in August of 2003, a student captured several passwords from other students by inserting a keystroke logging device between the keyboard and the system unit in several computers in a computing lab. The device was smaller than a tube of lipstick. Passwords are cheap and easy to use, but they may be compromised when users share them, write them down, or choose ones that are easy to guess. Some computers and the files therein may be valuable enough to justify more sophisticated user identification measures.

Biometrics applies statistics to biology. Biometric devices can match the patterns of a person's iris, retina, voice, fingerprint, or handprint with patterns stored in a database to confirm the identity of authorized users (see Figure 6.3). The computing power needed to scan, analyze, and retrieve data for this type of security used to restrict its use to mainframe systems with very valuable databases to protect. Because of the rapid increase in the power of personal computers, this type of security measure is now available for individual computers. A fingerprint identification scanner and software can be added to a personal computer for under $100 and iris identification costs under $250.

Object possession is a method that requires the user to carry an object like a swipe card with a magnetic stripe that contains identification (see Figure 6.4). Other types of identification devices have antennas and microprocessor chips built into them that react to scans from radio transmitters and respond with identification codes. This type of identification is used at gas stations, tollbooths, and some drive-through restaurants. These interactive identification devices, especially the ones used in automobiles, should be stored in a metal container when not in use to prevent someone from obtaining the code by activating the device with a radio transmitter similar to the one used at the tollbooth or gas station.

FIGURE 6.3

Biometric devices scan (a) eyes, (b) fingerprints, and (c) hand shape to verify identity.

Some companies use a combination of these confirmation methods to provide security for important systems. For example, a bank automatic teller machine requires a card with a code on a magnetic strip and a password to grant access.

To improve the physical security of your computer, consider the following tips:

❯ Attach your desktop system unit to the desk with a cable and lock.

❯ Record the serial numbers of your system unit, monitor, or laptop in another location.

❯ Attach an identifying tag, or inscribe your name in the metal of the case.

❯ Back up your important files on a regular basis, and store the files in another location.

❯ Lock the door to your office when you are not there.

❯ Set your operating system to require a password if the system is unused for more than a few minutes.

❯ Pick a password based on a phrase or saying that is a mix of upper- and lowercase letters, numbers, and symbols.

❯ If you need higher security, install a biometric device like a fingerprint or iris scanner, or use an object possession system like a magnetic swipe card.

SECURE CONNECTIONS TO OTHER COMPUTERS

Individual computers are connected to each other to share resources and aid communication. Computers may be connected within a company on a LAN or intranet, or they may be connected through the Internet. Managing

FIGURE 6.4

Cards may have user identification codes on magnetic strips or microprocessor chips embedded in the card.

these connections and preventing unauthorized access are an important part of providing security and privacy.

Intranets and LANs

If a company controls each of the computers on a network, security is easiest. Many company computer systems use the same client-server software used on the Internet but do not connect the network to the Internet backbone. Such systems are called intranets (see Chapter 2). Within a company intranet or on the local network, there are barriers that prevent users from unrestricted access to all areas of the network. A network administrator creates groups and assigns privileges to each group. Next, the administrator assigns user names to each group. For example, the most powerful group would be the administrator group, which has the ability to change group privileges. The least powerful office group might be assigned to two printers, a shared network drive, and company e-mail but little else. If an outsider discovers the user name and password of a user in a low-level group, access is limited to the access granted to that user group. Users can connect to an intranet using VPN (see Chapter 2) that uses encrypted packets (see Encryption below).

Internet Connections

When computers or networks of computers are connected to the Internet, methods must be used to block intruders from breaking into computers where they can cause harm or use that computer as a tool to harm others. In this section, we look at methods for blocking intruders from entering a network or individual computer.

Firewall   To describe the types of threats or illegal activities encountered on computers, we often use terms borrowed from warfare, firefighting, or infectious diseases. For example, a firewall in a building is a fireproof wall between adjacent sections that stops the spread of a fire. In computer parlance, a *firewall* protects your computer from the spread of a destructive influence from the Internet (see Figure 6.5). A firewall is software that monitors and controls data flowing between the computers. It may be installed on a single computer that is connected to the Internet or between a group of computers on a LAN and the Internet. It has a set of adjustable filters that detect and block certain types of activities. A firewall can check packets of data that flow through it for words or phrases, such as those from an adult site that has *XXX* in the title, and then block access to that site. Some firewall filters can accidentally block access to benign sites. For example, promoters were disappointed to find that many people who had firewalls installed on their computers set to block adult Web sites could not look at the Super Bowl XXX site.

It is common for the network administrator to configure the firewall to allow only one computer on the network to interact with the Internet. The firewall can control several interactions that we studied earlier, such as TCP/IP (packet switching), HTTP (Web pages), FTP (file transfer), Telnet (remote login), and SMTP (e-mail) protocols. Other protocols that may be controlled by the firewall are *User Datagram Protocol (UDP)*, used for managing streaming audio and video; *Internet Control Message Protocol (ICMP)*, used by routers to exchange information with other routers; and *Simple Network Management Protocol (SNMP)*, used to collect system information from a remote computer. A computer that serves as the contact point between a network of computers and the Internet for one or more of these functions is called a *gateway*. For example, a network administrator may choose to have one computer act as a gateway for company e-mail and another to act as a gateway for Web pages. The firewall could be set up to block all mail or Web page exchanges except for those on the designated gateways.

FIGURE 6.5

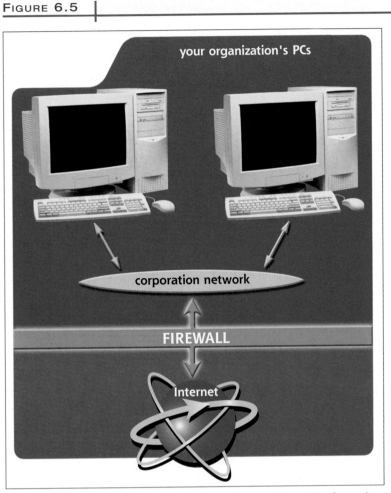

A firewall provides protection from unauthorized intrusion from the Internet.

Proxy server   As you learned in Chapter 4, Web pages may contain small programs known as applets. These programs can be used to break into a computer, so Web pages deserve special security measures. A proxy server is software that acts as a go-between for computers on the network and Internet Web pages. It also keeps a cache of recently downloaded Web pages for quick access. A request for a particular Web page goes to the proxy server, which checks its cache to see if it has a recent copy of the page already downloaded. If it does, it uses the copy from its cache to fulfill the request instead of asking for a download. If it does not have a recent copy in its cache, it requests the page from the appropriate Web server and passes the page along to the user. Proxy servers make a log of all traffic between the user and the Internet to help detect and trace attacks. If users request Web pages for personal entertainment or shopping, these requests will be part of the proxy server's log, as well. By funneling all the Web page requests through one computer, the firewall software filters have a better chance of blocking known threats and finding and fixing new problems as they arise.

If you have a home network connected to a broadband Internet service, you can buy a single device, often called a router or gateway, that combines a firewall, proxy server, and Ethernet hub for less than $100. It plugs into the cable, satellite, or DSL modem, and the computers in your home plug into it. This gives you sophisticated protection from most external threats. You can test the security of your Internet connection by using a free service at a Web site like ShieldsUP!! that tests your connection for vulnerability (see Mastering Technology in this section).

DMZ   Filtering and protecting computers takes time and computing power, which may slow down transactions. If one of your company's functions is to provide information or free downloads and these functions do not require communication with other company computers, you can set up a computer that handles those functions and place it on the Internet side of the firewall. The zone between the computers protected by the firewall and the rest of the Internet is called the *DMZ*, for demilitarized zone (see Figure 6.6). (Mixed metaphors such as this one are common when discussing this topic.) The DMZ refers to a buffer zone between two opposing armies. Placing a computer in the DMZ simply means it is connected directly to the Internet without the protection of a firewall. It may respond to requests for Web pages quickly, but if it is broken into, it does not have any direct connections to other company computers.

Browser security settings   Your Web browser also has security settings that can block certain features that pose security risks. You can disable the Java or ActiveX applets in Web pages or prevent a Web page from storing cookies (see the section on business privacy) on your computer. In Internet Explorer, the High security setting disables these features. Unfortunately, this disables the user-friendly features of many Web pages. A combination of Medium or Custom security settings that allow cookies and applets in combination with additional security software described in the next section is a good compromise for most applications.

Automatic operating system updates   Institutions that license Microsoft products should be aware of a section in the Microsoft Licensing Product User Rights agreement that gives Microsoft the right to "provide updates or fixes to the Software that will be automatically downloaded to your Workstation Computer." System managers are concerned that allowing automatic changes to the software bypasses their security oversight and violates government contracts that have security regulations. See the companion Web page at **http://www.prenhall.com/preston** for a link to an article on this issue and Microsoft's licensing agreement.

FIGURE 6.6

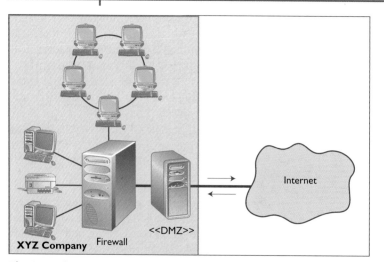

The DMZ is a zone outside the firewall's protection.

To improve the security of your connection to other computers, consider the following tips:

❱ Large companies can create an intranet that is independent of the Internet.

❱ Use a VPN connection from outside the secure network when traveling.

❱ Place a computer in the DMZ to serve Web pages rapidly and reduce traffic to computers inside the firewall.

❱ For home networks, install a router that provides an Ethernet hub, a proxy server, and a firewall.

❱ Set your browser's security setting to pick the types of applets that are allowed to run.

Types of Attacks and Countermeasures

The firewall and proxy server help defend against a variety of attacks. The automatic features may cause problems for you by blocking desired communication and may require periodic adjustments to the filter settings of the firewall. The types of communication you choose to allow through the firewall may still pose a risk. Knowing what types of attacks you are likely to encounter helps protect you from anything that may get past the firewall and proxy server.

Virus A biological virus infects host cells and tricks them into creating more viruses, often destroying the cell in the process. A computer *virus* is a small program that enters your computer and tricks it into producing copies that are transmitted to other computers. Viruses can attach copies of themselves to other programs or e-mail messages and infect computers that run the program or open the e-mail attachment (see Figure 6.7). A virus can cause a computer to slow down due to its use of computer resources to replicate itself, or it can contain a *payload*, which is a program that performs an operation on the computer such as erasing the disk. There are many different viruses, and new ones are written every day. Dedicated antivirus software is required to combat this threat. There are several effective programs from which to choose, and some of them are free (see the companion Web site at **http://www.prenhall.com/preston**). A good antivirus program includes an update service that provides countermeasures to new viruses as they appear.

Worm A worm takes advantage of holes in computers' security. It scans the network for computers that have the security hole and infects them with a copy of itself. It can order the infected computers to request the same Web page repeatedly or send junk mail to the same e-mail address, flooding the targeted servers with requests for service. Hiding a computer's IP address behind a proxy server and using a firewall to block individual computers from accessing the Internet is effective against most worms. As security holes become known to the manufacturers of operating system software, they issue updates to repair the problems. Watch for announcements of updates, and install them.

Macro virus Some application programs like Microsoft Word and Excel allow the user to automate repetitive tasks. A series of commands may be combined and given a single name for execution with a combination of keystrokes. Such a group of commands is called a *macro*. Macros written with the intent of causing harm to the user are called *macro viruses*. Recent versions of Microsoft Office are set to automatically disable macros. You may choose to run a file's macros if it is from a trusted source.

FIGURE 6.7

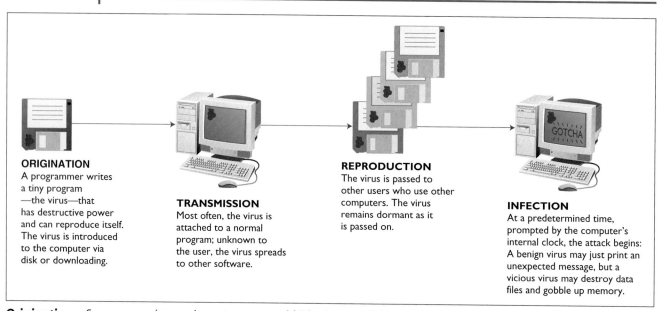

ORIGINATION
A programmer writes a tiny program —the virus—that has destructive power and can reproduce itself. The virus is introduced to the computer via disk or downloading.

TRANSMISSION
Most often, the virus is attached to a normal program; unknown to the user, the virus spreads to other software.

REPRODUCTION
The virus is passed to other users who use other computers. The virus remains dormant as it is passed on.

INFECTION
At a predetermined time, prompted by the computer's internal clock, the attack begins: A benign virus may just print an unexpected message, but a vicious virus may destroy data files and gobble up memory.

Origination—Someone writes a virus program and hides it on a disk or in an e-mail attachment.

Transmission—The disk or e-mail attachment is used in a computer that does not have antivirus software capable of detecting and blocking the virus.

Reproduction—The virus program copies itself to any new disk placed in the computer. An e-mail virus attaches itself to outgoing e-mail to numerous recipients.

Infection—Other computers that use infected disks or open the infected e-mail attachment will spread the virus.

Trojan horse   A *Trojan horse* is a program that claims to do one thing but in fact does another. It may claim to be a game or application software, but when you run it, it may damage your files. This problem is most common in pirated software. Be sure to buy software from a known company.

E-mail virus   An *e-mail virus* spreads by attaching itself to e-mail messages that it automatically creates and sends. If the recipient opens the attachment, the virus program runs. It generates fake e-mail messages with the virus attached and sends them to people using the names and addresses found in the address book in your e-mail program. It may choose one of the names in the address book to use as the sender of the e-mail so when someone gets an infected e-mail, they contact the wrong person to warn them of the problem; this type of misdirection is called *spoofing*. Antivirus programs and firewalls check e-mail attachments to see if they are executable programs. Most company firewalls block this type of e-mail attachment. Be very careful if you choose to open an executable e-mail attachment like a cute animated greeting, even if it appears to come from someone you know and it uses your first name in the greeting. Read the rest of the message to confirm that it is not a generic message but is really from your friend.

E-mail bomb   An *e-mail bomb* is not a single e-mail message but a huge number of e-mail messages sent to the same address to overwhelm the e-mail service by sheer quantity. Firewalls can be set to block mail if the quantity exceeds a set limit. E-mail clients like Outlook can be set to sort mail into folders based on the sender or words in the subject. This feature may be used to divert the duplicate messages into a folder that is separate from your real mail until the problem is resolved.

Hoax   You may be tricked into damaging your own computer. Someone may pose as an expert who is warning you of a dangerous file on your computer. The file may be a necessary part of the operating system. The mes-

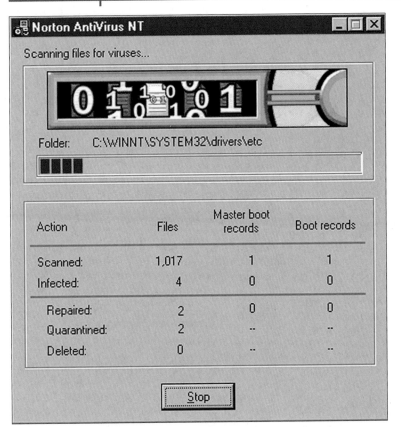

CRITICAL THINKING

DISCUSSION

1 Why do some people write malicious software?

2 If someone you know brags about writing a harmful virus, what should you do?

3 Is it OK to write viruses that attack companies to point out their security weaknesses and embarrass them publicly if you do it in a way that does not do too much actual damage?

4 In the futuristic movie *Minority Report*, starring Tom Cruise, the security system scanned people's eyes to pass them into top-security areas. While Cruise's character was a fugitive, he got past the system by letting it scan one of his eyes. What simple measure could the security forces have taken to prevent his entry? While he was being sought, advertisements on the wall of the mall were showing him targeted advertising. What would this imply about the coordination of the advertising system with the police system?

sage gives instructions on how to remove this file, and it advises you to send the message to your friends. People spread a hoax voluntarily, thinking they are doing their friends a favor. Because this file may be necessary when the computer starts up, the computer will fail to start the next time it is turned on. Never delete files from your computer on the basis of advice in an e-mail message, even if the advice has been passed along by a well-meaning friend. If you receive such advice, be suspicious that the warning may be a *hoax*. Go to one of the Web sites on the companion Web page at **http://www.prenhall.com/preston** where common and recent hoaxes are listed. If your computer's operating system really needs to have a security problem fixed, you can find instructions on what to do on the operating system's company Web site or on reputable security Web sites.

To protect your computer from these attacks, consider the following options:

❱ Install an antivirus program that updates its list of viruses regularly (see Figure 6.8).

❱ Choose an antivirus program that also checks e-mail attachments.

❱ Do not open executable e-mail attachments unless they are checked by an antivirus program, even if you know the sender, to protect against spoofing.

❱ To block worms, install updates and patches to your operating system when they come out.

❱ Disable macros in MS Office, or require that you be prompted before they run.

❱ Do not install pirated software; it may be a Trojan horse.

FIGURE 6.8

Antivirus software scans your disks looking for virus programs.

- If you are the target of an e-mail bomb, notify your Internet service provider or set your firewall to block the message.
- Do not delete files on the basis of advice in an e-mail message.

ENCRYPTED COMMUNICATIONS

Whether you are sending your credit card number or just a simple greeting over the Internet, you need to be confident that some unknown person is not reading it or tampering with it and the recipient is who they say they are. Fortunately, reliable security measures are available. If you understand them, you will feel more confident using the Internet for personal and financial communications.

Encryption

The Internet consists of a network of computers that transmit data in packets. These packets travel by the most convenient and available route, and people who have access to these computers can intercept the packets. When warfare became much more mobile in World War II, it became apparent that communication by telephone wire would not work for submarines, airplanes, and tanks. The alternative was using radio messages that could be received anywhere by anyone but were written in secret code so that only the intended recipient could read them. Changing plain text into unrecognizable text is called *encryption*, and changing it back into plain text is *decryption*. Encryption has been used to protect military communications for thousands of years. Most encryption techniques make decrypting the message so difficult that by the time existing methods can decrypt the message, the information is out of date and useless. The British recognized that the survival of their country depended on intercepting and *deciphering*—decrypting—enemy messages rapidly. They invented Colossus, one of the world's first computers, to speed up the decryption process so they could read enemy messages quickly enough to take advantage of them. Since then, the science of *cryptography* has developed ways to use computers to create coded messages that are too difficult for other computers to decipher quickly. These tools are critical for secure or private communications over the Internet.

Symmetric-key encryption   A *key* is a binary number that is usually between 40 and 128 bits long. A computer uses a specific set of rules called an algorithm to combine parts of the key with the binary numbers that normally represent the characters and numbers in a message. This produces a series of numbers that do not appear to make sense to anyone reading them during transmission. Longer keys provide greater security because there are more possible combinations of numbers. If the same key is used to encrypt and decrypt the message, the system is called *symmetric-key encryption*. The key must be kept secret and be possessed by both the sender and the recipient. This method of using one key to encrypt and decrypt the message is fast, but it poses the problem of getting the key safely into the hands of the intended recipient. For example, many applications allow you to protect a document with a password. The password is used to create a symmetric key. The recipient of the document must know the password and have the same application software that can use the password to generate the symmetric key, and then use the key to decrypt the document.

Public-key encryption   A much slower but more secure method is to use two keys that are created as a pair. One of the keys is kept secret (the private key) and never transmitted. The other key is published and available to anyone (the public key). This asymmetric use of a pair of keys, public and private, is commonly called *public-key encryption* even though it uses a public and a private key. If a message is encrypted with either of the keys, it cannot be decrypted by the same key. It can be decrypted only by the other key in the pair. For example, when you send an order to a merchant that contains personal information, you retrieve the merchant's public key and use it to encrypt the information before you send it. The merchant is the only one with the private key necessary to read the message. This encryption is performed automatically by your browser when you choose to use a secure server to complete a transaction.

Symmetric-key encryption is faster and easier to use than public-key encryption, but symmetric-key encryption has the significant problem of how to get its key to the recipient safely. The problem is solved by using both methods. First, the message is encrypted using symmetric-key encryption. Public-key encryption is used to send the recipient the symmetric key, which is then used to decrypt the message.

Certificate authority When you get a driver's license, the state driver's license bureau checks your identity before it issues you a license because it knows you will use the license as a form of identification. Once you have a driver's license, you can use it as a form of identification that has been verified by the state. Similarly, if you want to use the public-key encryption method to send an encrypted message to someone, you need to obtain the public key from a source you can trust to have verified the identity of the public key's owner. This service is provided by a *certificate authority (CA)*, which maintains a database of user names and their public keys. To assure the identity of the sender, the sender uses his or her private key to encrypt part of the message. The recipient goes to the CA and retrieves the public key for that person. The CA may be used to identify the merchant when you make a purchase online, or it can be used to verify the content of an important document and its sender. A CA like VeriSign charges about $15 a year for generating a public/private key pair and making the public key available on its Web site.

For more information and a well-illustrated tutorial on public-key cryptography, see the companion Web site at **http://www.prenhall.com/preston** for links to related Web sites.

How Encryption Addresses Security Concerns
There are four main communication security concerns: *eavesdropping*, *spoofing*, *misrepresentation*, and *tampering*. These problems can all be solved using a combination of symmetric and public-key encryption.

Eavesdropping If someone eavesdrops on your communication, he or she reads it but does not change it. Eavesdropping can be thwarted by encrypting the body of the message using symmetric-key encryption. Someone who intercepts the message cannot read it without the key.

Spoofing Spoofing is impersonating the sender. To authenticate the identity of the sender, the sender can use public-key encryption. The sender encrypts part of the message with his or her private key. The recipient gets the sender's public key from the CA and uses it to decrypt that part of the message. If the recipient can decrypt the message with the public key, that confirms the identity of the sender.

Misrepresentation Misrepresentation can be impersonating a legitimate recipient such as a well-known Web site, or it can be setting up a fake business that just accepts payment without delivering goods. You can defeat misrepresentation by obtaining a business's public key from the CA and encrypting your message. Only the party identified by the CA can decrypt the message using its private key. If a Web site misrepresents the legitimate function of a business, such as accepting orders but not delivering goods, the injured party can complain and have the CA remove its public key.

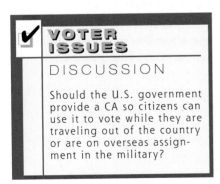

Tampering Tampering is changing the content of a message. Two methods are commonly used to prevent tampering. The easier is to use a symmetric key. The software used to create the document, like Word, WordPerfect, or Excel, can encrypt a file and require a password to decrypt it. The password is used to create the symmetric key. The weakness of that method is that the recipient must have the same password to decrypt the file. A more secure method uses the public- and private-key method to create a *digital signature*. To create a digital signature, the message is processed with an algorithm to produce a single number called a *one-way hash*. For example, an algorithm could tell the computer how to take the binary numbers that represent the characters in the message and arrange them in a table. Each row and column of the table could be summed and the hash assembled by listing this series of sums as a single number. When the message is transmitted, this number and the algorithm used to create it are encrypted with the private key, producing a *digital signature*. The recipient uses the public key to decrypt the hash and its algorithm. The recipient's computer uses the algorithm to create a new hash and compare it with the decrypted hash. If they match, the recipient knows the message was not altered during transmission and can verify the identity of the sender.

Examples

Credit card purchases: Many people are unwilling to use their credit cards to make purchases over the Internet for fear that the card number will be stolen and they will be forced to pay for whatever purchases are made by the thief. Using a credit card online is usually safer for the cardholder than giving it to a waiter at a restaurant. The waiter could copy down the numbers from the card and order something on the Internet during his next break. When you got the bill, you would challenge the unauthorized purchase, and the credit card company would not charge you for it. They would require you to fill out a statement that the charge was fraudulent so they could prosecute the waiter. If someone stole your credit card number online and charges something, you would follow the same process. Credit card companies are willing to accept the risk to make the cards attractive to use. The credit card number is much harder to steal online than it is in the back of the restaurant because your order and card number are encrypted before they are sent. When you place an order, most merchant sites use a *secure server*, which uses public-key encryption. You can tell if a server is using encryption by looking at the status bar in your browser. A lock or key symbol appears when a secure server is in use. Another way to tell whether the server is secure is that the URL of secure servers begins with https:// instead of the default http://. The extra *s* indicates a secure server that encrypts the data it sends and receives. Your browser uses the merchant's public key to encrypt your credit card and other personal information. The merchant checks with the credit card company to confirm that your card number matches the expiration date, name, and mailing address. Some card companies like Visa also allow you to choose a password for use online, which the merchant can use to confirm your identity.

Signing a document or e-mail: We attest to the authenticity of a paper document by writing our signature at the bottom of the document. We can confirm the authenticity and integrity of a digital document using encryption techniques. The message itself does not have to be encrypted. To create a public and private key for use with e-mail, you go to the CA's Web site and request this service. The CA creates the pair of keys and stores the public key on its Web site. It sends you an e-mail message with a program attached that installs the private key on your computer. You then change the security settings of your e-mail program or word processing program to use the key when you choose to encrypt your e-mail mes-

FIGURE 6.9

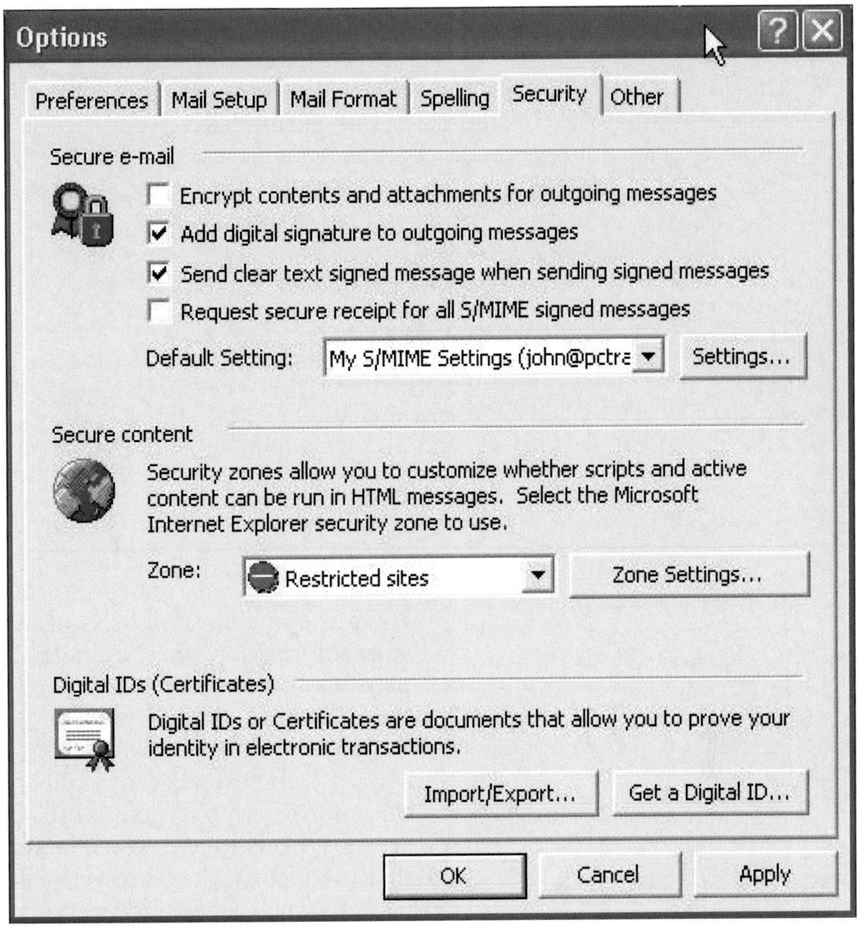

Options

Preferences | Mail Setup | Mail Format | Spelling | Security | Other

Secure e-mail

☐ Encrypt contents and attachments for outgoing messages
☑ Add digital signature to outgoing messages
☑ Send clear text signed message when sending signed messages
☐ Request secure receipt for all S/MIME signed messages

Default Setting: My S/MIME Settings (john@pctra ▼)   Settings...

Secure content

Security zones allow you to customize whether scripts and active content can be run in HTML messages. Select the Microsoft Internet Explorer security zone to use.

Zone: ● Restricted sites   ▼   Zone Settings...

Digital IDs (Certificates)

Digital IDs or Certificates are documents that allow you to prove your identity in electronic transactions.

Import/Export...   Get a Digital ID...

OK   Cancel   Apply

Security option for Microsoft Outlook set to add a digital signature to outgoing e-mail

sages or include a digital signature (see Figure 6.9). When someone receives your e-mail, it has a symbol on it that indicates the digital signature. If the recipient clicks the symbol, it shows the information about you and verifies your identity.

Encrypting documents using public-key encryption: Both parties must have registered public keys to exchange encrypted messages. The application programs must be set to use the keys. They are used to verify the identity of the sender as well as the recipient. See "Mastering Technology" in this section for details on how to set up encrypted communications on your computer.

To use encryption to protect your communications, consider the following tips:

❱ Choose to use the secure server option when making purchases online.
❱ If your credit card offers the additional protection of a password to use for online purchases, go to its Web site and sign up for it.
❱ Use the application software's password protection (see "Mastering Technology" in this section).
❱ Digitally sign important messages or documents.
❱ Encrypt important secret documents.

- Check your computer's security from attack. Use your Web browser and go to ShieldsUP!! at **https://grc.com/x/ne.dll?bh0bkyd2**. Make notes to share with the class about the types of security problems it checks.

- Find the size of the encryption key used by your browser. To do this, open Internet Explorer or Netscape Communicator and from the menu, choose Help, About (Internet Explorer or Netscape). Look through the information to see what the encryption strength is. Look for the numbers 128 or 64, which are the two most likely sizes.

- Save a Word document with a password.

- Add a digital signature to an e-mail message.

PRIVACY

Computers are very good at storing and correlating information, and they are in use in almost all parts of our lives. While they are in use, they can store information about us in databases, which can be analyzed to discover patterns in our behavior. As individuals, we can access these databases online to find old high-school classmates anywhere in the country, run background checks on blind dates, or look up tax values and sales history of a house and those adjacent to it before we buy. Web page designers may use this information to customize the pages we see to present products that we are most likely to buy, which increases the efficiency of shopping online. If they can identify the person requesting a Web page, they can look up information previously entered so that it only has to be entered once. The databases may be used by law enforcement agencies to find and prosecute those who break laws. Government officials use databases to help determine how to allocate resources most effectively to the people who use government services. These databases may also be used by individuals to locate us and find out information we prefer to keep private. They can be used to fill our mailboxes with unwanted e-mail or deny some of us health insurance coverage. It is also possible that law enforcement agencies and politicians may abuse their access to this information.

Finding the right balance between our needs for privacy and security is pivotal to the functioning of our society. In this section, we consider privacy issues related to individuals, businesses, and the government. We look at the methods used to know more about us, as well as actions we can take to protect our privacy.

INDIVIDUALS

Before the Internet was available, if you wanted to find an old high-school friend who had moved out of state and you knew only that he lived somewhere in the Midwest, you might have had to hire a detective or spend weeks in a public library looking at telephone books. Now, a free service like US Search can find someone's telephone number in any state in a matter of moments. If a woman wants to know more about a man with whom she has a blind date, she can look up his age, phone number, and address for free. For an additional fee, she can check his background for relatives (including spouses), roommates, bankruptcies, tax liens, small claims court judgments, real estate ownership and its value, and criminal convictions.

FIGURE 6.10 |

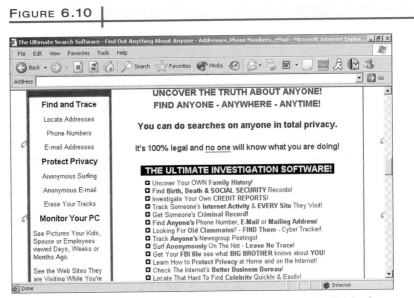

Web sites are available that provide information about individuals.

Some cities and towns make tax records available online. If you want to know the assessed value of your neighbor's house and its sale price when it has been sold, the information is available. This information may also be available about you and your house. It is unnerving to meet a complete stranger who knows a lot of information that you considered private. To find all this information about people, all you need to know is their name and the city and state where they live. Public records like these are readily available (see Figure 6.10).

To keep others online from learning your name, which can be used to look up information, you may choose to use a service that hides your identity while you browse the Web or take part in a chat room (see Figure 6.11).

FIGURE 6.11 |

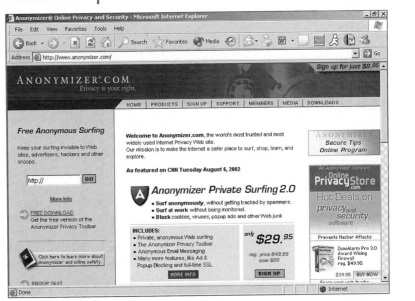

Services may be used to hide your identity while you surf the Web.

1 In response to a question, Scott McNealy, president and CEO of Sun Microsystems, a major computing company, pronounced publicly on January 1, 1998, "You have zero privacy anyway. Get over it." What do you think? Should we simply get used to living without privacy?

2 If you have read George Orwell's book *1984*, which was published in 1949, describe the surveillance technology used in the book. Is the technology Orwell considered futuristic in 1949 available today?

Children's privacy is protected by law. The Children's Online Privacy Protection Act applies to children under 13 years of age. The law requires operators of Web sites to:

❯ Post a privacy policy on the home page of the Web site and provide a link to the privacy policy on every page where personal information is collected.

❯ Provide notice about the site's information collection practices to parents and obtain verifiable parental consent before collecting personal information from children.

❯ Give parents a choice as to whether their child's personal information will be disclosed to third parties.

❯ Provide parents access to their child's personal information and the opportunity to delete the child's personal information and opt out of future collection or use of the information.

❯ Not condition a child's participation in a game, contest, or other activity on the child's disclosing more personal information than is reasonably necessary to participate in that activity.

❯ Maintain the confidentiality, security, and integrity of personal information collected from children.

Parents may also use the Content Advisor in Internet Explorer (IE) or install third-party software to filter software from Web sites (see "Mastering Technology" in this section). See the companion Web page at **http://www.prenhall.com/preston** for links to sites that provide additional information and software.

If you prefer to make it difficult for strangers to find out personal information about your children, have them follow these tips from the Federal Trade Commission's Kidz Privacy Web site (the link is available on the companion Web site at **http://www.prenhall.com/preston**):

❯ Never give out your last or family name, your home address, or your phone number in chat rooms, on bulletin boards, or to online pen pals.

❯ Don't tell other kids your screen name, user ID, or password.

❯ Look at a Web site's privacy policy to see how the site uses the information you give them.

❯ Surf the Internet with your parents. If they aren't available, talk to them about the sites you're visiting.

❯ Talk about the site's privacy policy with your parents so that you and your parents will know what information the site collects about you and what it does with the information.

❯ Web sites must get your parent's permission before they collect many kinds of information from you.

❯ If a Web site has information about you that you and your parents don't want it to have, your parents can ask to see the information—and they can ask the Web site to delete or erase the information.

❯ Sites are not supposed to collect more information than they need about you for the activity you want to participate in. You should be able to participate in many activities online without having to give any information about yourself.

❯ If a site makes you uncomfortable or asks for more information than you want to share, leave the site.

BUSINESS

Most businesses exist to make money. They do this by providing products and services we want to buy. Their choice of business methods is guided in part by the requirement to make money for investors, avoid penalties for breaking the law, and limit money paid out in civil lawsuits. The pressure of competition may cause some businesses to use methods that are legal but unethical. In this section, we consider privacy issues related to legal practices by businesses. We also consider the special problems of privacy related to personal medical records and health insurance.

Marketing

An important function of the marketing department in a company is to find the most effective way to advertise and sell the company's products or services to the people who are willing to buy them. One method is to advertise to everyone, hoping that some of the people will buy the product. Using highway billboards is an example of this type of advertising. Another approach is *targeted advertising*, which limits advertising to a segment of the population most likely to buy the product. If a company sells disposable diapers, they want to target their advertising to people who are most likely to have very young children. Both types of marketing may be done legally and ethically, but some companies use methods that are intrusive and unethical. Both types of advertising are possible using computers. First, we consider how computers may be used to advertise to many people at low cost.

Spam   Direct mail advertising is often called junk mail because people do not ask for it and end up throwing almost all of it away unread. Junk mail fills up our mailboxes and landfills with paper. Direct mail advertisers pay the cost of distributing their letters, flyers, and inserts but do not ask our permission to send it to us or pay us for the time and expense of disposing of it. Some people do respond to these ads or consider them valuable when they happen to want a particular product. *Spam* is similar to direct mail advertising in that it is sent to us without our permission, but it is different from direct mail advertising because the advertisers do not pay the people who deliver the e-mail messages. At this time, approximately half of e-mail traffic is spam and it is increasing. Spam costs American businesses more than $9 billion a year. Spam is like a billboard in that it is expected to be seen by many people at a low cost per person. Because it costs the sender so little to send out millions of e-mail advertisements, even small rates of successful sales yield large profits. It is unethical because an objective observer would not consider this practice fair to the Internet service provider that must buy extra equipment to distribute spam. Some businesses that use direct e-mail marketing include an address to which recipients can respond to remove their names from the mailing list. This practice by ethical direct mail advertisers is undermined by unethical spammers who simply use these responses to confirm that your e-mail address is active, which makes it more valuable.

Here are some tips for limiting unwanted e-mail advertising:

❭ Check registration forms carefully for check boxes that indicate you are willing to accept e-mail with product information from companies or their business partners, and deselect the check boxes.

❭ Read a Web site's privacy policy before you provide personal information.

❭ Check to see if your Internet service provider offers extra e-mail accounts that you are not using. Activate one of these accounts to give out when necessary. Advertising will accumulate in that account along with an occasional useful message, but you may choose when to read these messages. Some authorities suggest using one of the free e-mail accounts available through Yahoo! or MSN Hotmail for this purpose. Intentionally pointing large amounts of e-mail toward their servers when you are not paying for them is not fair to them. If you use one that is provided by a service you pay for, you will share the expense as it is passed along to you in your monthly fees.

❱ Firewalls may be set to block e-mail from some known sources of spam, but experienced *spammers* (purveyors of spam) easily change domain names to get past these protections.

❱ Buy software that helps the firewall block sources of spam and scan e-mail messages for key words or phrases that may identify them as spam. Known lists of spam sources are updated regularly.

❱ If you use Netscape mail or Microsoft's Outlook Express mail client at a public computer, be sure to remove any personal e-mail addresses before you leave so the next user does not provide additional Web sites with this information.

❱ Encourage state and federal lawmakers to pass laws similar to the *do not call* laws that make it illegal to make telemarketing calls to people who choose not to receive them.

Profiling Computers facilitate targeted advertising because the information is already in a computer somewhere—it just needs to be gathered and sorted properly to define specific groups of people who are likely buyers for particular products. For example, if you buy a book from Amazon.com, the company stores this information and the next time you visit the site you will be greeted by name and shown advertisements for books on the same topic. To keep track of your transactions, a company keeps records of personal information such as your mailing address, phone number, credit card number, and e-mail address. When you use a browser to go to a Web site to shop, you have the option of providing a user name and password to identify yourself to the server so it can look up your records. This method is useful for high-security sites like a bank, but is cumbersome when surfing from one site to another. The solution to this problem is to allow the server to generate a user identification number that is stored on your computer's hard drive the first time you visit the site. The next time you request the same Web page, your browser also sends this ID number with the request, and the server may respond with a Web page that greets you by name and is customized to your shopping preferences. The ID number is stored as a text file, called a *cookie*, on your computer. Cookies are widely misunderstood. They are not programs that search your hard drive for information. Your Web browser controls their use and confirms that they are simple text files without executable code. Cookies are usually stored in a folder called Cookies and may be read with a word processing program (see Figure 6.12).

A company with whom you do business can keep track of your visits to its Web site and any personal information you provide. What the company does with it is covered by its *privacy policy*, which few people read. The company may remove your personal information and report the behavior of it customers as a group, or it may sell details of your transactions and personal information to marketers who use this information to send unsolicited mail or e-mail or make unsolicited telephone calls. Many sites that provide free services or information in exchange for registering make

FIGURE 6.12

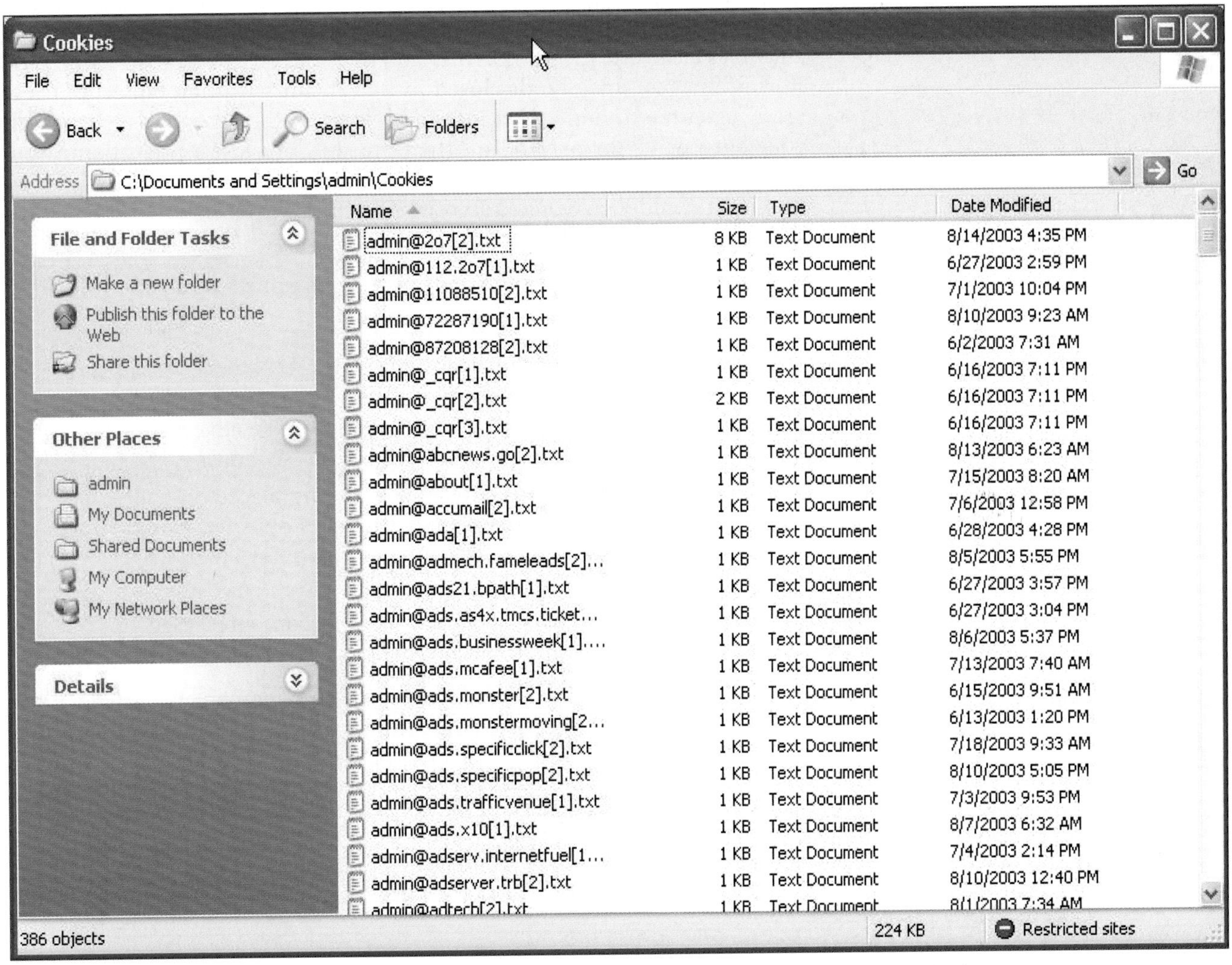

Cookies are small text files that are stored in the Cookies folder on computers that use Windows.

money by selling the information you provide to marketers. Ethical companies ask if you agree to allow your personal information to be used; other companies assume your permission unless the you make a special effort to decline this use. Companies that gather information about individuals from several sources develop a *profile* of the person that describes the person's Web browsing habits across a variety of sites. This profile is a valuable tool for efficient, targeted advertising, but it also makes people uncomfortable.

The privacy policies of individual companies were bypassed by DoubleClick, a company that provides banner ads that appear as part of thousands of different Web pages. The banner ads use a ***Web bug***, which is hidden on the banner ad as a small graphic image that is only one pixel and is often the same color as the background. The Web browser is tricked into requesting this extremely small image from the DoubleClick Web server, which uses the opportunity to place its own cookie on the user's hard drive without asking. DoubleClick uses this technique to obtain information about a user's Web browsing from every site they visit that has one of their banner ads. When DoubleClick acquired Abacus Direct, a company that bought information about individuals, many people objected that the combination of individual information and browsing behavior that was secretly obtained was too great an invasion of privacy. The use of Web bugs, also known as clear GIFs, 1-by-1 GIFs, and invisible GIFS (*GIF* is a format for storing images), may be disclosed in a Web site's privacy policy, but few users take time to find and read it. Web bugs are not programs that search your hard drive for private information; they are just a way of storing a cookie on your computer. The concern is that they were used by a company that could view your Web browsing habits from many different sites and form a profile of your activity.

This form of targeted advertising can be controlled using the following tips:

❱ Set your browser to prompt you each time a Web page attempts to place a cookie on your computer. If the source of the cookie is not the Web site you are using, it is probably from an advertiser using a Web bug. (See Mastering Technology in this section.)

❱ Set your browser to block cookies from being placed on your computer. This method defeats the conveniences of using cookies, but it stops them from being added to your computer's hard drive (see Figure 6.13).

❱ Delete the cookies that are already on your computer. (See Mastering Technology in this section.)

Read a Web site's privacy policy before you provide personal information. Do not use the site if you are not willing to allow your personal information to be sold or shared with business partners.

Spyware   When you install a program on your computer, you are required to read and agree to the end user license agreement (EULA). In some EULAs, there is a clause that gives the company permission to install

FIGURE 6.13

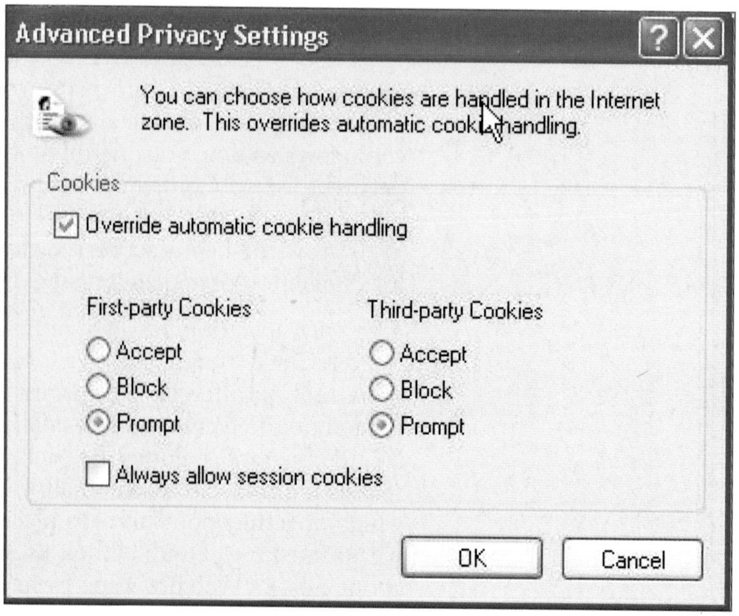

Browsers allow you to control cookies.

additional programs that track your behavior from inside your computer. Unlike DoubleClick's use of Web bugs, this method catches all of your Web browsing activity. These programs can contact a company's Web server and transfer the information automatically the next time you are attached to the Internet. Programs that track your Web browsing for use by marketers are called *adware*. The same type of program may be used to monitor any other activity on your computer that its owners want to know about; these programs that go beyond tracking Web browsing are called *spyware*. Spyware programs usually do not show up on your list of programs or on a list of programs you can delete.

Spyware and adware may be stopped using the following tips:

❯ Read the EULA to see if installing the "free" software gives permission to install spyware.

❯ Use free software to scan your computer for adware and spyware, and remove it. (See Mastering Technology in this section and the companion Web site at **http://www.prenhall.com/preston**.)

Pop-up and pop-under ads Another form of targeted advertising is an ad that is activated when you move the mouse pointer over a particular part of a Web page. A new window opens with an ad in it. Responding to the message in the ad, even just a choice to close the Window, can activate other ads. The windows do not fill the screen but appear to pop up in front of the current screen (see Figure 6.14) so they are called *pop-up* ads. Other ads pop up behind the other windows and do not come into view until the others are all closed. This type is called a *pop-under* ad. Pop-up window technology may be used by Web pages to provide useful information so if you want to use third-party software to block these ads, it is important that it be able to distinguish between pop-up windows you have requested and those you have not. To stop pop-up and pop-under ads, use the following tips:

❯ If pop-up windows are proliferating out of control on your screen and you are using the Windows operating system, halt operations

FIGURE 6.14

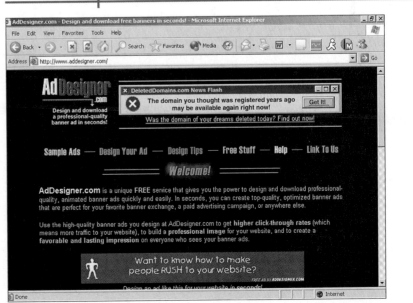

Pop-up ads appear in windows in front of the page you are viewing.

and delete the offending processes (see Mastering Technology in this section and the companion Web site at **http://www.prenhall. com/preston**).

〉 Download a free program to block pop-up and pop-under ads such as the Google Toolbar (see the companion Web site at **http://www. prenhall.com/preston**).

〉 If you have a personal firewall installed, check the settings to see if it already has an option to block pop-up ads.

Presence technology   Computer technology makes it possible to determine when you are using a computer and where you are. These are two features of *presence technology*. Knowing where you are and that you are looking at your computer provides another type of targeted advertising opportunity. If you use instant messaging (IM), the program knows when you are looking at your computer screen by your active exchanges. If you use a cell phone, it is easy to tell which cell phone tower is closest to you (see Figure 6.15). By using a computer to analyze the relative strength of your cell phone signal from several towers, it is possible to determine your location to within a city block. A computer device with Global Positioning System (GPS) capability uses signals from multiple satellites to calculate location within a few feet. Presence technology has many potential benefits—for example, the *enhanced 911 (e911)* emergency response system allows emergency responders to 911 calls from cell phones to respond to a

FIGURE 6.15

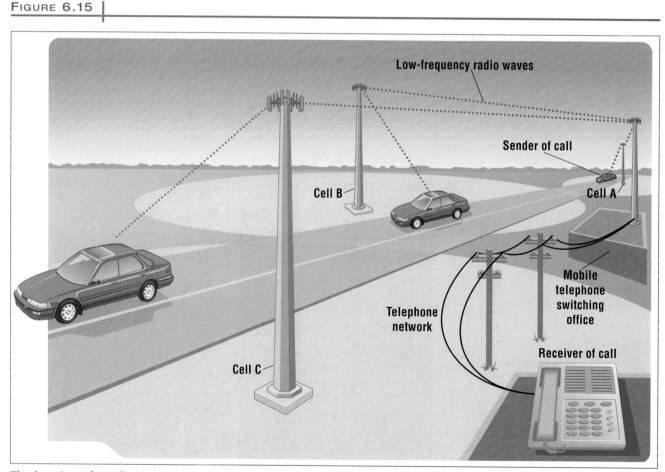

The location of a cell phone may be determined by its signal strength at nearby cell towers.

specific location. Some cell phones or personal digital assistants (PDAs) use presence technology to enable advertisers to respond to requests for information about restaurants and nightclubs with details about those businesses that are near the caller's location. Presence technology is used on automobiles to provide navigation and assistance. Use of this technology also gives someone a detailed record of your physical movements. These records may be stored and used to profile your behavior. If your cell phone is on, it is communicating with the cell towers in your area, providing continuous information about your location. To limit the availability of this type of information, you may choose to turn off your cell phone when you do not want your location tracked. Legislation has been proposed by Senator John Edwards (D-NC) to limit the recording of this type of location information from cell phones (see the companion Web site).

In general, to control marketers' intrusion into your privacy, consider the motivations mentioned earlier. If the intrusions are unprofitable, they will slow down, so do not buy products advertised via unsolicited e-mail or pop-up ads unless you want to see more of them. Because unethical practices give some advertisers an advantage, these intrusions will not be reduced unless they are made illegal. Individuals can contact their government representatives to support the creation of laws that limit advertising that violates our privacy.

Employer-Employee Relationship

When you are using a company's computer equipment, do not expect personal privacy. Your e-mail may be read and your Web browsing recorded. Each keystroke may be recorded. *Transponders*, which communicate using radio waves, may be used to track your location while you are on company property, or a GPS system may track the location of your company vehicle. It is best to conduct any personal business using your own computer or cell phone. If you use a company cell phone, the record of your calls is company property. For example, when the *New York Times* investigated its reporter Jason Blair, it found that many of his phone calls that were supposedly made in various cities to call in his stories actually originated in New York. Because he used a cell phone that was provided by the newspaper, the paper did not need a court order—it simply requested the phone records for that month. Companies may monitor workspaces with video cameras, which are useful for evaluating sexual harassment claims. The human resources department can locate significant amounts of information about someone before offering the person a job. Read your company's policy on monitoring employee activities. If there is a union where you work, it may be able to negotiate an agreement to limit employee monitoring.

Health Care Providers and Health Insurance Companies

Information about our bodies is very personal, and businesses that deal with our health have a special responsibility to safeguard our privacy. Unfortunately, this makes computerizing medical records and billing difficult, especially when there are hundreds of different insurance companies involved that do not use standardized forms. A study of 6,400 hospitals reported in the *New England Journal of Medicine* in 1993 revealed that administrative costs in the United States constituted 24.8 percent of hospital spending, which was more than twice as high as in Canada. For each practicing doctor, there are four people managing records and performing administrative tasks. We have the technology to reduce this cost, but its adoption is slowed by the concern for privacy. If patient records were

DISCUSSION

1 The FBI investigated and kept records of activities of civil rights leaders in the 1960s. Do you think that the information-gathering apparatus being put together by the Department of Homeland Security will be used against the interest of minorities? What should be done to ensure that government surveillance is not used to deny the rights of minorities?

2 Should children have a right to privacy from their parents while they surf the Internet?

3 Do you think it is ethical for parents to check the browser history on the family computer to see if their teenager has been visiting Web sites they consider unacceptable?

4 Do you think it is ethical for parents of a teenager to record the keystrokes on the teenager's computer to enable them to read their chat and IM conversations?

5 Should a woman be able to check a man's financial and criminal record before she goes out on a date with him? Should women have rights of this sort that are not granted to men?

pooled into a single database, which could be accessed by insurance and health care companies as well as the government, costs for billing could be greatly reduced. However, there are significant risks to personal privacy in compiling this much personal information in one place. One concern is that employers would refuse to hire someone if they knew there were a family history of disease that might affect the employee in the future. The health insurance industry is built on the concept of sharing risk of the unknown future across a large group of people. As we use computers to learn more about DNA and genetic diseases, it is possible to divide this large group of people into different groups with different degrees of risk. Insurance companies that are trying to make a profit may use this information to refuse insurance to people in higher-risk groups, eventually negating the basic assumption of buying insurance in the first place. Health care providers were required to provide detailed information about privacy rights to patients in 2003. To learn more about your rights to privacy of health information, see the link to the Department of Health and Human Services on the companion Web page at **http://www. prenhall.com/preston**.

GOVERNMENT

All U.S. congresspersons and military officers take an oath to "... defend the Constitution of the United States against all enemies, foreign and domestic. . . ." Their ability to do so is limited by the constitution itself (see Figure 6.16), which guarantees that citizens be secure from unreasonable searches. Determining what is a reasonable search in today's computerized world is a challenge for the courts. Enemies may attack our computer systems electronically or use e-mail and Web pages to coordinate attacks by agents within the country. Defending our country against such foreign enemies may require that the government perform the type of electronic searches and profiling that we find so disturbing when performed by businesses. Domestic enemies could include government officials themselves who seek to secure their hold on power by using computerized surveillance by government agencies to gain an advantage over political opponents. In this section, we consider the importance of privacy to the political process, as well as the trade-offs between privacy and security related to national defense and law enforcement.

Government Officials

Our political process depends upon the freedom to form dissenting political parties that try to win elections and replace the group in power. If the politicians currently in office use their power or office to spy upon those who oppose them in order to defeat their opponents and maintain power, the basis of our representative democracy is threatened. President Nixon resigned the presidency because his efforts to obtain records from

FIGURE 6.16

The right of the people to be secure in their persons, houses, papers, and effects, against unreasonable searches and seizures, shall not be violated, and no Warrants shall issue, but upon probable cause, supported by Oath or affirmation, and particularly describing the place to be searched, and the persons or things to be seized.— U.S. Constitution, Fourth Amendment

The Constitution limits unreasonable search.

Democratic Party headquarters and Daniel Ellsberg's psychiatrist were uncovered. President Clinton's director of personnel security resigned when it was discovered he had obtained confidential FBI files on hundreds of Republicans. These activities were detected because they involved physical break-ins or paper files. If these intrusions had involved computer files, they may have gone undetected.

The United States is fighting a war against terrorists who use the Internet to communicate with each other. To fight that war, law enforcement officials want more authority to record and evaluate private e-mail. They also want to check up on people who have airline reservations to see if there is any unusual activity in their bank records, credit card purchases, visa status, criminal record, or any other database to spot potential terrorists and subject them to additional screening before they board the plane. Older laws that governed the behavior of agencies like the Central Intelligence Agency (CIA) and the National Security Agency (NSA) were based on geography and limited their spying to activities taking place outside the United States. The attacks on September 11, 2001, prompted the government to reorganize and form the Department of Homeland Security and pass the USA Patriot Act (see the companion Web page). In the National Strategy for Homeland Security from the Office of Homeland Security, government officials stated that we must link our various databases together to fight this threat (see Figure 6.17).

We depend upon the government to protect us from many forms of intrusion into our privacy by businesses and individuals. It is therefore

FIGURE 6.17

National Strategy for Homeland Security from the Office of Homeland Security, page 10

Information Sharing and Systems. Information systems contribute to every aspect of homeland security. Although American information technology is the most advanced in the world, our country's information systems have not adequately supported the homeland security mission. Databases used for federal law enforcement, immigration, intelligence, public health surveillance, and emergency management have not been connected in ways that allow us to comprehend where information gaps or redundancies exist. In addition, there are deficiencies in the communications systems used by states and municipalities throughout the country; most state and local first responders do not use compatible communications equipment. To secure the homeland better, we must link the vast amounts of knowledge residing within each government agency while ensuring adequate privacy. The National Strategy for Homeland Security identifies five major initiatives in this area:

- Integrate information sharing across the federal government;
- Integrate information sharing across state and local governments, private industry, and citizens;
- Adopt common "meta-data" standards for electronic information relevant to homeland security;
- Improve public safety emergency communications;
- Ensure reliable public health information.

The National Strategy for Homeland Security indicates a plan to integrate databases from government, business, and public health.

frightening to many when the government itself wants to integrate databases from government, health, and business to monitor the activities of individuals, many of whom wish to replace the current officials in the next election. The separation of powers among the three branches of government, along with a free press, has corrected for the abuse of power in the past. Abuses of power by the executive branch involving computerized data may be much harder to detect than past offenses that involved break-ins and boxes of paper files. We must be careful when we allow one branch of government to collect and analyze data on every judge, congressperson, news reporter, and political opponent.

National Defense and Law Enforcement

Federal agencies have all the computer tools businesses do, plus several more. They may use court orders to gain access to financial databases, telephone conversations, and e-mail correspondence within the United States and monitor any foreign traffic without a court order. They also have significant budgets to devote to developing new technologies. Government computers can monitor e-mail traffic on the Internet backbone and look for key words in the messages that might indicate terrorist or illegal activity. The system used for this monitoring was originally named *Carnivore*. People who do not want the government reading their e-mail, files, or instant messages can use encryption software like PGP that is very difficult to decipher, even for government computers (see the companion Web site at **http://www.prenhall.com/preston**). To counter this type of encryption, government programmers wrote a program to record keystrokes that could be transferred to a suspect's computer as the payload of a virus. This operation was code-named *Magic Lantern*.

Law enforcement and other security agencies have video cameras that monitor public areas in major cities. Computers may be used to look for faces that match those in a database of suspects and notify authorities if someone who matches is seen.

Two other controversial technologies are under consideration: a national identification system and individual computer processor identification numbers. Social Security numbers are often used to identify individuals, but that number is not combined with any physical identification like a fingerprint or iris pattern that can be checked by computer, which makes identity theft relatively easy. States provide driver's licenses with pictures, but state transportation departments have not traditionally shared driver's license data, which limits their use for nationwide identification. The federal government is taking steps to use the Social Security number as a national ID number. In 1996, the Welfare Reform bill required all employers to report the Social Security number of each new employee to the federal government. The government also requires that children be given Social Security numbers when they are born to qualify as a tax deduction. The Illegal Immigration and Immigrant Responsibility Act instituted standards for state driver's licenses that require them to include an individual's Social Security number in machine-readable form. This portion of the act was repealed in 1999. In 1999, Intel announced that it would include an identification number in each microprocessor chip in order to make communications over the Internet more secure. Consumers were concerned that this number could be used to tie Web browsing activity to individuals. Under threat of a boycott of its products, Intel announced in 2000 that it would not include this feature in its future chips. Although both of these technologies were rejected as too much of a threat to privacy, we may see them reintroduced to provide law enforcement with powerful tools to enforce laws and track terrorists.

Deciding how much privacy to cede to the government in exchange for security is a decision that we must make as a society. Our choices will determine the nature of our democratic government and how much government is part of our personal lives (see Figure 6.18).

FIGURE 6.18

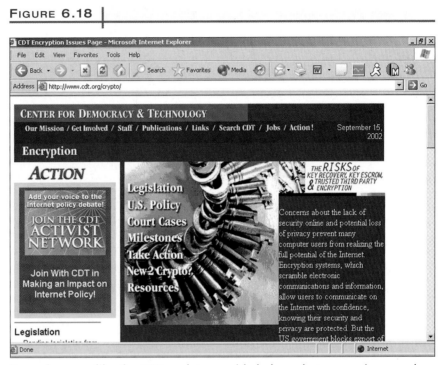

Several groups like the CDT work to provide balance between privacy and security.

1. Set the Content Advisor in Internet Explorer to filter Web pages, by choosing Tools, Internet Options, Content. In the Content Advisor section, click the Enable button. Choose the ratings levels for language, nudity, sex, and violence. Click the General tab and choose the rating system, password, and other user options of your choice.

2. Find the directory of cookies on your computer, and read some of them. To do this, look for a folder on your hard disk named cookies. Use a word processing program like Word to open the files. You may have to set the Files of type box to All Files to see these text files.

3. Download and install a free program to detect spyware and adware to see what's on your computer. To do this, use your browser to go to **http://beam.to/spybotsd**, and follow the directions to download and install this program. Then search your hard drive for spyware.

4. Set browser security to prompt you when a cookie is about to be saved on your computer so you can see how often this occurs.

   a. To do this in Internet Explorer 6.0, from the Tools menu, choose Internet Options. Click the Privacy tab, then click the Advanced button. Select *Prompt* for the first-party and third-party cookies. Click OK to close the dialog boxes.

   b. To do this in Netscape Communicator 7.1, from the Edit menu, choose Preferences, and double-click Privacy & Security. Click Cookies, and choose *Ask me before storing a cookie.* Click OK to close the dialog box.

5. Clear history and files after browsing in IE or Netscape Communicator. The History feature makes is easy to go back to a Web page that has been viewed previously. Clearing the history removes this convenience. Clearing the history is recommended when you leave a public computer or you do not want anyone else who uses the same computer to know what Web sites you have been visiting.

   a. To do this in IE, choose Tools, Internet Options. Click the General tab, if necessary. In the *Temporary Internet files* section, click Delete Files. If you have never done this, it may take several minutes to delete all the stored Web pages and temporary files. In the History section, click the Clear History button. Close the dialog box, and return to the browser. Click the arrow at the right end of the Address box. Normally this would show a history of your recent visits to Web pages. Now there is nothing in this list.

   b. To do this in Netscape Communicator, from the Go menu, choose History. From the menu in the History dialog box, choose Edit, Select All, and then choose Edit, Delete.

6. Learn more about Web sites. A company named Alexa.com compiles profiles on Web sites just as some companies compile profiles on individuals. To see these profiles of how Web sites are used, go to **http://www.alexa.com** and enter URLs for your favorite Web sites.

TEST PREPARATION

The following section does not replace reading the text, nor does it contain all the information that will be tested. It is designed to provide examples and identify sections that need review.

summary by objective

PHYSICAL SECURITY

- **Know methods used to identify and secure computer equipment:**
  - Record equipment serial numbers and attach or inscribe identifying code numbers
  - Use cables with locks for desktop computers
- **Understand how to back up data:**
  - Save data to optical media like a CD-R
  - Save to a network drive
- **Understand how to choose secure passwords:**
  - Avoid birth dates, real words
  - Use a mix of upper- and lowercase letters with numbers
- **Identify types of biometric identification:**
  - Fingerprint recognition
  - Iris recognition
- **Give examples of types of possessed objects:**
  - Card with magnetic strip
  - Card with computer chip and transponder

SECURE CONNECTIONS TO OTHER COMPUTERS

- **List types of software used for secure Internet connections:**
  - Firewalls
  - Proxy servers
  - Browser security settings
- **Define types of attacks and countermeasures:**
  - Virus—antivirus software
  - Worm—update operating system as updates are issued
  - Macro virus—turn off macros within software like Word, Excel, and WordPerfect
  - Trojan horse—do not install pirated software or software from an unknown source
  - E-mail virus—do not open attachments that are executable files without scanning them with an antivirus program
  - E-mail bomb—set firewall to block mail from the source or set it to limit the number of e-mail message to a particular address
  - Hoax—do not remove files based on advice in an e-mail; check the hoaxes Web site or the Web site of the software's manufacturer

ENCRYPTED COMMUNICATIONS

- **Explain how encryption works:**
  - Symmetric—key encryption uses the same key to encrypt and decrypt the message
  - Public—key encryption uses a pair of keys; one is secret and the other is available from a public source
  - Certificate authority—organization that maintains a database of public keys
  - Digital signature—The contents of the message are reduced to a single number using an algorithm. The number and algorithm are encrypted with the private key to create a digital signature that is sent with the message. The recipient decrypts the digital signature with the public key and uses the algorithm to recreate the single number. If the digital signature can be decrypted, you know it is from the sender; and if the algorithm produces the same number, you know the plain text message was not altered.
- **Explain how encryption is used to protect communications:**
  - Eavesdropping—encrypted messages may not be read without the key
  - Spoofing—a digital signature defeats spoofing
  - Misrepresentation—send a message encrypted with the legitimate Web site's public key; if the recipient does not have the private key, he or she cannot read the message
  - Tampering—use a digital signature to confirm identity and integrity
  - Credit card purchases—use secure Web servers that encrypt their communications

INDIVIDUAL PRIVACY

- **Use online sources to find personal information about individuals—Information is available on phone numbers, home prices, criminal records, and credit history.**
- **Minimize availability of your own personal information to other individuals:**
  - Do not give your real name to strangers
  - Use a service that hides your identity to browse Web pages

BUSINESS PRIVACY

- **Explain how databases are compiled for targeted advertising:**
  - Registration forms
  - Shopping
- **Understand how spam works and how to reduce it:**
  - Advertising sent to millions of e-mail addresses
  - Don't buy the products
  - Use an alternate e-mail address from your ISP
- **Explain how cookies are used:**
  - Managed by the browser
  - Created by the Web server
  - Data stored on server, ID number stored in a cookie on the hard drive
- **Understand how to block cookies and Web bugs—Change settings inside the browser to prompt when cookies are saved.**
- **Be aware of spyware and how to block it—Read the EULA of free software or any new software and look for section that permits installation of other programs to monitor activity.**
- **Describe how presence technologies determine your location:**
  - IM is in use
  - Signal from cell phone to towers
  - GPS determines location and transmits it
- **Know what privacy to expect while using computers at work—None.**
- **Be aware of problems managing health records:**
  - Privacy concerns slow computerization, which raises costs
  - Better knowledge of genetic diseases may undermine the basis for health insurance by for-profit companies

GOVERNMENT PRIVACY

- **Understand the risks of government officials gaining access to private information—May be used to perpetuate and concentrate power.**
- **List tools used by security agencies and law enforcement that look at personal information:**
  - Carnivore—sniffs e-mail for key words
  - Magic Lantern—infects suspect's computer with a Web bug to report activity
  - Face recognition

true/false questions

1. ____ Biometric devices combine biology with statistics to identify individuals by measuring characteristics of their bodies.

2. ____ Browsers may be set to block the use of cookies.

3. ____ Cookies are executable programs installed on your computer's hard drive that report on your activity and your hard drive's contents to a Web server.

4. ____ Passwords are used to create a symmetric key.

5. ____ Computers can be used with video surveillance cameras to identify individuals in public places.

1. Which of the following is the least secure method of backing up your data?
   a) Save the data on a CD-R, and place the disc in your desk drawer.
   b) Save a copy of your files in another folder on the same hard drive.
   c) Save a copy of your files on a different computer on the company's local area network.
   d) Make copies on a removable hard disk that is stored in a safe at night.

2. Which of the following tricks you into taking action that damages your own computer?
   a) hoax
   b) e-mail bomb
   c) worm
   d) macro virus

3. Which of the following is not a function of a firewall?
   a) serving Web pages in the DMZ
   b) filtering Web pages or e-mail that contain objectionable material

   c) limiting certain types of protocols like HTTP and SMTP to particular gateway computers
   d) logging traffic between a LAN and the Internet

4. Which of the following is not true about cookies?
   a) They are managed by the Web browser.
   b) They are text files that may be read with a word processing program.
   c) They may be stored on your computer by a Web bug.
   d) They typically contain your name, shipping address, and credit card number so you do not have to enter this information each time you buy something.

5. Which of the following is not true about spyware?
   a) If you agree to the EULA without reading it, you may unknowingly give permission to install spyware.
   b) Freeware software may include spyware.
   c) Cookies often contain spyware.
   d) Adware is a form of spyware.

1. A company or group that verifies a person's identity, issues public-key encryption keys, and serves public keys on Web pages is called a _____ _____ (two words, not just the acronym).

2. The emergency response system that can locate a cell phone is known as _____.

3. A program that claims to be one type of program but contains another type of program is called a _____ _____ (two words).

4. Falsifying the sender's name in a virus-bearing e-mail message to divert efforts to find and fix the virus is called _____.

5. A digital signature may include a _____-_____ _____ (three words) that may be used to verify that the nonencrypted message has not been altered.

Match each term with its definition.

_____ **1.** biometrics
_____ **2.** certificate authority (CA)
_____ **3.** cookie
_____ **4.** digital signature
_____ **5.** e-mail bomb
_____ **6.** encrypt
_____ **7.** enhanced 911 (e911)
_____ **8.** firewall
_____ **9.** gateway
_____ **10.** Global Positioning System (GPS)
_____ **11.** hoax
_____ **12.** key
_____ **13.** misrepresentation
_____ **14.** one-way hash
_____ **15.** payload
_____ **16.** proxy server
_____ **17.** public-key encryption
_____ **18.** secure server
_____ **19.** spoofing
_____ **20.** spyware
_____ **21.** symmetric-key encryption
_____ **22.** Trojan horse
_____ **23.** virus
_____ **24.** Web bug
_____ **25.** worm

a. binary number used to encrypt or decrypt messages
b. change using a specific method to hide the meaning
c. claiming to be a legitimate Web site to divert communication to the false site
d. connection to the Internet
e. emergency response system that can determine the location of cell phones
f. false message used to trick someone into taking an action
g. graphic element in a Web page that secretly calls an advertising Web page, which sets a cookie that monitors a user's browsing habits
h. group that maintains a database of user names and public keys
i. intermediary between the user's computer and the Web page server
j. single number produced from an entire message
k. portion of a message encrypted with the sender's private key to verify the identity of the sender
l. practice of sending large numbers of messages to an e-mail address to overwhelm the mail server
m. possibly destructive program carried by a virus
n. program that claims to be something else
o. unauthorized program that replicates itself using computer resources and then spreads copies to other computers
p. program that tracks behavior and the contents of a computer's hard drive without permission
q. providing a false name as the sender of an e-mail message
r. method of encryption that uses the same key to encrypt and decrypt a message
s. program that searches for vulnerable computers on the Internet and installs programs that allow someone to take control of them
t. software that filters connections to the Internet
u. statistics applied to biology
v. text file stored on the hard drive that is sent by the browser to a Web site to identify the person requesting the Web page
w. Two different keys used for encryption and decryption
x. Uses public key encryption to transfer data on a Web page form
y. Uses satellites to determine location

beyond the facts

Factual knowledge provides the basis for higher levels of learning. In the following sections, you work with the concepts and facts presented in the chapter to develop critical-thinking and problem-solving skills. You practice research, analysis, and communication and become aware of diversity issues while exploring the impact of computer technology on career choices, the workplace, social interactions, and home life. The Leadership section helps you identify ways in which you can lead others in organizing and implementing projects that meet worthwhile community needs. In the Lifelong Learning exercise, you build a set of learning resources that you can use after this course to continue learning.

objectives for beyond the facts

END OF CHAPTER EXERCISES	Achievement for the objectives of the end-of-chapter exercises requires evaluation of documents, class discussions, or presentations.
Critical Thinking—Research	Compare privacy rights in the EU versus in the United States. Demonstrate the following skills: ability to locate relevant information online, analyze the information and form an opinion based on the research, consider diversity issues, work with others where appropriate, and communicate the results in writing or by public presentation.
Problem Solving	1) Work with someone else to send and receive encrypted documents using public-key encryption. 2) Write a detailed description of the process for obtaining a public-key encryption capability from a CA like VeriSign. Describe any problems you encountered and how you addressed them. 3) Communicate the experience to the class.
Anticipating Career Challenges and Opportunities	If management of health care records and insurance payments is reformed and the amount of paperwork is cut in half, what impact will that have on jobs in health care administration and health insurance? Demonstrate the following skills: 1) Teamwork: coordinate research on jobs affected by improvements in efficiency in managing health care records and insurance billing 2) Research: find articles related to the topic 3) Diversity: consider the potential for services 4) Analysis: analyze the change in the way health care records are managed and insurance bills are paid. Predict new job opportunities and which types of jobs will be diminished. 5) Communication: communicate the results in writing or by public presentation
Impact on the Workplace	Find out how your company handles legal documents at a distance. If it does not use digital signatures or public-key encryption to transmit documents, determine what effect changing to that system would have. Demonstrate the following skills: 1) Teamwork: coordinate research with other students 2) Research: identify company policies toward security and authenticity of documents transmitted electronically 3) Diversity:Compare practices with those in other countries or cultures 4) Analysis: form an opinion about the degree to which your organization is willing to change its methods to use electronic document authentication 5) Communication: communicate the results in writing or by public presentation
Impact on Social Interactions	Are we ready to trust electronic voting? Consider the issue of electronic voting in light of what you have learned about security and privacy. Demonstrate the following skills: 1) Teamwork: allocate tasks for research on secure communications and voting 2) Research: review articles and polls concerning voting online. Compare people's trust of physical punch-card voting systems versus more advanced electronic voting systems. Find articles that discuss how votes could be verified. 3) Diversity: look for different attitudes among political and ethnic minorities about trusting electronic and online voting 4) Analysis: compare recent attitudes toward electronic voting with those in articles written before the presidential election of 2000. Comment on any findings related to diversity. 5) Communication: communicate the results in writing or by public presentation

Impact on Home Life	Find out about options for protecting young children while they use the Internet.
	Demonstrate the following skills:
	1) Teamwork: allocate tasks for finding options
	2) Research: find free options and software from third-party vendors to filter and monitor a child's online activity
	3) Analysis: prepare an example of how a set of options would address the concerns common to most parents
	4) Communication: communicate the results in writing or by public presentation
Leadership	Describe a plan to lead a group of people toward a worthy goal. In this case, provide a service to parents to set up their computers to protect children. Demonstrate the ability to inspire others to follow your vision.
Lifelong Learning	Identify three or more online resources that may be used to learn more about the topics introduced in this chapter.

critical thinking–research

The European Union and the United States have different approaches to privacy rights. Find out what rights people have in the EU to deal with unsolicited advertisements such as spam.

1. **Teamwork**—Join one to three other students. Decide how to divide up the work. Possible divisions could be: research, editing the group paper, and preparing the class presentation.

2. **Research**—Use a Web browser and go to the companion Web site at **http://www.prenhall. com/preston**. Follow the links by clicking on the Web addresses that are highlighted and underlined. Read about the trends in software piracy, starting with the link to the BSA Web site. Use a Web search engine such as **Google.com** or **Yahoo.com** to search for key words and phrases such as "European Union" and "Internet rights." Make a list of relevant sources that you may want to reference later. Include the title of the page or article, the name of the organization responsible for the Web page, the date the page or article was written, and the Web address. You may also

go to the library and look up books, articles, and news reports that are relevant to this topic. Many libraries have the full text of articles and news reports online in proprietary databases that are not available to the public.

3. **Diversity issues**—Look for differences based on culture, politics, geography, religion, and economic status.

4. **Analysis**—Write an essay that compares privacy rights online in the EU and in the United States. Go beyond simple reporting of the facts. Support your opinion with references to the articles you read. Ask your instructor for guidance regarding the required length of the essay.

5. **Communication**—Prepare a presentation in which you present your opinion and supporting facts to the class. Depending on your computer skill, you could give the presentation using a program like PowerPoint and save it as a Web page, or you could prepare a paper handout with your Web references for use while you talk to the class.

problem solving

The objective of this exercise is to learn valuable processes for solving computer-related problems, not just the solution to this particular problem.

Work with at least one other person to transmit encrypted documents using public-key encryption.

1. **Search for help on the topic**—Use the link on the companion Web site at **http://www. prenhall.com/preston** to the VeriSign site, and read about public-key infrastructure (PKI). Use Outlook or Netscape mail, and search for help on using encrypted communication.

3. **Read the instructions and try it**—Follow the instructions at the VeriSign site for enrolling for a free 60-day trial version. At least two members of your group must try it. Send an encrypted document as an e-mail attachment.

4. **Troubleshoot**—If your early attempts are unsuccessful, contact VeriSign and ask for help.

5. **Communicate**—Describe your experience. Prepare a presentation for the class that describes what you learned.

anticipating career challenges and opportunities

If the administration of health care and health care insurance is reformed and the cost is reduced by half to match that of Canada, most of that cost reduction will come from reducing the workforce that handles the paperwork. What challenges and opportunities will that present?

1. **Teamwork**—Join one to three other students. Decide how to divide up the work. Possible divisions could be: hospitals, doctors' offices, and insurance providers.

2. **Research**—Use a Web browser to search for articles on reducing health care paperwork through computerization.

3. **Diversity issues**—Consider how other countries manage health care records and billing. Are they more or less efficient? Would those methods work well in the United States?

4. **Analysis**—Write an essay that describes the future of the health care records and billing industry as you see it. Which jobs are likely to be eliminated, and which jobs may be in greater demand? Go beyond simple reporting of your opinion. Support your opinion with references to the articles you read. Ask your instructor for guidance regarding the required length of the essay.

5. **Communication**—Prepare a presentation in which you present your opinion and supporting facts to the class. Depending on your computer skill, you could give the presentation using a program like PowerPoint and save it as a Web page, or you could prepare a paper handout with your Web references for use while you talk to the class.

impact on the workplace

Find out how your company handles legal documents that must be signed in another state or country. If the company does not use digital signatures or public-key encryption to transmit legal documents, determine what effect changing to that system would have. If the company already does use this system, find out when it changed and what difference it made.

1. **Teamwork**—Join one or two other students who work where you do or in a similar type of business or organization. Decide how to divide up the work. Possible divisions could be: company policy statements, past examples in your company or in your industry, and practices in other countries.

2. **Research**—Talk to someone in the legal department about company policy.

3. **Diversity issues**—Is the use of digital signatures and electronically encrypted documents more or less accepted in other countries?

4. **Analysis**—Write an essay that describes how digital signatures and encryption are used in your company. Form and express an opinion about the degree to which your organization trusts this method and if it uses it for international documents. Support your opinion with interviews and articles. Ask your instructor for guidance regarding the required length of the essay.

5. **Communication**—Prepare a presentation in which you present your opinion and supporting facts to the class.

impact on social interactions

Are we ready to trust electronic voting? Consider the issue of electronic voting in light of what you have learned about security and privacy.

1. **Teamwork**—Join one or two other students to find out about online voting initiatives. Decide how to divide up the work. Possible divisions could be: Public trust of online voting, methods of securing online voting systems from tampering, and companies that provide online voting software and services.

2. **Research**—Find several organizations that are for or against voting online. Review articles and polls concerning voting online. Compare people's trust of physical punch-card voting systems versus more advanced electronic voting systems. Find articles that discuss how votes could be verified.

3. **Diversity**—Find out whether groups that represent minorities have taken a position.

4. **Analysis**—Write an essay that compares recent attitudes toward electronic voting with those in articles written before the presidential election of 2000. Comment on any findings related to diversity. Ask your instructor for guidance regarding the required length of the essay.

5. **Communication**—Prepare a presentation in which you present your findings to the class.

impact on home life

Find out about options for protecting young children while they use the Internet.

1. **Teamwork**—Join one or two other students. Decide how to divide up the work. Possible divisions could be: free filtering software, sites with guidance for parents, and options available within IE, Netscape Communicator, and AOL.

2. **Research**—Find free options and software from third-party vendors to filter and monitor a child's online activity. Try some of the free software and the content settings in IE.

3. **Analysis**—Write an essay that describes what can be done to protect children under the age of 13 while they browse the Internet. Form an opinion, and support it with references to articles you have read. Prepare an example of how a set of options would address the concerns common to most parents.

4. **Communication**—Prepare a presentation in which you present your findings to the class. Do **not** include examples of images or language that would offend classmates or that would be inappropriate in the classroom.

leadership

Many parents feel at a loss when it comes to protecting their children while they use the Internet. You can show leadership by devising a plan that allows teenagers and college students who are familiar with this issue to assist parents to set up filtering on home computers to protect young children.

1. **Vision**—Write a vision statement that describes what you want your group to achieve. It should motivate people to volunteer to help.

2. **Research**—Do not reinvent the wheel. Determine whether anyone has tried this in your community.

3. **Plan of Action**—Write a simple plan of action. Test the plan by following it yourself on a small scale. Locate parents who would like you to configure their browsers or install filtering software to protect their children while browsing the Internet.

4. **Analysis**—Write up an analysis of what you learned by testing your plan.

5. **Communication**—Present your plan to the class. Describe what you learned by testing your plan and how you think it could be expanded if others joined you. Share your vision statement, and try to inspire others to join you in your worthwhile effort.

lifelong learning

Add links to your browser's favorites list.

1. Start your Web browser, and open the list of favorite sites. Create a folder named *Security* and another named *Privacy*. (Look for Organize Favorites in Internet Explorer and Manage Bookmarks in Netscape Communicator.)

2. Go to the companion Web page for this chapter at **http://www.prenhall.com/preston**, and select one of the Web links on security or privacy that you found useful.

3. Add this link to your browser's favorites list in the Security or Privacy folder.

4. Repeat this process for other links on the companion Web page for this chapter, and add them to either the Security or Privacy folder.

Add learning goals to your journal.

1. Identify areas in which you feel you know the least. List three specific topics related to this chapter that you would like to learn more about in the future.

2. You will add to this journal after each chapter to compile a personal list of references and topics for future study.

The Past
Shapes the Future

outline&objectives

In the last 25 years, the widespread application of computer technology has changed our society. The developments in computers and how they are used as tools in other areas of our lives are likely to cause even more change in the next 25 years. Now that you know something about software, hardware, the Internet, ethics, security, and privacy, you can discuss these issues knowledgeably in light of other factors that influence the future. In this chapter, you learn about those factors that combined to produce the computer revolution in the United States, and then you look at how they are likely to influence the future.

WHY DO I NEED TO KNOW THIS?

To cope with our rapidly changing society, you need to combine what you have learned in previous chapters with an understanding of the past and then apply this combined knowledge to understand new developments. Review of the past is necessary to understand how a variety of factors interacted. This helps you anticipate how changes in those factors may affect the future. Anticipating the future helps you prepare for changes in your job and personal life. It gives you a better opportunity to exert control over changes that will affect your life and provides a basis for decisions regarding career direction and ethical actions you should take when the need arises.

THE PAST SHAPES THE PRESENT

In Chapter 1, we discussed how pervasive computers have become in our lives. This age of ubiquitous personal computers and networked connectivity would have been hard to predict in the 1970s when mainframe computers were dominant. In the 1970s and early 1980s, the Japanese were taking market share away from U.S. manufacturers with high-quality products and a business model that coordinated efforts by government, banks, and manufacturers. Many people thought this model was much more efficient than the U.S. model. In 1982, Japan's Ministry of Trade and Industry (MITI) announced a plan to become the world's leader in supercomputing. Some people predicted that America's days as a world leader in manufacturing and computing were numbered. However, new factors came into play, some of which were unique to the United States. In the following section, we look at nine factors and discuss how they interacted to create a society in which personal computers play an integral role:

❱ Rule of law—copyright and patent protection
❱ Spirit of entrepreneurism
❱ Post-World War II arms race and economic prosperity
❱ Company and university research labs
❱ Venture capital and reduced capital gains taxes
❱ Counterculture of the 1970s
❱ Hardware increasing in power exponentially
❱ Value of connectivity increasing exponentially
❱ Entrepreneurs still running large companies

RULE OF LAW—COPYRIGHT AND PATENT PROTECTION
The founders of the United States recognized the importance of patent and copyright laws, which had developed in England. The U.S. Constitution specifically guarantees the rights of authors and inventors (see Figures 7.1 and 7.2).

FIGURE 7.1

> Article I, Section 8
>
> The Congress shall have the power to … promote the progress of science and useful arts, by securing for limited times to authors and inventors the exclusive right to their respective writings and discoveries….

Constitution of the United States of America

FIGURE 7.2

Protection of copyright and patents is a founding principle.

Since that time, most Americans have recognized the fundamental right of authors and inventors to profit from their work.

SPIRIT OF ENTREPRENEURISM

American children learn about Thomas Edison, Alexander Graham Bell, Henry Ford, and others who became rich and famous because of their inventions and the businesses they founded. Some of them dream about following in the footsteps of these famous inventors. Immigrants come to the United States with a dream of a better life, and many come with a dream of striking it rich. A person who takes the risk of starting a new business is an *entrepreneur*. In many countries, an individual's creative work would simply be taken by the state or by an established company. People who immigrate to the United States know that in America there are laws that protect the individual's patent or copyright. They know that other immigrants to the United States have made inventions or written books, songs, or software that have made them rich. Many of the world's brightest and most creative people come to the United States to work with computers because of this possibility. Even though other countries have similar laws, people know that Americans generally respect and support copyright and patent laws.

POST-WORLD WAR ARMS RACE AND PROSPERITY

In the closing days of World War II, Soviet and American forces sought to capture the German rocket scientists who had developed the rockets used against England. The Soviets gained valuable information about making the booster rockets, and the United States captured scientists with valuable experience and information about making the guidance systems. In the cold war that followed WWII, the Soviet rocket program was much better than the American, and the Soviets succeeded in putting the first satellite in orbit. The United States was forced to make its satellites smaller and lighter because its rockets were less powerful. Ultimately, this worked to the benefit of the United States because it became expert at miniaturizing the electronic components that went into the satellites, which led to development of transistors and integrated circuits. The United States also had a significant economic advantage because World War II was not fought in its homeland, leaving its factories and economy intact. In the decades following WWII, the United States prospered, and many people had money to spend or invest.

COMPANY AND UNIVERSITY RESEARCH LABS

Laboratories that conduct *applied research* are seeking ways to make practical use of an invention or discovery. Other labs do *basic research* to discover completely new phenomena that may or may not have a commercial application. Some large companies fund basic research labs because discovery of new phenomena may be very profitable if it can be applied to a product they can sell. Government agencies fund basic research for the same reasons, but they may also fund basic research simply to discover the unknown, even if it has little likelihood of commercialization. Three companies whose labs have had a significant impact on computing are IBM, Bell, and Xerox.

FIGURE 7.3

Fiber-optic cable carries data as bursts of light.

Bell Laboratories discovered or pioneered:

- transistors
- lasers
- optical fiber communications (see Figure 7.3)
- cell phones
- communications satellites
- digital signal processors (A-D and D-A converters)
- the UNIX operating system

IBM labs discovered or developed:

- one-transistor dynamic RAM memory (DRAM)
- magnetic disk storage—hard disks
- relational databases
- the FORTRAN computer language
- Data Encryption Standard—public/private-key encryption
- scalable parallel systems that can use multiple processors
- speech recognition software
- Deep Blue—a computer with 32 processors that won the world's chess championship

Xerox established the Palo Alto Research Center (PARC) in 1970 (see Figure 7.4), which developed most of the features of modern personal computers between 1970 and 1980:

- laser printers
- Smalltalk—the first object-oriented programming language
- client/server computer architecture
- graphic user interface—mouse, menus, icons
- Ethernet—local area network

FIGURE 7.4

Most of the elements of a modern PC were conceived at Xerox PARC.

- word processing with what-you-see-is-what-you-get (WYSIWYG) printing, cut-and-paste text manipulation
- solid-state lasers—later used in optical disc reading and recording
- pop-up menus
- a worm program—later used by others as an attack method on the Internet
- linguistic technology—enables spell checkers, thesauruses, and dictionaries

University research labs also played an important role. Some universities allowed students to keep the rights to any inventions or software developed using university facilities; others did not. Stanford University is an example of one that allowed students to keep the rights to inventions and spin off companies. Three major computer companies were founded by students who lived in the same dormitory, Margaret Jacks Hall:

- SUN Microsystems—Internet servers and software; the company name stands for Stanford University Network
- Silicon Graphics (SGI)—workstations
- CISCO Systems—network infrastructure devices

These three companies have a combined worth of close to $100 billion, as well as appreciative and generous Stanford alumni.

In contrast, the University of Illinois is famous for denying Marc Andreessen the rights to the Mosaic Web browser concept he developed, forcing him to rewrite the code to create Netscape. The university licensed the rights to Mosaic to a competitor, named Spyglass. Spyglass made a deal with Microsoft, which then incorporated the browser in Windows as Internet Explorer (IE).

VENTURE CAPITAL AND REDUCED CAPITAL GAINS TAXES

A person may have a great new invention and own the rights to it, but to start a company to produce and sell it, he or she needs money. Conservative institutions like banks are not in business to take risks with their depositors' money so most high-risk investments come from individuals. A famous venture capitalist was Queen Isabella of Spain, who decided to fund a high-risk venture by a fellow named Christopher Columbus. Within a few years, ships were returning from the new world filled with gold. In modern times, people with money look for ways to make much higher than normal profits on their investments by taking higher than normal risks. The money they risk to help people start new companies is called *venture capital*. In the mid-1950s, the U.S. Government recognized that start-up companies needed capital and promoted Small Business Investment Companies (SBIC), which acted on the behalf of individuals to pool their venture capital to fund larger projects. Profits made from investment in business are called *capital gains*, and prior to 1974 they were taxed at 35 percent. In order to stimulate growth, Congress, though a series of bills, cut captial gains taxes down to 20 percent by 1982. As a result, more money was available to fund risky new ventures in the early '80s.

COUNTERCULTURE OF THE 1970S

The Vietnam War sparked the development of a counterculture among young people who rejected many of their parents' values. Repulsed by the greed and hypocrisy of some who valued personal profit and power over the good of people, the counterculture valued sharing without profit. People in

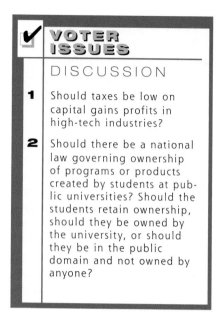
the counterculture had little respect for large companies or the government. Young men who went to college were granted a deferment from the draft until they graduated, and this led to a concentration of antiwar sentiment on college campuses. The Vietnam War era coincided with the spread of mainframe computers, and colleges around the country installed them and taught students how to use them. Following the end of U.S. involvement in Vietnam in 1973, many students did not want to work for established companies against which they had protested and found that they could use their computer skills to support themselves working for new software or hardware companies where they could express their beliefs in the way the products were marketed and sold. Many of these people also stayed in the education system as computer professionals or as teachers. The free software and open-source software movements have their roots in the counterculture.

HARDWARE INCREASING IN POWER EXPONENTIALLY

One of the factors influencing personal computing is the unusual rate at which computer power increased while falling in price. To get some idea of how differently the price and performance of computers has changed compared to other types of hardware, consider the changes in price and performance of automobiles and personal computers since 1982. Prices from 1982 are accompanied by prices shown in parentheses that are adjusted for inflation to show what the price would be in today's dollars.

- In 1982, a Mustang GT automobile cost $8,400 ($16,000). In 2003, a similar Mustang GT costs $22,000. The new car costs $6,000 more than the 1982 model in inflation-adjusted dollars. The new car is safer and pollutes less, but it is not faster, nor does it carry more people.

- In contrast, a 1982 IBM PC (4.7 megahertz processor with 64 kilobytes of RAM and a 20-megabyte hard drive) with a three-color monitor and an Epson dot-matrix printer cost about $4,500 ($8,600). In 2003, a Dell PC (2.2 gigahertz processor with 256 megabytes of RAM and a 40-gigabyte hard drive) with a 16 million–color flat-panel monitor and a color ink-jet printer/scanner/copier costs about $1,000. The new PC system is more than 400 times as fast with 4,000 times as much RAM and 2,000 times as much hard disk space. The monitor and printer can show 5 million times more colors. The new system costs less than an eighth as much as a 1982 IBM PC.

The rate at which computer power is increasing while its price is falling is amazing. One of Intel Corporation's founders, Gordon Moore, predicted in 1965 that integrated circuits would increase in complexity while falling in price at an exponential rate (see Figures 7.5, 7.6, and 7.7). His prediction may be simplified to state that the computing power of integrated circuits will double every two years. His prediction, known as ***Moore's law***, has

FIGURE 7.5

Linear growth is when the same amount is added to the preceding number to obtain the next number in a sequence. For example, if you start with 2 and add 2 each time, you get the following sequence of numbers; 2, 4, 6, 8, 10, 12, 14, 16, 18, 20. Increasing a value by a multiple in each interval is ***exponential growth***. For example, in this sequence, the numbers double each time: 2, 4, 8, 16, 32, 64, 128, 256, 512, 1,024.

Exponential growth rates are much faster than linear growth rates.

FIGURE 7.6

Intel Processor	Year of Introduction	Transistors
4004	1971	2,250
8008	1972	2,500
8080	1974	5,000
8086	1978	29,000
286	1982	120,000
386™ processor	1985	275,000
486™ DX processor	1989	1,180,000
Pentium® processor	1993	3,100,000
Pentium II processor	1997	7,500,000
Pentium III processor	1999	24,000,000
Pentium 4 processor	2000	42,000,000

The number of transistors per processor increased exponentially for the first 30 years.

FIGURE 7.7

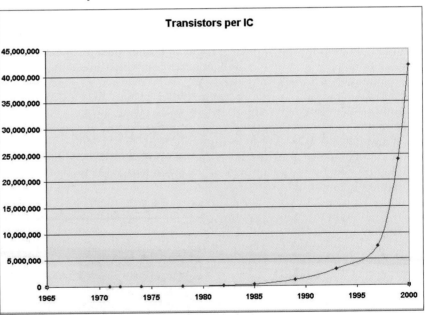

The number of transistors per chip is increasing exponentially.

proven remarkably accurate over a span of 38 years. Moore's law predicted that the power of integrated circuits per dollar of cost would experience exponential growth. The exponential growth of integrated circuit power combined with low cost was a major factor in making high-powered computing devices affordable for a variety of everyday tasks.

VALUE OF CONNECTIVITY INCREASING EXPONENTIALLY

The inventor of Ethernet, Robert Metcalfe, stated, "The value of a network grows as the square of the number of users," which became known as *Metcalfe's law*. It, too, deals with exponential growth. Metcalfe's law is harder to quantify than Moore's law because "value" is a subjective term, but most businesses connect their computers together in a network to take advantage of the multiplying effect on their productivity. With the advent of the Internet, individual home computers can become part of a network as well, which multiplies their power. In Chapter 5, you learned that networks of personal computers can be used as distributed file servers to share MP3 files and that they can also be used for distributed processing in ways that exceed the power of the most powerful supercomputers. In 1983, fewer than 1,000 people were connected to ARPANET, the predecessor of the Internet. In 2003, the number of people connected to the Internet exceeds 600 million. There are far more computers connected to LANs and the Internet in the United States than in other countries, conferring a distinct advantage over other nations.

ENTREPRENEURS STILL RUNNING LARGE COMPANIES

The exponential growth of processing power and the expansion of the Internet have produced companies that are among the richest and most powerful in the world, even though they did not exist 30 years ago. Many of these companies were founded by very young people who have retained control and have dealt with each other continually during this period. The entrepreneurs who founded companies like Microsoft, Apple, SUN, Oracle, and Dell are still in control (see Figure 7.8). The personalities of these people still strongly influence the companies they run and the products they make. These companies can react to events more quickly than those run by committees and boards, and they often make bolder business decisions. Entrepreneurs who still run large computer companies are:

- Bill Gates—Microsoft
- Steve Jobs—Apple
- Michael Dell—Dell
- Scott McNeely—SUN
- Larry Ellison—Oracle

FIGURE 7.8

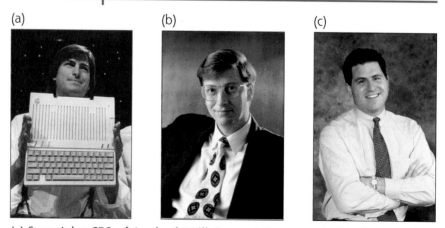

(a) Steve Jobs, CEO of Apple, (b) Bill Gates, chairman and CSA of Microsoft, and (c) Michael Dell, CEO of Dell.

EXAMPLES—MICROSOFT AND APPLE

To illustrate how the factors listed above came together in the United States and still play a strong role in our society, consider a brief history of two companies that have shaped the personal computer world—Microsoft and Apple.

Microsoft

The story of Microsoft is one of traditional values. It begins with a junior high school fund-raiser by which mothers raised money to buy a teletype machine for the school so students could connect to a local company's mainframe computer and learn to program it (see Figure 7.9). Bill Gates, an eighth-grader, and Paul Allen, a sophomore, became friends while learning to program. Gates went on to Harvard and was a freshman when Intel released the 8008 microprocessor and the first personal computer, the Altair, became available. He dropped out of Harvard and started Microsoft with Allen to adapt the BASIC programming language for use on the new computer. When others started to copy his program, Gates sent an open letter to other computer programmers admonishing them for stealing his work.

When IBM realized that many of its mainframe customers were using personal computers like the Apple (see next story), it decided to get into the PC business. IBM did not have time to develop one itself so it designed a PC from components that were available from other companies. It hired Microsoft to develop the operating system, which IBM called PC-DOS, and introduced the IBM PC in 1981. IBM was a major company intruding in the territory of small, inexperienced companies. It had the money and the marketing power to take over. However, the company had been sued previously for antitrust violations in its mainframe business so it did not want more than half the personal computer market. It allowed Microsoft to retain the rights to sell the operating system, which Microsoft called MS-DOS, to other computer manufacturers. As a result, competitors could easily build a rival computer from available parts and install Microsoft's operating system. These rival computers were *clones*—functional copies of the IBM personal computer. The IBM PC reached about 40 percent market share in the late '80s; the IBM PC and clones combined had a market share that was over 80

FIGURE 7.9

Milestone	Year
Gates and Allen learn to program	1969
Microsoft founded	1975
BASIC language adapted to the Altair PC	1975
IBM PC with DOS by Microsoft introduced; MS retains rights to sell to clone makers	1981
Microsoft Office for Macintosh introduced	1989
Graphic user interface added to DOS, Windows 3.0	1990
Windows 95 introduced; competes successfully with Apple GUI	1995
Internet Explorer introduced	1997
Microsoft found guilty of unfair competitive practices and ruled a monopoly	2001

Milestones in the history of Microsoft.

percent. Microsoft received a royalty from the sale of each of the non-IBM computers that used its operating system. The clone makers eventually became stronger than IBM and took market share away from it, while still increasing Microsoft's profits. The only significant rival to the IBM PC and its clones was Apple, which used different hardware and its own operating system. Starting in 1984, Apple computers used a graphic user interface.

Gates used the income from sales of MS-DOS to develop other software, including its own version of the graphic user interface, which it named *Windows*. The Windows operating system is really a package that contains an operating system and many utility programs, such as a Web browser and disk management software. In addition to Windows, Microsoft developed or purchased other application software to produce a suite of software that had a similar interface for each program. The suite consists of Word, Excel, PowerPoint, and Access and dominates the market for business software. Microsoft is a highly competitive, very profitable company, and Bill Gates is one of the richest people in the world. Unlike the extremely rich capitalists of the nineteenth century, Gates did not amass his wealth at the expense of his workers. Employees at Microsoft share in the success of the company, and its success has made more than a thousand millionaires within the ranks of company employees. Critics of Microsoft claim that it uses its ownership of Windows to give it an advantage in the design of applications that use the Windows operating system. In 2001, the U.S. Supreme Court ruled that Microsoft was guilty of unfair business practices but stopped short of dividing the company into two companies—operating systems and applications—as requested by those suing the company. Microsoft faces similar lawsuits in Europe over its business practices.

Apple

The story of Apple is one of the counterculture and its interaction with big business. Universities in California such as the University of California at Berkeley and Stanford were at the center of the counterculture in the early 1970s. When integrated circuits and microprocessors became available, groups like the Home Brew Computer Club, which met in a hall rented from Stanford University, openly shared their inventions and discoveries without regard to ownership. This openness led to rapid development of ideas because the groups were large and varied. Steve Wosniak, a member of the Home Brew Computer Club, loved to tinker with the new chips and circuits. He found that he could make a box with circuits, called a blue box, that could bypass the phone company's security system and let people make free calls to anywhere in the world. Wosniak used his anonymous free access to the international phone system to impress his friends. He tells stories about making false reservations at a hotel in London and waking up administrators in the Vatican in the middle of the night by impersonating Henry Kissinger. Wosniak's ability to manipulate the phone company impressed Steve Jobs, who started to realize the potential of these chips. In an interview for PBS, Jobs commented, "I don't think there would have been an Apple computer had there not been blue boxes."

When the microprocessor became available, Wosniak started work on his own personal computer and showed it off at the Home Brew Computer Club. He made several innovations that greatly improved the basic design and reduced its cost. Wosniak was a genius inventor, but his friend Steve Jobs was the visionary entrepreneur. Jobs saw the potential market for personal computers that were more than hobbyist toys. He sold his car and convinced Wosniak to sell his expensive calculator to raise money to make

••• CRITICAL
••• THINKING

DISCUSSION

1 Do you think Steve Wosniak acted ethically when he used and sold blue boxes? How does his activity compare with college students who use the Internet to distribute MP3 files? What would happen to a student who tried this today and got caught?

2 If you were entering college as a computer science major, would you prefer Stanford's or the University of Illinois' approach to ownership of intellectual property?

a prototype called the Apple I. Wosniak was working for Hewlett-Packard Electronics at the time and felt that to be ethical he should offer the company the first option, which it turned down. Jobs and Wosniak started the Apple Computer company and sold 50 of their prototype Apple I computer, which was enough to convince Jobs the market was real. Jobs needed money to take the company to the next level. Banks were not interested in lending two teenagers the money to start a company so Wosniak and Jobs started looking around for investors. A. C. Markkula invested an undisclosed amount of money and assumed control of the company as chairman of the board. They needed more money and approached Arthur Rock, a venture capitalist who had also funded Intel when it started up. Rock received $600,000 of venture capital from the Rockefellers to fund the launch of the Apple II. Venture capitalists usually require a majority of the stock in a company they fund so that they can control how the money is spent. Most inventors find this deal to be favorable because part of something big is better than all of nothing, but they lose control of the company. The Apple II was a great success. Within a few years, its market share was 50 percent and Jobs was worth $20 million dollars. However, his investors owned a majority of the stock, and they had control of the company.

Shortly after the Apple II became commonly available, a graduate student at Harvard, Dan Bricklin, developed a software program called *VisiCalc* that performed financial projections using a computerized table of rows and columns called a spreadsheet. This financial software made personal computers popular in businesses. When IBM salespeople came to call on their mainframe customers and found them doing some of their work on Apple II personal computers, they knew they had to enter the personal computer market. In 1981, IBM introduced the IBM PC, which was similar to the Apple II, but its screen had three primary colors—red, green, and blue—instead of only black and white. It immediately took significant numbers of customers away from Apple.

The researchers at Xerox PARC had already invented a computer called the Alto that had all the major components of today's computers. It cost over $10,000, and Xerox did not see its potential value. In 1979, Jobs toured the Xerox Palo Alto Research Center where he saw the graphic user interface (see Figure 7.10).

FIGURE 7.10 |

Steve Jobs—Interview with PBS (see the companion Web site at **www.prenhall.com/preston**)

… They showed me really three things. But I was so blinded by the first one I didn't even really see the other two. One of the things they showed me was object-orienting programming; they showed me that, but I didn't even see that. The other one they showed me was a networked computer system … they had over a hundred Alto computers all networked using e-mail et cetera, et cetera; I didn't even see that. I was so blinded by the first thing they showed me, which was the graphical user interface. I thought it was the best thing I'd ever seen in my life. Now remember, it was very flawed; what we saw was incomplete—they'd done a bunch of things wrong. But we didn't know that at the time, but still, though, they had the germ of the idea was there and they'd done it very well and within, you know, 10 minutes it was obvious to me that all computers would work like this someday.

Jobs sees the GUI interface for the first time at Xerox PARC.

Jobs dropped his current development projects and devoted all the company's resources to creating the Macintosh, an affordable computer with a graphic user interface. The processors available at that time were limited in power so he had to compromise. The first Macintosh still had a black and white screen that was smaller than the IBM PC's screen. However, it was much better at displaying graphics and text that could be shown in a variety of fonts. The operating system was designed from scratch to work with the graphic user interface (GUI), and it was not backward compatible with software that ran on the Apple II. Jobs saw the GUI as the embodiment of the values of counterculture, which embraced the humanities rather than corporate finance and profit-making (see Figure 7.11).

Jobs introduced the Macintosh with an ad that ran during the 1984 Super Bowl. He made use of the coincidence of the year of the Macintosh's introduction, 1984, with the title of a famous book, *1984* by George Orwell. In Orwell's book, individualism is crushed in an effort to make everyone into mindless, obedient servants of the state. Orwell wrote the book in 1948 to warn people of what might happen if tyrants ruled the world. The ad shows a tyrant on a giant television screen ranting to a room full of people dressed in gray. A beautiful girl dressed in red and white is shown running from security forces. She runs into the room and hurls a large hammer through the screen. The tag line is "On January 24th, Apple Computer will introduce the Macintosh, and you'll see why 1984 won't be like '1984.'" The ad paints corporate Americans as mindless drones who use IBM PCs while creative people use Macintoshes. The ad did little to endear Apple to buyers of corporate PCs and did not help overcome the $1,000 price difference; however, it established the Macintosh as the computer of choice for creative artists, and the Macintosh became an icon of the counterculture.

When Microsoft introduced Windows 3.1, with a GUI interface, it was designed to run in addition to MS-DOS on a computer so computers could still run all the older software. The Windows GUI was not as good as the Apple interface, but it was good enough to keep corporate buyers from switching until better versions of Windows came out. Apple sued Microsoft for copying its GUI to delay the introduction of Windows 95, but the suit was dropped when Xerox pointed out that Apple copied the idea from Xerox in the first place.

The Macintosh sold well to graphic artists and to educational institutions, but it was in trouble. Because Jobs did not own a controlling inter-

FIGURE 7.11

Steve Jobs—Interview with PBS (see the companion Web site at **www.prenhall.com/preston**)

Ultimately it comes down to taste. It comes down to trying to expose yourself to the best things that humans have done and then try to bring those things in to what you're doing. I mean Picasso had a saying: he said good artists copy, great artists steal. And we have always been shameless about stealing great ideas … and I think part of what made the Macintosh great was that the people working on it were musicians and poets and artists and zoologists and historians who also happened to be the best computer scientists in the world.

Comments like this one hurt Apple's claim that Microsoft copied the GUI interface from them.

est in the company, the board of directors chose a business plan proposed by John Sculley, a former Pepsi executive who had been hired to run the operations of the company. Jobs left Apple in 1985 and started two new companies, NeXT Computing and Pixar. Without Jobs, the company floundered and was almost sold or broken up. Larry Ellison, CEO of Oracle, announced he was considering buying the company. The board asked Jobs to return in 1996 when he sold NeXT to Apple. Since that time, he has revitalized the company with innovative, high-quality products. In 1997, Microsoft invested $150 million in Apple and increased technology collaboration. Jobs's departure and return illustrate how important the visionary entrepreneur can be to a computer company (see Figure 7.12).

FIGURE 7.12

Event	Year
Jobs drops out of college and immerses himself in the counterculture	1973
Jobs travels to India seeking enlightenment	1974
Jobs attends the Home Brew Computer Club with Wosniak; they start the Apple company	1974
Apple introduces the Apple I computer	1976
A. C. Markkula invests and becomes chairman of the board; Arthur Rock and the Rockefellers invest $600,000 of venture capital	1977
Apple II introduced	1977
Apple III introduced at a price of $10,000; the first 14,000 units were recalled, losing the company money	1981
John Sculley leaves Pepsi to run Apple	1983
Macintosh with GUI introduced in famous Super Bowl ad	1984
Sculley ousts Jobs, who leaves Apple and founds NeXT. Apple lays off 1,200 employees	1985
Apple sues Microsoft over Windows	1988
Apple lays off 15,600 employees	1991
Apple loses lawsuit against Microsoft	1992
Apple introduces the Newton PDA; Sculley replaced; 2,500 employees laid off	1993
IBM offers to buy Apple	1994
Apple recalls new laptops when two burst into flames	1995
Apple lays off 1,300 employees; Apple and SUN discuss merger; second-quarter loss of $700 million predicted	1996
Apple buys NeXT, and Jobs returns to Apple	1996
Larry Ellison considers buying Apple; Jobs appointed interim CEO at a salary of $1 per year until return to profitability	1997
Apple introduces iMac, PowerBook G3; company returns to profitability	1998
Jobs named full CEO	2000

Milestones in the history of Apple

FIGURE 7.13

Apple typically has more stylish computers that are usually more expensive than other PCs.

Jobs's vision of the Apple Computer company as an icon of creativity born in the counterculture has created a loyal following. Apple computers are typically more stylish than other brands (see Figure 7.13). Users of Macintosh computers often refer to themselves as "Mac people" to identify themselves with Jobs's vision. Since IBM withdrew from the desktop PC business, Mac users now view Microsoft as the embodiment of the corporate ethic against which they rebel. Because of this view, emotions may run high when committees meet to decide what type of computer to buy for a school and need to choose between an Apple and another brand's computer.

mastering
technology

1 View the Macintosh ad from 1984—Go to **http://www.uriah.com/apple-qt/1984.html** and view the famous commercial that introduced the Macintosh computer. If you use IE 6.0, you may need to download the latest version of QuickTime Player from **http://www.apple.com/quicktime/download/**.

2 Download and run VisiCalc, the first spreadsheet program. The program runs in a special DOS window on computers running Windows. Go to **http://www.bricklin.com/history/vcexecutable.htm** and follow the instructions to download a copy of the program and its manual.

THE PRESENT SHAPES THE FUTURE

RULE OF LAW

Protecting the rights of authors and inventors is a constitutional responsibility of the U.S. Congress, but it is difficult to achieve in the face of accurate digital copying and distributed file servers operating over the Internet. Current methods of distributing music, videos, and software on CDs will probably be replaced by other methods. A model that is likely to become more popular is paying a relatively small amount per song or video. One model works like a phone card: you deposit money to the account online, and whenever you want to buy something from a participating merchant, you click an icon on the Web page and its price is deducted from your account (see BitPass on the companion Web site at **http://www.prenhall. com/preston**). Software piracy must also be minimized. Microsoft is positioning itself through the .NET strategy to charge for software on an annual license renewal basis. Others ask for voluntary payment.

A study by the National Science Foundation in 1999 reported that of the computer scientists working in America who held advanced degrees, 29 percent of those with master's degrees were foreign born, and 39 percent with doctorates were foreign born. The prosperity of the U.S. computer industry depends upon attracting the best minds from around the world. One of the factors that attracts these people is the protection of their right to profit from their ideas.

ENTREPRENEURISM AND VENTURE CAPITAL

Entrepreneurs often seek to make a fortune. They need to know that if they produce a very popular product or service, they have the chance to make it big (see Figure 7.14). Venture capitalists will fund entrepreneurs if they have surplus money to risk and if they stand to make big profits when they back the right entrepreneur. The government made the payoffs bigger when it cut capital gains taxes in the late 1970s and early 1980s from 35 percent to 20 percent. Capital gains taxes rose to 28 percent in 1987 and were reduced in 2001 to 18 percent. Congress can affect the availability of venture capital by deciding how much to tax the gains made by risking private capital to fund start-up companies.

Many people are concerned that Microsoft keeps start-up companies from growing by abusing its ownership of Windows and the large amount of money the operating system earns. Many small companies create specialized software that performs a valuable function. If Microsoft chooses to create a competing product and include it with Windows at no additional

FIGURE 7.14

Many young entrepreneurs bought an Apple II or IBM PC and started small software companies (authors Robert Ferrett at left and John Preston seated).

cost, the smaller company cannot compete and goes out of business or sells out to Microsoft. Some point out that this results in lower costs to the consumer, but others fear that this practice discourages entrepreneurs from starting new software companies. Another concern is that Microsoft gives its applications developers an advantage by sharing secrets about its operating system with them.

Another motivation for entrepreneurs is fame. Thomas Edison and the Wright brothers were famous American inventors who founded successful businesses. They were famous in their lifetimes and were held up as examples to schoolchildren for years afterward as American success stories. Few children in the United States today can name a living inventor. Many know who Bill Gates is, but he is seldom held up as an example to emulate. Students who major in computer science or computer engineering are often labeled nerds or geeks, but they are the ones who are likely to discover or invent the products that will form the basis for jobs in the future. To build a strong economy in a future based on computers, young people need to be encouraged by their peers and elders to pursue interests in basic science, programming, and computer science. One way to do that is to provide examples of men and women from diverse backgrounds who have made major inventions or discoveries that provide us with jobs today (see links to relevant resources on the companion Web page).

RESEARCH AND POST–WORLD WAR II PROSPERITY

Because the United States did not have its homeland industries attacked in World War II, it had the advantage of time and money to build a large lead in new technologies. The Soviet system could not compete successfully with the United States and collapsed in 1990, leaving the United States as the sole superpower. U.S. domestic resources, such as the oil that paid for WWII and the cold war, are diminishing, and we are paying for imports of oil and manufactured goods by exporting high-tech goods and services. Non-manufacturing now accounts for 71 percent of the nation's economy. Continued exportation of high-tech goods such as computers and software depends upon basic research that keeps U.S. technology ahead of foreign competition. The United States leads the world in research, but the difference between the United States and other countries is shrinking. One way to measure a country's performance is to look at its balance of trade with other countries. The Census Bureau started tracking the trade balance for advanced technology products 14 years ago. The balance originally favored the United States but shrank steadily until it went negative for the first time in 2002. The long-term health of the U.S. economy depends upon basic research. Companies must have a regulatory and tax environment that encourages this investment in the future, and the government must fund basic research efforts. As individuals, we need to support policies by the government and companies that support basic research.

DIVERSITY OF CULTURES

One of the great strengths of the United States is the diversity of its culture, and this is true of its computing culture. The counterculture of the 1970s played an important role in the development of personal computers, and its influence is still evident when you browse the Internet. There is a wealth of information that is freely shared, and there are numerous freeware, shareware, and open-source software programs available. The diversity of the computing environment must be protected to ensure healthy growth in the future. You can contribute by paying the voluntary fees for shareware if you use a program beyond its trial period, as well as by supporting government action to make the competitive markets for software fair and open to new entrepreneurs. It is important to recognize the contributions made by the counterculture, the competitive entrepreneur, and big business and to value all of them. It is also important to maintain a welcoming environment that encourages creative people from around the world to come to the United States.

HARDWARE AND SOFTWARE

Moore's law predicts a doubling of computer power every year or two. Exponential growth has to stop at some point because it consumes the available space or resources or runs into fundamental theoretical limits. Integrated circuits built on traditional silicon are reaching their theoretical limits. Experts at Bell Laboratories estimate that the theoretical limits of silicon-based transistors will be reached by 2012. Researchers are looking ahead to new ideas for constructing smaller, faster, more powerful computer chips by working at the molecular level. Devices this small are measured in *nanometers*, which are billionths of a meter, and the technology of these devices is called *nanotechnology*. Sumio Iijima, a scientist at NEC, is developing a promising nanotechnology based on the discovery of *carbon nanotubes*. He discovered that carbon atoms could be arranged in tubes, some of which conduct electricity like a metal and some of which are semiconductors, similar to silicon transistors. The potential exists to arrange these tubes into circuits that would replace silicon transistors and wires. In 2001, IBM researchers devised a method to separate the two types of carbon nanotubes. Nantero, a start-up company in Massachusetts that has attracted more than $6 million in venture capital funding, hopes to produce memory chips from carbon nanotubes that would work like flash memory chips, which do not require constant power. The company hopes to have a prototype chip within two years that has a capacity of 2 gigabytes (2,000 megabytes). The company hopes to produce chips with a *terabyte* (1 million megabytes) of memory eventually. Even if new materials do not live up to expectations, we can expect Moore's law to continue for at least another eight years, during which time the power of computers would double four more times. For example, if we have processors that work at 2 gigahertz now, that would imply that we can expect processors to work at 32 gigahertz by 2012. These computers will be able to run software that is more sophisticated than that of today. Futurists and scientists are already at work on ideas to take advantage of this new power. Here are some examples of technologies that are likely to show significant advances when more powerful hardware and software become available in the near future.

Changes in the Computer/Human Interface

Today's desktop computer has changed dramatically inside the system unit, but the monitor, keyboard, and mouse have changed little in the last 20 years. Research is being conducted to change the way we communicate with computers.

Replacing the monitor   Monitors are changing from CRTs to flat panels, but newer ideas are being developed. One method is to mount a small screen on a pair of glasses with a lens that makes the screen appear to float in the air in front of us. Another method that makes the screen appear to float in front of us uses low-power lasers to project the image directly onto the retina in the back of the eyeball. Some researchers are exploring the possibility of bypassing the eyeball and stimulating the optic nerve or brain directly, which would eliminate the need for glasses and enable blind people to see.

Replacing the keyboard and mouse Learning to type on a keyboard is a barrier to using computers that has been with us from the beginning. Voice recognition is a technology that is steadily improving. Many companies already use it for routing customer calls. Microsoft includes voice recognition software with Word 2002, but many people who have Word 2002 do not even know it because the technology is still less accurate than most people want. It is likely that voice recognition will improve significantly in the next 10 years to the point where it is a viable alternative to typing. We may see a new "digital divide" between young people who have not learned to type and older people who have. The mouse may be replaced by fingertip clips that sense the position of the user's fingertips in three dimensions (see Figure 7.15). This technology was represented in the movie *Minority Report*, in which users sorted through data and images by waiving their hands in the air.

Virtual reality and avatars If the sensory inputs of vision and touch can be controlled by a computer and the computer can react to the actions of the user, then an individual can interact with an artificial world called ***virtual reality (VR)***. VR is already used to design automobile passenger compartments and to train pilots and astronauts. VR equipment is bulky and expensive. If external monitors and speakers can be replaced with visual displays that are projected into the eye or directly into the brain, then costs would be greatly reduced. Gamers are driving this technology to make the game environment increasingly realistic. People can interact with each other in virtual reality using animated images called avatars. With increasing computer power, these avatars become more realistic. Computers can

FIGURE 7.15

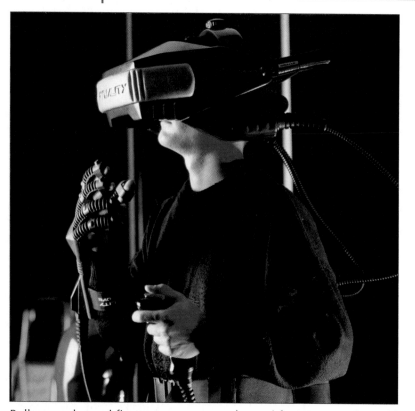

Bulky goggles and finger sensors currently used for VR research are likely to be replaced by much smaller devices.

FIGURE 7.16

Alan Turing devised a simple test of machine intelligence.

also be used to create entirely artificial characters in movies or on television.

Artificial Intelligence

When computers began performing tasks that were similar to those performed by humans, people began to wonder if computers would ever possess the ability to think like a human or think in a completely new way that might be superior to human thought. This ability is called *artificial intelligence (AI)*.

The possibility of an intelligent machine forces people to try to define human intelligence, a task that has proven to be elusive. In the 1950s, Alan Turing (see Figure 7.16) devised a simple test. He said that you start by placing a person at a keyboard that communicates with either a computer or a person. If the person at the keyboard cannot tell the difference between the responses of a computer and those of another person, the computer has achieved intelligence. Computers can pass the Turing test for short periods of time in very limited circumstances.

Computers are able to play games that have well-defined rules. In 1997, an IBM computer named Deep Blue defeated the world champion in chess using methods that IBM calls *deep computing* (see Figure 7.17). IBM's Deep Computing Institute applies the technology it developed to solve complex problems like pairing crews with flights, assessing insurance risks, focusing Web searches, and comparing plant compounds with genetic information to identify potential applications as drugs.

Computers are also able to provide advice on complex problems in which they take on the role of an expert consultant. They can be used to provide advice on fixing an automobile or investing money. This type of system is called an *expert system* (see Figure 7.18). Sophisticated programs can also analyze huge databases, looking for patterns that would not be apparent to humans due to the size of the database. For example, a computer could be programmed to look at sales of fashionable clothing at hundreds of retail stores to determine how sales are affected by seasonal and regional factors to help buyers make decisions. Finding patterns in large databases is called

FIGURE 7.17

IBM's Deep Blue program defeats chess master Garry Kasparov in 1997.

FIGURE 7.18

Expert systems can give advice on complex problems such as analyzing automotive problems.

data mining. As computers continue to increase in power, deep computing and expert systems will become available on desktop computers.

These abilities are part of AI, but they are only the beginning. Several factors limit the development of AI. One is that humans draw from a vast store of knowledge about our world to provide context for ambiguous instructions or terms, and another is that the human brain does not work like a digital computer.

People use their knowledge of the world and their previous experience to interpret instructions and words. Even a young child draws on this background knowledge when you tell her to put on her shoes and socks. She knows from experience that the socks go on first, even though the sequence of the instructions implies otherwise. Humans use the same word to mean many different things, depending on the situation. For example, the word *wash* can function as a verb, noun, or adjective. *The American Heritage Dictionary* lists 42 ways to use the word. Depending on context, the word can refer to a thin layer of water color on a drawing or the air from a propeller. A company named Cycorp is developing a database of facts it calls *common sense* that computer programmers can use to assist their development of AI.

Written language does not capture the additional meanings that may be conveyed by tone of voice or body language. Computer languages were created because computers could not deal with the ambiguity of human languages. In a computer language, a word can only have one meaning, and the organization of commands must follow strict rules. Computer programmers have to work hard to learn how to write specific, step-by-step instructions called algorithms to work with computers. This method works well when all the information for solving the problem is provided. Algorithms do not work well when important information is assumed or is incorrect. The hard part is to get a computer to do what you mean rather than what you say. Instead of trying to write algorithms that anticipate every possible context or interpretation, computer scientists are trying to approach problems the way human brains do.

A fundamental problem of developing computers with AI is that the human brain is constructed differently than a digital computer. People are not programmed—they learn from experience. We know that brain cells connect to thousands of other cells and that *thinking* causes waves of communication activity. The transistors that make up a digital circuit are connected directly to only a few other transistors. Researchers are trying new ways of connecting computer circuits to improve their ability to function like a human brain.

The human brain is good at arriving at solutions that are right most of the time. Digital computers traditionally work with zeros and ones and work well with things that can be on or off, true or false. However, many things are somewhere in between. Rules may be written for dealing with less exact situations in which being close most of the time is good enough. These rules are called **fuzzy logic**. Fuzzy logic circuits are already in use in hand-held digital video cameras to remove the shaking of the image due to small movements of the person holding the camera. The same logic is used to hold the barrel of an Abrams tank on target while it is moving.

Another example of a task in which close is good enough is **pattern recognition**, which means the ability to identify something from the characteristic arrangement of its features. Recognizing visual patterns and associating them with a person's face is something we learn from birth but is difficult for a digital computer. A caricaturist can draw a few lines on a piece of paper and people will immediately recognize a parody of a well-known politician or actor, even though there is not a single line in the drawing that matches an actual contour of the person's face. People can look at two objects and identify them both as chairs even if they do not have any common components. Even limited pattern recognition problems are challenging for digital computers. Computers are better at recognizing patterns of behavior and may be used to detect behaviors that should not occur. Research scientists at IBM labs are working on a computer immune system to fight viruses that is similar to the human immune system. The human immune system uses white blood cells that recognize organisms that do not belong in the body and attack them. We may see the creation of computer programs that behave like white blood cells that automatically identify viruses by recognizing patterns of behavior and attack them as soon as they appear.

One approach to solving problems that digital computers find difficult is to arrange microprocessors in a network with connections to each other similar to the way nerve cells in the brain are connected to many other nerve cells. This arrangement is called a **neural network**. Digital computers are likely to continue to increase in power according to Moore's law for at least another 20 years, so it is likely that they will get better at approximating human behavior using traditional digital circuit designs. Real breakthroughs in AI are more likely to occur when new technologies like carbon nanotubes are used to create neural networks that are interconnected like neurons in the brain. Computers that use these new technologies may learn from experience the way humans do and may not need to be programmed in the traditional sense. If the exponential growth of circuit element density continues at the pace Moore predicted using new non-silicon technology, some predict human-level AI by 2030 (see the companion Web page at **http://www.prenhall.com/preston** for links to related articles).

CRITICAL THINKING

DISCUSSION

1 If the advantage of a robot is that it works three shifts and costs less money than humans, why shouldn't workers who man the same workstation get together and buy a robot? In other words, why should companies be the only ones to benefit from the work of the robot?

2 Should a unique strand of your DNA be recorded at birth to provide a world ID number?

3 What are some of the accessory programs that are included with Windows? If you bought these programs separately from third-party vendors, would you end up paying more or less for software?

4 If computer programs that mimic the human immune system are written to attack computer viruses, could they suffer the same types of problems humans have when their immune systems cause allergic reactions? What are some examples of autoimmune diseases in humans that might have analogous problems in a computer immune system?

Robots

Early science fiction writers envisioned machines with artificial intelligence that could do the work of humans. The Czech playwright Karel Capek adapted the Czech word *robota*, which means *work*, to describe these machines.

Robots may be too small to see with the unaided eye. They may be built using nanotechnology and assembled atom by atom. Such small robots could travel through a person's arteries and veins clearing out blockages or repairing weak spots. Most robots are much larger and are used in manufacturing industries.

❭ In the United States, 52 robots are used per 10,000 manufacturing workers.

❭ In Germany, 127 robots are used per 10,000 manufacturing workers.

❭ The U.S. automobile industry uses 700 robots per 10,000 manufacturing workers.

❭ Approximately 100,000 robots are in use in factories in North America.

These robots do welding and hazardous work and do not look like humans (see Figure 7.19). They have some ability to recognize patterns using cameras, and some have a simple sense of touch to determine how hard to grasp an object.

Most science fiction writers envision humanoid robots that can talk and interact like people. This raises moral and ethical questions about rights for AI machines. One term for sentient AI computer systems is ***silicon-based life***, which differentiates them from carbon-based life forms like us. If estimates are correct, we may need to decide this issue within our lifetimes.

FIGURE 7.19

Auto industries use robots for hazardous welding operations.

CONTINUOUS CONNECTIVITY

Many college students do not bother to sign up for telephone service at their apartments because it makes more sense for them to use a cell phone. They do not have to change phone numbers when they move each year, and they can talk whenever and from wherever they please. Cell phones continue to shrink in size and may eventually be replaced by tooth or ear implants. Communications technologies like cell phones, pagers, instant messaging, e-mail, and videoconferencing are converging. If they are combined with new visual displays directly to the brain or eye, then people will be able to communicate in a variety of ways at any time. For example, someone may decide to combine voice recognition, cell phone, and IM technologies to transcribe everything they say or hear onto an Internet blog site.

The Internet will become faster when **Internet2** is widely available. It is designed for better videoconferencing and security. Faster computers may provide accurate, real-time translations of languages on Web pages and in postings in chat sessions, breaking down one of the largest barriers humankind faces in communications. Another option is that the Internet will fragment into regional nets and make communication more difficult due to duplicate domain names and uncoordinated standards.

AGING OF LEADERSHIP

The leaders of the computer revolution were young when they founded their companies in the late '70s and early '80s. Consider this list of leaders and when they were born:

- Bill Gates, CSA and chairman of Microsoft—born in 1955
- Steve Balmer, CEO of Microsoft—born in 1956
- Steve Jobs, CEO of Apple—born in 1955
- Michael Dell, CEO of Dell—born in 1965
- Scott McNeely, CEO of SUN—born around 1960
- Larry Ellison, CEO of Oracle—born 1945

Michael Dell is still in his thirties; Gates, Jobs, and McNeely are in their late forties; and Ellison is the senior of the group in his late fifties. In the next 10 years, it is likely that these people will remain at the head of their respective companies, although Gates has already handed over the position of CEO to Steve Balmer, who is also in his late forties. Gates retains control of the company as chairman of the board of directors and chief software architect. As these men age into their fifties and sixties, their attitudes will likely differ from the ones they had as young men, and their firm grasp on power may prevent more vital leaders from gaining control. Another possibility is that they will tire of the pressure and long hours and retire. When Steve Jobs left Apple Computer, the company almost went under. The importance of having the visionary founder of the company at its helm was demonstrated when he resumed leadership and revitalized the company. Eventually, these leaders will retire. Because they are all within 15 years of each other in age, that could happen in a relatively short time span. This may result in uninspired leadership by committees, or it could provide opportunities for new leaders with new vision to take charge.

EXAMPLES

The exponential increase in processor power is expected to continue for at least the next 8 years in the absence of fundamental breakthroughs. There will also be changes in the other factors that provided the basis for

America's growth in this field. Projecting past trends into the future is always subject to error, but it is still useful to do so in order to make plans and be prepared for the changes that will come. Here are three examples of what to expect in the next 15 years, along with some speculation about what could happen in our lifetimes.

Health

Computers have provided health-care professionals with tools that have allowed amazing advancements already. We can expect revolutionary changes in biology and human health care that rival the computer revolution of the 1980s and 1990s.

Microprocessors will become even smaller and may be implanted in our hearts and other organs to monitor and report some types of problems before they become acute. During our lifetimes, we may see robots smaller than blood cells that can circulate through our bodies looking for problems and repairing damage. They could provide an effective cure for many types of cancer.

Computers are already used with lasers to sculpt the cornea to eliminate the need for glasses. This process is likely to become cheap and commonplace so that few people will wear glasses. Surgeons may use expert systems to provide advice on the latest procedures and even to control laser scalpels during some procedures (see Figure 7.20). High-speed Internet2 connections will allow more reliable teleconferencing and high-resolution images. Human surgeons may be able to perform operations remotely by controlling robotic arms.

Computers are used to process images and provide artificial vision. One method uses an artificial retina that attaches to the optic nerve at the back of the eyeball, and another stimulates the visual cortex of the brain directly. Crude prototypes of both systems are already being tested on humans with encouraging results.

Computers were used to map human DNA. Due to the exponential increase in computers' power, the project was finished earlier than expected and under budget. Project directors declared they had finished the project to better than 99.99 percent accuracy on April 14, 2003. We now know how the genes are arranged in human DNA, and the same computer techniques are being applied to the DNA of other lab animals commonly used in research. Applications of computers to biology will mean more to human health than the invention of the microprocessor meant to the computer industry. Computers will be used as important tools for designing drugs and determining treatments for genetic diseases. Scientists hope to find out how to control the mechanisms that turn genes on and off. If they do, people with spinal cord injuries may grow new nerve tissues and leave their wheelchairs. We may see the elimination of most birth defects in our lifetimes. Some people expect to find out why the human body stops repairing itself effectively, resulting in the effects of old age. We may find the cure for aging in our lifetimes.

Military

The U.S. military places a high premium on the lives of its soldiers and uses technology whenever possible to reduce risk to its personnel. Robots are used to enter caves or buildings to find the enemy and deliver explosives. Unmanned aircraft are used to patrol large areas like Afghanistan. They may be controlled remotely and their weapons fired from the safety

FIGURE 7.20

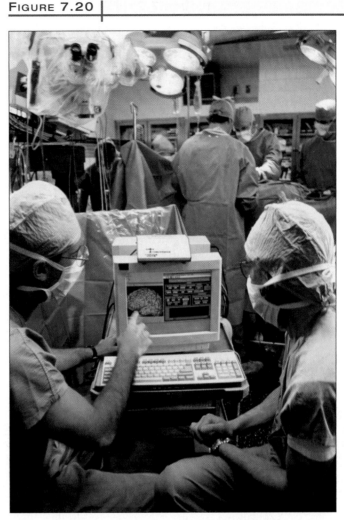

Expert systems and teleconferencing with human experts will bring the best of both types of experts to the operating room.

of the rear areas. Computers are even used to design camouflage fabrics for soldiers' uniforms. The military trains its soldiers using computer-operated simulators to reduce expense and improve safety. Reliance on technology and placing a premium on human life make the U.S. military the strongest conventional force in the world and enable it to be staffed by volunteers. This trend is likely to continue as advances in computer technology continue to be applied to military equipment and training. High technology is not the answer to all of the military's problems. The recent war in Iraq demonstrated that surveillance from a safe distance is no substitute for information obtained from people inside the country (see Figure 7.21) and managing a conquered population is very different from operating a tank.

The military advertises to potential teenage recruits by emphasizing the similarity of warfare to a video game (see Figure 7.22). This type of training does not prepare them for dealing with a population that speaks a different language and has a different culture and religion. The role of the military is likely to include more nation-building in years to come, which will require more emphasis on low-tech skills such as knowledge of languages and culture.

FIGURE 7.21

Knowledge of the spirit world is to be obtained by divination; information in natural science may be sought by inductive reasoning; the laws of the universe can be verified by mathematical calculation; but the dispositions of the enemy are ascertainable through spies and spies alone.

Sun Tzu, *The Art of War,* approximately 500 B.C.

Technology is no substitute for knowledge obtained from people.

Government

The government faces several challenges in the coming years that are due to changes in computing and Internet capabilities.

❱ Following the controversies involving punch-card ballots in the 2000 presidential election, there is momentum behind the idea of voting

FIGURE 7.22

Recruiters use video games to develop young people's interest.

online. Riverside, California, is using an electronic touch-screen voting system that does not involve paper ballots. Riverside saved $600,000 in printing costs and is able to provide ballots in Spanish at no extra cost. Online voting is unlikely to spread rapidly until voters are confident the system is secure and a reliable method for recounts is in place. This is likely to occur but not rapidly.

❱ Law enforcement agencies will probably take more advantage of DNA testing and biometrics. The U.S. Patriot Act will be fully implemented, and a variety of databases will be joined together to profile individuals, resulting in less privacy.

❱ Use of computer databases and computerized analysis of DNA will change the basic assumptions of health insurance by identifying who is likely to get sick or die prematurely. Traditional companies may use this information to reduce their risk and maximize profits by refusing to cover those who they know are most likely to make claims. The government may be forced to take over the health insurance business to provide benefits to everyone—including those who are genetically prone to disease.

❱ A de facto system of national ID numbers is likely to appear. The system may use Social Security numbers or numbers that represent a unique part of a person's DNA sequence.

❱ If terrorist attacks on cities using weapons of mass destruction are successful, more people may move from cities to the suburbs and use telecommuting and teleconferencing for daily work activity.

❱ Confrontations with countries that have sophisticated computer programmers could produce the government-sponsored use of viruses to attack U.S. computer systems. Fighting wars online is called *cyber war*. This type of conflict could lead to the breakup of the Internet into defendable regions with firewalls between them.

❱ Increased reliability on foreign imports of oil and manufactured goods puts more reliance on exporting high-tech products. The government will probably try to increase the revenue from software sales by helping industry install antipiracy measures.

COPING WITH COMPUTERS IN A CHANGING SOCIETY

The changes that are coming to our society in the next 20 years will be greater than those we have experienced in the last 20 years. It is easy to become overwhelmed without developing strategies to cope with change. Here are some tips for keeping up with the changes that are going to take place in our lives:

❱ Search out diverse and balanced sources of information—Assume that any single newspaper or television station represents a limited view of events and the world.

   • Read about technology advances from a financial newspaper like the *Wall Street Journal* as well as the popular press.

   • Read news coverage from other countries to gain an international perspective. Several English-language newspapers from other countries are available on the Internet.

❱ Read or watch quality science fiction that extrapolates trends into the future in a plausible manner and examines impacts and moral dilemmas. We need time to consider how to apply our moral principles to changing technology. By considering possibilities before they happen, we may be able to anticipate events and how we should react to them.

❱ Evaluate how emerging technologies will affect your job. Look for opportunities as well as threats.

❱ Talk with children to find out what the newest trends in communication and Internet use are. Discuss with them how to apply your family's values to new situations. Monitor their behavior with their knowledge when appropriate.

❱ Make lifelong learning a goal. Your current job skills will not suffice for your whole career. Plan to change responsibilities within your company or to change jobs completely. Work on skills that will be valuable in the future rather than just those that are popular now.

❱ Take periodic breaks from technology. One reason we preserve our wilderness areas and parks is to give us the luxury of escaping from technology for a while. Go camping or hiking, and appreciate the beauty of nature to gain perspective.

For more information and other ideas about the future of computers in our changing society, see the companion Web site at **http://www.prenhall.com/preston**.

TEST PREPARATION

The following section does not replace reading the text, nor does it contain all the information that will be tested. It is designed to provide examples and identify sections that need review.

summary by objective

THE PAST

- **Factors that influenced computer development in the United States**
  - Rule of law
  - Entrepreneurism
  - Victory in WWII and Cold War
  - Research
  - Venture capital
  - Counterculture
  - Exponential increase in computer power
  - Exponential increase in value of connectivity
  - Entrepreneurs run large companies
- **Relationship of patent and copyright to the U.S. Constitution**
  - Constitutional right in Article I Section 8
- **Examples of entrepreneurs**
  - Pre-WWII: Edison, Bell, Ford, Wright brothers
  - Computer era: Gates, Jobs, Dell, McNeely, Ellison
- **Motivations of entrepreneurs—Fame and fortune**
- **Advantages after World War II**
  - Factories not destroyed
  - Space race pushed miniaturization
- **Types of research conducted by companies and the government**
  - Applied—making products based on discoveries
  - Basic—seeking new knowledge
- **Examples of computer technology developed by IBM, Bell, Xerox, Stanford University, and University of Illinois**
  - Bell Laboratories—transistor, laser, optical fiber, cell phones, communications satellites, digital signal processors, UNIX operating system
  - IBM labs—DRAM, hard disks, relational databases, FORTRAN language, public-key encryption, scalable parallel processor systems, speech recognition, Deep Blue chess, and problem solving
- **Xerox PARC—laser printers, object-oriented programming, GUI, Ethernet, WYSIWYG printing, solid-state lasers, pop-up menus, worms, spell checking**
- **Policies regarding ownership of inventions at Stanford and U of I**
  - Stanford allowed students to own their discoveries
  - University of Illinois claims ownership
- **Role of venture capital in technology start-ups—Funded Intel and Apple but not Microsoft**
- **Contributions of counterculture**
  - Freeware, shareware, open-source programs
  - Apple computer company
- **Implications of Moore's law—Power increases by a factor of two every year or two**
- **Implications of Metcalfe's law—Value of a network increases with the square of the elements connected to the network**
- **Leadership of computer companies by founding entrepreneurs—Due to rapid increase in power, early leaders still run companies, e.g., Microsoft, Apple, Dell, Oracle, SUN**
- **Key elements of Microsoft's history**
  - 1969—Gates and Allen learn to program
  - 1975—Gates and Allen found Microsoft and adapt BASIC to the Altair
  - 1981—IBM PC introduced with PC-DOS from Microsoft
  - 1989—MS Office adapted for Macintosh operating system
  - 1990—Windows 3.0
  - 1995—Windows 95
  - 1997—Internet Explorer
  - 2001—found guilty of unfair competition and ruled a monopoly

- **Key elements of Apple's history**
  - 1976—Apple I
  - 1977—Apple II
  - 1984—Macintosh
  - 1985—Jobs ousted
  - 1988—Sues Microsoft over Windows
  - 1996—On verge of bankruptcy, Jobs returns
  - 1997—Jobs made interim CEO
  - 1998—iMac and PowerBook G3, return to profitability
  - 2000—Jobs made full CEO

THE FUTURE

- **Legal environment—Royalty payment systems must adapt to new environment to protect copyright and attract foreign talent**
- **Effect of capital gains taxes**
  - Lower capital gains taxes on profits from tech investments stimulates investment
  - Lowered to 18% in 2001
- **Factors that encourage entrepreneurs—Fame and fortune**
- **Importance of basic research to future growth—Provides basis for applications research and new products**
- **Value of cultural diversity and tolerance—Creative new ideas combined with basic research and capitalism provide a unique mix that can be very productive**
- **Example of new technologies that may extend Moore's law—Nanotechnology like carbon nanotubes**
- **Expected changes in the computer/human interface**
  - Monitors replaced by projected images or visual implants
  - Keyboard replaced by voice recognition
  - Mouse replaced by fingertip sensors
  - Virtual reality environments with avatars representing people
- **Developments in artificial intelligence**
  - Deep Blue wins chess match
  - Expert systems give advice
  - Data-mining programs look for patterns
  - Fuzzy logic deals with situations that are partly true or false
  - Pattern recognition
  - Neural networks mimic human brains
- **Use of robots**
  - 100,000 used in manufacturing in North America
  - Silicon-based life possible within our lifetimes
- **Effect of more connectivity**
  - Some become comfortable with loss of privacy
  - Internet may split into regions
- **Effect of aging leadership in the computer industry**
  - Possibly less innovative
  - Entrenched power
- **Examples of impact on health, military, and the government**
  - Health—implants that monitor organs, nanotechnology that repairs and maintains organs, DNA deciphered, possible cures for nerve damage and old age
  - Military—increased sophistication of surveillance and weapons with risk of becoming dependent on technology rather than human intelligence sources
  - Government—online voting slowly accepted, biometrics and DNA used widely for law enforcement, government may take over health insurance, government sponsored cyberwar.
- **Coping strategies**
  - Diverse sources of information
  - Reading or watch quality science fiction
  - Evaluating emerging technologies for effects on your job
  - Discussing new developments with children; monitor them openly when appropriate
  - Lifelong learning to maintain current job skills
  - Taking breaks from technology

1. ___ To secure a loan, venture capitalists require collateral in the form of real property like land or houses.

2. ___ Counterculture is characterized by rebellion against the traditional values of corporations.

3. ___ The United States became adept at miniaturization as a result of the space race with the Soviets.

4. ___ The Macintosh computer was introduced in 1984 with an advertisement that made use of the theme from a book titled *1984*.

5. ___ Metcalfe's law says that the density of computer chips will grow exponentially.

multiple choice

1. Which of the following is not a significant development of Microsoft?
   a) It introduced Windows 95.
   b) It made a deal with IBM to provide an operating system for the IBM PC.
   c) Jobs assumed the role of interim CEO.
   d) The company was found guilty of unfair competition.

2. Which of the following is not a significant development in the history of Apple?
   a) The Macintosh was released.
   b) Jobs was forced out by Sculley.
   c) *Toy Story* was released.
   d) Jobs returned.

3. Which of the following was not discovered or developed at Bell Laboratories?
   a) the transistor
   b) cell phones
   c) UNIX
   d) Ethernet

4. Which of the following was not discovered or developed at IBM labs?
   a) GUI
   b) DRAM
   c) FORTRAN
   d) Deep Blue

5. Approximately how many industrial robots are in use in North America?
   a) less than 50,000
   b) between 50,000 and 150,000
   c) between 150,001 and 250,000
   d) more than 250,000

completion

1. An animated image that represents a person in virtual reality is called a(n) _____.

2. A nanometer is a(n) _____ th of a meter.

3. Computers that were built to the same design specifications as the IBM PC and that used Microsoft's operating system were called _____.

4. The prediction that integrated circuit density would increase exponentially is called _____ law.

5. A million megabytes is a(n) _____ byte.

Match each term with its definition.

_____ **1.** algorithm
_____ **2.** applied research
_____ **3.** artificial intelligence (AI)
_____ **4.** avatar
_____ **5.** basic research
_____ **6.** capital gains
_____ **7.** carbon nanotubes
_____ **8.** clones
_____ **9.** data mining
_____ **10.** entrepreneur
_____ **11.** expert system
_____ **12.** exponential growth
_____ **13.** fuzzy logic
_____ **14.** linear growth
_____ **15.** Metcalfe's law
_____ **16.** Moore's law
_____ **17.** nanometer
_____ **18.** nanotechnology
_____ **19.** neural network
_____ **20.** pattern recognition
_____ **21.** terabyte
_____ **22.** venture capital
_____ **23.** virtual reality (VR)
_____ **24.** VisiCalc
_____ **25.** Windows

a. the ability to perceive identity of objects from their image
b. arrangement of carbon atoms into tubes
c. artificial character that represents a person in virtual reality
d. billionth of a meter
e. computers made to the same specification as the IBM PC
f. connections of processors that mimic the function of neurons
g. the technology of devices whose size is measured in nanometers
h. the first electronic spreadsheet
i. step-by-step specific instructions
j. looking for new knowledge
k. looking for patterns in large amounts of data
l. the ability of machines to display properties similar to a human's ability to think
m. making a product from a new discovery
n. methods of dealing with situations that are not completely true or false
o. Microsoft's GUI interface
p. a million megabytes
q. money lent without collateral in exchange for part ownership of a new company
r. person who organizes a business and assumes the risk
s. prediction that integrated circuits would increase in capability by a factor of two every year or two
t. profits from the sale of assets such as investment in a company
u. provides advice on how to solve a problem
v. sequence of numbers that increases by a multiple of the preceding value
w. sequence of numbers that increases by the same amount
x. simulations that can appear to be real
y. the value of a network is proportional to the square of the number of elements connected to it

beyond the facts

Factual knowledge provides the basis for higher levels of learning. In the following sections, you work with the concepts and facts presented in the chapter to develop critical-thinking and problem-solving skills. You practice research, analysis, and communication and become aware of diversity issues while exploring the impact of computer technology on career choices, the workplace, social interactions, and home life. The Leadership section helps you identify ways in which you can lead others in organizing and implementing projects that meet worthwhile community needs. In the Lifelong Learning exercise, you build a set of learning resources that you can use after this course to continue learning.

objectives for beyond the facts

END OF CHAPTER EXERCISES	Achievement of the objectives for the end-of-chapter exercises requires evaluation of documents, class discussions, or presentations.
Critical Thinking–Research	Which intellectual property rights policy has benefited the university more, that of Stanford University or of the University of Illinois? Demonstrate the following skills: locate relevant information online, analyze the information and form an opinion based on the research, consider diversity issues, work with others where appropriate, and communicate the results in writing or by public presentation.
Problem Solving	1) Transfer files between word processing programs on different operating systems, such as Star Office in Linux, Word in Mac OS, and Word in Windows. 2) Write a detailed description of the process for exchanging word processing documents between applications that run on Linux, Mac OS, and Windows. Describe the problems you encountered and how you addressed them. 3) Communicate the experience to the class.
Anticipating Career Challenges and Opportunities	How can expert systems be utilized in your type of work? Demonstrate the following skills: 1) Teamwork: coordinate research on the use of expert systems in the workplace with other students 2) Research: identify company policies and services that would be compatible with an expert system 3) Analysis: form an opinion about the potential for using expert systems at your workplace 4) Communication: communicate the results in writing or by public presentation
Impact on the Workplace	If monitors, keyboards, and mice are replaced by virtual devices that do not require significant desk space, what effect would that have on the place where you work? Demonstrate the following skills: 1) Teamwork: coordinate research on the impact of removing monitors, keyboards, and mice from the workplace. 2) Research: identify company needs for workspace, furniture, privacy, and connectivity. 3) Analysis: form an opinion about the impact on your workplace of removing these devices. 4) Communication: communicate the results in writing or by public presentation.
Impact on Social Interactions	Compare the impact of artificial vision for blind people with the impact of cochlear implants for the deaf. Demonstrate the following skills: 1) Teamwork: allocate tasks for research on artificial vision. 2) Research: review articles and polls concerning artificial vision; find articles that discuss different methods of artificial vision. 3) Diversity: find out about problems deaf people have related to cochlear implants and peer group acceptance. 4) Analysis: compare the attitudes toward deaf people who get cochlear implants and possible attitudes of blind people who get artificial vision implants. 5) Communication: communicate the results in writing or by public presentation.
Impact on Home Life	Which of Bill Gates's expectations of the impact of computers on home life actually happened? Which ones are actively under development, and which ones will probably not happen? Demonstrate the following skills: 1) Teamwork: allocate tasks.

2) Research: read an interview with Gates, search for available home technology, and search for products in development.

3) Analysis: determine the accuracy of Gates's 1994 predictions. Form an opinion about the accuracy of similar predictions made today about the next 10 years.

4) Communication: communicate the results in writing or by public presentation.

Leadership

Describe a plan to lead a group of people toward a worthy goal—in this case, acquiring financial support for blind people getting artificial vision. Demonstrate the ability to inspire others to follow your vision.

Lifelong Learning

Identify three or more online resources that may be used to learn more about the topics introduced in this chapter.

critical thinking–research

Which intellectual property rights policy has benefited the university more, that of Stanford University or of the University of Illinois?

1. **Teamwork**—Join one to three other students. Decide how to divide up the work. Possible divisions could be: research, editing the group paper, and preparing the class presentation.

2. **Research**—Use a Web browser, and go to the companion Web site at **www.prenhall.com/preston**. Follow the links by clicking on the Web addresses that are highlighted and underlined. Read about Marc Andreessen and his experience with the University of Illinois. Use a Web search engine such as Google.com or Yahoo.com to search for information about alumni support at U of I and at Stanford. Make a list of relevant sources that you may want to reference later. Include the title of the page or article, the name of the organization responsible for the Web page, the date the page or article was written, and the Web address. You may also go to the library and look up books, articles, and news reports that are relevant to this topic. Many libraries have the full text of articles and news reports online in proprietary databases that are not available to the public.

3. **Diversity issues**—Provide background on the two universities that gives insight into the differences in cultures that may have resulted in the different policies.

4. **Analysis**—Write an essay that compares the intellectual property rights policies of the two universities. Describe the money each gets from royalties derived from copyrights it holds based on work done by students on campus versus how much money they each get in donations from alumni who have become rich from ownership of ideas developed in college. Go beyond simple reporting of the facts. Support your opinion with references to the articles you read. Ask your instructor for guidance regarding the required length of the essay.

5. **Communication**—Prepare a presentation in which you present your opinion and supporting facts to the class. Depending on your computer skill, you could give the presentation using a program like PowerPoint and save it as a Web page, or you could prepare a paper handout with your Web references for use while you talk to the class.

problem solving

Before Microsoft's software and operating system dominated the workplace, there were a variety of programs, each with its own interface and file format. Transferring a document between two computers was difficult. If Linux-based software becomes more common, transferring files between applications that run on Linux and those that run on Mac OS and Windows may become more commonplace. Find out whether this is likely to be a problem by creating a document in Star Office and transferring it to a word processing application on an Apple computer or on a computer running Windows.

The objective of this exercise is to learn valuable processes for solving computer-related problems, not just the solution to this particular problem.

Work with two or three other people to transfer a word processing file.

1. **Form a team with diverse computers and operating systems**—Form a team whose members have an Apple computer, a computer with Windows and Microsoft Word, a computer with Microsoft Works, a computer with Star Office or Open Office on Linux, and a computer with WordPerfect. (Star Office is a version of Open Office that runs on Windows computers as well as Linux and costs about $50.) If you do not know people who have each one, see your instructor for approval to use a selection of them.

2. **Create a document to transfer**—Create a document that has some formatted text, a table, and embedded clip art that represents the types of documents you might wish to exchange.

3. **Troubleshooting**—Attempt to exchange the document with each member of your team using each type of application by exchanging floppy disks and by e-mail attachments. Record the problems and how you overcame them.

4. **Communicate**—Describe your experience. Prepare a presentation for the class that describes what you learned through this experience.

anticipating career challenges and opportunities

How can expert systems be used in your type of work? What challenges and opportunities will that present?

1. **Teamwork**—Join one to three other students who have similar careers. Decide how to divide up the work. Possible divisions could be: advising customers calling into the company, fixing malfunctioning products, and making complex company decisions.

2. **Research**—Use a Web browser and search for articles on expert systems.

3. **Diversity issues**—Consider how other countries use expert systems. Would those methods work well in the United States?

4. **Analysis**—Write an essay that describes the future use of expert systems in your career. List which jobs are likely to be eliminated and which jobs may be in greater demand. Go beyond simple reporting of your opinion. Support your opinion with references to the articles you read. Ask your instructor for guidance regarding the required length of the essay.

5. **Communication**—Prepare a presentation in which you present your opinion and supporting facts to the class. Depending on your computer skill, you could give the presentation using a program like PowerPoint and save it as a Web page, or you could prepare a paper handout with your Web references for use while you talk to the class.

impact on the workplace

If monitors, keyboards, and mice were replaced by virtual devices that do not require significant desk space, what effect would that have on the place where you work?

1. **Teamwork**—Join one or two other students who work where you do or in a similar type of business or organization. Decide how to divide up the work. Possible divisions could be: research, writing the paper, and making the presentation.

2. **Research**—Find out about the savings on computer desks and space, as well as privacy issues.

3. **Analysis**—Write an essay that describes what effect it would have on the workplace if employees could interact with text by speaking or waving their fingers. Assume a wireless connection so people would not be tethered to the workstation by wires. Form and express an opinion about the effect. Support your opinion with references to articles. Ask your instructor for guidance regarding the required length of the essay.

4. **Communication**—Prepare a presentation in which you present your opinion and supporting facts to the class.

impact on social interactions

Consider the social impact of artificial vision for blind people. Compare it to the social impact of cochlear implants for the deaf.

1. **Teamwork**—Join one or two other students to find out about artificial vision and cochlear implants.

2. **Research**—Find articles about artificial vision for the blind and cochlear implants for the deaf.

3. **Diversity**—Find out how the hearing-impaired community reacts to those who attempt to have their hearing restored with cochlear implants.

Seek information from Web sites or organizations for the visually impaired to see if there is a similar feeling about those who would seek to use artificial vision.

4. **Analysis**—Compare the attitudes toward cochlear implants in the hearing-impaired community with any reactions you may find in the visually impaired community.

5. **Communication**—Prepare a presentation in which you present your findings to the class.

impact on home life

Which of Bill Gates's expectations of the impact of computers on home life actually happened? Which ones are actively under development, and which ones probably will not happen?

1. **Teamwork**—Join one or two other students. Decide how to divide up the work. Possible divisions could be: research, essay writing, and preparation of the presentation.

2. **Research**—Use the link on the companion Web site to read the 1994 interview with Bill Gates.

Then look up each of the products he mentions that may be used in the home.

3. **Analysis**—Determine the accuracy of Gates's predictions from 1994. Form an opinion about the accuracy of similar predictions made today about the next 10 years.

4. **Communication**—Communicate the results in writing or by public presentation.

leadership

Prepare talks for groups like the Kiwanis and Lions on artificial vision and other therapies that some people may require assistance to afford.

1. **Vision**—Write a vision statement that describes what you want your group to achieve. It should motivate people to volunteer to help.

2. **Research**—Do not reinvent the wheel. Determine whether anyone has tried this in your community.

3. **Plan of Action**—Write a simple plan of action. Test the plan by following it yourself on a small scale. Locate a service group that would like you

to make a presentation on what technologies may be available to those who need them but who cannot afford them without help.

4. **Analysis**—Write up an analysis of what you learned by testing your plan.

5. **Communication**—Present your plan to the class. Describe what you learned by testing your plan and how you think it could be expanded if others joined you. Share your vision statement, and try to inspire others to join you in your worthwhile effort.

lifelong learning

Add links to your browser's favorites list.

1. Start your Web browser, and open the list of favorite sites. Create folders named *History*, *Future*, and *Coping*. (Look for Organize Favorites in Internet Explorer and Manage Bookmarks in Netscape.)

2. Go to the companion Web page for this chapter and select one of the links from this chapter that you found useful.

3. Add this link to your browser's favorites list in the *History*, *Future*, or *Coping* folder.

4. Repeat this process for other links in the companion Web page for this chapter and add them to the *History*, *Future*, or *Coping* folder.

Create a journal in a word processor to set learning goals.

1. Identify areas in which you feel you know the least. List three specific topics related to this chapter that you would like to learn more about in the future.

2. You will add to this journal after each chapter to compile a personal list of references and topics for future study.

Answers to Test Preparation Questions

CHAPTER 1

True/False Questions
1. CD-R is a processor by AMD **(F)**
2. A "smart bomb" is a computer designed drug that targets specific tumors. **(F)**
3. Ergonomics is the applied science of design to reduce operator fatigue and discomfort. **(T)**
4. A veiling reflection causes eye fatigue because the muscles of the iris adjust constantly. **(F)**
5. The "Digital Divide" refers to the separation between the processor and RAM memory **(F)**

Multiple Choice
1. Which of the following is not one of the four functions that defines a computer?
   a) Algorithm
   b) Output
   c) Storage
   d) Processing
2. Which of the following uses of computers are mismatched with their area of application?
   a) Military—smart bombs, training, maintenance, GPS
   b) Business—documents, spreadsheets, project management
   c) Health—MRI, CAT scan, insurance records
   d) Recreation—bar codes, fuel load, traffic control
3. Which of the following statements is least appropriate for ergonomic design of a computer workstation?
   a) Use bold, primary colors near the computer to reduce boredom.
   b) Your feet should be flat on the floor or on a footrest.
   c) Adjust the height of the chair to prevent using the keyboard with your wrist bent.
   d) The monitor should be placed where its screen does not reflect the light from a window to the operator's eye
4. Which of the following is true about the Digital Divide?
   a) 75% of children between 5 and 17 use the computer.
   b) 50% of people older than 65 reported they had at least one disability that limited use of a computer.
   c) Countries that charge a flat fee for Internet have a lower rate of computer use than those countries that charge by the minute.
   d) One of the factors that limits Internet use in poor countries is the lack of reliable electricity.
5. Which of the following is not a storage device?
   a) MRI
   b) EPROM
   c) RAM
   d) CD

Completion
1. If a distance education class is conducted online using live communication at the same time each week, it is using **synchronous** communication.
2. A message like a memo or letter sent electronically is called **e-mail**.
3. The center of the monitor should align with the **centerline** of the body.
4. **LCD** is a type of display used in thin monitors.
5. A **relational** database has two tables that have a field in common.

Matching Key Terms with Definitions
Write the number of the definition in the Ans. column next to the matching term.

9	**a.** Asynchronous	1	A curved portion of the back of a chair that provides additional support for the lower part of the back
7	**b.** Avatar	2	An image of a bright light source on a computer screen that partially obscures the object behind the reflective surface
3	**c.** Bar code	3	A series of vertical bars and spaces that can be read by a computer
13	**d.** CAT scan	4	A type of chart which uses horizontal bars to represent tasks, the time they take, and their relationship to the start and end of other tasks

12 e. CD

5 A type of storage that is used to record information for later retrieval, and does not require constant power to retain the information that is stored.

8 f. Center line

6 An arrangement of cells in rows and columns that can be used to display and calculate financial information, some of which is dependent on the results of calculations in other cells.

11 g. CPU

7 An image that represents a person online

19 h. Database

8 An imaginary line that bisects the human body vertically

16 i. Disc
9 At different times

17 j. Disk
10 At the same time

14 k. E-mail

11 Part of the computer that performs calculations

25 l. Ergonomics
12 An optical memory device

24 m. Flash

13 An imaging system that uses x-rays and computers

4 n. Gantt

14 Mail exchanged between computers

15 o. GPS

15 A system that uses radio signals from satellites to determine locations accurately on earth

18 p. LCD

16 Optical storage term that is similar to a term used for magnetic storage

1 q. Lumbar support

17 Magnetic media term that is similar to a term used for optical storage

20 r. Magnetic

18 A type of screen used in laptop computers and some desktop monitors which are typically much thinner than older style monitors

21 s. Optical

19 Lists of data organized in tables where each column is a type of information and each row is one person, event, or interaction

22 t. Processing

20 materials like plastic or metal (hard) disks coated with a material usually containing iron used to store data

23 u. RAM

21 materials like reflective discs that can store data and retrieve it using light, usually in the form of a reflected laser beam.

5 v. Secondary Storage

22 One of the main four functions of a computer—manipulating data according to a set of instructions to create information which can be stored.

6 w. Spreadsheets

10 x. Synchronous

2 y. Veiling reflection

23 High-speed memory on computer chips

24 similar to RAM but does not require constant power

25 The applied science of equipment design to reduce operator fatigue and discomfort

CHAPTER 2

True/False Questions

1. Intranet is another term for backbone. **(F)**
2. VoIP has been around since the early days of ARPANET. **(F)**
3. The government encouraged academic networks to seek commercial customers to expand the use of the Internet. **(T)**
4. A LAN with a T1 line is a faster connection to the Internet than a cable modem. **(T)**
5. A domain name can have only one IP address. **(F)**

Multiple Choice

1. Which of the following is not a function of e-mail?
   a) posting daily thoughts for anyone on the Internet to read
   b) CC
   c) BCC
   d) Reply to All

2. Web-based training is not appropriate under which of the following conditions?
   a) geographically dispersed workforce
   b) workforce dispersed among different shift schedules
   c) high travel costs to assemble workforce
   d) content of training changes often and requires regular updates

3. Which of the following is not a method or device used to connect to the Internet?
   a) cell phone
   b) CD-RW
   c) satellite television dish
   d) modem

4. Which of the following people was not directly involved in creating or developing important products for use on the Internet or World Wide Web?
   a) Tim Berners-Lee
   b) Mark Andreessen
   c) J. C. R. Licklider
   d) Leslie Groves

5. Which of the following is the best ranking of connection speed from slowest to fastest?
   a) dial-up, LAN with T1, cable
   b) LAN, satellite, DSL
   c) DSL, cable, cell phone
   d) dial-up, DSL, LAN with T1

Completion

1. An IP address is 32 binary digits long. It is divided into four groups called **Octets**, which are represented as decimal numbers separated by periods.
2. The abbreviation CC in an e-mail message stands for **courtesy copy or carbon copy** (two words).
3. The new domain name extension for museums is **.museum**.
4. Icons used to show emotion are called **emoticons**.
5. The acronym HTML stands for **hypertext markup language** (three words).

Matching Key Terms with Definitions

Match each term with its definition.

G	**1.** blog	A	method of transferring files on the Internet
X	**2.** checksum	B	a group of connected computers
V	**3.** client	C	a high-speed connection to the Internet from a company or ISP
I	**4.** disk cache	D	a method used to retrieve Web pages from a server
J	**5.** DNS	E	a name that often resembles the name of the organization and is easier to remember than a number; it often includes www as a prefix and always has an extension to indicate the category
E	**6.** domain name	F	a program that searches the Web for Web pages and indexes them for use by a search engine
N	**7.** DSL	G	a series of dated journal entries available online
W	**8.** FAQ	H	a programming language used to write applets
A	**9.** FTP	I	area of the computer where recently visited Web pages are stored for quick retrieval
P	**10.** HTML	J	computer with a database of domain names and IP addresses and the relationships between them
D	**11.** HTTP	K	company or group that provides a connection to the Internet backbone
L	**12.** IM	L	direct communication between users with windows that display text or video
K	**13.** ISP	M	encrypts packets within packets that are sent to an intranet via the Internet
H	**14.** JAVA	N	high-speed connection technology that uses existing telephone lines over distances of a few miles
B	**15.** LAN	O	identifies the method of interaction with the server, a domain name or IP address, the local folder, and file name
T	**16.** POP3	P	language used to create Web pages that can be displayed on any computer
U	**17.** SMTP	Q	method of running programs on a remote computer
Y	**18.** spam	R	method of sending telephone conversations using TCP/IP packets
F	**19.** spider	S	method of transmitting packets on the Internet
C	**20.** T1	T	program to handle mail being received by the user
S	**21.** TCP/IP	U	program to handle mail being sent from the user
Q	**22.** Telnet	V	program that communicates with the server and usually resides on the user's computer
O	**23.** URL	W	questions and answers posted so new participants can catch up
R	**24.** VoIP	X	sum of numbers within a packet
M	**25.** VPN	Y	term used to describe unsolicited e-mail

CHAPTER 3

True/False Questions

1. Computer applications such as simulating the behavior of an airplane are good candidates for distributed processing. **(F)**
2. A byte is eight bits. **(T)**
3. An A-D converter changes continuously varying signals into a stream of numbers. **(T)**
4. A circle that is open at the top with a vertical line through the opening is a symbol used on power buttons to indicate that this button does not turn the power completely off. **(T)**
5. OCR programs are used with scanners to convert images of documents into editable text. **(T)**

Multiple Choice

1. Which of the following is not a device that can use a USB port?
   a) mouse
   b) monitor
   c) printer
   d) keyboard
2. Which of the following storage devices can use both sides of the disc?
   a) CD-R
   b) DVD
   c) CD-ROM
   d) CD-RW
3. Which of the following is not a keyboard key that is commonly used in combination with other keys to perform functions?
   a) Alt
   b) Num Lock
   c) Ctrl
   d) Fn

4. An eight bit binary number can represent how many different numbers or characters?
   a) 64
   b) 128
   c) 256
   d) 512

5. Which of the following is the slowest connection?
   a) SCSI
   b) USB 1.1
   c) FireWire
   d) serial port

Completion

1. A device that converts a series of numbers into smooth variations in an electrical signal is an **D to A** converter.

2. The **Unicode** standard expands upon the ASCII standard to provide codes for letters and symbols in many other languages.

3. A round flat piece of plastic used to record data optically is called a **disc**.

4. A round flat piece of plastic or metal used to record data magnetically is a **disk**.

5. A USB 2.0 connection is about **40** times faster than a USB 1.1 connection.

Matching Key Terms with Definitions

Write the letter(s) of the definition in the Ans. column next to the matching term.

E	**1.** A to D converter	A	ability to convert speech into digital files or commands
H	**2.** Unicode	B	Removable electronic memory
X	**3.** liquid crystal display (LCD)	C	communication device with a keyboard and monitor that depends on another computer for processing and storage
A	**4.** voice recognition	D	optical storage that can record in layers on both sides
C	**5.** dumb terminal	E	device that converts analog electric signals to a series of numbers
M	**6.** flat screen	F	projection that requires the proper orientation of plug and receptacle
N	**7.** network interface card (NIC)	G	round connector used for mice and keyboards
G	**8.** PS/2	H	code that uses 64-bit numbers to represent characters from numerous languages
P	**9.** hub	I	group of eight bits used to represent characters, decimal numbers, and other special characters

I	**10.** byte	J	integrated circuits that work with the CPU
J	**11.** random access memory (RAM)	K	standard telephone connector
U	**12.** CD-RW	L	optical disc to which data may be written
L	**13.** CD-R	M	CRT with a less curved screen
D	**14.** digital versatile disc (DVD)	N	device used to connect a computer to other computers
F	**15.** key	O	thin display that often uses LCD technology
V	**16.** flash memory	P	used to provide additional USB connections
B	**17.** USB drive	Q	device that sends out pulses used to coordinate computer component activity
Q	**18.** clock	R	similar to Standby on Apple computers
Y	**19.** virtual memory	S	type of bus connection for high-speed data transfer between devices and the computer
W	**20.** ASCII	T	standard Ethernet connector
T	**21.** RJ-45	U	optical disc from which data may be read and to which data may be written, erased, and rewritten
K	**22.** RJ-11	V	remembers data even when disconnected from a power source; used with electronic devices like cameras
O	**23.** flat panel	W	code for assigning eight-bit numbers to characters and commands
S	**24.** SCSI	X	type of display the uses electric fields to change the transparency of liquids cells
R	**25.** sleep	Y	space on a hard disk used to supplement physical memory

CHAPTER 4

True/False questions

1. First generation languages use hexadecimal numbers and command codes. **(F)**

2. BIOS is an operating system designed to work with medical research devices and programs. **(F)**

3. Script languages are simpler than most 3GLs. **(T)**

4. CGI is a script language. **(F)**

5. Fifth generation languages may be compiled by 3GL or 4GL compilers. **(T)**

Multiple Choice

1. Which of the following is not a characteristic of OOP?
   a) Methods
   b) Messages
   c) Operations
   d) Structured queries
2. Which of the following applications is the first to run when you turn on a computer?
   a) Microsoft Office
   b) Operating system
   c) BIOS
   d) HTML
3. What term describes the development of code writing that eliminated use of the GOTO branching method and replaced it with IF-THEN-ELSE statements?
   a) Structured code
   b) Procedural code
   c) Spaghetti code
   d) Logical Synchronicity
4. Which of the following is a characteristic of object-oriented programming that is not a feature of event-driven programming?
   a) Uses graphic elements
   b) Polymorphism
   c) May be compiled by a 3GL compiler
   d) Higher level than 2GL
5. Which of the following is not an operating system?
   a) MVS
   b) LINUX
   c) C++
   d) Mac OS X

Completion

1. A programming method that reuses blocks of code using standardized inputs and outputs is **modular** programming.
2. The **ADA** language was named in honor of an early programming pioneer and adopted by the military.
3. The first program a computer runs when it is turned on is the **BIOS**.
4. The **compiler** converts source code to machine code.
5. Reorganizing the data on a disk to place data from the same file on adjacent sectors is called **defragmenting** the disk.

Matching Key Terms with Definitions

Write the letter(s) of the definition in the Ans. column next to the matching term.

Ans.	Term		Definition
X	1. applets	A	a 2GL language one step higher than machine language
A	2. assembler	B	a fourth-generation language that is used for extracting specific sets of data from a database
J	3. attributes	C	a group of objects with common attributes and methods
D	4. byte code	D	a partially compiled program that can be run by a Java virtual machine
Q	5. C#	E	a program on a Web server that handles requests for scripts
C	6. class	F	a program that converts higher-level programs into machine language
E	7. Common gateway interface (CGI)	G	an action by the user such as clicking a button on the screen
F	8. compiler	H	characteristic of modular programming
Y	9. drivers	I	characteristic of object-oriented program in which objects can accomplish a stated message independently
G	10. event	J	characteristics of an object
T	11. event driven	K	compiles byte code for execution on a particular platform
P	12. Extensible Markup Language (XML)	L	derivative of UNIX that is free and open source
H	13. information hiding	M	instruction in object-oriented programming
O	14. Java	N	language that is in written in binary code that a computer processor can interpret directly
K	15. Java virtual machine (JVM)	O	language that uses byte code and a virtual machine to create interactive Web pages
L	16. Linux	P	method of attaching additional information to text or pictures on a Web page
N	17. machine language	Q	Microsoft's version of Java
M	18. message	R	nonprocedural method that uses attributes, methods, classes, and messages
V	19. methods	S	programming entity with attributes and methods that belongs to a class
R	20. object-oriented programming (OOP)	T	characteristic of programs that are executed when the user chooses an option
S	21. objects	U	rules for a software language that must be followed when writing code
I	22. polymorphism	V	sets of instructions on how to accomplish a task in OOP

W 23. scripts   W short programs that reside on the Web server that are used with Web pages

B 24. Structured Query Language (SQL)   X small application programs included with Web pages

U 25. syntax   Y small programs that provide communication instructions between a peripheral and the operating system

CHAPTER 5

True/False Questions

1. A copyright is in effect only if the author provides a notice. **(F)**
2. Patents are issued only to protect the design of physical objects. **(F)**
3. Cybersquatting involves using a company's trademark as part of a domain name. **(T)**
4. Plagiarism is the use of a trademark without permission. **(F)**
5. Downloading and playing copyrighted music from file-sharing sites without paying a royalty is like listening to music on the radio. Both are legal. **(F)**

Multiple Choice

1. Which of the principles does not belong with the others in this group?
   a) respect yourself
   b) respect your school
   c) respect your profession
   d) respect your self-interest
2. Which of the questions used to determine ethical behavior does not belong with the others in this group?
   a) Would you be proud to have your parents and neighbors know?
   b) Do most of your friends do it?
   c) If the people affected by your decision knew all the details, would they think they had been treated fairly?
   d) If your action involves your place of employment, would your boss or the company's customers agree with what you have done?
3. Which of the following is not considered plagiarism?
   a) quoting something from a government publication without using quotation marks or an indented block of single-spaced text
   b) copying text from a Web page without indicating the source
   c) writing your own opinion that is based on a variety of facts and readings
   d) writing down what your roommate dictates while you type and then turning in the paper with only your name on it

4. Which of the following is true about using course packs in college classes?
   a) Royalties do not have to be collected or paid, regardless of the amount of text copied, because it is for educational purposes.
   b) Web sites exist that make it much easier than it used to be for people to pay to use excerpts of articles and books.
   c) Determining fair use is a simple matter of applying the standards set forth in the copyright laws.
   d) Reproducing copyrighted material for use in classes is permitted if the people doing the reproduction do not profit from including the copyrighted material.
5. Which of the following is true about most end user license agreements, excluding those for freeware and shareware?
   a) You are allowed to deconstruct the machine code and use up to 49 percent of the program in other programs.
   b) You are allowed to make and distribute copies on the Internet.
   c) You are allowed to install the software on one computer.
   d) You are allowed to install the software on all the computers you personally own.

Completion

1. Reporting an illegal activity is called **whistleblowing**.
2. A difficult choice between two moral behaviors is called a moral **dilemma**.
3. A person owns the copyright on his or her writing unless it is done as a **work for hire** (three words).
4. An agreement that covers software installations on all the computers at a particular location is called a **site license** (two words).
5. Parts of copyrighted works may be used for criticism, commentary, news reporting, teaching, scholarship, or research without paying a royalty under certain conditions. This policy is called **fair use** (two words).

Matching Key Terms with Definitions

Match each term with its definition.

C 1. course packs   A agreement to allow installation of software on all the computers at one location

X 2. cybersmearing   B checking someone's background for indications of character

O 3. cybersquatting   C collections of copied works

Y 4. cyberstalking   D compression technique for video

F 5. end user license agreement (EULA)   E compression technique used with music files

N 6. fair use   F contract between the software copyright holder and the user

G	7. freeware	G	copyrighted work that is available without charge
M	8. frequently asked questions (FAQ)	H	creative product for which the copyright is owned by the company that paid for the creator's services
L	9. honor code	I	creative work that is not copyrighted
W	10. identity theft	J	critical analysis of fundamental assumptions and beliefs
U	11. moral dilemma	K	device that records television programs and can share them over the Internet
E	12. MP3	L	ethical conduct agreed to by a group's members
D	13. MP4	M	lists of questions and answers that help a new user take part in a group rapidly
S	14. open source	N	policy that allows use of copyrighted works without permission or payment under certain circumstances
K	15. personal video recorder (PVR)	O	profiting from a trademark as part of a domain name without permission
J	16. philosophy	P	reporting illegal activity
Q	17. plagiarism	Q	representing the work of others as one's own
I	18. public domain	R	sound delivered over the Internet
A	19. site license	S	programming code that is available to the public
V	20. software piracy	T	symbol or logo used to identify a product
R	21. streaming audio	U	two conflicting moral behaviors
T	22. trademark	V	using copyrighted software without permission
B	23. vetting	W	using private facts to impersonate
P	24. whistle-blowing	X	using the Internet to defame
H	25. work for hire	Y	using the Internet to harass

CHAPTER 6

True/False Questions

1. Biometric devices combine biology with statistics to identify individuals by measuring characteristics of their bodies. **(T)**
2. Browsers may be set to block the use of cookies. **(T)**
3. Cookies are executable programs installed on your computer's hard drive that report on your activity and your hard drive's contents to a Web server. **(F)**
4. Passwords are used to create a symmetric key. **(T)**
5. Computers can be used with video surveillance cameras to identify individuals in public places. **(T)**

Multiple Choice

1. Which of the following is the least secure method of backing up your data?
   a) Save the data on a CD-R, and place the disc in your desk drawer.
   b) Save a copy of your files in another folder on the same hard drive.
   c) Save a copy of your files on a different computer on the company's local area network.
   d) Make copies on a removable hard disk that is stored in a safe at night.
2. Which of the following tricks you into taking action that damages your own computer?
   a) hoax
   b) e-mail bomb
   c) worm
   d) macro virus
3. Which of the following is not a function of a firewall?
   a) serving Web pages in the DMZ
   b) filtering Web pages or e-mail that contain objectionable material
   c) limiting certain types of protocols like HTTP and SMTP to particular gateway computers
   d) logging traffic between a LAN and the Internet
4. Which of the following is not true about cookies?
   a) They are managed by the Web browser.
   b) They are text files that may be read with a word processing program.
   c) They may be stored on your computer by a Web bug.
   d) They typically contain your name, shipping address, and credit card number so you do not have to enter this information each time you buy something.
5. Which of the following is not true about spyware?
   a) If you agree to the EULA without reading it, you may unknowingly give permission to install spyware.
   b) Freeware software may include spyware.
   c) Cookies often contain spyware.
   d) Adware is a form of spyware.

Completion

1. A company or group that verifies a person's identity, issues public-key encryption keys, and serves public keys on Web pages is called a **Certificate Authority** (two words, not just the acronym).
2. The emergency response system that can locate a cell phone is known as **e911**.
3. A program that claims to be one type of program but contains another type of program is called a **Trojan horse** (two words).
4. Falsifying the sender's name in a virus-bearing e-mail message to divert efforts to find and fix the virus is called **spoofing**.
5. A digital signature may include a **one-way hash** (three words) that may be used to verify that the nonencrypted message has not been altered.

Matching Key Terms with Definitions

Match each term with its definition.

U	1. biometrics	A	binary number used to encrypt or decrypt messages
H	2. certificate (CA) authority	B	change using a specific method to hide the meaning
V	3. cookie	C	claiming to be a legitimate Web site to divert communication to the false site
K	4. digital signature	D	connection to the Internet
L	5. e-mail bomb	E	emergency response system that can determine the location of cell phones
B	6. encrypt	F	false message used to trick someone into taking an action
E	7. enhanced 911 (e911)	G	graphic element in a Web page that secretly calls an advertising Web page, which sets a cookie that monitors a user's browsing habits
T	8. firewall	H	group that maintains a database of user names and public keys
D	9. gateway	I	intermediary between the user's computer and the Web page server
Y	10. Global Positioning System (GPS)	J	single number produced from an entire message
F	11. hoax	K	portion of a message encrypted with the sender's private key to verify the identity of the sender
A	12. key	L	practice of sending large numbers of messages to an e-mail address to overwhelm the mail server
C	13. misrepresentation	M	possibly destructive program carried by a virus
J	14. one-way hash	N	program that claims to be something else
M	15. payload	O	unauthorized program that replicates itself using computer resources and then spreads copies to other computers
I	16. proxy server	P	program that tracks behavior and the contents of a computer's hard drive without permission

W	17. public-key encryption	Q	providing a false name as the sender of an e-mail message
X	18. secure server	R	method of encryption that uses the same key to encrypt and decrypt a message
Q	19. spoofing	S	program that searches for vulnerable computers on the Internet and installs programs that allow someone to take control of them
P	20. spyware	T	software that filters connections to the Internet
R	21. symmetric-key encryption	U	statistics applied to biology
N	22. Trojan horse	V	text file stored on the hard drive that is sent by the browser to a Web site to identify the person requesting the Web page
O	23. virus	W	method of encryption and decryption that uses two different keys
G	24. Web bug	X	a server that uses public-key encryption to transfer data
S	25. worm	Y	a device that uses satellites to determine its location

CHAPTER 7

True/False Questions

1. To secure a loan, venture capitalists require collateral in the form of real property like land or houses. **(F)**
2. Counterculture is characterized by rebellion against the traditional values of corporations. **(T)**
3. The United States became adept at miniaturization as a result of the space race with the Soviets. **(T)**
4. The Macintosh computer was introduced in 1984 with an advertisement that made use of the theme from a book titled 1984. **(T)**
5. Metcalfe's law says that the density of computer chips will grow exponentially. **(F)**

Multiple Choice

1. Which of the following is not a significant development of Microsoft?
   a) It introduced Windows 95.
   b) It made a deal with IBM to provide an operating system for the IBM PC.
   c) Jobs assumed the role of interim CEO.
   d) The company was found guilty of unfair competition.
2. Which of the following is not a significant development in the history of Apple?

a) The Macintosh was released.
b) Jobs was forced out by Sculley.
c) Toy Story was released.
d) Jobs returned.

3. Which of the following was not discovered or developed at Bell Laboratories?
a) the transistor
b) cell phones
c) UNIX
d) Ethernet

4. Which of the following was not discovered or developed at IBM labs?
a) GUI
b) DRAM
c) FORTRAN
d) Deep Blue

5. Approximately how many industrial robots are in use in North America?
a) less than 50,000
b) between 50,000 and 150,000
c) between 150,001 and 250,000
d) more than 250,000

Completion

1. An animated image that represents a person in virtual reality is called a(n) **avatar.**
2. A nanometer is a(n) **billionth** of a meter.
3. Computers that were built to the same design specifications as the IBM PC and that used Microsoft's operating system were called **clones.**
4. The prediction that integrated circuit density would increase exponentially is called **Moore's** law.
5. A million megabytes is a(n) **tera** byte.

Matching Key Terms with Definitions

Match each term with its definition.

I	1. algorithm	A	the ability to perceive identity of objects from their image
M	2. applied research	B	arrangement of carbon atoms into tubes
L	3. artificial intelligence (AI)	C	artificial character that represents a person in virtual reality
C	4. avatar	D	billionth of a meter
J	5. basic research	E	computers made to the same specification as the IBM PC
T	6. capital gains	F	connections of processors that mimic the function of neurons

B	7. carbon nanotubes	G	the technology of devices whose size is measured in nanometers
E	8. clones	H	the first electronic spreadsheet
K	9. data mining	I	step-by-step specific instructions
R	10. entrepreneur	J	looking for new knowledge
U	11. expert system	K	looking for patterns in large amounts of data
V	12. exponential growth	L	the ability of machines to display properties similar to a human's ability to think
N	13. fuzzy logic	M	making a product from a new discovery
W	14. linear growth	N	methods of dealing with situations that are not completely true or false
Y	15. Metcalfe's law	O	Microsoft's GUI interface
S	16. Moore's law	P	a million megabytes
D	17. nanometer	Q	money lent without collateral in exchange for part ownership of a new company
G	18. nanotechnology	R	person who organizes a business and assumes the risk
F	19. neural network	S	prediction that integrated circuits would increase in capability by a factor of two every year or two
A	20. pattern recognition	T	profits from the sale of assets such as investment in a company
P	21. terabyte	U	provides advice on how to solve a problem
Q	22. venture capital	V	sequence of numbers that increases by a multiple of the preceding value
X	23. virtual reality (VR)	W	sequence of numbers that increases by the same amount
H	24. VisiCalc	X	simulations that can appear to be real
O	25. Windows	Y	the value of a network is proportional to the square of the number of elements connected to it

Credits

CHAPTER 1

01.02: Micron Electronics, Inc.

01.03a: © PhotoDisc, Inc.

01.03b: © Shambroom/Photo Researchers, Inc.

01.09: David Young-Wolff PhotoEdit

01.11: Courtesy of Microsoft Corporation

01.14: Mark Harmel/Tony Stone Images

01.16: Bob Mahoney The Image Works

01.20: Peter Vadnai Corbis/Stock Market

01.21: © Jeff Greenberg/Omni

01.22: © Sony Computer Entertainment America, Inc.; portions ©2002 Sony Online Entertainment Inc. Everquest is a registered trademark of Sony Computer Entertainment America Inc. in the U.S. and/or other countries.

CHAPTER 2

02.01: © 2002 Ingenta. Inc.

02.02: © Netscape Communications Corporation

02.03: © 2002 AT&T

02.09: Image courtesy of Matrix NetSytems, Inc.

02.11: Courtesy of Aladdin Systems, Inc.

02.14: Jon Feingersh CORBIS

02.15: © Yahoo! Inc. YAHOO! and the YAHOO! logo are trademarks of Yahoo! Inc.

02.16: Netscape website © 2004 Netscape Communications Corporation. Screenshot used with permission.

02.19: © 2004 Goggle

02.21a-c: © 2002 Cheap Tickets/ ©Autobytel, Inc./ These materials have been reproduced with the permission of eBay Inc. Copyright ©eBay Inc. All rights reserved.

02.23: © 24 Hour Museum

02.25: © Joe Cornish/TSI

CHAPTER 3

03.02: Dennis MacDonald/PhotoEdit

03.03: © Palm, Inc.

03.04: © J. Greenberg/The Image Works

03.05: Spenser Grant/ PhotoEdit

03.13: © Logitech Inc.

03.14: © Logitech Inc.

03.15: © Saitek Industries

03.17: AP/Wide World Photos

03.18: Courtesy of International Business Machines Corporation. Unauthorized use not permitted.

03.21: Courtesy of Intel Corporation

03.22: Micron Electronics, Inc.

03.23: Imation Enterprises

03.24: © Iomega Corporation

03.25: Courtesy of Seagate Technology Corporation

03.28a: © View Sonic Corporation

03.28b: © View Sonic Corporation

03.29a: Infocus

03.29b: Infocus

03.31: Epson America, Inc.

03.36: Tripp Lite Worldwide

03.37: American Power Conversion Corporation

CHAPTER 4

04.04: Courtesy of the Naval Historical Center

04.10: Courtesy of Apple Computer, Inc.

04.12: Toshiba America Information Systems

04.13: The Linux penguin, "Tux", was created by Larry Ewing using The GIMP (General Image Manipulation Program).

04.14: Courtesy Lotus Development Corporation. Lotus Notes is a registered trademark of Lotus Development Corporation.

CHAPTER 5

05.03: © SourceForge.net

05.04: © Disney Enterprises, Inc.

05.05: Courtesy of the Software Publishers Association

05.07: © Tom Stweart/CORBIS

05.08: © Mark Richards/PhotoEdit

05.09: TIME MAGAZINE, Copyright TIME, INC.

05.10: © AFP/CORBIS

05.11: SW Productions/Getty Images

05.12: © buy.com

CHAPTER 6

06.01: Courtesy of Kensington Technology Group, a division of ACCO Brands, Inc.

06.02: Seagate Technology, Inc.

06.03a: AP/Wide World Photos

06.03b: AP/Wide World Photos

06.03c: © Mark Peterson/Corbis Saba

06.04: © P. Franch/Corbis Sygma

06.10: © DPI, Inc.

06.11: © Anonymizer.com

06.14: © AdDesigner.com

06.18: © The Center for Democracy and Technology

CHAPTER 7

07.03: © Digital Arts/ Corbis

07.04: Courtesy of the Palo Alto Research Center

07.08a: AP/Wide World Photos

07.08b: Silver Burdett Ginn

07.08c: Daemmrich Corbis/Sygma

07.13a: Courtesy of Dell Computer Corporation

07.13b: Courtesy of Apple Computer, Inc.

07.16: Photo Courtesy of The Computer History Museum

07.19: Adam Lubroth/Getty Images, Inc.

07.20: © Mark Harmel/Tony Stone Images

Glossary

A

A to D converter Device that converts analog electric signals into a series of numbers

Active Server Page (.asp) A page created upon request but not stored

ActiveX control Applet used with Internet Explorer

ADA A modularized language that uses information hiding, named in honor of Augusta Ada Byron, who is considered by some to be the first programmer. It was chosen for use by the U.S. military.

Advanced Research Projects Agency (ARPA) Government agency that developed the Internet

Algorithm A set of specific instructions that a computer can follow to accomplish a task

Alt (Alternative) key Keyboard key used with other keys to provide new functions (see Ctrl)

American Standard Code for Information Interchange (ASCII) Group that chooses which eight-bit numbers would represent letters, decimal numbers, and special function characters (see byte)

Analog Electric signal that varies in time in a way that is similar to the event it is portraying

Apache Open-source Web server software

Applet A small application program that runs with a Web page

Appliances Computers that are dedicated to particular tasks

Application program A program that is written to accomplish a specific task

Applied research Making a product from a new discovery

ARPA See Advanced Research Projects Agency

ARPANET Network managed by ARPA

Artificial intelligence (AI) Machines that can display similar properties to a human's ability to think

Assembler A 2GL one step higher than machine language

Assembly language See assembler

Asynchronous Not occurring at the same time

Attributes Characteristics of an object (see Object-oriented programming)

Avatars Artificial characters that represent a person in virtual reality

B

B to B See Business to business

Backbone The long-distance, high-capacity communication links that consist of undersea cables, microwave antennas, satellite relays, and large bundles of traditional telephone lines

Backlight Fluorescent light used with LCD screens

Backslash (\) The symbol that is used to separate one folder name from the next

Bar code A series of vertical bars and spaces that represent a code that can be read by a computer

BASIC A general-purpose language created to help students learn programming

Basic Input/Output System (BIOS) The program that runs when you turn on your computer. It checks the connections to each of the major components such as the monitor, keyboard, mouse, RAM, CPU, and ports.

Basic research Looking for new knowledge

BCC Blind courtesy copy; the recipients do not see the address of those who receive a blind copy

Beep code A pattern of beeps that sound to indicate a problem has occurred in the start-up process of a computer

Binary numbering system Numbering system that uses two digits, 0 and 1, to represent numbers

Biometrics Statistics applied to biology

Bit Single digit, 0 or 1, in a binary number

Blog See Web log

Bookmarks List of Web pages that can be returned to conveniently (Netscape)

Branching The ability of a program to complete different operations based on certain conditions

Broadband A high-speed connection

Browser Graphic interface used to view Web pages and link to other Web pages

Bug An error found in a program that causes the program to fail to complete its operation successfully

Bus Pathway for data

Business to business (B to B) Special Web pages for direct communication between businesses that buy from and sell to each other

Business to consumer Type of commercial interaction on the Internet, typical of most Web pages

Byte Group of eight bits used to represent characters, decimal numbers, and other special characters (see ASCII)

Byte code A partially compiled program that can be run by a Java virtual machine

C

C# Microsoft's version of Java

Calendar An electronic calendar in a computer application that can track events and meetings

Capital gains Profits from sale of assets such as investment in a company

Carbon nanotubes Arrangement of carbon atoms into tubes

Carnivore Government program used to detect key words or phrases in e-mail messages

Carpal tunnel syndrome Pain or irritation associated with compression of a nerve, often in the wrist.

Cathode ray tube (CRT) Glass tube that uses an electron beam to create pictures on the end of the tube, which is covered with light-emitting phosphors

CC Courtesy copy, used to indicate what addresses will receive copies of the message. Also known as carbon copy, which refers to the old method of placing a sheet of paper with carbon black between pages while typing to produce a copy

CD-R Optical disc from which data can be read and to which data can be written

CD-ROM Optical disc from which data can be read

CD-RW Optical disc from which data can be read and to which data can be recorded and rewritten

Centerline An imaginary line that bisects the human body vertically

Central processing unit (CPU) Device for performing calculations in a computer (see microprocessor)

Certificate authority (CA) Group that maintains a database of user names and public keys

Chat A synchronous text communication in a group setting organized by topic

Cheating Falsifying information on evaluation tools

Checksum Sum of numbers within a packet

Chip See integrated circuit

Circuit breaker Safety device to disconnect electric power

Circuit switching Method of linking circuits to connect two parties

Cite Indicate the origin of the information in a paper

Class A group of objects with common attributes and methods (see Object-oriented programming)

Client Program that communicates with the server, usually residing on the user's computer

Client software Resides on the user's computer and communicates with server software

Clock Device that sends out pulses used to coordinate computer component activity

Clones Computers made to the same specification as the IBM PC

Cluster Data spanning two or more sectors on a hard disk

COBOL Common Business Oriented Language—an early programming language that was written for use with business functions like accounting and payroll

Code of ethics Specific behaviors condoned or prohibited

Common gateway interface (CGI) A program on a Web server that handles requests for scripts

Compact disc (CD) Optical storage medium

Compact flash card Removable electronic memory

Compiler A program that converts higher level programs into machine language

Computerized axial tomography (CAT) scan An imaging system that uses x-rays and computers

Consumer to consumer Type of commercial interaction on the Internet in which consumers bypass the usual retail middleman

Cookie Text file stored on the hard drive that is sent by the browser to a Web site to identify the person requesting the Web page

Corel WordPerfect Office A suite of applications that includes the WordPerfect word processing program

Course packs Collections of copied works

Cryptography The science of encrypting and decrypting messages

Ctrl (Control) key Keyboard key used with other keys to provide new functions (see Alt)

Cyber war Attacking a country's computer infrastructure

Cybersmearing Using the Internet to defame

Cybersquatting Profiting from a trademark used as part of a domain name without permission

Cyberstalking Using the Internet to harass

D

D to A converter Device that converts a sequence of numbers into a smoothly varying electric signal

DARPA Defense Advanced Research Projects Agency, name changed from ARPA

Data Raw, unprocessed facts and figures

Data bus Connection between parts on a motherboard

Data mining Looking for patterns in large amounts of data

Database Lists of data organized in tables where each column is a type of information and each row is one person, event, or interaction

Debugging The process of removing bugs or errors from a software program

Decimal numbering system Numbering system that uses 10 digits, from 0 to 9, to represent numbers

Deciphering The act of decrypting an encrypted message

Decompress The action of restoring a compressed file to its original condition so it can be opened and read

Decrypt Change a message whose content is hidden back to plain text

Deep computing IBM program to develop advanced problem-solving programs

Defragmenting Rearranging data on a hard disk so files are written on adjacent sectors

Demilitarized zone (DMZ) Buffer position between a firewall and the Internet

Desktop computer Personal computer that is too large to be portable

Digital computers Computers that work with facts and variables that can be represented by numbers

Digital signature Portion of a message encrypted with the sender's private key to verify the identity of the sender

Digital Subscriber Line (DSL) High-speed connection technology that uses existing telephone lines over distances of a few miles

Digital versatile disc (DVD) Optical storage on which data can be recorded in layers on both sides

Direct mail advertising Mail sent through the postal system for which the advertisers pay delivery charges

Directories Programs that search the Web for pages and then categorize them

Disc Optical medium

Disk Magnetic medium

Disk cache Area of the computer where recently visited Web pages are stored for quick retrieval

Disk-on-key Flash memory device that is recognized as a removable hard disk

Distributed database Related records stored on more than one computer

Distributed processing Dividing a task into component parts that can be distributed to multiple computers

Docking station Device into which a laptop computer connects to provide permanent connections for the portable computer

Document sharing A feature of an online course in which documents are made available to students

Domain name server (DNS) Computer with a database of domain names and IP addresses and the relationships between them

Domain names A name that often resembles the name of the organization and is easier to remember than a number. It often includes www as a prefix and always has an extension to indicate the category.

Dot-matrix printer Type of impact printer

Dots per inch (dpi) Measure of printed image quality

Drive Device that reads data from and writes data to magnetic or optical media

Drivers Small programs that are written to provide communication instructions between a peripheral device and the computer's operating system

Dumb terminal Communication device with a keyboard and monitor that depends on another computer for processing and storage

E

Eavesdropping Reading an e-mail message without alerting the sender or recipient

ECMAScript The proper name for Netscape's Jscript language

E-mail Electronic mail exchanged between computers

E-mail bomb Practice of sending large numbers of messages to an e-mail address to overwhelm the mail server

E-mail virus Unauthorized program that spreads to other computers by attaching itself to e-mail messages

Emoticons Icons that express an emotion

Encrypt Change using a specific method to hide the content

End user license agreement (EULA) Contract between the software copyright holder and the user

Enhanced 911 (e911) Emergency response system that can determine the location of cell phones

Enterprise resource package (ERP) Horizontal and vertical software that is combined by service providers in a single software solution

Entrepreneur Person who organizes a business and assumes the risk

Erasable programmable read only memory (EPROM) A type of memory that is usually programmed at the factory and is used to start the computer

Ergonomics The applied science of equipment design to reduce operator fatigue and discomfort

Ethical principles Guides to making decisions about moral behaviors

European Computer Manufacturers Association (ECMA) Group that standardized the Jscript programming language

Event   An action by the user, such as clicking a button on the screen

Event driven   Programs that are executed when the user chooses an option

Expert system   Provides advice on how to solve a problem

Exponential growth   Sequence of numbers that increase by a multiple of the previous value

Extended Binary Coded Decimal Interchange Code (EBCDIC)   Code for representing characters and control commands with eight-bit binary numbers used by IBM 390 mainframes

Extensible Markup Language (XML)   Method of attaching additional information to text or pictures on a Web page

F

Fair use   Policy that allows use of copyrighted works without permission or payment under certain circumstances

Favorites   List of Web pages for convenient return; a feature of Internet Explorer

Fifth-generation language (5GL)   A software language that is most like human language in the way it is structured and states instructions; it uses a knowledge-based system

File allocation table (FAT)   A place in the computer's memory that records and tracks the location of files

File compression   The process of reducing the size of files by compressing the data in the file

File name extensions   Three-letter codes following a period at the end of a file name

File server   Computer that finds files or data and delivers the information to the user, as well as manages updates to the files

File Transfer Protocol (FTP)   Method of transferring files on the Internet

Finite element analysis   Dividing a model into small elements and calculating how they interact to simulate behavior of a real system

Firewall   Software that filters connections to the Internet

FireWire   High-speed connection often used for transferring video data

First-generation language (1GL)   A software language written in binary code, or machine language

Flash memory   Memory for use in electronic devices like cameras that remembers data even when disconnected from a power source

Flat panel   Thin display that often uses LCD technology

Flat screen   CRT with a less curved screen

Flatbed scanner   Device to transfer documents and pictures one sheet at a time

Floppy disk   Removable magnetic storage medium

Formatting   Marking the tracks and sectors on a disk

FORTRAN   FORmula TRANslation—an early programming language that was used primarily for complex formulas

Fourth-generation language (4GL)   Very high-level language for use by both novices and experts

Frames per second   Rate at which blocks of data are created

Freeware   Copyrighted work that is available without charge

Frequently asked questions (FAQ)   List of questions and answers that help a new user take part in a group rapidly

Function (Fn) key   Keyboard key used with numbered function keys to provide additional functions

Fuzzy logic   Methods of dealing with situations that are not completely true or false

G

Gantt   A type of chart that uses horizontal bars to represent tasks, the time they take, and their relationship to the start and end of other tasks

Gateway   Connection to the Internet

Gateways and routers   Computer devices at the nodes of communication links that pass packets along to the next computer en route to their final destination

GIF   Image format

Global positioning system (GPS)   A system that uses radio signals from satellites to determine positions accurately on earth

Graphical user interface (GUI)   The use of icons, buttons, a mouse, dialog boxes, and menus for communication between the user and a computer

Groupware   Software that enables groups to coordinate calendars and meetings

H

Hard disk   Magnetic medium made of metal

Hard drive   Device to read and write hard disks (see hard disk)

Hardware   Physical components of a computer

High-level languages   Another term used for third-generation languages

Hoax   False message used to trick someone into taking an action

Honor code   Ethical conduct agreed to by a group's members

Horizontal software   Applications that may be used by a variety of organizations

Host Computer on which software resides. Another name for a server.

Hot-swappable Used to describe connected devices that can be connected or disconnected without shutting down the computer

Hub Multiple port connector

Hyperlink A link to another Web page activated by a mouse click

Hypertext Markup Language (HTML) Language used to create Web pages that can be displayed on any computer

Hypertext Preprocessor (PHP) Script language used to create interactive Web pages that may end with .php or a similar extension

Hypertext Transfer Protocol (HTTP) A method used to retrieve Web pages from a server

I

Identity theft Using private facts to impersonate

Impact printer Printer that transfers ink to the paper by striking an ink-impregnated cloth ribbon

Information Data that has been processed so it is organized, meaningful, and useful.

Information hiding Characteristic of modular programming

Inherit In object-oriented programming, to take on attributes and methods of a higher class

Ink-jet printer Printer that creates an image by spraying ink on a page

Input One of the four main functions of the computer—the action of adding instructions and data to a computer.

Instant messaging (IM) Direct communication between users with windows that display text or video

Integrated circuit (IC) Arrays of transistors and other electronic devices that perform a function

Intellectual property laws Laws that protect rights of copyright, trademark, and patent holders

Internet Control Message Protocol (ICMP) Protocol that manages information exchange between routers

Internet Corporation for Assigned Names and Numbers (ICANN) Coordinates use of domain names

Internet Explorer (IE) A popular Web browser owned by Microsoft, distributed with Windows

Internet Message Access Protocol (IMAP) Mail program that allows screening and sorting of incoming e-mail messages on the server before they are downloaded to the client computer

Internet Protocol (IP) addresses Specific number used as an address on the Internet

Internet service provider (ISP) Company or group that provides a connection to the Internet backbone.

Internet2 Next generation of the Internet

Intranet Similar to the Internet, using TCP/IP but separate

J

Jack Any connection for telephones

Java Language that uses byte code and Java virtual machine programs to create interactive Web pages

Java 2 Platform Enterprise Edition (J2EE) Cross-platform programming language

Java virtual machine (JVM) Compiles Java byte code for execution on a particular platform

JavaScript Subset of Java language, used for writing scripts

Joystick Pointing device that is a rod connected to a track ball

Jscript Script language created by Netscape (see ECMAScript)

Junk mail Unwanted mail

K

Key (hardware) Projection that requires a plug and receptacle to be properly oriented

Key (software) Binary number used to encrypt or decrypt messages

Knowledge-based system A characteristic of fifth-generation languages that can interpret instructions in a more humanlike manner

L

Language A set of structured communication protocols used to write software programs

Laptop computer See notebook computer

Laser printer Printer that uses a light beam to transfer images or text to paper in which powdered ink is attracted and melted onto the paper

Laws Formalized codes of ethical behavior enforced by the courts and police

Licensing agreement An agreement between a software vendor and a user that governs the terms of use of the software

Linear growth Sequence of numbers that increase by the same amount

Linux Derivative of UNIX that is free and open source

Liquid crystal display (LCD) Type of display that uses electric fields to change the transparency of liquid cells and are typically much thinner than older style monitors

Local area network (LAN) A group of connected computers

Lotus SmartSuite   Suite of application programs that includes the Lotus 1-2-3 spreadsheet program

Lumbar support   A curved portion of the back of a chair that provides additional support for the lower part of the back

Lumens   Measure of brightness of light sources

Lurking   Watching without taking part in a chat

M

Machine code   See machine language

Machine language   Language that is written in binary code that a computer processor can directly interpret

Macro   Group of commands activated by an action; used in Microsoft Office

Macro virus   Group of commands in an MS Office program that replicate and distribute themselves without authorization (see virus and macro)

Magic Lantern   Government program that uses a virus to set spyware on a suspect's computer

Magnetic media   Materials like plastic or metal (hard) disks coated with a material usually containing iron that will remain magnetized to store data

Magnetic resonance imaging (MRI)   An imaging system that uses magnetic fields and computers

Mainframe   Powerful computer typically used to manage databases

Many-to-many relationship   Describes the relationship between domain names and IP addresses where there can be more than one of each related to one of the other

Megabyte   Approximately a million bytes. The actual number is 1,048,576 which is 2 to the 20th power

Megahertz   One million cycles per second

Memory   A type of storage that is used while the computer is processing data and instructions, also called primary storage.

Message   Instruction in object-oriented programming

Metasearch sites   Sites that report the results of several other search engines

Metatag   Hidden text at the beginning of the HTML code for a Web page that identifies key words and other information used by spiders to index the page

Metcalfe's law   The value of a network is proportional to the square of the number of elements connected to it

Methods   Sets of instructions on how to accomplish a task in OOP

Microcomputer   Smallest class of computers

Microprocessor   Integrated circuit that performs mathematical or logical functions on data

Microsoft Disk Operating System (MS-DOS)   An early nongraphical operating system that was introduced by Microsoft when personal computers first became popular

Microsoft Office   Suite of application software from Microsoft that includes Word and Excel

Microsoft Works   Suite of application software from Microsoft for home use

Microsoft.NET   Cross-platform programming environment from Microsoft

Midrange computer   Similar to a mainframe computer but less powerful

Milestones   A particular date that marks a goal such as the date a phase of the project is finished

Minicomputer   A computer that is larger than a microcomputer and smaller than a midrange computer

Misrepresentation   Claiming to be a legitimate Web site to divert communication to the false site

Mobile communication devices   Devices that use radio waves to transfer voice or messages

Modeling   Using formulas to simulate the behavior of real systems

Modem   A device that converts computer data into a format compatible for transmission by another device such as telephone, Digital Subscriber Line, or cable television

Modular programming   Style of programming in which blocks of code with standard input and output may be reused and exchanged

Monitor   Display device used with computers

Moore's law   Prediction that integrated circuits would increase in capability exponentially by a factor of two every year or two

Moral behavior   Behavior that conforms to standards of right and wrong

Moral dilemma   Conflict between two moral behaviors

Mosaic   Early graphic Web browser

Motherboard   Connects integrated circuits and other devices

Mouse   Pointing device that moves on the desktop and controls a screen pointer

Mouse pad   Pad to give traction to the rubber ball in a mouse

Mozilla   Nickname for Netscape

MP3   Compression technique used with music files

MP4   Compression technique for video

Multi-user dungeon (MUD)   A gaming environment for simulating interactions between participants often using avatars

MVS   IBM mainframe language

N

Nanometers   Billionths of a meter

Nanoseconds   Billionths of a second

Nanotechnology   Devices whose size is measured in nanometers

Netscape   A popular Web browser owned by AOL

Network interface card (NIC)   Device used to connect a computer to a computer network

Network server   Computer that coordinates communication on a local area network

Neural network   Connections of processors that mimic the function of neurons

Nonprocedural   Characteristic of fourth-generation languages (see object-oriented programming)

Notebook computer   Portable computer also known as a laptop computer

NSFNET   Network operated by the National Science Foundation for academic research

Num Lock   Keyboard key that toggles the function of the numeric keyboard keys from navigation to numeric functions

O

Object   Programming entity with attributes and methods that belongs to a class

Object possession   Security technique that requires the user to present a card or device to aid identification

Object-oriented programming (OOP)   Nonprocedural method that uses attributes, methods, classes, and messages

Octets   Groups of eight binary digits represented with decimal numbers

One-way hash   Number produced from text (see digital signature)

Online courses   College classes taught using the Internet

Open architecture   Not secret or owned by anyone

Open source   Source code that is available to the public

OpenOffice   Suite of productivity applications available for free download that works with Linux

Operating system (OS)   The software program that provides common functions and controls communication between a computer and its various attached components

Operations   Synonym for methods (see object-oriented programming)

Optical character recognition (OCR)   Converts images of text into editable text

Optical media   Materials like reflective discs that can store data and retrieve it using light, usually in the form of a reflected laser beam.

Optical mouse   Mouse that detects motion using the reflection of a beam of light

OS/390   IBM mainframe operating system that is an update of an operating system that dates back to the IBM 360 mainframe used in the 1960s

Output   One of the four functions of the computer— the process of displaying, printing, sharing, or otherwise communicating information that has been processed by the computer.

P

Packet switching   Managing packets in a network, as opposed to circuit switching

Palm OS   The operating system used by the popular Palm Pilot personal digital assistant

Palm Pilot   Popular personal digital assistant

Partition   Logical division of a large hard disk

Password   Secret group of letters and numbers used along with a user name for identification

Pattern recognition   Ability to perceive identity of objects from their image

Payload   Possibly destructive program carried by a virus

Peer-to-peer network   Method of connecting computers that doesn't require a designated computer to handle traffic

Peripheral   Device attached to the system unit, or case

Perl   Script language for use with UNIX and Linux operating systems

Personal computer   Alternative term for microcomputer (see microcomputer)

Personal digital assistant (PDA)   A small handheld computer device that is used for recording appointments, calendar events, contact information, and other data and may be expanded to include other functions like e-mail

Personal video recorder (PVR)   Device that records television programs and can share them over the Internet

Pert   A type of chart that uses boxes connected by lines to represent work flow and relationships between tasks

Philosophy   Critical analysis of fundamental assumptions and beliefs

Physical memory   High-speed integrated circuits that work directly with the CPU to temporarily store data

Piracy   Using copyrighted works without permission

Pixel   Picture element

Plagiarism   Representing the work of others as one's own

Platform   The combination of a particular operating system and the processor that it controls

Plug strip   Device with several power outlets

Pointing stick Pointing device that senses directional pressure

Point-of-sale terminal (POS) Type of dumb terminal used for recording transactions

Polymorphism A characteristic of object-oriented programs in which objects can accomplish a stated message independently

Pop-under Window that appears automatically behind other windows

Pop-up Window that appears automatically in front of other windows

Port Connection device on the computer

Portal A Web page that seeks to provide for all your needs without your leaving the page

Post Office Protocol 3 (POP3) Program to handle mail being received by the user

Power supply Device that converts household electricity for use inside the computer

Presence technology Technology that makes it possible to determine someone's location

Primary storage A type of storage that is used while the computer is processing data and instructions, also known as memory.

Privacy policy Statement of methods used to deal with personal information

Procedural language Third-generation language in which the programmer gives a specific set of instructions on how to handle the data and processing

Processing One of the four main functions of a computer—manipulating data according to a set of instructions to create information that can be stored.

Productivity applications Programs intended to assist with common processes like word processing

Profiling Developing a database of user activities to predict behavior

Programmer Person who writes programs

Programming The process of writing software

Proxy server Intermediary between a user's computer and the Web page server

PS/2 Round connector used for mice and keyboards

Public domain Creative work that is not copyrighted

Public-key encryption Method of encryption and decryption that uses two different keys

Q

Query A request for information from a database

R

Random access memory (RAM) Integrated circuits that work with the CPU (see physical memory)

Register A holding place in a computer's memory

Registered Jack Term used by AT&T for standard telephone connectors

Relational database A database with two or more tables that are related to each other by a common field

Resources People or equipment that may be assigned to tasks

Rexx Script language from IBM

RJ-11 Standard telephone connector

RJ-45 Standard Ethernet connector

Router Connects and routes signals between computers

S

Scanner Device used to transfer documents and pictures into a digital computer file

Scanning Act of converting a document or picture into a digital file

Scripts Short programs that reside on the Web server and are used with Web pages

Search engine A program that finds Web pages based on key words and other information provided by the user

Secondary storage A type of storage that is used to record information for later retrieval, and does not require constant power to retain to the information that is stored.

Second-generation language (2GL) A computer language that allows use of limited command words and decimal numbers

Sectors Segments of tracks on a disk

Secure server A server that uses public-key encryption to transfer data

Sensor A device that reacts to changes in the environment and produces an electrical signal that corresponds to the change.

Serial Sequentially

Server Computer that stores and provides Web pages and other services

Server software Provides files or Web pages to client software

Shift Keyboard key that can be used to produce capital letters or can be used in combination with other keys to access special functions (see Alt and Ctrl)

Silicon-base life See artificial intelligence

Simple Mail Transfer Protocol (SMTP) Program to handle mail being sent from the user

Simple Network Management Protocol (SNMP) Protocol used to collect system information from remote computers

Simple Object Access Protocol (SOAP) Microsoft's method of incorporating programming from other sources to offer services

Site license Agreement to allow installation of software on all the computers at one location

Sleep See standby

Small Computer System Interface (SCSI) Type of bus connection for high-speed data transfer between devices and the computer

Smalltalk First object-oriented programming language

Smart weapon Weapon that can steer itself onto a target

Software Written instructions that direct a computer's processor on how to complete tasks, also called programs

Source code Instructions written by a programmer

Spaghetti code Code that uses GOTO statements and is particularly complex and difficult to follow

Spam Term used to describe unsolicited e-mail

Spam blocker Program to prevent unsolicited e-mail from being downloaded to the user's computer

Spammers People who send unsolicited e-mail advertising

Spider A program that searches the Web for Web pages and indexes them for use by a search engine

Spoofing Providing a false name as the sender of an e-mail message

Spreadsheets An arrangement of cells in rows and columns that can be used to display and calculate financial information, some of which is dependent on the results of calculations in other cells.

Spyware Program that tracks behavior and the contents of a computer's hard drive without permission

Standby Partially powered state

StarOffice Commercial version of OpenOffice

Storage One of the four main functions of the computer—the action of recording instructions and data for processing by the computer, or for retaining processed data for later retrieval.

Streaming audio Sound delivered over the Internet

Structured programming Uses structured commands to handle branching

Structured Query Language (SQL) A fourth-generation language that is used for extracting specific sets of data from a database

StuffIt A program used to compress files that works on Macintosh and Linux systems

Subwoofer Audio speaker designed for low-range sounds and music

Suite Group of applications

Supercomputer The most powerful kind of computer

Surge suppressor Protects the computer from pulses of higher-than-normal electric voltage

Symmetric-key encryption Method of encryption that uses the same key to encrypt and decrypt a message

Synchronous Occurring at the same time in a coordinated manner

Syntax Rules for a software language that must be used when writing code

System unit The case that houses the processing and storage functions of a computer

T

T1 A high-speed connection to the Internet from a company or ISP

Tampering Changing the content of a message

Targeted advertising Matching ads to consumers who are most likely to buy the product

Tasks Items of work to be done that may be associated with a calendar program or with a project management program

TCL Script language from Sun Laboratories

Telnet Method of running programs on a remote computer

Terabyte Million megabytes

Terminator Required device at the end of some types of buses such as SCSI connections

The last mile A phrase that refers to the millions of miles of connections between a company's high-speed system and consumers' homes

Third-generation language (3GL) High-level programming language that uses compilers to create machine code for specific processors

Threaded discussion A series of asynchronous text messages connected together to show the relationship of posting and response

Thumb drive Brand of removable memory (see flash memory)

Toner Powdered ink used with laser printers

Touch pad Pointing device that senses the motion of a finger

Trackball Pointing device in which the user moves a ball in a cradle

Tracks Concentric paths on a disk for recording data

Trademark Symbol or logo used to identify a product

Transistors Electronic devices that can switch on or off in response to an external signal

Transmission Control Protocol/Internet Protocol (TCP/IP) Method of transmitting packets on the Internet

Transponder A device that uses radio transmissions to track location

Trojan horse Program that claims to be something else

Type A USB plug Connector on the upstream, or computer, end of a USB cable

Type B USB plug Connector on the downstream, or device, end of a USB cable

U

Unicode Code that uses 64-bit numbers to represent characters from numerous languages

Uniform Resource Locator (URL) Identifies the method of interaction with the server, a domain name or IP address, the local folder, and file name

Uninterruptible power supply (UPS) Plug strip with a battery that provides electricity for a short period

Universal Serial Bus (USB) Connection method that replaces many other types of connectors

UNIX Operating system common on mainframe computers

Unzipping The processing of restoring a compressed file to its original condition so it can be opened and read

USB 1.1 First version of USB (see Universal Serial Bus)

USB 2.0 Second version of USB (see Universal Serial Bus)

USB drive Removable storage (see flash memory)

User Datagram Protocol (UDP) Protocol that manages streaming audio and video

User name Identifying term that usually contains part of a person's name (see password)

V

VB.Net Programming language that uses object-oriented programming (see Visual Basic)

VBScript Simplified version of Visual Basic used for writing scripts

Veiling reflection A reflection of a bright light source on a surface that partially obscures the object behind the surface

Venture capital Money loaned without collateral in exchange for part ownership of a new company

Vertical software Applications written for specific market segments such as medical offices, restaurants, supermarkets, manufacturers, or tax return preparation

Vetting Checking someone's background for indications of character

Video graphics adapter (VGA) Standard method of attaching monitors to computers

Virtual memory Space on a hard disk used to supplement physical memory (see physical memory)

Virtual private network (VPN) Encrypts packets within packets that are sent to an intranet via the Internet

Virtual reality (VR) Simulations that can appear to be real

Virus Unauthorized program that replicates itself using computer resources and then spreads copies to other computers by copying itself to disks or by attaching itself to e-mail messages

VisiCalc First electronic spreadsheet

Visual Basic (VB) An event-driven language that uses a graphical interface that includes buttons, dialog boxes, scroll bars, and menus

Voice over IP (VoIP) Method of sending telephone conversations using TCP/IP packets

Voice recognition Ability to convert speech into digital files or commands

W

Web bug Graphic element in a Web page that secretly calls an advertising Web page, which sets a cookie to monitor a user's browsing habits

Web camera Video device intended for use over the Internet

Web crawling The process of searching the Web

Web log (Blog) A series of dated journal entries available online

Web page A page written in HTML for display by a browser

Web server Computer that runs software that provides Web pages and runs scripts

Web-based training Skill and product familiarization using the Internet

Webcam A video camera that is connected to the Internet

Whistle-blowing Reporting illegal activity

Windows Microsoft's GUI interface

Windows 2000 Datacenter Operating system by Microsoft for use on mainframe computers

Windows CE The operating system program written by Microsoft for use with PDAs

Wintel Platform of Windows operating system and Intel microprocessor

WinZip A program used to compress files that works on Windows systems

Wireless Uses radio to connect devices

Word processing The process of using a computer to write, store, retrieve, and edit documents.

Work for hire Creative product for which the copyright is owned by the company that paid for the creator's services

Workstation A high-performance desktop computer

Worm Program that searches for vulnerable computers on the Internet and installs programs that allow someone else to take control of them

Z

Z/OS New IBM operating system for mainframe computers

Zip disk Brand of high-capacity floppy disk

Zipping The process of compressing files

Index

See also applications
antivirus, 187, 189
business licenses for, 161–162
calendar, 10
client, 126–127
compatibility of, 114
compression, 49, 131
in computer labs, 159
custom, 134
defined, 113
end user license agreements for, 151, 157, 200
filtering, 196
freeware, 152, 169
groupware, 127
horizontal, 134
installed on several computers, 169
open-source, 126, 152–153
presentation, 8–9
server, 126–127
shareware, 169
site licenses for, 151
student discounts on, 159
vertical, 134
voice recognition, 87, 222, 236
software development careers, 114
software distribution, copyright protection and, 232
software piracy, 154, 156, 160, 162, 233, 245
solid-state lasers, 222
sound, 82
source code, 116–117, 123, 138
Soviet Union
arms race with, 221
collapse of, 234
spaghetti code, 118
spam, 48–49, 197–198
spam blockers, 134
speakers, 95, 100
special needs, users with, 23–24
speech recognition software, 87, 222, 236
spiders, 56
spoofing, 188, 191
spreadsheets, 8–9
Spyglass, 223
spyware, 200–201
SQL (Structured Query Language), 120
standby mode, 83
Stanford University, 223
StarOffice, 129
Startup tab, customizing automatically started programs using, 134
storage, 6, 89, 91–92
See also memory
devices, 5
primary, 4
secondary, 4–5
streaming audio technology, 166
Structured Query Language (SQL), 120
StuffIt, 50
subwoofers, 95
suites, application, 127–129
SUN Microsystems, 223
supercomputers, 79–80
supercomputing, Japan's role in, 220
surge suppressors, 101
surgery, computer technology and advances in, 242
symmetric-key encryption, 190
synchronous classes, 11
synchronous communication, 50
syntax, 115, 117
system units, 76

T

T1 connections, 42
tags, 135
tampering, with messages, 192
targeted advertising, 197–198, 200–202
tasks, 10
tax evasion, on the Internet, 154
taxes
capital gains, 223, 233
sales, on online purchases, 168
TCL, 138
TCP/IP, 37
teachers, communication between parents and, 10
technological advances, coping with, 245–246
telephone conferencing, 51
telephone jacks, 99
television industry, 165–166
Telnet, 37
terabyte, 235
terminals
dumb, 79
point-of-sale (POS), 79
terminators, 99
terrorism
effect of, 245
privacy issues and war on, 205
third-generation languages (3GLs), 116–119
BASIC, 117–118
C, 119
COBOL, 117–118
FORTRAN, 117–118
GOTO commands and, 117–118
modular, 119
for the Web, 119
thumb drives, 92
toner, 95
touch pads, 76, 86
trackballs, 76, 85
tracks, 132
trade, balance of, 234
trademarks, 152–153
traffic signals, 15
trains, influence of computers on, 16
transistors, 81, 88, 221
Transmission Control Protocol/Internet Protocol (TCP/IP), 37
transponders, 203
transportation industry, influence of computers on, 13–16
travel, recreational, 17
Trojan horse, 188
trucks, computers used by, 13, 15
Turing, Alan, 237
Turing test, 237
Tuvalu, 46
type A USB plugs, 97
type b USB ports, 97

U

U.S. balance of trade, 234
U.S. Constitution
copyright protection in, 220–221
privacy safeguarded in, 204
U.S. economy, long-term health of, 234
UDP (User Datagram Protocol), 185
Unicode, 81
Uniform Resource Locators (URLs), 44, 46
uninterruptible power supply (UPS), 101
United States
1970s counterculture in, 223–224
arms race between Soviet Union and, 221

copyright protection in, 220–221, 232–233
digital divide between world and, 21–23
digital divide in, 21
diversity of cultures in, 234
prosperity in, following WWII, 221
spirit of entrepreneurism in, 221
venture capital in, 223
universal access, 21–23
Universal Serial Bus (USB) ports, 92, 97, 102
University of Illinois, 223
university research labs, 223
UNIX operating system, 126, 222
unzipping, 132
UPS (uninterruptible power supply), 101
URLs, 44, 46
USA Patriot Act, 205, 245
USB (Universal Serial Bus) ports, 92, 97, 102
USENET, 37
User Datagram Protocol (UDP), 185
user names, 181–182
utilities, 129–134
antivirus, 134
defragmentation, 133
erasing, 132
file compression, 131–132
file management, 129–131
formatting, 132
scanning, 132
spam blockers, 134
Web security, 134

V

VB (Visual Basic), 120–121
VB.NET, 122
VBScript, 138
veiling reflections, 20
venture capital, 223, 229, 233–234
vertical software, 134
vetting, 159
VGA connectors, 99, 102
video cameras, 87
video distribution, copyright protection and, 232
video graphics adapter (VGA) port, 99, 102
video tape recorders, 164
videoconferencing, 51–52
Vietnam War, 223–224
virtual memory, 89
virtual private network (VPN), 42
virtual reality (VR), 236–237
viruses, 187–189
vision, artificial, 242
VisiCalc, 229
Visual Basic (VB), 120–121
visually-impaired users, Windows XP features for, 24
Voice over IP (VoIP), 52
voice recognition software, 87, 222, 236
voting online, 52, 244
VPN (virtual private network), 42

W

war on terrorism, privacy issues and, 205
weapons, advanced, 13
Web browsers, 53, 136
graphical, 38–39, 223
Mosaic, 38, 223
Netscape, 223
security settings, 186–187
Web bugs, 199–200

Web cameras, 10, 87, 167
Web crawling, 56
Web logs, 36, 51
Web mail, 49
Web pages/sites, 39
    interactive, 114, 136
    languages for creating, 135–137
    misrepresentation of, 191
    personal, 36, 51
    searching, 56
    stored, 53
Web security utilities, 134
Web server languages, 137–138
Web servers, 126
Web-based training, 62
Webcams, 10, 87, 167
whistle-blowing, 163

Windows, 124, 126, 228
Windows 3.1, 230
Windows 2000 Datacenter, 126
Windows CE, 126
Windows XP, 24, 125
wintel machines, 126
WinZip, 49, 132
wireless
    connections, 78
    keyboards, 99
    mice, 99
word processors, 7
work for hire, 151
workstations, 78
    ergonomics of, 17–19
World War II, prosperity following, 221, 234

World Wide Web (WWW), 36
    See also Internet; Web pages/sites
    advertising on, 197–202
    development of, 38–39
    downloading content from, 160
worms, 188–189, 223
Wosniak, Steve, 228–229
WYSISYG, 222

X-Y-Z

Xerox PARC, 222, 229–230
XML (Extensible Markup Language), 137
Z/OS, 126
Zip disks, 90–91
zip files, 49
zipping, 132